UNDERSTANDING CINEMA

A Psychological Theory of Moving Imagery

Understanding Cinema analyzes the moving imagery of film and television from a psychological perspective. Per Persson argues that spectators perceive, think, apply knowledge, infer, interpret, feel, and make use of knowledge, assumptions, expectations, and prejudices when viewing and making sense of film. Drawing on the methods of psychology and anthropology, he explains how close-ups, editing conventions, character psychology and other cinematic techniques work, and how and why they affect the spectator. This study integrates psychological and culturalist approaches to meaning and reception in new ways, anchoring the discussion in concrete examples from early and contemporary cinema *Understanding Cinema* also examines the design of cinema conventions and their stylistic transformations through the evolution of film.

Per Persson is currently researcher at the Nokia Research Center, Helsinki.

Understanding Cinema

A Psychological Theory of Moving Imagery

Per Persson

CAMBRIDGE
UNIVERSITY PRESS

PUBLISHED BY THE PRESS SYNDICATE OF THE UNIVERSITY OF CAMBRIDGE
The Pitt Building, Trumpington Street, Cambridge, United Kingdom

CAMBRIDGE UNIVERSITY PRESS
The Edinburgh Building, Cambridge CB2 2RU, UK
40 West 20th Street, New York, NY 10011-4211, USA
477 Williamstown Road, Port Melbourne, VIC 3207, Australia
Ruiz de Alarcón 13, 28014 Madrid, Spain
Dock House, The Waterfront, Cape Town 8001, South Africa

http://www.cambridge.org

First published 2003

Printed in the United Kingdom at the University Press, Cambridge

Typeface Palatino 9.75/12.5 pt.   *System* LATEX 2_ε [TB]

A catalog record for this book is available from the British Library.

Library of Congress Cataloging in Publication Data

ISBN 0 521 81328 x hardback

Contents

List of Illustrations   *page* ix

Preface and Acknowledgments   xi

1   **Understanding and Dispositions**   1
    Psychology: Understanding and Dispositions   6
    Parameters of Dispositions   13
    A Psychological Model of Reception   19
    Discourse and Meaning   21
        Level 0   26
        Level 1   28
        Level 2   29
        Level 3   30
        Level 4   32
        Level 5   33
    Some Specifications of the Model   34
    Conclusions   43

2   **Understanding Point-of-View Editing**   46
    Historical Context of Point-of-View Editing   48
        Early Point-of-View as Attraction – Not as
            Spatial Articulation   50
        Spatial Immersion Begins   52
        Editing between Adjacent Places: Movement   54
        Editing between Adjacent Places: Gazing   56
        Functions of Point-of-View Editing   63
    Deictic Gaze   66
        The Structure of Deictic-Gaze Behavior   67
            Development   68

Functions 70
Universality and the Question of Origin 72
How Does Point-of-View Editing Work? 74
Eight Hypotheses 75
Conclusions 92
Explaining the Presence of the Point-of-View Convention
in Mainstream Cinema 97

3 **Variable Framing and Personal Space** 101
Personal Space 102
Personal-Space Invasions 105
Personal-Space Behavior: A Vehicle for Communication 108
Conclusions 108
Visual Media and Personal Space 109
Personal Space and Variable Framing 110
Early Cinema 110
Threatening Imagery of Early Cinema 113
Emblematic Shots: Marks of Intimacy and
Emotional Repose 118
Variable Framing in Mainstream Narrative Cinema 121
"Closer-ups" 121
Analytical Editing: Exploiting Personal-Space Intimacy 127
The Important Foreground 130
Threat Revisited 131
Voyeurism 138
Conclusions 141

4 **Character Psychology and Mental Attribution** 143
Introduction 143
Textual Theories of Characters 144
Reception-Based Theories of Characters 146
The Psychology of Recognition and Alignment 149
Levels of Meaning 150
Level 0 152
Level 1 152
Level 2 152
Level 3 152
Level 4 153
Level 5 153
Level 6 154
Why Mental States? 158
"Subjective Access" versus "Mental Attribution" 158

Mental Attribution in Everyday Life   159
  Ability with Body and Gesture Cues   159
  Folk Psychology: Reasoning about Mental States   161
    The Mind and Its Parts   163
    Emotions and Their Causes   169
    Deep Psychology   173
  Additional Remarks   173
    Folk Psychology is a Cultural Understanding   174
    People with Different Folk Psychologies   176
    Relativism versus Universality   177
    Anthropomorphism: Intentional Stance and
      Psychological Causality   178
    Instrumental Value of Folk Psychology   181
    Folk Psychology = Normality   181
Mental Attribution Processes in Reception of Cinema   182
  Some General Principles   183
  The Minds of Cinematic Characters   186
    Goals Bring Coherence to Events   186
    Emotions are Important Motivators for Goals
      and Actions   192
    Perceptions Inform Beliefs that Constrain Goals
      and Actions   193
  The Emotions of Cinematic Characters   201
    Positive/Negative Emotions   202
    Surprise   204
    Events Caused by Circumstance, Other, or Self   206
    Appetitive/Aversive Emotions   209
    Certain/Uncertain Events   210
    Low/High Control Potential   211
  Additional Remarks   211
    Intradiegetic Attributions   211
    Mental Attributions and Time   213
    What is a Round/Flat Character?   216
    Narrative Causality is Primarily a Psychological
      Causality   217
Text and Mental Attribution   220
  Textual Techniques   220
    Acting versus Situation   221
    Creating Psychologically Rich Situations   222
    Nonarbitrary Conventions   231
    Good/Bad Conventions   232

The Narrativization and Psychologization of Early Cinema   232
    Psychology as Complement?   236
Concluding Comments   242

5   The Case for a Psychological Theory of Cinema   247

Notes   251

References   261

Index   277

List of Illustrations

1 Meaning emerges from understanding.   *page* 24
2 Some gestalt effects of perceptual organization.   27
3 *Komposition in Blau* (1935).   35
4 Levels of coherence and their interaction.   37
5 Understanding visual discourse affects the structure
   of dispositions.   39
6 *Dr. Jekyll and Mr. Hyde* (1912).   51
7 *Le Chien de Montargis* (1909).   55
8 *The Musketeers of Pig Alley* (1912).   58
9 The filming of a studio interior scene from *Vor Tids Dame*
   (1912) at the Nordisk studio in Copenhagen.   59
10 *The Egyptian Mummy* (1914).   60
11 *Ladies' Skirts Nailed to a Fence* (1900).   61
12 *Easy Street* (1917).   61
13 *Le Voyage dans la lune* (1902).   63
14 *Rear Window* (1954).   77
15 *The Lady and the Mouse* (1913).   89
16 *The Man With a Movie Camera* (1929).   93
17 *The Salvation Army Lass* (1908).   95
18 Surreal POV in *Un chien Andalou* (1929).   96
19 *The Great Train Robbery* (1903).   111
20 *L'Arrivée d'un train à la Ciotat* (1895–6).   113
21 *How It Feels to Be Run Over* (1900).   114
22 *The Big Swallow* (1900).   114
23 *The Great Train Robbery* (1903).   115
24 The Müller–Lyer illusion.   116
25 Title unknown (1904).   118
26 *Bangville Police* (Keystone, 1913).   119
27 *Le Chien de Montargis* (1909).   120

28 *Das Cabinet des Dr. Caligari* (1920).   123
29 *The Egyptian Mummy* (1914).   124
30 *Nosferatu* (1922).   127
31 *Citizen Kane* (1941).   129
32 Unknown (1904).   132
33 *Die Hard* (1988).   133
34 *Psycho* (1960).   134
35 *Friday the 13th: The Final Chapter* (1984).   135
36 *Nosferatu* (1922).   136
37 Promotional poster for *House of Wax* (1953).   137
38 *Sommaren med Monika* (1953).   140
39 *Seven Samurai* (1954).   151
40 The Western model of the mind.   164
41 Model of appraisal parameters.   170
42 *Die Hard* (1988).   194
43 *North by Northwest* (1959).   195
44 *Seven Samurai* (1954).   196
45 *Steamboat Bill, Jr.* (1928).   197
46 *Der Letzte Mann* (1924).   199
47 *Rear Window* (1954).   200
48 *The Big Parade* (1925).   208
49 *Die Hard* (1988).   213
50 *Die Hard* (1988).   215
51 *Die Hard* (1988).   230
52 *The Great Train Robbery* (1903).   235

Preface and Acknowledgments

A number of people have contributed to this project. Although I have exposed my supervisor, Jan Olsson, to many long and tedious texts over the years, he has patiently endured and given fast feedback in the intelligent and verbally equilibristic way that is only his. In the same spirit, many fellow students and teachers at the colloquium in the Department of Cinema Studies, Stockholm University, have given me constructive criticism when it was best needed. I would like to express my thanks to David Bordwell, who took the time to read and comment on some of my draft chapters and inspired me academically with his lectures and professionalism. David Modjeska's meticulous revision of my English provided invaluable help, and his corrections often led to clarifications of content. Younghee Jung and my brother, Ola Persson, delicately provided the form and layout of the book. Maxime Fleckner Ducey granted me access to the archives of Wisconsin Center for Film and Theater Research, from which most of the photographic material in this book originates. The staff at the Department of Cinema Studies helped me with technical and economical matters all through the project. The Sweden–America Foundation allowed me the financial means to stay abroad for a year. Additional funding was provided for by Holger och Thyra Lauritzens Stiftelse, Wallenbergsstiftelsens Jubileumsfond, Run-Jannes Stipendium, and the Swedish Institute of Computer Science. I would also like to express my gratitude to all people at the HUMLE lab at the Swedish Institute of Computer Science for their generous support and constructive discussions. In particular, Kristina Höök's persistent encouragement – economically, academically, and personally – took me through many of the dark labyrinths that all projects of this nature eventually always run into. Finally, I thank Ewa Björnsson and Jonny Persson, my mother and father. If it were not for their joint support, constructive encouragement, and unconditional love all through the years, this study would simply not exist.

Understanding Cinema

A Psychological Theory of Moving Imagery

CHAPTER ONE

Understanding and Dispositions

This book is meant to be a contribution to the psychology of film. (Tan, 1996, p. ix)

The phenomenal world of humans is indeed remarkably rich and complex. It involves the understanding and the experience of the world around us, including sensation, perception, thought, and emotion. The phenomenal is the common-sense appearance of the world ("in here"), and it is the *Lebenswelt* (living world) on which we base our actions and behavior. To use the computer metaphor, the phenomenal world becomes the interface to the environment around us, structuring and directing behavior. As we receive response and feedback from the physical, social, and cultural habitat, the phenomenal transforms and adapts; thus enters a continuous loop among phenomenal–behavior–response–phenomenal. The phenomenal world is not the same thing to all individuals, but large parts of it are shared globally or locally.

The following list gives examples of the phenomenal:

- In the external world, colors exist only as light frequencies, but in the phenomenal world we see colors.
- In the phenomenal world, we perceive and categorize entities called objects that have certain properties, such as color, weight, and position. We can create new objects (artifacts), and we develop habits with objects, in addition to attaching a symbolic–emotional meaning to them.
- In the phenomenal world, things not only exist: Things *happen*. Billiard balls collide, plants grow, prices are raised, people lose their jobs, children beat up their siblings, and friends become sad once in a while. Most of us do not treat these events as random and whimsical, but rather we construct causal relations between them and other events. Causality is one of the most fundamental parameters of the phenomenal world.

1

- In the phenomenal world, we make clear distinctions between living and nonliving matter, between agents and things. Agents have personality and character and are driven by emotions, perceptions, and intentions. We use specialized communicatory, social, and moral codes in our interaction with agents. In the phenomenal world, we entertain social stereotypes, which we project on people based on their surface appearance (skin color, face and bodily appearance, gender, clothing).

- In the phenomenal world, we experience events and social situations that can be said to be coherent routines and habitual activities that involve a temporal chain of events, standard roles to be played as well as specialized activities often involving props or artifacts. Examples include dining at restaurants, going to bed, having breakfast, and visiting the doctor. Retelling and making sense of our day at night often invoke situations of this kind.

- In the phenomenal world, we have complex social relations with other people, for example, family relations, partners, relatives, friends, business contacts, doctors, and priests. Such relations are important experiential hubs around which the lives of many people circle.

- Cultural, religious, and personal rituals are important in the phenomenal world to give sense and meaning to the world and to provide formalized social interactions.

- Narratives and fictional worlds are key phenomenal entities that are created by others (novelists, filmmakers, game producers, porno producers) or ourselves through play, toys, and games of make-believe. We enter such fictional worlds, and they affect our experience and behavior in short- and long-term perspectives.

- Many narratives purportedly deal with actual events and characters of historic, national, and religious natures. Shared "grand narratives" occupy a key position in people's lives.

- Emotions are mechanisms by which we relate to and make meaningful the world around us. Emotions are experiences that regulate and synchronize our behavior with others.

Thus the phenomenal world is the world we perceive, experience, feel, desire, think about, talk about, and have attitudes about; it comprises the things with which we live and through which we live. The phenomenal world is multilayered and multifaceted, involving an intricate system of bodies, minds, culture, artifacts, history, social processes, and individual experiences. There is no reason to believe that natural systems of atoms, nuclear particles, molecules, cells, or macrocosmos are more complex than human systems. It is the task of the humanities and the social sciences to explain how this system emerges (from behavior, bodies, and culture) and transforms and affects behavior, as well as to describe the mechanisms by which it operates. In academia, there are now at least four broad approaches to describe the phenomenal world of humans.

In philosophy – until recently the only systematic investigation of the phenomenal – metaphysics and epistemology are concerned with the relation between the phenomenal and the objective, observer-independent, external world "out there." Do the entities in the phenomenal world have their equivalents in this *Ding-an-sich* (object in itself) world? Do objects continue to exist even if we do not perceive them? If so, do they have the same properties as phenomenal objects? Are there actual causes in the world, and do they have the same features as phenomenal causes? Do mental states, such as intentions and emotions, exist in our *Ding-an-sich* reality? Do these phenomena exist independent of human observers, or are they abstract frameworks and conceptualizations of our constructive capacities? If we are looking for a justification for knowledge and scientific inquiry, these questions need answers.

The phenomenal is also a topic within the philosophy of consciousness (Churchland, 1988), which investigates how conscious experiences (in philosophy called *qualia*) emerge. Are such phenomenal entities products of neurons or do they arise because of the functional architecture of our minds and bodies? The philosophy of aesthetics discusses the ontological status of fictional experiences (Walton, 1990) and describes the functions of art and aesthetic experiences.

A second approach to the phenomenal is through culture. The introduction of culture – with its artifacts, tools, technology, rituals, images, and words – has been acknowledged as one of the key mechanisms by which our species started to develop a rich phenomenal world (Cole, 1996:146ff). Cultural artifacts such as knives, spears, fire, telephones, restaurants, computers, and moving imagery instigate new ways of thinking about the world, new practices, and new phenomenal worlds that did not exist before. Collectively and in interaction with those artifacts, members of a culture develop practices, conventions, norms, and codes (this is true of tangible artifacts as well as more ephemeral artifacts, such as spoken words or moving imagery). Several strands within cultural studies, history, and cultural psychology investigate how the introduction of new technology, artifacts, and instruments is appropriated by a culture and how it changes its members' (phenomenal) view of the world (the plough, writing technology, the printing press, the camera, the car, the airplane, space technology, or, more recently, gene technology). Within the humanities – for example, in cinema studies – there are research traditions that focus on how individual works of art, music, film, or literature create not only temporary phenomenal experiences, but also change the cultural climate. A film (or a genre of films), for instance, might introduce a new theme, style, or convention that transforms the way in which critics, authors, and audience understand literature and the rest of the world.

Other cultural approaches investigate to what extent phenomenal worlds are shared among members of a group. Because cultural artifacts are mass distributed, these new phenomenal worlds become shared by many individuals, synchronizing or homogenizing thought and behavior within a group or culture. On what level and to what extent are phenomenal worlds shared universally, culturally, or socially? Is there a panhuman unity? In what ways do cultures, nations, and social groups differ in terms of the phenomenal? And how can one phenomenal world be understood by and translated to another? These are research questions within anthropology, cultural studies, sociology, and cultural psychology.

From a communication point of view, shared phenomenal worlds enable personal and mass communication. On the other hand, cultural homogenization and culture's ability to synchronize individual minds threaten to lessen cultural variation. The ways in which cultural practices create a hegemony in the distribution of phenomenal worlds, promoting one phenomenal world at the expense of others, have been the focus of much recent cultural and critical theory. In these research traditions, "marginalized voices," minorities, and nonofficial cultural practices have been brought to the fore to counter the dominant phenomenal world of a culture. Critical investigations of mass media are particularly crucial in this respect, as mass-media technology boosts the cultural homogenization process in scope as well as in speed.[1]

Third, we may describe the phenomenal within a Darwinian perspective. The phenomenal world did not emerge in a day. It was developed through phylogenetic and cultural history. Evolutionary theories argue that this development was not completely ad hoc and random, but that contents of the phenomenal world adapted to features in our habitat. Our experiences of objects, space, and causes are relevant in an environment in which it is critical for us to perceive and manipulate objects, navigate in space, and understand (mechanical) causal relations between events. The highly social skills of humans must have provided a great advantage in a complex social environment (Byrne & Whiten, 1988; Whiten, 1991). The ways in which we categorize, evaluate, predict the behavior of, and morally judge other people lay the groundwork for decisions about whether to exchange greetings, converse, socialize, impress, flirt, enter partnership, trust, or even marry and have children (Barkow, Cosmides & Tooby, 1992). Positive emotions of empathy and social bonding seem to promote social cooperation, and thus they have a strong survival value

(Grodal, 1997:94). The ability to initiate fantasies and games of make-believe enables us to simulate events and situations in our minds before we play them out for real in the social world. Such a faculty of mind performs useful functions in the life of humans and must reasonably have had great evolutionary value.

Moreover, if we accept that biology and genetics are put to work within this evolutionary framework, we may even expect to see some of the "successful" phenomenal entities and mental capacities encoded and hardwired into our genetic structure, making the ontogenetic development of these phenomenal abilities more or less automatic and less dependent on stimuli from the environment. Because these processes are extremely slow, we can expect that the "evolved structure of the human mind is adapted to the way of life of Pleistocene hunter–gatherers, and not to our modern circumstances" (Cosmides, Tooby & Barkow, 1992:5).

Of course, changes in the sociocultural environment affect the phenomenal world a great deal faster than do changes in the physical–perceptual environment. Thus, to use the words of cultural psychology, "[a]t some point in evolutionary history, an ability to adapt to cultural changes must have become much more critical than a genetic/biological ability to adapt to changes in the physical/natural habitat, since the former transforms so much faster than the latter" (Cole, 1996:163). In a sense, then, culture takes on a greater responsibility in the creation of the phenomenal. However, rather than creating wholly new realms of the phenomenal, cultural artifacts and cultural practices build upon existing evolutionary-developed mental capacities, "exploiting" them to generate culturally diverse realms of meaning.[2] Culture also provides a fundamental infrastructure to uphold, maintain, and stimulate phenomenal entities, for example, through cultural practices, artifacts, and written and image-based communication.

Finally, we may approach the phenomenal from the perspective of the *mental* mechanisms by which the phenomenal emerge in the mind or psyche of the individual. This is the *psychological* approach, investigating physiological, perceptual, cognitive, and emotional processes involved in the creation of the phenomenal. What knowledge, assumptions, and hypotheses about the world are used, and how are these mental structures organized? What cues and stimuli from the "outside" are pertinent to the mind? How do we create a *meaningful* experience of our environment? Once created, how do phenomenal entities provide the basis for action and behavior?

Scholars and researchers need not take all of these perspectives into account in their descriptions of phenomenal entities. What they do need to acknowledge, however, is that they are all needed in an integrated and full account. They all investigate the different evolutionary, mental,

cultural, social, and historical systems that enable complex phenomenal worlds to emerge and thrive so successfully in and around humans. Whereas the natural sciences describe natural systems of particles,
molecules, cells, and stars, the humanities and the social sciences investigate human–sociocultural systems. Acknowledging that philosophy,
psychology, sociology, cultural studies, communication studies, anthropology, and Darwinism are all in the same boat, however, is not to say
that all of them can be reduced to one. The existence of each is called for
because each describes separate levels of the phenomenal. For instance,
although individual mental states form the basis of the phenomenal, sociological and communication-based frameworks are needed to describe
the effects of many people sharing the same phenomenal worlds and how
those phenomenal worlds are propagated in a social setting. The psychological and the social are different levels of description, each with its own
properties and relationships. This is not too dissimilar from the natural
sciences. Although genes and cells ultimately are made up of quantum
particles, a biological description cannot be reduced to physics, as the
biological level has its own properties and laws.

Unlike the natural sciences, however, the disciplines in the humanities and the social sciences have achieved little conceptual integration
(Cosmides et al., 1992:4). Whereas terminology, theories, and methodology of physics, chemistry, biology, and the engineering sciences are compatible, few researchers in the humanities and the social sciences make
much effort to understand other academic approaches; they fail to adjust
their theories to comply with the insights of the neighboring field. If we
want to achieve the fullest description of the phenomenal and the human
systems that have brought it into existence, scholars and researchers have
a responsibility to integrate their – now rather disparate – frameworks.
This book is an effort in this direction. Although the focus is on psychology and mental processes, historic, cultural, and communicational
perspectives are integrated into the theories and descriptions. This ecumenical ambition is essential to keep in mind as we now move on to a
closer description of psychology and a psychological theory of cinema.

Psychology: Understanding and Dispositions

Compared with cinema studies, the academic discipline of psychology is a
giant and includes a number of subfields. Social psychology is concerned
with our understanding of other people and multiparticipant situations.
Personality psychology studies abstract traits of people, for example,
introversion, extroversion, and agreeableness, and develops the criteria
for measuring such features. Cognitive psychologists investigate perception, memory, thought, knowledge, and problem solving. Developmental

psychology investigates how mental capacities and processes are transformed during life, in particular during childhood and adolescence. Clin-
ical psychologists study and treat pathological and deviant psychological
processes and behavior. Industrial or organizational psychologists deal
with the physical and the social aspects of people's work environments
and how they affect work output. Evolutionary psychologists are interested in studying the evolved structure of the mind and how human mental capacities differ from or overlap those of animals. Neuropsychology
looks into the relation between the mental sphere and its neurological basis. Cultural psychology investigates how behavior and thought processes
are affected by cultural artifacts, technology, and language. Environmental psychology examines the interrelationship between environments and
human behavior. In short, psychologists are all over the place.

Being a book about film and psychology, this study does not do justice
to the whole field. Neither do I concentrate on one psychological sub-
field. In contrast to psychoanalytical cinema studies, which draws on one
small, marginalized segment of psychology, the framework developed in
this book is broad, involving traditions in the center of and on the mar-
gin of academia psychology. Psychology, according to most handbooks,
is the systematic study of *behavior* and *mental processes* – and their interaction. Mental processes involve perception, comprehension, interpretation,
evaluation, judgment, inference making, and emotion. From an individual perspective, these are the processes by which the phenomenal world
emerges in our consciousness. Thus, preceding the phenomenal world is a
complex and multilayered web of processes that take cues from the physical, social, and cultural environment, but also transform, add to, and make
richer those cues. Mental processes enable the leap from the transcenden-
tal, observer-independent *Ding-an-sich* reality to the internal phenomenal
world that we know and are able to handle. Mental processes ultimately
are operations by which the individual mind infuses *meaningfulness* and
coherence into a fragmented and nonmeaningful objective world, generating holistic chunks of phenomenal entities (e.g., objects, events, intentions,
and causes). In the subsequent text, *understanding* is the general term for
these processes, reflecting a striving for meaningfulness on all levels of
process (see Johnson, 1987; Lakoff, 1987). Understanding is an ongoing
interaction between an organism and its environment:

Understanding does not consist of merely after-the-fact reflections on prior experiences; it is, more fundamentally, the way (or means by which) we have those
experiences in the first place. It is the way the world presents itself to us. And
this is the result of the massive complex of culture, language, history, and bodily
mechanisms that blend to make our world what it is. . . . Our subsequent propositional reflections on our experience are made possible by this more basic mode of
understanding. (Johnson, 1987:104)

Understanding is the process by which we come to "have a world," forming the basis for our physical, cultural, social, and ethical behavior in the world. Although understanding connotes "cold" processes (perception, cognition), it is deeply involved in the "hot" processes of emotions and feelings.

Understanding, however, does not operate in a void. It is enabled, constrained, and guided by *mental structures*. The idea of mental structures is not new. Both Kant and Hume, for instance, postulated some mediating *schemas* or *categories* between the phenomenal and the observer-independent world (in the domains of space, time, and causality). Areas of psychology have picked up and developed the concept of mental structures to explain why mental processes and our understanding of the world have such a stability and regularity as they do and why the phenomenal world in many cases seems to be different from the "real world." Mental structures can be seen as patterns or mediators, transforming, enhancing, enriching, and generalizing the incoming stimuli to generate the phenomenal world.

Within psychology, mental structures have been described and investigated on many levels. Our system of visual perception, for instance, is able to infer a three-dimensional (3D) object in the phenomenal realm from a two-dimensional (2D) retina projection of objects at the back of the eye. Although seemingly without effort, this remarkable task is performed with the guidance of perceptual expectations held by the visual system. A straight line in two dimensions, for instance, could in 3D space be interpreted as a straight line, but also as a circle seen from the side, a wiggly curve from the side, or a square from the side. To bring 3D coherence to and untangle input such as this, it is believed that the vision system operates according to forty or so rules or perceptual assumptions, specifying how to interpret incoming stimuli and how to reach stable 3D solutions to a 2D array (Hoffman, 1998). The visual illusions generated by artists and psychologists exploit such assumptions, often leading the observer to apply oppositional rules to the same information. In establishing stable worlds of objects and space, our systems for vision, hearing, and touch rely on a number of such perceptual assumptions.[3]

More complex mental structures are often referred to as models, theories, hypotheses, common-sense knowledge, or background knowledge. These are more or less systematic conglomerates of beliefs (not necessarily conscious) that are causally, temporally, or otherwise linked with one another. These mental structures form the basis for the ways in which everyday reasoning is performed in everyday life. Some of them may be more foundational, whereas others are quite domain specific. Everyday logical reasoning, for instance, is a foundational capability that is applied to many domains in life. The ways in which peoples' everyday deductions, inductions, syllogisms, and other forms of conclusions differ from those of formal logic have been considered in cognitive psychology (e.g., Evans, Newstead & Byrne, 1993). Johnson's (1987) *image schemas*, which are thought structures that emerge from our embodied interaction with a gravitational environment, are also foundational in this sense. They bring organization to experience in many different domains.

Domain-specific everyday knowledge structures have been investigated in a number of fields. Hume (1739), Piaget (1954), and White (1995) have argued that children and adults acquire and use *theories of causality* when they establish causality in the mechanical world. Such models of causality often overlap with and are creatively expanded into common-sense or *folk theories* of physics and chemistry (Gentner & Stevens, 1983; McCloskey, 1983).

When giving causes of human behavior, on the other hand, people often ascribe these causes to intentions, emotions, sensations, perceptions, or beliefs. The methods by which such mental states are given causal status and how people reason around these are thought to rely on complex and often culturally specific models of folk psychology (FP) (Dennett, 1987, 1991b; Lakoff & Kövecses, 1987; Omdahl, 1995; Roseman, Antoniou & Jose, 1996; van den Broek, Bauer & Bourg, 1997; White, 1995; Whiten, 1991; Chapter 4 of this book).

Environmental psychology is concerned with how people acquire mental models of a given environment (a room, a building, a city, a landscape) and make use of such *mental maps* in navigation (Weatherford, 1985).

Another field of inquiry has been human interaction with mechanical and technical systems such as computers, copying machines, home heating systems (Kempton, 1986), VHS recorders, and cars. In trying to understand and interact with a system, users develop *mental models* about how the system works, often drawing on mental models from other domains (e.g., the desktop metaphor of computer interfaces). To design systems that trigger appropriate mental models and interaction patterns, system developers and designers need to know how mental models are structured and used.

In the social realm, people entertain a number of common-sense knowledge structures. In addition to making use of folk-psychology to attribute mental states to others, we ascribe personality traits to them (Andersen & Klatzky, 1987). We may, for instance, make sense of John's tendency to be late by referring to "his carelessness." People seem to have consistent and shared models about traits and how to apply them to behavior (see Chapter 4, the section on the Psychology of Recognition and Alignment, and Cantor & Mischel, 1979). Traits give us handy ways to summarize and abstract complex chains of behaviors, as well as to create first impressions of new acquaintances. In addition, people categorize others through *social roles* and *stereotypes*. We have cultural knowledge about *occupancy roles* (e.g., police, waiters, officers, farmers, and programmers), *family roles* (e.g., mother, father, daughter, and cousin), and *situation roles* (e.g., lecturer–student, buyer–seller, waiter–restaurant guest, and master–slave). People in different cultures hold complex assumptions and theories about how such social roles should be acted out, which affects not only how other people's behavior is perceived, but also how to behave in everyday life (Augoustinos & Walker, 1995:39; Taylor & Crocker, 1981:91). In addition, *social stereotypes* are idealized and simplified assumptions of groups of people along the lines of ethnicity, religion, political convictions, gender, handicap, profession, physiognomy, and social class (Augoustinous & Walker, 1995:207; Ruble & Stangor, 1986). In Western society, for instance, women are considered to be emotional, bachelors are held to be macho and interested in sexual conquests, and the stereotypical Japanese person is industrious, polite, and clever. In cultural studies, social stereotypes are often described on a representational level, that is, how stereotypes are represented in and circulated by public discourse such as newspapers, film, literature, and computer games. However, social stereotypes are also represented in the minds of the individuals in a given culture and operate in their understanding of the world (and in their generation of discourse – see, e.g., Holland & Skinner, 1987). Like all social roles, stereotypes are often tightly linked to external marks, clearly discernible and salient: skin color, hair color, body size, man or woman, clothing, and age (Augoustinos & Walker, 1995:39ff). In first-encounter categorizations of another person, this "visuality" acts as a trigger of stereotype expectations. In contrast to traits and occupancy roles, stereotypes often involve moral judgments that may lead to acts of social injustice (Tan, 1996:168). Many social stereotypes act as objectified knowledge in collective and social life.

Event schemas are mental structures that contain (often culturally specific) expectations about social situations, such as dining at restaurants, going for a bus ride, going to a soccer game, having a birthday party, having breakfast, courting, and changing diapers (Abbott, Black & Smith, 1985; Bower, Black & Turner, 1979; Cole, 1996:187ff; den Uyl & van Oostendorp, 1980; Graesser, Gordon, and Sawyer, 1979; Mandler, 1984; Schank & Abelson, 1977; Taylor & Crocker, 1981; van den Broek et al., 1997).

Event schemas are the knowledge structures that enable people to appraise the basic nature of a situation and act in a socially appropriate manner. They hold expectations not only about social roles to be played, but also about typical locale, typical instruments and props, typical conditions for entering the situation, a standard sequence of scenes or actions in which one action enables the next, and some standard results of successfully performing the activity. The presence and operations of implicit event schemas can be tested by text-recall experiments. Bower et al. (1979), for instance, found a strong tendency for subjects to falsely recall actions that were not part of an original text, but that were strongly implied by the event schema. For example, if the text stated that John ordered food and later left the restaurant, subjects tended to remember that John also ate the food and paid for it, although it was not explicitly mentioned in the text. The understanding and the memory of the text were constructed based not only on textual structures, but also on common-sense expectations about restaurant visits. It is believed that we appropriate approximately a hundred or so event schemas as we develop as cultural beings in the socialization process.

(Cognitive) anthropology and cognitive semantics are concerned with mental structures that are manifested in language or cultural practice, so-called cultural models. The authors in the book edited by Holland and Quinn (1987), for instance, describe a number of cultural models, such as Americans' systematic view on marriage, how the cultural model of anger is expressed in American English, how illness is understood and talked about among Ecuadorians, and how Americans define the notion of a lie. Lakoff (1987) follows the same approach through more detailed linguistic evidence and sketches what he calls *idealized cognitive models* of, for example, colors, animals, plants, bachelors, mothers, going somewhere, over, and there. Lakoff and Johnson (1999) investigate the structural metaphors of time, events, causes, mind, self, and morality in the discourse of cognitive science and philosophy. Shore (1996) lists a number of Western and non-Western cultural models. All of these approaches overlap, to some extent, traditional sociology, anthropology, and cultural studies insofar as they investigate cultural understandings of various phenomena. Cognitive approaches to anthropology or semantics, however, treat culture less as the external customs, traditions, practices, or representations but rather as the knowledge people need "in order to act as they do, make the things they make, and interpret their experience in the distinctive way they do" (Quinn & Holland, 1987:4). Of course, culture exists as artifacts, habits, and behavior in the actual world. Equally important, however, those artifacts, habits, and behaviors are represented in the minds of people in the form of mental structures (see Shore's [1996:52] distinction between *culture-in-the-world* and *culture-in-the-mind*[4]).

Many facets of the social sciences investigate similar cultural models. When sociologists, cultural researchers, television researchers, ethnographers, and opinion-poll researchers conduct interviews or ask subjects to answer questionnaires about various cultural phenomena, they investigate shared cultural models. In our culture, people have complex theories about and attitudes toward Dallas, fan magazines, MTV, Pokemon, winners of the Nobel prize for literature, traffic congestions, modern art, consumerism, mobile telephones, smoking, Leonardo Di Caprio, Hitler, prime ministers and politicians, or any other cultural entities. People also entertain complex models of historical events, wars, conflicts, historical figures, and the causes of historical events. In most cultures, theories, myths, and narratives about history are vital to maintaining social, national, and ethnic identities and are thus powerful thought structures (White, 1990). Of course, these investigations into cultural models can also be conducted within a historical perspective, describing cultural models that used to operate but no longer circulate in our present-day culture. However, in history, the history of ideas, cultural and media history, interviews and questionnaires have to be replaced with an analysis of archival material such as written or printed material, archeological evidence, and historical artifacts. Of course, few of these approaches to cultural models treat them as mental structures in the mind of individual inhabitants of a culture of historical era. A psychological approach to culture, however, does.

It is important to note that cultural models are not exclusively concerned with facts and real entities. Cultural models may contain expectations of facts as well as of fiction and fantasy. People have sophisticated knowledge about the destiny, personality, social relations, attitudes, and physical appearance of Odysseus, Ally McBeal, Santa Claus, Macbeth, Winnie the Pooh, and Robinson Crusoe, although these characters are fictional in nature. People have fictional expectations of character types, e.g., the hero, the villain, the princess, and the Mafioso, as well as expectations of what type of fiction these characters are typically involved in. Audiences have sophisticated assumptions about genre (typical plotlines, typical character galleries, typical actions and behavior, typical moral structure, typical instruments, and locales). As children and adults, we engage in games of make-believe through play, toys, literature, film, television, and dreaming, and we come to develop complex mental structures about fictional worlds (Walton, 1990). As fictions are shared within a community or a culture, such fictional expectations often become socially shared.

Mental structures also encompass even more abstract phenomena such as people's image of politics, morals, righteousness, individual freedom, responsibility of the state, industrialization, urbanization, or modernity. In addition, religious thought structures of fate, death, life, God(s), forgiveness, and confession are central in many people's understanding of and behavior in the world. Again, these quite abstract and general apprehensions are often investigated from a culturalist–historical perspective (within cultural studies, history of ideas, and history of politics), but they can also be treated as mental structures represented in the minds of individuals.

This sample list of mental structures is not comprehensive, but it gives a flavor of the breadth and the wealth of the various levels that shape the processes of understanding. Although academic investigations have not referred to them as individual and mental phenomena (knowledge, schemas, assumptions, expectations), these types of foreknowledge are represented in the minds of humans, socialized individuals, and members of a culture. Moreover, although they exist on widely different levels of processing, they belong together because they provide the mental tools by which individuals make sense of their physical, social, and cultural environments. In concert, they enable individuals to *understand* and to *act* within these environments. To mark this functional connection between the levels, I use one broad term to denote all of them. Although *knowledge* and *cognitive models* tend to exclude cultural aspects and *cultural models* seem to disregard noncultural mental structures, *disposition* seems to be the most neutral term to cover all levels. Dispositions are the totality of expectations, assumptions, hypotheses, theories, rules, codes, and prejudices that individuals project onto the world. Through these capacities, humans are *disposed* to understand the world in a certain preconfigured way, already prepared for some regularities of the world. Equipped with dispositions, the mind–body complex is already "halfway in the world" (cf. Heidegger's *in-der-Welt-sein* [existence in the world] or Brentano's *intentionality*). Through our acquired dispositions, we "reach out" toward reality even before we start taking things in. Together, dispositions and understanding constitute the basic building blocks of psychology.

Parameters of Dispositions
In the mental architecture, dispositions perform a number of essential functions. Dispositions guide the encoding of information, bring coherence to the incoming stimuli, and lend structure to experience. Because dispositions often contain internal coherence, placing stimuli into those frames of mind usually means that the phenomenal world becomes stable and reliable. Even though stimuli are scarce and poor, dispositions provide the background and the "carpet of assumptions" that enable the mind–body complex to make sense of the data presented, filling in where information is missing. This occurs in "here-and-now" situations, as well as in recalling, fantasizing, dreaming, and other reconstructive enterprises. For instance, a great number of studies within cognitive psychology have shown how mental schemas supplement in situations in which memory fails (e.g., Bower et al., 1979).

Dispositions also enable reasoning, explanations, and predictions. Dispositions come in different forms of sophistication, but all have structures that enable inferences. For instance, if I categorize a man as an introvert, I can draw the conclusion that he is also quiet and shy (according to the trait model). If a man has finished eating at a restaurant, he has probably already ordered (according to the going-to-a-restaurant event schema). Because dispositions often specify probable temporal, spatial, and causal relations among objects, events, and behavior, such everyday reasoning becomes possible. Because dispositions are shared across individuals in a given culture, there is often a general social consensus about the (non)validity of such explanations and predictions, at least in common-sense reasoning. Predictive inferences allow people to make qualified predictions of how physical and social reality will behave in the future. For sure, such folk-theoretical predictions are primitive and simplified, but they are almost certainly more valuable to the organism than no predictive ability at all (in terms of Folk Psychology, see the discussion in Chapter 4, the subsection on the Instrumental Value of Folk Psychology).

Because dispositions are general, simplified, and idealized models of the world, they save cognitive energy. Hoffman's perceptual rules, a restaurant schema, social stereotypes, or the diverse heuristics in attributing cause and effects are simplified conceptions of the world, by which we "uncomplicate" reality and thereby "make sense" of it. Event schemas, for instance, are not fleshed-out memories of particular restaurant visits or bus rides, but abstract models of what restaurant visits *generally* include, in what order events in those situations *prototypically* happen, and what props and roles are most *typically* involved. Using such idealized models in understanding or recalling a situation, event, or object liberates the mind from the impossible task of making sense of and recalling every nitty-gritty detail. Instead, unique phenomena are placed within abstract frameworks. All behavior and events taking place at Mickey's last night are placed in "a restaurant visit." Many actions of John are simply subsumed under the trait "careless." In gaining our first impressions of people, we often tend to ignore complexities in behavior and appearance and to categorize them along social, ethnic, religious, and other stereotypical lines.

Even though such "top-down" processes are fast, do not require us to model reality from scratch, and may work well in some situations, the simplified nature of dispositions may make them contraproductive. Consider the following riddle:

A FATHER AND HIS SON ARE DRIVING ALONG A MOTORWAY WHEN AN ACCIDENT OCCURS. THE FATHER IS KILLED. THE SON IS SEVERELY INJURED AND TAKEN TO THE HOSPITAL. IN THE OPERATING ROOM, THE SURGEON LOOKS AT THE CHILD AND EXCLAIMS, 'MY GOD, IT'S MY SON!' HOW COULD THIS BE?[5]

The failure (?) to identify the answer to the seeming contradiction is attributed to the fact that our society maintains a social stereotype that associates surgeons with men. When our tacit assumptions fail to distinguish between male and female surgeons, we also fall short in solving the riddle. As more and more surgeons of today are women, a person operating with such a stereotype will surely run into more serious social dilemmas than failing to solve riddles. Although disposition-driven processes ("simplification") help to make a fragmented world appear meaningful without much cognitive strain, stimuli-driven processes enable us to detect new distinctions and hierarchies in the world, as well as to modify and transform the structure of the dispositions that we already have. Learning, science, scholarship, criticism, and art, for instance, seem to require that we (make an effort to) put some of our dispositions and foreknowledge aside and attend to things with "a fresh mind," taking things at "face value" or "from another, unusual perspective." To deal with a constantly changing physical and social habitat, balancing between these two cognitive modes seems to be crucial to any animal.

Dispositions are not singular and isolated structures of knowledge, but the mind maintains sophisticated mechanisms by which to combine dispositions. Metaphors and analogies are forceful tools by which the mind extends dispositions in one domain to another (Johnson, 1987; Lakoff, 1987; Lakoff & Johnson, 1980, 1999). Such conceptual mappings may be deliberate acts of speakers, but they also seem to be built into the language use and the cultural models we evoke when we talk.

Many dispositions emerge in or habitual interaction with reality. Their operations become habitual thinking, and we seldom reflect on the fact that we use dispositions in our understanding of reality. To use Hutchins's (1980:12) words, once dispositions are learned they become "what one *sees with*, but seldom what one *sees*." Because many dispositions are transparent in this way, phenomenal reality appears as if it existed objectively, independent of our perception of it. To Feldman (1987), this tendency to endow the phenomenal world with a special, external ontological status may be a human universal. She calls this "ontic dumping."[6] Of course, the fact that humans in their everyday business many times fail to reflect on their active dispositions does not mean that they are doomed to ignorance. Science, social science, the humanities, art, and public discourse often investigate and remind us about the foreknowledge by which our minds operate, making us aware of the ways in which we understand the physical, social, and cultural world. Dispositions do not reside in the Freudian unconscious, but rather in the *cognitive unconscious* (Lakoff & Johnson, 1999:9) or *preconscious*. Such mechanisms of awareness making are important for individuals as well as for cultures. Making explicit tacitly held and taking for granted dispositions and knowledge and putting them up for intimate scrutiny are essential for a culture to avoid stagnate consensus and intellectual decline. The possibility for awareness making also means that humans' destinies are not determined by dispositions, cultural or otherwise. Even though dispositions govern and constrain understanding and behavior, they also enable creativity and awareness-making processes. Humans and human cultures are able to break free from traditional thinking and to understand the world in novel ways. The cultural–psychological theory presented here is compliant with the fundamentals of Modernity and Enlightenment on individual and cultural levels.

Although we take an individual perspective of dispositions, we find that it is important to acknowledge the extent to which many of them are shared locally or even globally. To be sure, dispositions can be idiosyncratic and restricted to an individual. I may, for instance, have a mental map of the route to my work, or I may have memories from last year's Midsummer's Eve festivity that differ radically from those of my party friends. Many dispositions, however, are spread within a group, a community, a culture, or a species. We share dispositions and methods by which we understand the world. In this way, a great many people come to have overlapping phenomenal worlds. This fact, that individuals are not islands of solitary and idiosyncratic phenomenal worlds, is not a happy coincidence. Considering its communicatory, cultural, and evolutionary advantages, synchronizing minds and understandings of the world is invaluable. It enables smooth cooperation in activities, work, tasks, and communication. The fact that group members share dispositions about the environment – and are aware that they all share dispositions about the environment – enables members to predict the behavior of other group members in ways that profoundly improve cooperative activities. In this way, sharing habitual thinking and behavior makes altruistic tendencies more effective and thus more advantageous from a Darwinian point of view. Shared assumptions about the world also make oral, written, or image-based communication more efficient, easier, and less ambiguous. Sharing dispositions enables communication to leave out a great number of details and "context" that otherwise would have been required for making sense of the discourse. The more shared dispositions, the less information needs to be explicitly communicated. The ways in which (visual) communication relies on tacitly shared dispositions and the ways in which the dispositions of the spectator–reader guide the decoding of the discourse are the most central themes of this book.[7]

Shared dispositions also seem to provide a sense of group belonging and social identity that are crucial to the perseverance of any given culture or nation.

The extent to which people share dispositions and phenomenal worlds is, of course, not a settled question. Anthropologists, sociologists, communication researchers, psychologists, and others do not agree on panhuman universals, cultural homogeneity, and group consensus, nor the levels at which such shared phenomenal worlds should be best described. Moreover, as globalization gains speed, the objects of study seem to change faster than empirical studies can cope with, literally making anthropological results obsolete (or rather, historical) within months. In cinema studies, however, one thing seems to be clear. In describing the reception of visual media, *differences* in dispositions along lines of gender, ethnicity, and class have been prioritized at the expense of investigating the degree to which spectator groups *share* dispositions and understanding of a film. In this respect, in this book I hope to make a difference. In the following chapters I make the case for (semi)universal dispositions and describe the ways in which these contribute to a shared understanding of certain layers of cinematic meaning.

The issue of shared dispositions and phenomenal worlds is often confused with the question of their origin. Finding out whether a disposition is shared universally or locally restricted is a straightforward empirical endeavor. Explaining the causes of those results, however, is trickier. How and why do dispositions end up in the minds of people? Whereas Kant and Hume assumed that their categories were implanted there by a benevolent God, modern academia discusses other origins. Evolutionary approaches assume that some dispositions, proven to be valuable in the everyday lives of humans, over time become genetically encoded. This would ensure disposition continuity across generations. For instance, a basic ability to visually perceive 3D objects and determine their position in space in order to manipulate them and navigate among them is probably valuable to any creature of our size living on a planet such as ours. Another example would be the basic social skills required for coping with a social environment like that of humans. For instance, paying attention to the eyes of other people – their movements and directions – seems like such an old and basic social strategy that it may have been "hard–wired." Although this seems straightforward enough, it still needs to be determined how influential such genetic predispositions are and the extent to which environmental features spark, inform, enable, and change those emerging dispositions. This is the old nature–nurture issue. How much of our ability to perceive and categorize 3D objects is because we were born with an ability or a predisposition to develop an ability, and how much is caused by the fact that we inhabit and develop in a rich object environment that structures and shapes our visual system? Are the sensory–motor, cognitive, and emotional stages of Piaget's developmental psychology mainly caused by a genetic predisposition to develop those skills at a various point in time, or does a child actively have to learn, construct theories, and form dispositions from the embodied interaction with the environment?[8] These are difficult questions. Perhaps dispositions that are basic and critical for higher-level dispositions are genetically pushed into the mind of the child. If the child, for instance, fails to pay attention to another's eyes and has trouble establishing a mutual gaze with his or her caretaker, he or she will have problems developing basic empathic, social, and emotional skills in later developmental stages. Giving eye fixation a reflexological status in the newborn would impede such malfunctions.

Although interesting and important, the nature versus environment debate is centered on the individual. Culturalist approaches take this to another level, claiming that the so-called environment with which we interact is not something naturally given (consisting only of natural objects), but is something that we "artificially" create. I can design artifacts that structure my thoughts and incite new and innovative thinking (e.g., a sketch or a drawing). Most cultural artifacts and practices, however, exist before and beside my own intervention. Looking around my apartment, for example, I find very few objects that are either "natural" or manufactured by myself. Instead, culture, history, and economy have "created" tools, instruments, utensils, pottery, technology, props, buildings, clothes, computers, knives, and vehicles. In addition, each such artifact mediates and supports some form of habitual or routine activity that not only structures my behavior, but also allows me to "see" and imitate the practices of others. This also includes cultural practices in which no "physical" artifacts are involved, for example, rituals, dances, ceremonies, greetings, singing, customs, and body language. Cultural environment includes social and cultural rules, laws, and conventions, as well as the institutions for reprimanding those people who do not follow these rules. Finally, discourse and imagery forcefully influence the ways in which people acquire dispositions.[9] Although some species may be thought of as "artifact species" (think, for instance, of nesting activities among birds), none produce cultural environments with such complexity, range, and quantity as humans do (Cole, 1996).

As far as the origin of dispositions is concerned, the culturalist asks two questions. How and to what extent does the cultural environment (locally or globally distributed) determine individuals' dispositions? This may be seen as the traditional nature–nurture question, although the notion of *environment* probably differs between psychologists and cultural researchers. Second, cultural studies are not so much concerned with how dispositions end up in the minds of a cultural inhabitant (culture-in-the-mind), but rather to explain how cultural environments emerge and exist (culture-in-the-world). Describing the mechanisms by which dominant, semidominant, and subversive cultures struggle to design the cultural environment and to define the practices and codes in those environments constitutes a sociological level of description. This includes critical analysis of institutions, commercial forces, political lobbying, and the message of mass-communication channels. The sociological perspective extends the classical nature–nurture question and encompasses a much broader view of the origin of dispositions.

According to the stance I take in this book, dispositions originate from all of these sources. Genetics may be responsible for some dispositions, phylogenetically as well as ontogenetically. Our embodied interaction with and manipulation of physical reality are critical for many dispositions (Johnson, 1987). Cultural practices, conventions, and artifacts provide a rich habitat out of which many dispositions arise in the minds of people. Finally, to explain how and why people acquire a given set of cultural dispositions, history, cultural studies, media studies, cultural psychology, and anthropology need to describe how cultural environments exist and are transformed. This broad and integrative stance, of course, does not give answers to the origin of individual dispositions; it only acknowledges that causes of dispositions must be sought on many levels in an ecumenical spirit. To paraphrase Johnson (1987:xix), humans are *cultural* animals, but also cultural *animals*.

We now need to specify how dispositions and understanding operate in the reception of cinema and the ways in which spectators create meaning out of moving imagery.

A Psychological Model of Reception

The image is not an end in itself; it is a start. (Mitry, 1997:51)

Reception theories seek to explain the production and the emergence of meaning in the broadest sense of the term. The basic assumption is that spectators, or some aspect of the spectator, use or do things with the film object and that these activities decidedly influence the meaning of it. The film is not seen as an autonomous object that contains its own meaning, but rather as a structure that acquires its meaning in the confrontation or interaction with spectators' knowledge, world views, morals or, in my terms, dispositions: "[I]t is in the reader that the text comes to life" (Iser, 1978:19).

Over the years, film theory has produced or recruited models of reception (for overview and criticism, see Mayne, 1993; Persson, 2000). Soviet film theorists embraced reflexologic and behaviorist models of the spectator, in which meaning was thought of as (shock) effects of the film text. Eisenstein's (1988) spectator, for instance, is not a mind negotiating the text or evaluating alternative understandings, but is one who simply reacts involuntarily. In spite of Eisenstein's revolutionary ambitions for the film medium, he does not seem to recognize that different background assumptions (cognitively, culturally, social class, or gender) might be the source for different understandings of the film. Münsterberg's (1916/1970) purportedly psychological approach seems to promise a somewhat more complex theory of the spectator and meaning production. However, instead of explaining how close-ups, flashbacks, and point-of-view (POV) shots are understood and processed by the spectator, he suggests that these conventions imitate and materialize the mental processes of the spectator. The close-up, for instance, is said to "objectify" the mental process of attention (Münsterberg, 1916/1970:38). The screen almost seems to acquire a mind of its own, making it the site of meaning production – not the spectator. In the 1970s, the spectator was widely considered as a *subject*, driven by psychoanalytical or capitalist mechanisms. Often decontextualized from his or her psychological, cultural, and historical situation, the spectator assumed the role of a "position" rather than an embodied recipient. The implied reader–spectator, for instance, was "not the flesh-and-bones you or I sitting in our living rooms reading the book, but the audience presupposed by the narrative itself" (Chatman, 1978:149ff). This rather odd conception of the spectator was in fact less a theory of reception and more a theory of texts: "[I]t can be argued that contemporary psychoanalytic criticism, despite its claim to offer a theory of 'spectatorship,' is in fact not particularly concerned with the viewer" (Thompson, 1988:28).

Growing out of dissatisfaction with the abstract notion of spectator, cultural studies differentiated the audience in terms of ethnicity, culture, subculture, class, and gender, and claimed that these parameters of social identity decidedly influenced the reception process. The influential distinction of Hall et al. (1980) among *dominant*, *negotiated*, and *oppositional* readings of media took into consideration not only the socioeconomical background of the spectator, but also assumed that the spectator could (in theory) resist any dominant position offered by the text. Many researchers of cinema studies took this as yet another framework within which they could pursue introspectionist textual–critical analysis (for criticism, see Bordwell, 1989b); others started to turn to empirical methods by which they could validate different forms of reception. The ethnographic approach developed by the University of Birmingham's Centre for Contemporary Cultural Studies (of which Stuart Hall was a member), included *qualitative* methods (e.g., group interviews, individual interviews, participatory observation) and *quantitative* (e.g., questionnaires distributed among a large number of spectators). Although popular in media studies, few of these methods caught on with researchers in cinema studies, who instead turned to historical evidence. Through a meticulous study of reviews, fan magazines, promotional campaigns, exhibition conditions, trade papers, architecture, museums, postcards, censorship cards, and other legal documents, the "turn to history" in the middle of the 1980s sought to describe the social, historical, and media context in which reception took place (Abel, 1994; Bordwell, Staiger & Thompson, 1985; Burch, 1990; Elsaesser, 1990; Fullerton, 1998; Gomery, 1992; Gunning, 1994; Hansen, 1991; Jauss, 1970; Musser, 1990a; Pratt, 1973; Staiger, 1992; Tsivian, 1994; Uricchio & Pearson, 1993). By reconstructing long-forgotten media forms, genre systems, styles, screen practices, and entertainment forms, these scholars sought to explain why early cinema looks the way it does as well as how it was received by the audience. The production and the reception of early cinema, for instance, seem to have been influenced by the magic-lantern culture (Musser, 1990b; Rossell, 1998), vaudeville (Allen, 1980; Musser, 1990a;), museums (Griffiths, 1998), and other stage entertainment forms (Urrichio & Pearson, 1993). Finally, *cognitivism* is perhaps the newest and most multifaceted reception strand within cinema studies. It discusses low-level perception of moving imagery (Anderson, 1996). It deals with schema-based and assumption-based inference processes and investigates how such schemas are learned by the spectator from historical screen practices (Bordwell, 1985, 1989a; Thompson, 1988). It is concerned with the spectator's emotional involvement with fictional and documentary film (Carroll, 1990, 1996d; Grodal, 1997; Plantinga, 1994; Plantinga & Smith, 1999; Smith, 1995; Tan, 1996; Tan & Diteweg, 1996; Vorderer, Wulff & Friedrichsen, 1996). In addition, it engenders analytic philosophy discussions about the ontological status of fiction and moving imagery (Allen & Smith, 1997; Carroll, 1988, 1996a, 1996b, 1996c; Currie, 1995; Plantinga, 1997; Walton, 1990).

The psychological model of reception presented in this book is positively and negatively influenced by these theories, but it also takes cues from disciplines not considered within traditional cinema studies, e.g., psychological research on discourse understanding (Britton & Graesser, 1996; Graesser, Murray & Trabasso, 1994; Magliano, Dijkastra & Zwaan, 1996; van den Broek, 1997; van den Broek et al., 1997; Zwaan, 1993). Let us start with the concept of discourse and differentiate among the levels of meaning.

Discourse and Meaning

As mentioned, artifacts are of great importance to human experience. We develop tools, instruments, and technology (culture-in-the-world) with which individuals establish routines and habits. These habits then become internalized as dispositions (culture-in-the-mind), upholding cultural practice and enabling history. Discourse, natural language, and imagery are also artifacts in this sense, perhaps the most central ones (Cole, 1996:117). Instead of triggering concrete behavioral interaction patterns ("cutting," "driving," "sawing"), however, these artifacts prompt mental responses and thought processes. Nevertheless, they operate through the same mechanisms: Written words and imagery are culture-in-the-world structures, and through the culturalization process, individuals use and develop culture-in-the-mind habits with those structures. These habits constitute the cross individually shared dispositions (also known as codes, grammar, conventions, etc.), supporting not only the reception of discourse, but also the production of it. In this sense, even the ephemeral nature of spoken utterances can be seen as culture-in-the-world artifacts. In this way, "communication artifacts" are not principally different from more material artifacts such as tools and instruments.

In the following discussion, *discourse* denotes such communication artifacts. Discourse is not associated with natural language and linguistics (as it has tended to be within cinema studies), but covers all media and communication modalities: imagery, utterances, gestures, written words, moving imagery, and other forms of representations.

I previously described in general terms how individuals understand and make meaningful their physical, social, cultural, and historical environments. Assuming that discourse is one aspect of that environment, we can apply the same framework to how people understand or receive discursive structures. For instance, receivers of discourse – readers, spectators, listeners, players – will use their dispositions in trying to understand the discourse, in making it meaningful and coherent. Similar to "real-life" understanding, discourse understanding seeks to integrate the textual cues into internal meaningfulness based on dispositions. This strive for meaningfulness as the key driving force in the reception process constitutes the first postulate in our psychological theory of reception (see Graesser et al., 1994:371). This, of course, is not to say that spectators create the same kind of meanings in reality as they do with discourse, nor that spectators make use of identical set of dispositions in both realms (there are discourse-specific dispositions; see the subsection on Some Specifications of the Model). It is just to say that maximizing meaningfulness is a mental strategy shared by both discourse understanding and real-life understanding.

So then, what is meaning and meaningfulness in terms of cinematic reception? Some scholars are suspicious about the usefulness of this vague concept:

So many things might count as what is called "the meaning of film" that it is better to think of it in terms of the activity of diverse mechanisms, functioning to promote diverse purposes (some narrational, some emotional, some allegorical, and so on), which are conducive of diverse effects. The meaning of film is a rather baggy conception, somewhat loose or vague. (Carroll, 1996a:364)

However, just because a concept is "baggy" does not mean that we have to refrain from using it. It means only that we have to constrain its definition.

According to the psychological model of reception, meaning emerges out of the interaction between a disposition-equipped spectator and the film text. Just as in nondiscursive realms, meaningful experience is preceded by active mental processing by the spectator. Dispositions and processes of understanding transform, abstract, and add to the text to such an extent that we may talk about creative and constructive processes (shortly we shall learn how). Of course, text cues steer the production of meaning, but meaning requires a disposition-rich spectator who is actively searching for coherence in the film.[10] According to this approach, meaning is not contained in the film (or book, or image), but emerges in the constant negotiation between discourse and the dispositions of the spectator:

Textual structures and structured acts of comprehension are therefore the two poles in the act of communication, whose success will depend on the degree in which the text establishes itself as a correlative in the reader's consciousness. This 'transfer' of text to reader is often regarded as being brought about solely by the text. Any successful transfer however – though initiated by the text – depends on the extent to which the text can activate the individual reader's faculties of perceiving and processing. . . . This fact is worth emphasizing, because there are many current theories which give the impression that texts automatically imprint themselves on the reader's mind of their own accord. This applies not only to linguistic theories but also to Marxist theories. . . . Of course, the text is a 'structured prefigurement,' but that which is given has to be received, and the way in which it is received depends as much on the reader as on the text. Reading is not a direct 'internalization,' because it is not a one-way process, and our concern will be to find means of describing the reading process as a dynamic *interaction* between text and reader. (Iser, 1978:107)

Making the reader or spectator a coconstructor of meaning is not a new idea within cinema studies, literary studies, or other fields. What may be new in the psychological framework, however, is its emphasis on the *mental* nature of meaning and its production. Textual wholeness, unity, coherence, meaning, or whatever we may call it, is primarily a mental phenomena:

What do we mean, then, when we say that a conversational or written discourse is coherent? We probably mean that we are able to find relationships between the ideas based upon the contents of the discourse, and that the discovery of these

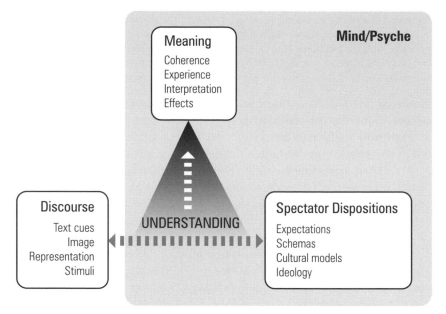

FIGURE 1. Meaning emerges from understanding. (Diagram by Younghee Jung.)

relations gives us the feeling of experiencing something holistic. The failure to find such relations would, conversely, lead us to feel that the discourse lacked coherence. Coherence, then, is a subjective state of mind that results from generating or evaluating ideas in relation to one another. (Trabasso, Suh & Payton, 1995:189ff)

According to this approach, the processes of understanding – as well as its meaningful "end products" – reside largely in the mental sphere of the spectator–reader (Figure 1). When Bordwell (1985:49) speaks about "the fabula" in terms of an "imaginary construct we create progressively and retroactively," he seems to mean something similar to the mental sphere.[11] This does not mean that all meanings are conscious; nor does it reduce the importance of the discourse. A reception theory needs to describe the ways in which discourse and spectator interact in order for meaning to emerge in the mind of the spectator. Or, as Bruner (1986:153) succinctly puts it, "how the meaning 'in' the text becomes a meaning 'in' the head of a reader."

We must further constrain our notion of meaning. When meaning is discussed, it is often spoken of in terms of *one* thing that overlaps or contrasts with others – e.g., "you and I have similar or dissimilar interpretations of this film." Meaning and coherence, however, are constructed not only in different *ways*, but also on different *levels* within the same reception. Written and image-based discourses are exceptionally rich sources of information from which a spectator can extract meaningful and coherent experiences on a wide variety of levels. If we want to define the notion of meaning and how meanings are constructed, we must specify the different levels at which reception may take place.

The idea of a multilevel meaning of discourse is not new. Staiger's (1992:18ff) distinctions among *reading, comprehension,* and *interpretation* somewhat overlap the following account, as do the frameworks of Bordwell (1989a:8ff), Grodal (1997:59ff), and Wilson' (1997). It is also reflected in the disciplinary departmentalization of psychology into low-level processing (perceptual psychology) and more high-level processes (cognitive psychology and schema theory).

My primary source of inspiration, however, has been psychological research about discourse processing. Although these researchers focus primarily on written discourse and not cinema (but see Magliano et al., 1996), their model of discourse understanding is transposable to the cinematic realm. Within this field, there is a general consensus that texts are constructed and mentally represented by readers on at least three levels (Graesser et al., 1994; van Dijk & Kintsch, 1983; Zwaan, 1996:243). At a *verbatim* level, readers construct coherence that is related less to the content of the text and more to its surface structure. This includes word-for-word memory of a text and in what order words appear in the text (independent of the underlying meaning of those words and sentences). Such memories of texts can be supported by rhymes and alliterations, as in litanies, jingles, and poems. In spoken language, we may memorize particular phonetic and prosodic features independent of the content (as in accents and speech types).

A *textbase*-level understanding involves the propositional description of a given text, concerning how the predicates (i.e., the verbs, adjectives, or conjunctions) stand in relation to the arguments (i.e., the nouns or embedded propositions). For example,

(1) MICHAEL'S CAR BROKE DOWN. HE TOOK THE BUS TO TOWN.

A textbase-level understanding of these sentences involves Michael's relation to his car (possession) and what happened to that car (it broke down). It may also be concerned with anaphoric references across sentences, e.g., that "he" in the second sentence refers to "Michael" in the first. Understanding at this level is thought to involve grammatical and semantic knowledge, but few knowledge-based inferences.

At a third level we find meanings that can be said to reflect the *situation* the discourse tries to convey. This is a much richer level of coherence. It involves the following inferences:

■ Causal relations between textual units (e.g., inferring a cause–effect relation between the broken-down car and the bus ride)

■ Temporal relations (the car broke down before the bus ride); spatial relations (the car broke down far from the town)
■ Goals and plans of characters (Michael wanted to go to town)
■ Emotions of the characters (Michael was disappointed and angry)
■ Properties of objects (the car was old)
■ Instruments (Michael gave the bus driver money to receive a ticket)
■ Expectations on impending events (Michael was going shopping in town)

Many of these meanings are not explicitly mentioned in the text but have to be inferred or constructed on the basis of textual cues and background knowledge of the reader. Much psychological research on discourse processing aims to describe the conditions under which readers actually construct these types of inferences (Britton & Graesser, 1996; Graesser et al., 1994) and how different genres of text (news, fiction, narratives) influence the ways in which such inferences are drawn (Zwaan, 1993).

The distinctions among verbatim, textbase, and situation levels of understanding are valuable when we are trying to come to grips with coherence making in cinematic discourse. By identifying equivalent levels in cinematic understanding (as well as adding a couple that discourse psychology may ignore), we can demonstrate the complexity and the flexibility of understanding cinematic discourse. What levels of meaningfulness exist in understanding cinematic discourse?

LEVEL 0. On the most basic level, all kinds of cinematic discourse and moving imagery can be taken as formal patterns, independent of their content or representational nature. Thus we may call this level of meaning *premeaning* or *level 0 meaning*. On this level, cinematic meanings are equivalents to the verbatim level of natural language discourse. Cinema scholars often refer to these types of meaning as "formal effects" of the surface of the visual channel. This may involve experiences of shapes, colors, rhythm, patterns, and size "considered purely as graphic configurations, as patterns of light and dark, line and shape, volumes and depths, movement and stasis – *independent of* the shot's relation to the time and space of the story" (Bordwell & Thompson, 1993:250; see also Hoffman, 1998:114). "This area is red," "that's a square," and "blobs of color are moving to the right" would be examples of level 0 understanding, as would effects of "patterns," symmetry, and gestalts (Figure 2). In addition, particular color configurations, for instance the color atmosphere in Technicolor films, would be an effect belonging to this level of meaning.

The phenomenon of apparent movement, which provides the basis for all moving imagery, has a strong experiential effect even before the

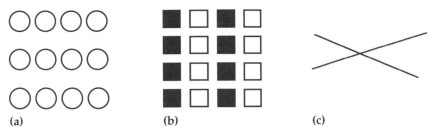

FIGURE 2. Some gestalt effects of perceptual organization: (a) Proximate objects tend to cohere together; we perceive "rows of circles" rather than "columns of circles." (b) Similar objects cohere together; the distance between all squares is the same, but we perceive columns rather than rows. (c) Good continuation; we perceive two lines crossing rather than two angles touching. (Diagram by Ola Persson.)

perceptual apparatus starts recognizing objects and spatial relation in the image. There are still disputes within perceptual psychology as to how this effect comes into existence in the mind of spectators (Anderson, 1996; Anderson & Anderson, 1993). Other examples of level 0 meanings could be formal effects of editing and shot juxtapositions, for instance, the *graphical match* of Bordwell and Thompson (1993:251) (in which the "[s]hapes, colors, overall composition, or movement in shot A may be picked up in the composition of shot B"). Eisenstein's (1957a:72) notion of *metric montage*, in which shot lengths create a pattern of increasing or decreasing rhythm, would also be included here. These are semimeaningful effects created independent of the representational or narrative content of those shots.[12]

At some point, Barthes writes about his notion of *third* or *obtuse meaning* as nonrepresentational, which would make it fit into my level 0 meaning:

The obtuse meaning is a signifier without a signified, hence the difficulty in naming it. . . . If the obtuse meaning cannot be described, that is because in contrast to the obvious meaning, it does not copy anything – how do you describe something that does not represent anything? (Barthes, 1977:61)[13]

Level 0 would also include simple "synchronization effects" between sound and image to which the spectator attributes the source of a sound to a feature in the image track (even though they are broadcast from separate places in the theater). Even minimal out-of-synch mistakes by editors or projectionists may disrupt this effect so central to the sound cinema.

Admittedly these effects are not meanings in the normal sense of the word. They do not represent or refer. Still, they produce coherent experiences in the spectator, in addition to having a certain "salience" (Grodal, 1997:64). Experiencing rhythm and visual patterns has a certain effect that lies closer to meaningfulness than nonrhythm and perceptual chaos do.

LEVEL 1. Entering the domain of representation or mimesis, spectators start to extract meanings by processes of *perception*, which refers to the means by which experiences of objects, events, sounds, tastes, and so on, are constructed by the perceptual systems. For instance, from formal and nonrepresentational patterns of lines, shades, and surfaces, we perceive objects – perhaps one of the most central categories in the phenomenal world of humans. Although objects enter the visual system through varying angles, light conditions, and motion patterns (in cinema as well as in real life), perceptual processes manage to hold together such impressions as one entity – "a knife" or "a dog." Although habitual and seemingly without labor, such meanings require a formidable effort by the human mind. Spectators of cinema are able to perceive such objects as 3D objects, although the projection on the retina is only 2D (Hoffman, 1998). Spectators are also able to categorize objects on different levels of abstraction, e.g., "That is an animal," "That is a bird," and "That is a crow." The construction of such meanings seems to involve complex mixtures of perception and linguistic knowledge (Arnheim, 1974; Biederman, 1987; Biederman, Mezzanotte & Rabinowitz, 1982; Deregowski, 1980, 1984; Jolicoeur, Gluck, & Kosslyn, 1984; Palmer, Rosch & Chase, 1981). The recognition of unique and familiar faces seems to hold a particular position within object recognition as it enables us to identify people in our everyday social world (Eysenck & Keane, 1995:65).

When several objects are juxtaposed within the frame, there may be impressions of *depth* in space (e.g., close, far away, in front of, and behind). Depth in space is not perceptible per se, but only as a *relation* between objects.[14] There are a small number of perceptual assumptions by which our vision system infers such spatial relations and in the end gives us our experience of 3D space. These include occlusion of one object by another, relative size differences between objects distant and objects close, height of object in the visual field, aerial perspective (differences in blueness of close and distant objects), motion perspective (so-called parallax), accommodation and binocular disparity, stereopsis, and diplopia (Cutting & Vishton, 1995). From a given juxtaposition of objects, a spectator may infer spatial relations between objects within the frame ("X is standing a couple of meters behind Y"; "X is lying under the table"; "X is walking away from Y and the spectator, down a long road").

Combined objects may also generate recognition and classification of "scenes," which are put on an even higher level of abstraction ("This is a living room," "This is a restaurant," "This is a march") (Grodal, 1997:65; Mandler, 1984; see also Walton, 1990:311ff). *Object* and *scene schemas*, with which objects and scenes are recognized, are structured in specific ways. Because of this, some angles of objects and some configurations of scenes will be recognized faster and with more certainty than others (Arnheim, 1974:106ff; Biederman, 1987; Deregowski, 1980, 1984; Palmer et al., 1981). All of these processes require knowledge and construction processes; they are what Bordwell (1985:30) would call perceptual conclusions.

LEVEL 2. At a deeper level, perceptual meanings become more sophisticated and abstract. Spectators may recognize and identify a character across different appearances in a film ("X in this shot is the same person as in the previous shot"). This aspect corresponds quite nicely with anaphoric references in verbal discourse ("he" refers to "Michael" in the preceding example), although it involves a different set of dispositions (e.g., facial-recognition abilities). Smith (1995) discusses this type of meaningfulness in terms of *recognition* and *identity* of characters.

In addition, the categorization of characters becomes more specific: "X is a Bolshevik," "X is a nerd," "that is Dracula," "X is the hero/villain." Visual culture is abundant in conventions that relate faces, grimaces, makeup, clothing, poise, manners, and voice to a character gallery (e.g., "Santa," "a Mafioso," "Jesus," "the crazy scientist," "a cowboy"). Such recognitions are instant and require little action on the part of the character. Once the iconography has been decoded, the spectator projects a host of cultural expectations onto the character and the events portrayed, for example, "nerds are socially and emotionally incompetent" (Smith, 1995:191ff). Of course, iconography of this kind changes with history.

Perception relates not only to static objects, but also to recognizing and categorizing simple "events." Here objects are put into temporal frameworks such as "the ball flies through the air and lands in the bushes" or "the leaves rustle." Simple events like this are implicated in physical–mechanistic models of causality (Dennett, 1987; Hume, 1739; Piaget, 1954; van den Broek et al., 1997; White, 1995:115; see also Chapter 4, the section on Mental Attribution in Everyday Life). "Behavior" is a particular form of event that involves agents. Similar to objects, behavior can be perceived on different levels of abstraction, e.g. "the Samurai lowers his arm and the hand grabs the flower" versus "the Samurai picks the flower" (Zacks & Tversky, 2001:7; Chapter 4, the subsection on Levels of Meaning).

Other experiences of events include "threat" and "intimacy" in scenes with variable framing. In Chapter 3 I argue that transpositions from long-shot to close-up (or vice versa) generate specific emotional effects that are due to spectators' personal space. These are low-level effects and can be said to be level 2 meanings.

Spatial meanings become increasingly complex on this level. The straightforward level 1 spatial relationships between objects explicitly within the frame are now complemented by meanings relating to objects in offscreen space. Such meanings can have different characters and strengths. On the basis of the spectator's knowledge and dispositions about objects, bodies, interiors, and exteriors, she or he may assume that objects and space continue outside the frame, although it is not explicitly visible at the moment ("This is a close-up of X, rather than of X's head cut off"). In a number of studies, Intraub, Gottesman, and Bills (1998) have shown that when subjects are asked to recall an image by making a drawing of it they tend to remember a much "larger" portion of the space than was contained within the frame. These results suggest that offscreen space is actively constructed and constitutes a vital part of the cognitive experience of imagery. If this is true with still images, this should be even more so with moving displays.

Other forms of offscreen expectations and meaning may be triggered by the direction of speed and gaze within the frame ("The car races out to the left," "X looks into offscreen space"). When several shots are juxtaposed we may have POV effects such as "X in shot A looks at the objects in shot B," or "X in shot A and Y in shot B look at each other." In the next chapter, I return to why such meanings arise and why they are relatively homogeneous across large groups of spectators. On this level, we may also have an understanding of spatial relations between diegetic places and objects ("X is now somewhere offscreen right or left," "This shot depicts another place other than or the same place as the previous one," "This place is adjacent to or far away from the former one"). POV editing, shot–reverse-shot techniques, and the 180° convention are important textual techniques to regulate and trigger these kinds of meaning.

On the auditory channel, we might also find the more complex relations between audio and visual tracks: recognizing the onscreen or offscreen source of sounds ("That is a car horn, and it comes from that car") or verbal references to visual objects ("X is talking about that knife on the table"). It must still be determined exactly what sort of knowledge and cognitive abilities such intermedia inferences involve.

LEVEL 3. An understanding of the *situation* or the *referential meaning* (Bordwell & Thompson, 1993:49) involves yet another set and level of processes that aim at constructing a mental model of the situation. van Dijk and Kintsch (1983) call this the *situation model*. Much of the meanings produced here are tied to characters and their behavior. For instance, the level 2 understanding of events and characters' behavior may be placed within the more abstract framework of a situation. "Picking flowers" may be a part of a "Sunday walk" and "ordering food" may be one aspect of a more abstract "restaurant visit." As previously mentioned, this level of understanding seems to be central to us in our everyday life. Such abstract meaning requires complex knowledge structures and inference mechanisms (Persson, Laaksolahti, and Lönnqvist, 2001; Schank & Abelson, 1977; van den Broek et al., 1997; see also the preceding section on Understanding and Dispositions, and Chapter 4, the subsection on Levels of Meaning). These knowledge structures also support spectators in establishing temporal relations between events or phases of events ("This event takes place before, after, or at the same time as the previous one").

More importantly, perhaps, is the spectators' ability to understand behavior in terms of character *psychology*. Attributing goals, beliefs, knowledge, and emotions, as well as more stable mental traits, to characters are central spectator activities on this level ("X wants to escape from prison," "X knows that his wife betrayed him," "X is angry with Y," "Marion does not know that Norman spies on her through the whole in the wall," "X is an extrovert," "X is a pessimist"). Mental attributions of this sort are central to making characters' behaviors coherent and comprehensible, complementing and extending the event-schema-based understanding. In Chapter 4, I argue that these processes are similar to mental attribution in nonfictional, everyday settings.

The situation model also contains most of the *causal* relations between events and scenes, which in terms of narratives is a thick and rich level of meaning. Often such causality is intimately tied to a character's mental states and traits ("X is angry with his wife because he believed she was unfaithful to him," "The villains in *North by Northwest* want Thornhill because they think he is Kaplan," "X gets scared because he sees a snake," "Norman spies on Marion because he is a hedonist"). Causal reasoning of this sort also enables *predictive inferences*, guessing at the causal consequences of an event: "X will be killed," "the prince will save her." According to some scholars (Vorderer et al., 1996; in particular Tan & Diteweg, 1996), the ability to produce such "forecast meanings" is a key requirement for emotions of suspense (which is central to many cinema genres). Predictive inferences may also involve speculations about the destiny of characters after the narration ("They will live happily ever after").

In addition to psychology and traits, spectators may also categorize characters along the lines of social roles ("He is a father," "he is a waiter," "she is a professor") and stereotypes of ethnicity, gender, religion, handicaps, etc. ("he is Japanese," "she is Muslim," "she is a lesbian"). Such meanings emerge out of cultural assumptions or prejudices about groups of people and may carry moral and judgmental value (see Chapter 4, the subsection on Levels of Meaning).

On the basis of the understanding of characters' psychology, personality traits, social roles, and stereotype – as well as the situation in which an action occurs – spectators produce *moral judgments* about actions. This include meanings such as "X is treating her badly," "Norman's spying is not appropriate and not very polite," "It was nice of X to give her a present," "X is a mean person," and "X is weak, but he is kind at heart." In contrast to other meaning processes, these kinds of meaning involve hot processes of emotion and affect – cf. Smith's (1995) notion of *allegiance*.

The processes at levels 2 and 3 are sometimes referred to as *comprehension* or *narrative interpretation* (Currie, 1995:228). The meanings produced at these levels are similar to formalists' and structuralists' notions of *fabula* and *story*.[15]

LEVEL 4. Level 4 involves meanings that are even more abstract. The understanding of situations and the establishment of temporal, causal, and spatial relations between situations enable scene and plot summarizations. These can be seen as abstract descriptions of a series of actions, scenes, and situations: "X leaves the prison"; "A man is mistaken for another and is drawn into a series of mysterious events and threats. Through courage and ingenuity, he is able to survive and disclose the identity of the villains." These kinds of meaning are often expressed in reviews and promotional material of films and books.

From situational meanings and plot summarization, we enter the twilight zone between comprehension and interpretation. *Thematic inferences* (Graesser, et al., 1994:372) or *explicit meanings* (Bordwell, 1996b:8) involve extraction of a *point* or *moral* of the film as a whole ("Love is stronger than death," "Drinking will lead to misery," "Seize the day," 'The Holocaust was indeed a terrible thing," "Practice what you preach"). Such meanings often take the form of (culturally distributed) proverbs. In contrast to many of the previous types of meaning, which are *local* in nature, thematic inferences have a more *global* character, spanning the whole of a given film or text (Graesser et al., 1994:378).

On this level we may also find more symbolical, associational, conceptual, and metaphorical understandings that transfer the literal meanings of motifs, events, and objects established on lower levels to a higher level. Examples include "The pince-nez in *The Battleship Potemkin* serves as a symbol of the bourgeoisie"; "The strikers in *Strike!* are shot down like cattle in a slaughterhouse"; "The eyes of the bird stand for the spying eyes of Norman"; and "The football in *Bigger than Life* is a symbol of Avery and his life" (Wilson, 1997:228). These meanings establish symbolic relations within the diegesis of the narrative, but the film may also make use of symbolic associations circulating in society at large, for example, symbols of nationalism and ethnic groups, symbols of cultural belonging, political symbols, and symbols of consumerism. Visual media have played a decisive role in introducing, circulating, and maintaining such symbols within popular culture. The ways in which spectators infer the meanings of such symbols are situated at level 4.

Related to this are *contrast editing* (Gunning, 1990b, 1994:134) and *propositional editing* (Messaris, 1994:106), which also invite the spectator to make conceptual parallels between discourse segments. Some films (and many commercials) specifically attempt to trigger such metaphorical inferences in the spectator. As Lakoff and Johnson (1980, 1999) and Lakoff and Turner (1989) have shown, metaphorical understanding within literary contexts often draws on cultural and universal knowledge and assumptions from everyday life.

LEVEL 5. Some level 4 meanings operate on the border between comprehension and interpretation (Wilson, 1997). Level 5 meanings, however, are univocally referred to as interpretative. This kind of understanding – which I take in a somewhat broader sense than do most cinema scholars (including Bordwell, 1989a) – goes beyond the thematic in several ways. It includes aesthetic judgments ("I liked it," "It was bad"), which often are connected with emotional reaction vis-à-vis the film. Interpretation may include inferences about the pragmatic and communicative context of the film, including the *attitudes* of the filmmaker ("I think the person who made this film is very politically aware") or the *purpose* of making the film ("*Die Hard* is made for nothing more than entertainment," "Oliver Stone made *JFK* to ignite a debate about the murder investigation," "Oliver Stone made *JFK* with nothing more than speculation and moneymaking in mind," "This film wants to teach us that history is a social construction") (see Staiger, 1992:19). This kind of meaning may also involve speculations as to what audience the film is directed at ("This film is definitely family oriented") and about what formal devices and conventions are used to achieve a desired effect. Interpretative inferences can be related to the ways in which a given film or a film in general functions in society, that is, the way in which mass media develop, maintain, or suppress values and cultural assumptions ("The negative portrayal of men in this film will have great impact on teenagers").

Furthermore, on an interpretative level there may be *motivational inferences* (Bordwell & Thompson, 1993:55), which seek to explain the presence of textual units ("The film shows us this in order to make us cry," "These teenage girls go to this far-away cottage so that they won't be able to call for help when the stalker shows up"). Level 5 meanings may also contain a moral or *critical* evaluation of the theme or message of the film ("Yes, I understand that this film tries to tell us that we should seize the day, but I happen to disagree with that philosophy") or some aspects of the film ("I really think this film's portrayal of women was misleading," "Life is never this good or easy," "I think the nationalism in *Top Gun* is stupid and ridiculous"). Such critical analysis often contains speculations about how thematic and explicit meanings reflect or maintain phenomena and ideologies in society at large, often evoking questions of *realism*. At the extreme end, such inferences may involve claims about how the film supposedly is bound up with certain ideas, values, or ideologies that it itself is not "aware of" – so-called repressed or symptomatic readings or readings *against the grain* (Bordwell, 1989b:9) ("*Psycho* is a worked-over version of an unconscious fantasy of Hitchcock's," "*Psycho* tries to conceal the male fear of female sexuality").

Although level 5 meanings emanate out of the film, many of them exist outside the fictional, diegetic world shown in the film (similar to level 0 meanings). Interpretative meanings "take a step back" from the film, investigating its fictional, narrative, communicatory, rhetorical, and societal functions rather than establishing its fictional meaning. Interpretations typically do not engage in the game of make-believe advocated by the film (Walton, 1990). Level 5 meanings treat the film as an *artifact* rather than as *fiction* (Tan, 1996). By analogy to the notion of a situation model, Zwaan (1993:152) calls this construction the *pragmatic model*.

It is difficult to estimate to what extent ordinary spectators construct interpretative meanings or the specific circumstances that trigger such processes. All we know is that some types of spectator are paid by academic and publishing institutions to produce and write down such understandings – reviewers and cinema scholars. There seems to be an urge for other people to read these interpretations, and this will definitely affect their understanding of a film or films in general.

Some Specifications of the Model

The point of this typology is not to argue that 6 is the appropriate number of meaning levels, nor to exclude other forms of meaning types that may exist on each level (surely there are additional types). Nor is the point to establish the exact line among perception, comprehension, and interpretation (Wilson, 1997) (to avoid semantics, levels are instead referred to by numbers). The purpose of this typology is to obtain an overview of the kinds of meaning typically produced by spectators in their understanding of a film and to start discussing how they emerge and interact. What unites them all, I argue, is a disposition-equipped spectator who constructs some form of coherent meaningfulness in the interaction with the film text.

The task of a psychological theory of visual media would be to investigate how and under what circumstances different meaning types actually are realized in the mind of the spectator before, during, and after

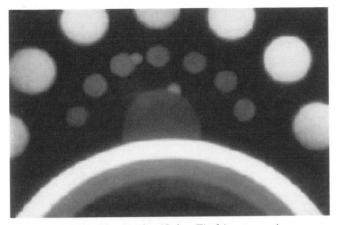

FIGURE 3. *Komposition in Blau* (Oskar Fischinger, 1935).

viewing. This is a formidably complex process, constrained by a number of parameters.

The film text surely has the potential to steer the spectator to "preferred" levels of understanding. *Die Hard* (1988), for instance, tries to focus on levels 3 and 4, whereas *Ballet mécanique* (1925) and Oskar Fischinger's cubes and circles in *Komposition in Blau* (1935) (see Figure 3) seek to constrain the meaning construction to level 0 or 1. Modern music videos can be said to be "lyrical" in nature insofar as their display of objects and events tries to stop the meaning construction process at levels 1 and 2 (Grodal, 1997:60).

The set of dispositions entertained by the spectator influences meaning production in substantial ways. Dispositions create a framework within which the spectator can make sense of cues from the text. Sharing dispositions means constructing similar meanings of a film; different dispositions lead to different understandings of the same film. Even though this general principle seems intuitive enough, we know little about the exact nature of these processes. Moreover, the real problem seems to determine when and how two spectators' dispositions differ or overlap.

However, dispositions not only influence the meaning construction on each level, they also influence what level of coherence the spectator focuses on. A child spectator, for instance, may lack certain skills in attributing mental states to characters (see Chapter 4) and may thus have problems in establishing coherence on that level and be content with coherence on levels 0–2. A spectator who knows little about a film's historic and industrial context is perhaps likely to avoid level 5 meanings. A non-Western spectator lacking experience with the horror genre may appreciate *Beetlejuice* (1988) on levels other than its frequent intergenre references. A modern user may lack the iconographic codes needed to establish the

precise distinctions among capitalists, Mensheviks, Bolsheviks, bourgeoisie, Communists, proletariats, tsarists, Cossacks, and Germans in the
films of Eisenstein. In all of these cases, the spectator establishes meaning
and coherence "to the best of her or his ability," that is, by focusing on
those levels of meaning construction at which she or he is "competent."
"The viewer can respond actively to a film only to the degree that he or
she notices its cues, and only if he or she has viewing skills developed
enough to respond to these cues" (Thompson, 1988:31). If a spectator cannot construct coherence on one level, she or he may prefer others at which
she or he is more competent (see Currie, 1995:228ff).

In addition to dispositions, spectators use different purposes or "reading stances" vis-à-vis the text that heavily affect what level of coherence
the spectator "settles for." This is to say that spectators "make use" of
films in a variety of ways. Special-effects experts may be primarily interested in levels 1 and 2, the Friday-night spectator in levels 3 and 4,
scriptwriters in levels 3 and 4, reviewers in levels 4 and 5, and film
history students in level 5. Spectators seem to be able to deliberately shift
such "roles" during the course of a film and between films and reception situations. In addition, films and their promotional material seek
to prescribe "appropriate" reading stances for the spectators. Genre
(Western, drama, or thriller) and discursive modes[16] (information, ed-
ucation, entertainment, documentary, art) are often part of the viewing
context for a given film, and the spectator may just "go with flow" and
adopt such prescribed stances. Irrespective of the origin of such reading
stances, they have been shown to affect the ways and levels in which
meaning is produced by readers of news and fiction texts (Zwaan, 1993).
Cinema spectators should be no different in this respect.

Theoretically, then, spectators can and are able to deliberately choose
the level of meaning construction, contradicting the "intended" ones (see
Hall et al., 1980). Spectators may "at will" understand Die Hard as a formal
pattern of color and shapes (level 0) or make abstract level 5 interpretations of Oskar Fischinger's cubes and circles. The question is, of course,
whether such "reading" levels are equally valid and correct (Currie, 1995;
Persson, 2000:64ff; Walton, 1990).[17] Moreover, just because spectators theoretically or under special circumstances can understand films at many
levels and in many ways does not mean that spectators normally do so in
their everyday reception of moving imagery. The former is a philosophical
matter, the latter psychological and ethnological.

Meanings are not constructed in isolation from each other. Levels presumably interact in complex ways. In many cases, the lower level of coherence must be in place before the spectator can move on to the next.
For instance, to make thematic inferences about the whole of a narrative

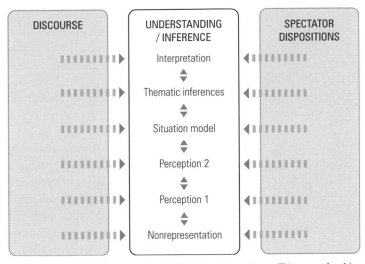

FIGURE 4. Levels of coherence and their interaction. (Diagram by Younghee Jung, after a figure in Kintsch, 1977:34.)

it seems intuitive that spectators must have understood the different situations of the plot. In Figure 4, these bottom-up processes are represented by the upward arrows. At the same time, high-level assumptions and hypotheses certainly guide the understanding of details: If a spectator assumes that the theme of a given story is "crime doesn't pay," this will affect the processes of perception and comprehension (the downward arrows). Such high-level hypotheses might have been formed by the beginning of the film or may have been provided by extratextual sources (e.g., the spectator has already read the book on which the film is based, heard an interview with the director, or been told by friends what they think the film is about). The difference between downward and upward directions in the processes relates to the discussion about simplified versus stimuli-driven thinking (see the subsection on Parameters of Dispositions). The shifts between the two can be swift and depend on pragmatic context (e.g., the spectator's purpose in the viewing).

Even though the spectator, according to this theory, actively searches for multileveled meaning and coherence, there are circumstances under which this appetite for sense making is brought to a halt (see Graesser et al., 1994:372; Iser, 1978:108):

- If the reader is convinced that the text is "inconsiderate," that is, it lacks coherence in any form (see the discussion of L'Année dernière à Marienbad [1961] in Thompson, 1988:31)

■ If the reader believes there is coherence in the text (on some level), but it will take too much effort relative to the purpose of the reading
■ If the reader lacks the tacit assumptions that permit the establishment of coherence on one or more level (see preceding discussion)
■ If the reader has goals that require little or no construction of coherence (e.g., proofreading a text for spelling errors or trying to disclose how special effects in a film have been produced).

Abandoning the search for coherence usually includes activities such as "losing concentration," "not giving the text a chance," "skimming through or scanning a text," or simply "leaving the theater or stopping reading." In these cases, the reader more or less "breaks the contract" with the text and starts spending his or her meaning construction efforts on other objects.

It is crucial to make clear the nature of the levels of meaning previously presented. They are not merely cold processes. Although mentally hot phenomena, such as affect, emotions, and feelings, are not the primary focus of this study, meanings on all levels are tightly associated with them: Beauty or rhythm in formal patterns (level 1); disgust from looking at the slaughtering of a bull (levels 2 and 3); affects connected to spatial immersion (level 2); close-up effects (levels 1 and 2); moral judgments of characters' motives and actions (levels 3 and 4); identification with characters (level 3); or strong emotions of suspense, fear, surprise, curiosity, hope, relief, sadness, hate, anger, and joy (levels 2–5). Dealing with close-ups effects and variable framing, in Chapter 3 I touch on level 1 and level 2 meanings and their tight links with affect. Links between cognition and emotion have been acknowledged within neuroscience and psychology (e.g., Damasio, 1994). This paves the way for psychological and philosophical theories of emotions and affect in cinema (Grodal, 1997; Plantinga & Smith, 1999; Tan, 1996; Vorderer et al., 1996), providing a complement to psychoanalytical and sexual approaches to emotion.

It is equally important to point out that meaning types on all levels require active deployment of spectator dispositions. This is true of all levels, including the lowest.

Some dispositions originate from media practices themselves (Figure 5). Genre norms and genre expectations, for instance, contain far-reaching expectations about character gallery, iconographic codes, typical actions, typical plot structure, and moral hierarchies between characters (Smith, 1995). Many films explicitly play on such dispositions of the spectator, for example, *Beetlejuice* (1988) and *Top Secret!* (1984). In addition, through promotional material, tabloids, and fan magazines, the media industry provides important dispositions that may influence the reception process. The star system seems exceptionally central in this respect

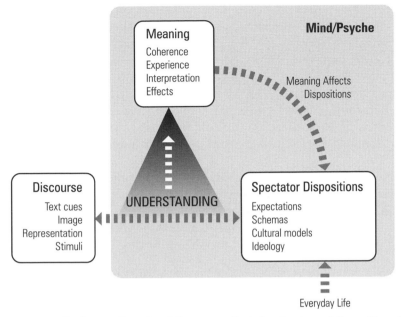

FIGURE 5. Understanding visual discourse affects the structure of dispositions. Some dispositions, however, come from sources unrelated to visual discourse ("everyday life"). (Diagram by Younghee Jung.)

(deCordova, 1990; Hansen, 1991). Fiction, narratives, and characters also appear in other media, such as books, computer games, and theater, and earlier acquaintances with these media equip the spectator with rich dispositions (Uricchio & Pearson, 1993).

However, although cinema and fiction constitute important aspects of our cultural habitat, especially in a media-dominated society such as ours, it cannot be the sole educator about the dispositions by which we decode moving imagery. Understanding moving imagery, on all levels, seems to use a great variety of dispositions originating from our interaction with our everyday physical, social, and cultural environment, rather than with fictions and narrative practices:

The inference mechanisms and world knowledge structures that are tapped during the comprehension of everyday experiences are also likely to be tapped during the comprehension of narratives; there is no justifiable reason to believe that readers would turn off these pervasive interpretive mechanisms during reading. (Graesser et al., 1994:372)

This point has been made by a number of scholars (Bordwell, 1989b: 134ff; Carroll, 1996b:35; Grodal, 1997:10; Iser, 1978:185; Lombard, 1995:241; Messaris, 1994; Plantinga, 1994; Walton, 1990:349; Wilson, 1997:234). In the previous subsections I tried to capture the richness and wealth of dispositions that have their origin in noncinematic, nonmedia, nonliterary, and nonfictional practices of everyday life (in Figure 5 called everyday life).

Of course, some meaning levels may require more media dispositions than others. For instance, lower levels may rely more on nonmedia dispositions than do higher ones. Moreover, visual media maintain, reinforce, transform, and add to everyday-life dispositions to the extent that distinctions between them are difficult to sustain – particularly in our media-dominated society. Media and nonmedia origins of dispositions blur.

There are nevertheless reasons why everyday dispositions seem to perform important functions in spectators' understanding of cinema. If we assume that cinema exploits dispositions that are specific to visual media and that the institution of visual media in this sense alone has educated its audience about its conventions, then it is difficult to explain the instant and universal success of mainstream cinema:

Part of the mass appeal of movies, that is, results from the fact that audiences can apprehend the basic symbols in this mode of communication without learning a language – like a code or specialized forms of inference or decipherment. (Carroll, 1996a:133)

That is, instead of creating new dispositions of the spectator, the visual discourse exploits or makes use of preexisting dispositions in the spectator to generate certain effects and meanings.

This means a new agenda for cinema studies, which heretofore greatly underestimated the importance of everyday dispositions and commonsense knowledge in their investigations of cinematic reception.[18] On the one hand, of course, we have to take seriously those disciplines that investigate everyday dispositions: psychology, anthropology, linguistics, and sociology. On the other hand, if large audiences share everyday dispositions we can assume that the film industry and its discursive conventions and norms will be adapted and designed with respect to those dispositions. Given the structure and functions of those dispositions, cinema scholars will be able to explain the presence of certain cinematic conventions and norms.

In the following chapters, I peruse all of these themes. I claim that POV editing, variable framing, and character psychology make use of dispositions that do not originate from visual media, but rather from basic aspects of our everyday life. After investigating the structure of those dispositions, I try to reconstruct the interaction between text and disposition. From this analysis, I then try to give explanations as to why certain cinematic practices look the way they do. I hope that such a psychological explanation will complement historically oriented ones (see Chapter 4, the subsection on Psychology as Complement?).

A psychological theory of cinema reception acknowledges that all six levels of meaning are components of the visual medium and the spectators' experience of it. In a full theory of reception of cinema, all of these levels must be addressed and described:

The perceptual, the cognitive, and the emotional, and the temporal as well as the spatial, are *a priori* equally important aspects of the viewing experience. Many normative discussions of film are implicitly futile discussions about hierarchies of mental functions: some prefer 'perceptual' films; others prefer associative-memory-activating films; yet others like mental problem-solving. (Grodal, 1997:9)

Perhaps because of the historically close relationship between film studies and aesthetics, film scholars have been eager to make hierarchies between and normative judgments of different levels of meaning. Barthes' search for the *filmnost* – the essence of the cinematic medium – in his "third meaning" is a typical example:

[I]t is at the level of the third meaning, and at that level alone, that the 'filmic' finally emerges. The filmic is that in the film which cannot be described, the representation which cannot be represented. The filmic begins only where the language and metalanguage end. Everything that can be said about *Ivan* or *Potemkin* can be said of a written text (entitled *Ivan the Terrible* or *Battleship Potemkin*) except this, the obtuse meaning; I can gloss everything in Euphrosyne, except the obtuse quality of her face. The filmic, then, lies precisely here, in that region where articulated language is no longer more than approximate and where another language begins. (Barthes, 1977:64ff)

In his article, Barthes favors the third meaning at the expense of others (e.g., "the message" or "symbolic meaning"). A psychological theory of cinema makes no such claims. It aspires to *describe* how meaning levels arise in different spectators and to *explain* the complex reception mechanisms involved, but it does not try to make the case for the most "important" or "cinematic" level of meaning. Of course, some meaning levels are more conscious, abstract, and deeper than others, but no level is simple or mechanical, and all levels contribute to the experience and phenomena of film. Thus the claims in this book are psychological, not aesthetic. This shift from *prescriptive* to *descriptive* would, I believe, benefit the whole field of cinema studies.[19]

Discarding hierarchization, however, does not mean that individual scholars and researchers of film must focus on and explain all levels of meanings. In fact, given the multilevel nature of meaning, it seems hazardous to talk about reception or meaning construction in general. Some researchers would argue that a grand, full-scale theory of film reception is unfeasible unless one starts with small-scale problems, medium-level questions, and piecemeal theorizing (Carroll, 1996c:58). Many film scholars do in fact concentrate on separate levels of meaning. Historians such as Tsivian (1994) and perception psychologists such as Anderson (1996) seek to describe how perceptual meanings are constructed. Cognitivism and formalism, as described by, for example, Bordwell (1985), Thompson (1988), and to some extent Carroll (1996a), focus primarily on comprehension and referential meanings (levels 2–4). Cultural and historical reception studies are often concerned with interpretative levels. For instance, when Staiger (1992:4ff) describes a study by Robert Darnton, concerned with the French and the Polish receptions of *Danton* (1982), she is primarily interested in how "the message" and "the point" of the film were received (levels 4 and 5). The distinction made by Hall et al. (1980) among dominant, negotiated, and oppositional receptions, which later was applied to many cinema studies' analyses and publications, deals specifically with the interpretative level of understanding. In the same manner, the case studies presented in the subsequent chapters also focus on specific levels of meaning (mainly levels 1–3). Naturally, film scholars are perfectly free, and perhaps also better off, to restrict their research to one or two levels. My point is only that such specialization must not prevent acknowledgment of the importance and separate processes of other levels. This relates to scholars working with low-level meanings as well as scholars investigating high-level meanings.

The reason I press this issue is that different approaches or schools in cinema studies, which have been portrayed as standing in opposition to one another, may be more similar than their proponents want to recognize. For instance, cultural studies and neoformalism both seem to study reception processes of cinema, but they do so on separate levels (levels 4 and 5 and levels 2–4, respectively). Perhaps they agree on many (tacitly held) principles of reception, although they disagree about what level to focus on. If this is the case, there is reason to believe that academic acts of hostility are pseudoconflicts rather than fundamental disagreements about how film works and is received.[20] Moreover, if some research questions that now are restricted to one level were to be addressed on other levels, then perhaps discrepancies among different fields of cinema studies would be reduced. For instance, philosophers' concerns about "representation" and realistic properties of the cinematic medium seem to focus on level 1 only (Allen, 1993; Carroll, 1988; Currie, 1995; Walton, 1990). Would they be more inclined to take more "cultural" approaches into account if they framed their research questions within level 2, 3, or 4 (see Currie, 1995:21ff)? And would scholars who claim cultural diversity in the reception of the same film still cling to extreme relativism if they investigated meanings at lower levels than 4 and 5? If the notion of meaning as *one* monolithic thing is avoided and its multileveled nature is acknowledged, it is possible to initiate a renewed discussion about classical problems within cinema studies, bringing together schools of thought that were heretofore academically detached. Such crossover discussions will not automatically lead to definite solutions, but they would force research communities to share vocabularies and take each other's research agendas seriously.

Conclusions

In a psychological framework, written and image-based discourse acts as triggers or cues for various kinds of cognitive–emotional reactions and meaning construction efforts. The spectator actively, although not necessarily consciously, uses a wide set of dispositions to make sense of the various levels of image-based discourse. To underscore this active role of the spectator, I prefer the term *understanding* rather than *reception*. The text is a *potential*, the *realizations* and *actualizations* of which are brought forward by "the understander." Moreover, the spectator is psychologically active on all levels, including the lowest. Psychologically speaking, meanings produced at level 4 or 5 are not more sophisticated than level 1 meanings. It is just that the understanding processes takes place on different levels with different degrees of automaticity and speed. Moreover, because there is often a high degree of interpersonal agreement about meanings at lower levels (because the dispositions used to generate those meanings are widely spread among the audience), these meanings often seem "obvious" and "mechanical" (and thus uninteresting?). On the surface, such meanings seem to exist independent of psychological processes. My focus on lower-level meanings in the following chapters tries to contest this misconception.

Another question – philosophical in nature – is whether these psychological processes *substantially transform* the input from the text or just *establish* relations and meanings that already existed in the text. Even though processes of understanding are active, philosophers want to know if the principal site of meaning lies in the spectator or in the structure of the text. Gaut (1995), for instance, discusses whether the spectator is to be seen as a *constructivist* (building meaning) or a *detectivist* (finding meaning). In both cases the spectator is psychologically active. In the former, however, the site of meaning production lies closer to the recipient; in the latter it lies closer to the textual structure. This question mirrors epistemological issues in traditional philosophy: Can our apprehension of reality (individually or through scientific inquiry) be said to *discover* features of objective reality, or is the phenomenal world drastically different, constructed by our minds and our cultures? Philosophically speaking, the question is vital. From a psychological point of view, however, scientific work can continue without resolving this question. Psychologists are concerned with the phenomenal world and the nature of mental processes situated in a physical, social, and cultural environment, not whether these correctly represent observer-independent features of external reality (or texts) (see White, 1995:12ff). Even though the question at some point needs answers, psychologists can still concentrate on their thing.

Moreover, to answer the question, a psychological method of inquiry may be preferred over a philosophical one. The philosophical question, it seems to me, deals with the nature of the mental processes involved. Are gap filling, additions, inferences, generalizations, abstractions, contributions, and transformations substantially attributing new features to the stimuli? Where this line is to be drawn between construction and detection may be a philosophical matter, but before philosophers can voice their arguments, we need a psychological description of those processes (which we do not have). Thus, before armchair philosophizing can do its job, lots of empirical work needs to be done.

This argument relates to an overall theme of this book, namely, its empirical ambitions. If we want to describe reception processes and put together theories of reception, we have to make "real" observations to support our claims. Observations cannot be restricted to the introspectionist, armchair philosophizing of cinema scholars, but must cover situated spectators (historically or culturally) and many receptions. There are several ways of empirically grounding one's claims: written spectator accounts in magazines, trade journals, censorship cards, newspaper reviews, ethnographic studies, or psychological or sociological experiments. Another approach is to bring in results from experiments and observations in other disciplines, for example, anthropology, sociology, psychology, or biology. In these cases, someone has done "the empirical work" and the generalizations before the cinema scholar appropriates these results for his or her reception theory. The following chapters use a combination of these sources.

The outline of the study is as follows. Each chapter can be read on its own. They are case studies, either bringing some particular form of disposition – closely studied by psychology – to the cinematic context or bringing some conventionalized and central cinematic technique to psychology. In either case, I aim to describe the processes of understanding and thereby to explain the effect and presence of that technique. In Chapter 2 I try to account for the popularity of the POV editing technique in mainstream cinema on the basis of psychological studies of *deictic gaze* competence. I try to explain why some POVs generate more certain POV inferences than do others. In Chapter 3 I am concerned with the relationship between personal space of the spectator and the cognitive–emotional effects of close-ups and variable framing. In the fourth chapter I describe research on our everyday ability to attribute mental states to other people, thereby explaining or coming to understand their actions and behavior. This ability, I argue, is crucial to understanding characters on the screen.

In each of the three chapters, I try to sketch the historical introduction and development of the convention being discussed, both in early cinema and in the narrative mode of filmmaking established between 1905 and 1917. Such historical contextualization is important in two respects. First, it is not enough merely to pair psychological dispositions with individual devices or conventions; we have to look at the context in which these devices are used. In the two radically different systems of discourse – the cinema of attraction and the classical Hollywood cinema – POV editing, variable framing, and characters had equally radically different functions. To describe processes of reception and the interaction between a given disposition and a textual device, we must investigate the overall system in which this interaction takes place. Second, the development of a given convention – how it gains new meanings and expressions over time – provides a good opportunity for us to study the psychological conditions for our understanding and reception of it. Studying changes of style and their meaning enables scholars to detect which spectator dispositions are active.

The three cases studies were chosen not because they represent the whole spectrum of understanding – they fall mostly on levels 1–3 – but because they seem to provide clear couplings between distinct phenomena on either the cinematic side or the psychological side. In principle, however, I could have chosen any level and any film–psychology interaction.

CHAPTER TWO

Understanding Point-of-View Editing

[W]hen we watch a movie, we take the separate spaces of the various sets and merge them into a continuous space that exists only in our minds.

(Murray, 1997:110)

[E]diting is not merely a method of the junction of separate scenes or pieces, but is a method that controls the "psychological guidance" of the spectator.

(Pudovkin, 1970:75)

If the term point-of-view (POV) is laden with multiple meanings in everyday discourse, cinema scholarship has done its best to add to this formidable semantic jungle. In narratology, the term can refer to the conceptual perspective of a character and the way knowledge is distributed by the narration among characters. It may also refer to the way in which characters comment on or relate to diegetic events. Moreover, it can designate the stance of the narrator or the implied author toward fictive events, and it can be used in reference to the filmmaker's personal POV. In all of these cases, POV is seen as a textual structure that can be investigated and revealed through meticulous textual analysis. According to one scholar,

[T]he category of point-of-view is one of the most important means of structuring narrative discourse and one of the most powerful mechanisms for audience manipulation. The manipulation of point-of-view allows the text to vary or deform the material of the fabula, presenting it from different points-of-view, restricting it to one incomplete point-of-view, or privileging a single point-of-view as hierarchically superior to others. (Stam, Burgoyne & Flitterman-Lewis, 1992:84)

The most straightforward sense of the term – which will be the only emphasis in this chapter – is perhaps *optical* or *perceptual* POV, or what I choose to call POV *editing*. (This term denotes the whole editing pattern, not only the POV shot.) The textual structure of this device has been described in textbooks: first, one shows a character glancing offscreen (let us call this the glance shot); then, one shows an object or event or scene (object shot); and between them there is some form of transition (pan, movement, or, prototypically, a cut). If the camera of the object shot is placed at the same place or at least along the same angle as that of the gazer, then we have a "true POV" (Brewster, 1982:6). If this place is not the same as the gazer's, than we have a *sight link* (Gunning, 1994:169) or an *eyeline match* (Bordwell et al., 1985:207). All of these cases supposedly create for the spectator continuity and the impression that "character C is looking at object O" (see Branigan, 1984:103ff).

One major question in contemporary film theory of the 1970s was the relation between the privileged optical perspective of a character, gender, or narrator and the way this situation regulated the implied or real spectator's moral or ideological relation toward characters and narrators (Browne, 1982; Mulvey, 1975; for a critique, see Smith, 1995:156). Here are a couple of examples of this line of argument:

Yet what the camera sees may also be what the characters in the drama see. This is what is called the *subjective* view, since it allows the audience to "take the place" of the heroes, to see and feel "as they do." (Mitry, 1997:207)

The shower scene starts with us seeing, for virtually the first time, something of which Marion is unaware: Norman's prying, during which we have in fact shared Norman's viewpoint. By its end Marion will be dead. So our identification with her must be released. Indeed it is a vital part of the design that we should be cut adrift emotionally by the shock removal of the picture's chief identification-figure, heroine, and star. In the course of the scene, as our viewpoint jumps in violent agitation from place to place, we see less and less through Marion's eyes: and towards the end of the attack our viewpoint is more often the murderer's than the victim's.[1] (Perkins, 1972:108)

Although I have doubts about the rhetoric and emotionally manipulative effects of optical POV in cinema – at least as far as the real spectator is concerned – those questions must be postponed to another occasion. Instead, the focus here is on the preceding processes of how the spectator *initially* infers that a given shot "belongs" to a diegetic character. In most textbooks, the POV status of a shot is generally already established by the scholar or the interpreter ("This is a subjective shot"). In this chapter, however, we deal with the process by which the spectator comes to such a conclusion in the first place. How and on the basis of what criteria does a spectator determine that a shot shows what a character sees? What form of knowledge or disposition is involved in understanding POV editing?

First, I sketch the historical context from which POV editing conventions emerged and the kind of narrative and spatial practices in which they are involved today. Then I describe the nature, structure, and function of *deictic-gaze* ability in the spectator (the ability to follow other people's direction of gaze). I (and others) propose that such an ability has a direct influence on the way POV editing is understood. Last, I compare the structures of deictic gaze and POV editing and suggest that we can explain the features of the POV editing convention by looking at this behavioral disposition of the spectator.

Historical Context of Point-of-View Editing

By 1917, the classical mode of narration had reached its full formulation. Although not all mainstream films had adopted this mode completely or wholeheartedly, most had in some form. In the 1920s, the system stabilized and settled, and later additions were of a complementary character (Thompson, 1985:159). POV editing and eyeline matches were at the core of this system; to discuss their form and function in mainstream cinema, we must investigate the context in which they arose, and to which much attention has been paid by scholars during the past twenty years.

The first ten years of filmmaking were heavily embedded in a context of science, vaudeville, museums, circus, amusement parks, travel, tourism, and the burlesque. It is difficult to overestimate these surrounding discursive practices. Following the thread from Muybridge, Edison, and Marey, cinema's connection to the scientific discourse was strong. How film could capture movement, and thus bring it to the dissection table of physiognomists, ethologists, and anatomists, was one of the first motivations for the development of the technology. Second, in the same vein as "professors" and lecturers toured town halls, circuses, fairs, museums, and vaudeville houses with lantern slides shows, so did cinema immediately take on didactic and informational functions. In fact, in the first years, nonfictional genres – such as travelogues and actualities – outnumbered the fictional (Thompson, 1985:159). The system of production was that of the individual cameraman, touring the city and countryside, taking pictures of newsworthy events and people of local and national interest. Visual media quickly adopted this informative function, and has continued to do so all through the previous century (newsreels, television news, documentaries, talk shows).

What we normally associate with highbrow art, however, did not saturate the new technology during its first years, although many production companies alluded to and exploited fine arts concepts to secure a wider and more stable patronage, preferably that of the middle class. Not until the 1920s did film receive interest from the artistic and modernist communities.

Instead, cinema was firmly established in the tradition of entertainment and became one of the first powerful means of creating popular culture in industrialized societies. As people had more money for leisure, amusement parks, burlesques, theatres, and museums were booming. It was perhaps in vaudeville that most forms of entertainment came together under one roof. A prototypical vaudeville evening consisted of many acts, including magic acts, dancing, slide show presentations of an educational or entertaining nature, songs, gags, clowns, and sketches, and even occasional exhibitions of inventions and machines. At the beginning of the twentieth century, this form of entertaining was fairly stable and had its own agency chains and trade papers, for example, *Variety*. It was within this context that cinema was introduced.

This connection had a strong influence on themes, motifs, and length of films. Of the films produced between 1896 and 1905, most consisted of shorts gags, magical tricks, or filmatizations of other vaudeville acts (Salt, 1992:40). More important to our discussion, however, vaudeville also provided the framework within which space was conceptualized and constructed:

As many historians have noted, the primitive cinema largely assumed that the spectator was equivalent to an audience member in a theater. Mise-en-scène often imitated theatrical settings, and actors behaved as if they were on an actual stage. The framing and staging of scenes in constructed sets placed the spectator at a distance from the space of the action, looking into it. Devices like crosscutting, montage sequences, and dissolves for elliding or compressing time were not in general use. The spectator witnessed either a continuous stretch of time over a whole film or discrete blocks of time in one-shot scenes with ellipses or overlaps between. (Thompson, 1985:158)

The camera actually worked as a stand-in for the spectator in the theater seat. This tight link between the camera and the viewer's place in the auditorium had fundamental consequences for the spatial practices of early cinema. There was a strong respect for the autonomy of the profilmic event, and events were showed in their entirety, just as a theater spectator would see them. There was little "camera work," but the narrative force was placed on the players and their acting abilities. What we call a shot was universally called a scene well into the 1920s (Thompson, 1985:196). The procedures of copyrighting each shot of a film (Gaudreault, 1985) suggest that the concepts of "film" and "shot" were tightly interwoven, reflecting the respect for the profilmic. "The esthetic of attractions stressed the autonomy of each shot, and even within certain multishot films individual shots still functioned as relatively independent attractions" (Gunning, 1994:66).

Now, because it involves radical camera changes, general usage of POV editing was introduced quite late. In the following discussion I try to illuminate how the immobile-spectator metaphor affected spatial practices until the classic period and only gradually allowed practices such as POV editing to become common. In fact, there seems to be a clear trend, from the static camera and the spectator sitting in front of the space (as in front of a stage), to the almost freely movable camera and a space surrounding the spectator on all sides.

Early Point-of-View as Attraction – Not as Spatial Articulation

Copying the vaudeville articulation of space, early film displayed actors with much space above and below in order to maintain the actual size of these characters when projected onto a larger screen (see the discussion in the subsection on Early Cinema). The frame of the image and the boundary of the stage overlapped. As on a stage, characters exited and entered parallel to the screen plane, through doors or other passageways – seldom close to the camera. Gazing or pointing off frame was typically not followed by a shot of the space gazed at, but – following the stage tradition – rather in anticipation of a character about to enter the stage. Offscreen space was equivalent to off*stage* space, and there were no editing techniques to engulf or immerse the spectator in fictive space. The spectator was placed *in front of* space.

The handling and the reception of the first POV structures are placed within this early regime. These examples are rare and do not in any way reflect formal trends of the time. In G.A. Smith's *Grandma's Reading Glass* (1900), a medium long shot of a boy holding the glass in front of different objects is alternated with close-ups of the objects isolated from surroundings by a circular mask. As the Warwick Trading Company catalogue puts it at the time, "The conception is to produce on the screen the various objects as they appeared to Willy while looking through the glass in their enormously enlarged form" (cited in Salt, 1992:49). A year later Smith repeated this device in *As Seen Through a Telescope* (1901), in which an older man operates a pair of binoculars to spy on a man fondling a woman's ankle while helping her onto a bicycle. The spying is evidently acknowledged by the man, who in the end strikes the old man with an umbrella, thereby ending the film. A later example occurs in Emile Cohl's *Les joyeux microbes* (1909). Here a professor takes cell samples of a patient and puts them under a microscope. The long shot of the two protagonists brackets the major portion of the film: animations within a circular mask, depicting different sorts of microbes taking figurative and imaginative forms.

In each of these cases, there are no efforts to create a continuous space, assisting the spectator to establish spatial relations between shots. Rather, the glance shot itself constituted and contained the major attraction (Brewster, 1982:7; Gunning, 1986, 1994:73): objects in an "enormously enlarged form" in *Grandma's Reading Glass*, the voyeuristic leg shot of *As Seen Through a Telescope*, the fantasy animations of Cohl's film. (Cohl was one of the first cinema animators.)

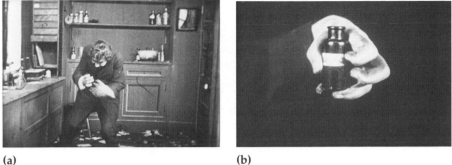

(a)   (b)

FIGURE 6. *Dr. Jekyll and Mr. Hyde* (Thanhouser, 1912). (Obtained from the Wisconsin Center for Film and Theater Research.)

The disinterest in creating continuous space across shots is apparent in many films and practices during the early years. In *Dr. Jekyll and Mr. Hyde* (Thanhouser, 1912), for instance, the editing from the long shot of *Jekyll and Hyde* [Figure 6(a)] to a bottle of poison he is holding in his hand and that eventually will end his life [Figure 6(b)] blissfully disregards any permanence. In long shot, Jekyll moves violently, whereas the hand of the insert is still. In contrast to the hand of the long shot, the hand of the close-up is (theatrically?) holding the poison bottle, signifying perhaps death angst and a psyche in disorder. Finally, the close-up is shot against an abstract, black background with no relation to the space of the long shot.

There is reason to believe that editing within a scene – at that time as well as later – was not conceived of in terms of camera movement to another place in fictive space (as modern spectators would apprehend it). The master shot was perceived as *the* fictive space, whereas inserts, close-ups, and other intrascene shots were somehow shown "separately," on the side, so to speak, belonging to a dimension other than the spatiality of the master shot:

He sits at the fireplace in his study and receives the letter with the news of her wedding. The close-up picture which shows us the enlargement of the engraved wedding announcement appears as an entirely new picture. The room suddenly disappears and the hand which holds the card flashes up. Again when we have read the card, it suddenly disappears and we are in the room again. (Münsterberg, 1916/1970:42)

After seeing off her husband 'she' sends a letter to Paul asking him to drop in. The letter contains all those little lover's phrases predescribed in the *Young Person's Guide to Letter-Writing* and is actually shown on the screen separately. Paul is round like a flash. (Yu. Engel' [Signed Yu. E.] (1908) "O kinematografe" [On the Cinematograph], *Russki Vedomosti*, no. 275, 27, November. Cited in Tsivian, 1994:331ff)

The actors playing Velinsky and Nadya, badly made up around the eyes, often pull terrible faces. The director ought not to have fastened the audience's attention on those grimaces, which are shown separately from the rest of the picture and much enlarged. (*Tsari Birzhi* [Kings of the Stock Exchange] (1917), *Kulisy* [The Wings], Nos. 9/10, 15–16. Cited in Tsivian, 1994:197ff)

Here the cutaway is described as an "entirely new picture," suddenly "flashing up" seemingly outside the narrative world of the film. This space apparently belonged to another realm than the room of the long shot[2] ("We are in the room again"). Still clinging to the notion of the camera as the stand-in for the immobile spectator, we see each shot as a scene of its own – in front of which the spectator sits – rather than as having a spatial relationship with other surrounding shots. Münsterberg does not try to build a mental spatial model of the fictive room (including letters), but treats each shot as an event in itself. This stance is also reflected in the terminology of censors and screen wiring manuals: *Close-up*, denoting a spatial movement of the camera in diegetic space was a part of later discourse; *enlargement*, focusing on bringing objects out of the fictive world to the spectator, was used in the early years:

Close shots were initially described as bringing the players closer to the camera . . .; later on, they were perceived as moving the camera closer to the players. . . . In earlier practice, the camera was deemed to occupy a fixed position and actors were drawn or attracted by it to make contact with the spectator. In later practice, it was the diegetic world that was on display; a practice in which the camera was understood to highlight important aspects, to transport the spectator close up. (Olsson, 1998:240)

Thus the few examples of POV editing from the first ten years of filmmaking were probably not apprehended as the complex spatial articulations that we take POV editing structures to be. The production and understanding of those POVs were still placed within the theatrical and the vaudeville context in which the spatial immersion of the spectator was not an issue. In such a context, "spatial" POV editing within the "same" diegesis, playing with offscreen expectations and complex spatial model building, was more or less impossible; it had to wait for increasing acceptance of editing and space-constructing techniques.

Spatial Immersion Begins

Between 1906 and 1909, national film industries around the world went through rapid transformations, of which the American one may be best accounted for (Bordwell et al., 1985; Elsaesser, 1990; Gunning, 1994; Musser, 1990a). Industry was forced to increase in size, organization, and stability. Although the cameraman and perhaps a director had managed to write, organize, stage, and edit films up to this time, during the next ten years or so, this duo gathered a team around them, dividing labor in increasingly specialized ways (Staiger, 1985). Moreover, the legal fights about techno-logical patents, which had lingered on from the early years, were finally settled.

Films became longer, and "multiscenes" became more common. In gen-eral, the medium turned to the narrative on all levels (Gunning, 1994; Thompson, 1985). One important protonarrative genre was the chase film, which consisted of full-shot scenes of a character being chased by a group of other characters from one location to the next – often exteriors – on the basis of some gag or joke shown in the very first shot (Gunning, 1994:67). The end of each shot was signaled by characters leaving the frame, and the next shot was initiated with their reappearance. This patterned con-tinued ten to fifteen times with more or less the same intensity, until the fleeing figure was captured, often at some rather arbitrary point, at which the film ended.

This pattern – popular from 1904 to 1908 – is interesting from a spatial point of view. Although it retains an emphasis on gags and vaudeville acts in each scene or shot, chase films also introduce spatial relationship between shot spaces. The films often take place in an anonymous city or countryside location, but the chase and the movement between shots suggest some form of spatial contiguity. Such contiguity is not necessarily one of adjacency, but it starts to break up the notion of cinematic space as confined by screen boundaries and starts playing with the notion of offscreen space. Movements of characters in chase films were often di-agonal (Brewster, 1990:45), with entrances and exits more or less close to the camera. This suggested a space behind the camera or the specta-tor from which the character emerged and disappeared. This marked a shift from the vaudeville conceptualization of space, in which exits and entrances ran parallel to the plane of the screen, thereby duplicating the space of the stage. Whereas early spectators were placed in front of the space, simple devices such as close-to-camera entrances constituted the first steps toward surrounding the spectator, placing him or her *in* fictive space.

In the following discussion, I try to sketch the nature and historic devel-opment of the set of conventions that embody this striving for immersion, of which POV editing is a central part.

Gags and vaudeville sketches soon began to transform into narratives, dealing with a causally connected and extended chain of events. These involved individualized characters with clear goals and mental lives (Thompson, 1985; also see Chapter 4). The crude and stereotyped stock characters in vaudeville were transformed into agents with idiosyncratic motivations, partly through the longer format of films (now extended to up to ten minutes). Often the narrative had to display events taking place at different times or in different places. For this reason, transitions and relationships between shot spaces became fundamental. *The Great Train Robbery* (1903), for instance, takes place at the train station office, loading station, the train, along the tracks where the actual robbery takes place, in a dancing hall, and at other locations. Titles, often in the form of lantern slides or spoken words by lecturers or projectionists, probably provided the first primary means for establishing such relations. Surviving prints of these films actually say little about the verbal context in which they were received – and produced.[3] Titles soon became a part of the physical film itself, first with heavy emphasis on summary or expository functions (including spatial anchors) and then, in the early 1910s, there was a heavier importance on dialogue (Thompson, 1985:183ff).

There were other techniques for establishing distance and noncontiguous relations between spaces. Both Pathé's *The Physician in the Castle*[4] (1908) and Griffith's remake of *The Lonely Villa* a year later made use of telephones (Abel, 1994:194; Gunning, 1994:196ff; Salt, 1992:92). Mise-en-scène often provided cues for understanding the relations, as in *The 100-to-One Shot* (1906), in which the film shifts from a man at the racing track to the interior of the house where his fiancée and her father are on the verge of eviction by debt collectors (Salt, 1992:57). Within a few years' time, repeated alteration between two places was to become the dominant visual method for designating simultaneity, often in connection with the run-to-the-rescue pattern, familiar from the films of Biograph and those of other studies.

Editing between Adjacent Places: Movement
More relevant to our discussion of POV editing, however, is the fact that films started to use the space adjacent to the place of action – the immediate offscreen space. The motivating force behind this transition was probably the same as the impetus for inserts: A scene consisted of many events and narratively important details; considering them in one full shot would make the figures too small for even the most experienced full-shot cameraman. In *Le Chien de Montargis* (1909), for instance, the aristocrat Macaire, out of jealousy, plans to ambush his comrade Montargis because the King favors him. In the forest, Macaire (in the tinted version appearing in a yellow cape) orders his men to dig a grave, in which the victim is later to be buried [Figure 7(a)]. Macaire looks and listens off frame [Figure 7(b)] and exits right with his men following. Cut to an oak; Macaire enters left, with Montargis approaching from the horizon on his horse [Figure 7(c)]. After an ambush, Montargis is stabbed from behind [Figure 7(d)].

Even though the grave and the tree are proximate, it is difficult to capture both the stabbing and the burial if both events are to be detailed enough for comprehension. Instead, the action is divided between two

(a)   (b)

(c)   (d)

FIGURE 7. *Le Chien de Montargis* (SCAGL, 1909). As with most enlargements in this study, these are from 16-mm prints. (Obtained from the Wisconsin Center for Film and Theater Research.)

adjacent spaces. Considering the fact that inserts and other types of dissections *within* the shot space did not come into popularity until 1911–1913 (Salt, 1992:92), this technique of "adding" a space beside the present one was indeed a natural solution.

Moreover, the camera can be said to imitate the theatrical practice of changing sets and thus does not violate the notion of the camera as a stand-in for an immobile theater spectator. The early practice of having all characters *leave* the shot before the transition to a new *empty* shot reflects this fundamental theatrical inheritance of early cinema. This practice is present in most chase films, as well as in the example from *Le Chien de Montargis* discussed here [all the grave diggers leave Figure 7(b) before the cut].

Movement and gazing across the cut provided the most important means by which adjacency could be rendered and understood by an audience:

When a film presents contiguous space in separate shots, it needs some method for showing the viewer that these spaces are indeed next to each other. There are different ways of providing cues: A character or objects moving from one space to another might link them together, or a character looking offscreen in one direction might lead the viewer to surmise that the next shot shows the space that character sees. (Thompson, 1985:203)

The effect of adjacency between shot spaces when characters move across cuts is quite strong. It seems that it is fundamentally perceptual and difficult to avoid (Carroll, 1996a:169ff; Hochberg, 1986). The effect seems to have been acknowledged quite early by both audiences and filmmakers, as in this review of Biograph's *The White Rose of the Wilds* (1911):

This is melodrama with sentimental trimmings, all of which is exceedingly interesting because it is so capitally done. One of the most striking features of the production, to the experienced eye, is the almost perfect mechanical precision with which each scene is timed; it all goes like well oiled clockwork and there are no jarring moments. In several instances the joining of scenes, where an entrance is made through a door and we instantly see the act completed on the other side, the action is so carefully put together that it seems the same movement. This is closely approaching perfection in the technique of picture directing. (From "Reviews of Licensed Films," *The New York Dramatic Mirror*, Vol. 65, No. 1693, May 31, 1911, p. 31. Reprinted in Pratt, 1973:91)

Occasionally the effect gave rise to "defects" in the picture that were readily noticed by some spectators, here discussing Biograph's The Seventh Day from 1909:

There is also another defect in the picture which has appeared in other Biograph subjects and which, it appears to the writer, could be corrected with advantage to those otherwise highly meritorious productions. Changes in scenes from one location to another are effected too suddenly. The characters leave the mother's parlor and immediately appear in the judge's chamber and vice versa, giving the impression that they are adjoining rooms, or at least in the same house. (From "Reviews of New Films," *The New York Dramatic Mirror*, Vol. 62, No. 1602, September 4, 1909, p. 17. Reprinted in Pratt, 1973:62)

However, although *movement* across the cut became widespread and perhaps the most crucial method to connect proximate spaces, *gazing* was used to a much lesser degree. For a possible psychological explanation of this, see the subsection on Eight Hypotheses, hypothesis 1.

Editing between Adjacent Places: Gazing
Soon enough, however, POV editing and eyeline matches were introduced more systematically. It is interesting to follow the development of the POV editing device – how and in what context it was first introduced – as this clearly demonstrates how the notion of the spectator as a theatergoer was transformed only reluctantly, and step by step.

The earliest examples of POV, as we saw, were often accompanied by some form of visual device (e.g., binoculars, magnifying glass, or microscope). This practice continued after 1906, often in combination with circular masking of the object shot. Around 1910–11, however, the interest in POVs without masking seemed to increase. According to Salt, Vitagraph was at the forefront of experimentation with this technique in the United States. Initially, such editing transitions were accompanied by explanatory intertitles, clearly stating the spatial relations between the shots. In films such as Larry Trimble's *Jean and the Waif* (1910) the ("true") POV shot was introduced by the title "What they saw in the house across the court," and in *The Switchman's Tower* (1911) with "What he saw" (Salt, 1992:96).

Soon, however, unvignetted POV structures appeared. Of the American 1911 films inspected by Salt, five out of thirty-one Vitagraph productions and three out of ninety-three productions made by other companies had POV. In 1912 and 1913 combined, twenty-eight out of ninety-two Vitagraph films and forty-five films out of 245 other studios contained some form of POV. Those figures include both true POV and eyeline matches, of which the latter seem to dominate:

> In other words, although film-makers outside Vitagraph were becoming interested in using the POV structure, they were having considerably difficulty mastering it. It is noticeable that Allan Dwan at American Film Manufacturing was one of those who could not get it quite right. (Salt, 1992:96)

It is worth noting that Salt conceptualizes the stylistic changes in an "evolutionary" manner, with the eyeline match as a typically inferior and "wrong" technique compared with the "correct" POV, in which the camera is explicitly placed at the location of the gazer, facing the way the gazer is looking. Thompson, on the other hand, regards the eyeline match as a convention in itself. In her sample, one quarter of the 1912 American films had at least one eyeline match. In 1913 that figure is approximately fifty percent, and in 1914 the majority of films have them. By 1915, Luna Production Company seems confident that the convention is stable enough to parody it in *Ye Gods! What a Cast!* (Thompson, 1985:212). In 1917, only occasional films lack eyeline matches. I am not aware of figures from other national cinemas, although we could – deductively – expect the European figures to be lower, considering Europe's general tendency to rely more on mise-en-scène and profilmic techniques.

From Thompson (1985:207) and Salt, we may conclude that the general use of eyeline matches preceded true POVs. That is, when gazing across a cut to connect adjoining spaces eventually became more widespread, changing the angle of view was done only reluctantly. Instead, the camera was moved sideways to the space beside it. For instance, in the gangster's

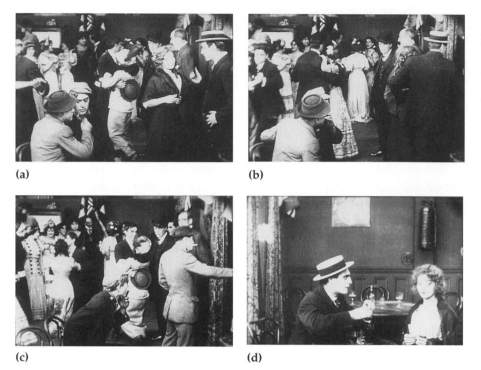

FIGURE 8. Sight link in *The Musketeers of Pig Alley* (D.W. Griffith, 1912). (Obtained from the Wisconsin Center for Film and Theater Research.)

ball scene in *The Musketeers of Pig Alley* (Biograph, 1912), the little lady goes into an adjoining room with a courting gangster [Figures 8(a) and 8(b)]. Snapper, in the dancing hall, rises and looks off frame [Figure 8(c)]. Cut to a shot of the adjoining room, into which Snapper first blows smoke [Figure 8(d)] and then enters. Here the camera refuses to cut to the exact visual position of Snapper, but displays both rooms from the same angle, although from somewhat different camera positions.

Why did sight links such as this precede the introduction of true POVs? Well, the conception of cinematic space was still under influence of the notion of stage space; although the camera was no longer restricted to one *point*, it did confine itself to one *side* of the space (that of the auditorium). The notion of the spectator as sitting in front of the fictive space still lingered on. This placed strict constraints on the freedom of the camera, enabling it to move sideways only (exemplified by both Figures 7 and 8). Generally, until 1913, a change of camera angle was rare (Salt, 1992:93). Instead, adding a space beside it, predominantly by movement across rooms through doors and other passageways, but occasionally also by

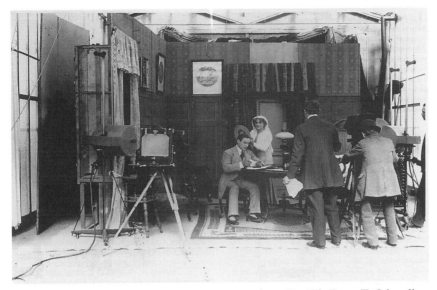

FIGURE 9. The filming of a studio interior scene from *Vor Tids Dame* (E. Schnedler-Sørensen, 1912) at the Nordisk studio in Copenhagen. (Reproduced from Salt, 1992:66.)

gazing, was the major intrascene spatial articulation. For Griffith, such practice became almost "obsessive" (Salt, 1992:98ff). In a regime like this, sight links are much more natural than true POV as the latter often requires a dramatic change of angle (often between 90° and 180° with a character facing the camera). Even though Griffith broke with the early respect for the profilmic by dissecting space into different rooms, displaying those rooms from the angle and location of Snapper was still too daring in the early 1910s.

This notion of space was, of course, also mirrored in the way sets were built at the time. In the early years, a flat perpendicular set, often only a painted back wall, was used. By around 1907, this had developed into an L-shaped construction, with walls at two sides (Figure 9; Salt, 1992:65ff). This allowed the camera to change angles somewhat, although still in a very confined manner, without the sets having to be changed. True POV editing and opposite angles are virtually impossible in a studio environment like this if one is to maintain a nine-feet distance to the actors and at the same time wants to avoid changing sets. Such constraints must have delayed the introduction of true POV editing.

The three to four wall sets with movable sections introduced in the early 1910s enhanced the possibilities. By then, however, the medium close-ups had been introduced, which enabled filmmakers to isolate characters

(a)   (b)

FIGURE 10. *The Egyptian Mummy* (Lee Beggs, 1914). The Professor sees the arrival of the "mummy" through his window. (Obtained from the Wisconsin Center for Film and Theater Research.)

from the background. In this way, only a small portion of background was needed, which defused many of the set-building problems altogether [see, for example, Figure 12(b)]. In such a system, the POV editing structure, with a camera taking reverse angles, is much more manageable in terms of both time and budget.

Moreover, if a POV structure contained a serious change of angle, it almost invariably included an exterior object shot. "Although shots taken from the opposite directions to a scene had been put together well before this date [1908], as far as I know this very infrequent practice had always involved at least one of the scenes being shot outdoors on location, which eliminates the set building problem" (Salt, 1992:93). If the L-shaped sets in combination with the nine-feet line provided difficulties with drastic changes of angles, placing the object of the gaze outside a window avoided these problems. Because the window was often placed in such a manner as the spectator was unable to look through it (having the window on the flank of a set, with its plane perpendicular to the film screen), exteriors could be chosen freely and there was no risk for continuity problem between interiors and exteriors (see Figure 10 or the shot in *The Lonedale Operator* [1911] in which the female operator waves goodbye to her fiancé through the window of the train station).

Changes of angle or even reverse angles *are* present in early cinema, but they seem to be used only under special circumstances, for example, when the understandability of the act or scene requires them. *Ladies' Skirts Nailed to a Fence* (Bamford, 1900) is perhaps one of the earliest examples. Here, the actions of the bad boys are visible only with a view from the other side of the fence[5] (Figure 11). Other typical situations in which drastic change of angle were used involved theaters, courts, or lectures, in

(a)   (b)

FIGURE 11. *Ladies' Skirts Nailed to a Fence* (Bamford, 1900) with a reverse angle simulated by moving the actors to the other side of the fence, without moving the camera. (Reproduced from Salt, 1992:56.)

which two people or groups more or less "must" confront each other spatially (theater audience in front of a stage, judge with courtroom, lecturer with students). Griffith, for instance, resorts to reverse angle only a couple of times during his career. When he does, the situation contains two confronting parties. The reverse-angle POV of *A Drunkard's Reformation* (1909) occurs when the father and his daughter sit in an auditorium watching a play (Gunning, 1994:167; Salt, 1992:93ff). *Easy Street* (Keystone, 1917), which to a remarkable extent rejects all change of camera angles and emphatically clings to the earlier style of sideways camera movement only, contains only one scene with reverse angles. This scene involves a missionary house sermon with a clearly frontal layout (Figure 12). All street scenes in *Easy Street*, which constitute the bulk of the film, are shot in

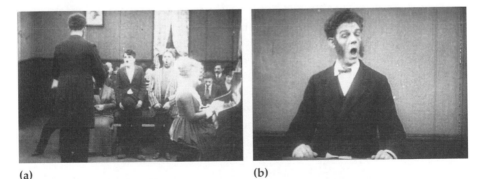

(a)   (b)

FIGURE 12. *Easy Street* (Lone Star Corporation, 1917). (Obtained from the Wisconsin Center for Film and Theater Research.)

the same style as Griffith's, moving the camera only sideways (and occasionally upward–downward). Not even when Chaplin and his fiancée at the end of the film meet on the sidewalk is the spectator given access to the space behind the camera. In a frontal medium shot, Chaplin gazes in a direction close to the camera and reacts happily, but the viewer never gets to see what he looks at or reacts to. The camera stays with Chaplin, and soon his fiancée enters from behind the camera left. In terms of spatial articulation, *Easy Street* surely belongs to the regime developed ten years earlier, rather than to the spatially more elaborate films that were produced the same year.

Eventually, however, changing the camera angle became a legitimate means by which cinematic space could be constructed, even though some constraints prevailed (e.g., the 180° convention). This, in combination with closer framing, enabled the cinema to break loose from its theatrical inheritance and to have the camera move more or less freely within the fictive space. To describe it from the spectator's perspective: With true POV editing, shot–reverse shot (SRS), and other devices, the spectator had to build more complicated spatial models than previously, enabling space to immerse her or him on all sides rather than remaining in front. These devices exploited the spatial abilities of the spectator and triggered offscreen expectations and inference making, thereby creating a (mental) "surround space" (Persson, 2001; Persson, 1999a).

In the classical period, POV inferences were not only supported by gazes across the cut, but by other cues as well. The so-called over-the-shoulder shot, which included body parts of the gazer in the object shot, is perhaps the clearest and most useful cue for inferring a POV link between two shots. Interestingly enough, although POV and SRS were systematically implemented during the late 1910s, the over-the-shoulder shot became popular in the 1930s. Until then, all object shots of POVs and SRSs were in-front-of-the-shoulder shots (Salt, 1992:94; Thompson, 1985:210). The cause for this delay may again have been the frontality of the theatrical practice out of which cinema had sprung. (This general resistance may also be related to the effect of personal-space invasion that over-the-shoulder shots generate[6]; see the discussion in Chapter 3, the subsection on Voyeurism.)

By having body parts of the gazer included in the object shot, over-the-shoulder shots fall in between pure POV editing, in which object and gazer are wholly separated and exist in different shots, and pure "full-shot" style, in which object and gazer are fully present in the same shot (e.g., Figure 13). The point here is that POV editing and other forms of rendering characters' gazing at objects are not clearly divided by boundaries, but rather exist on a continuum. Although over-the-shoulder shots are essential for understanding POV relations between shots, I exclude

FIGURE 13. *Le Voyage dans la lune* (Georges Méliès, 1902). The scientists perceive the rising earth from the surface of the moon. Gazer and target object coexist within the same shot. (Obtained from the Wisconsin Center for Film and Theater Research.)

them from the following discussion. I instead look at other types of cues. POV editing will henceforth refer only to cases in which object and gazer are placed completely within separate shots.

In the late 1910s, using masking and irises to indicate POV relations between shots regained popularity. In contrast to the earlier use before 1906, suggesting binoculars, magnifying glasses, or keyholes, the circular iris now became a convention for marking the POV as such (Thompson, 1985:208). In the 1920s, however, this practice disappeared.

Other ways of marking POV status include tracking shots and a handheld camera. If the glance shot is a tracking shot (perhaps following a walking character) and the object shot is moving with the same approximate speed, this situation constitutes a strong cue for POV (see, e.g., *Ladri di biciclette* [1948], in which the father scans a row of bicycles at the secondhand market). If the glance shot is shot with a stationary camera and the object shot with a swinging handheld one (perhaps signifying intoxication or dizziness), this is also a strong cue. These practices, however, are of later origin than the period we are discussing here.

Functions of Point-of-View Editing
So far, I have tried to sketch the timetable and the immediate context in which POV editing was introduced and how POV questioned and

changed the earlier theatrical regime of spatiality. It is not sufficient, however, to determine when conventions were first introduced; we must also consider the specific system of representation in which those devices were used (Bordwell et al., 1985:xiv). Just as the chase, the insert, and the tableau of cinema between 1895 and 1905 were later integrated into the narrative context, so too was the POV structure. If the magnification and the "trick" effects of early POV shots were part of the vaudeville and attractionist era, the eyeline matches and POV of the 1910s came to be a part of the new mode of representation that cinema adopted during those transitional years.

First, POV editing creates spatial relationships between different shot spaces. If a spectator infers that a shot displays objects that the character in the preceding shot is now looking at, then the character and the objects must at least be within sight range; that is, in the object shot, the gazer must be somewhere offscreen. Spatial bonding of this sort may take on important functions in the narrative, for example, in determining the closeness or the distance between a victim and his stalker. In *The End of St. Petersburg* (1927), POVs indicate important spatial relations among table, tea kettle, and window in the episode in which the Worker, warned by his Wife, escapes from soldiers in his basement flat (see Kepley, 1995).

Spatial understandings such as these fundamentally depend on the idea of a diegesis separated from the space of the theatre and that shot spaces somehow belong together spatially, temporally, causally, or conceptually. As we have seen, such conceptualization was not in place during cinema's first years. Instead, the characters and the space of gags belonged to the space of the auditorium, with the two spaces acknowledging each other through glances into the camera and audience reactions. The POVs of *Grandma's Reading Glass* or *As Seen through a Telescope* did not try to establish spatial relations within a fictive world, but constituted a magic trick along the lines of slow motion, reverse motion, substitution, or multiple exposure.

Besides building spatial relationships in diegetic space, POV structures were also used to serve one of the central parameters of transition through the years 1905–17: the psychologization of characters. I will have more to say about this in Chapter 4, but it suffices here to mention that POV or eyeline matches constituted one component in this change. First, eyeline matches and true POVs are powerful devices for narration, as far as they efficiently direct the spectator's attention to the object of the character's gaze. Through POV editing, the narration is able to isolate the object of gaze at any time that suits the purpose of the narrative, thus to a great extent manipulating the spectator's speculations and inferences about character psychology. Being able to control when and at what a character looks is important for conveying that character's emotions and intentions to the spectator.

Gunning's discussion about *The Redman and the Child* (1908, Griffith's third film) is pertinent in this respect. Here, an Indian loses and recovers his two most valuable possessions – his gold and his best friend (a white boy). While the Indian is away scouting territory with two surveyors, the boy is attacked by two men, who force him to reveal the hiding place of the gold, kill an old man who tries to save the boy, and then abduct the boy in their canoe. A climactic canoe chase follows, creating a coherent geography. It ends with a happy reunion and an emblematic shot, which shows the Indian canoeing toward the camera with the recovered gold and the rescued child (Gunning, 1994:69ff). The POV enters in one of the turning points of the film, in which the Indian is on a hill with the surveyors, setting up a telescope. As the Indian examines this technological wonder of the white man, he happens to see the abduction of the boy through the telescope. In the first long shot, the Indian sets his eye to the telescope, expresses surprise, and then appears alarmed. We cut to a masked shot of the white men killing the old man and abducting the boy in their canoe. We then return to the Indian, who reacts wildly and rushes off to the final canoe chase. Not only does this POV create a geography between the Indian on the hill and the boy by the river, but it allocates knowledge about the abduction and emotions vis-à-vis that event to the Indian: The boy is dear to him and the abduction is an affective disaster. In this way, the POV allows the spectator to understand some aspects of the character's psychology at a critical moment in the story, providing a major *psychological* motivation for the chase: "Although the psychology is not complex, the editing conveys the character's motivation" (Gunning, 1994:74). Of course, this psychological or narrative function probably worked side by side with the attractionist, as is shown by the following review from *Variety*, cited and commented on by Gunning:

"Here a clever bit of trick work is introduced to bring about an intensely dramatic situation . . . immediately the field of the picture contracts to a circle and the scene is brought before the audience as though through the eye of the Indian glued to the telescope." *Variety*'s description of the technique is revealing. Instead of an "invisible" narrative code expressing the character's point of view (as the sequence would probably be understood today), *Variety* describes it as a "trick work," relating the technique to the trick-film genre typified by the films of Méliès. (Gunning, 1994:72)

To put it in another way, the trick aspect of the device is placed alongside its narrative and psychologizing function ("to bring about an intensely dramatic situation"). Thus it is positioned in the twilight zone between the early mode of reception and its more classical form, here succinctly formulated by Thompson:

> The classical cinema's dependence upon POV shots, eyeline matches, and SRS patterns reflects its general orientation toward character psychology.... [M]ost classical narration arises from within the story itself, often by binding our knowledge to shifts in the characters' attention: we notice or concentrate on elements to which the characters' glances direct us. In the construction of contiguous spaces, POV, the eyeline match, and SRS do not work as isolated devices; rather they operate together within the larger systems of logic, time, and space, guaranteeing that psychological motivation will govern even the mechanics of joining one shot to another. As a result, the system of logic remains dominant. (Thompson, 1985:210)

POV editing is thus not only a central part of classical cinema's general striving for *spatial* immersion of the spectator, but also constitutes one of the first steps toward *narrative* immersion. Enabling the spectator to attribute emotions, beliefs, goals, and knowledge to characters is the first step toward the processes of alliance, empathy, and identification, all of which lie at the core of all narrative art forms.

Deictic Gaze

Historical reception studies of the sort just described are concerned with economical, productional, (non)narrative, and stylistical contexts within which conventions and discursive practices are used and understood by its audience. To a psychologist, this is vital information. To describe the mental processes of the spectator, however, we must now begin to sketch the mental dispositions involved and how they influence the understanding of POV editing.

My general approach is that understanding POV editing is fundamentally an *inferential* activity in the cognitive unconscious of the spectator. Whether in cinema or in real life, the spectator *infers* that a person is looking at a certain object. This inference is never objectively certain, but only more or less probable and always relative to understanding (like all cognition and inferences). Even when the gazer and the seen object are in the same shot, the spectator still must attribute a gaze (and the object of that gaze) to the character. "C looks at O" or "This is what C looks at" is thus never a textual structure per se, but a mental coherence created on the basis of textual cues and, as I argue, deictic-gaze ability. Some scholars have acknowledged this inferential feature of POV. Thompson (1985:203) uses terms such as *surmise*: "a character looking offscreen in one direction might lead the viewer to surmise that the next shot shows the space that character sees." Jean Mitry talks about the processes of *recognition*:

In any case, the subjective image is never more than a complement to another image. It has meaning only insofar as it relates to a character already objectively described and placed. I can see "what Pierre sees" only if I have already seen Pierre, and I can share his point of view only if I can relate it to him, recognizing it as *his*. (Mitry, 1997:209)

Although both of these passages indicate the importance of understanding processes in the spectator, none of them goes into detail. My emphasis on understanding – rather than on textual structure – contrasts with semiotic–structuralist approaches, which deal more or less exclusively with textual processes and "the reader" that the text implies or suggests (Branigan, 1984). A psychological approach does not deny that textual structures exist, but their shape and effects cannot be deduced solely on the basis of textual analysis. A description of POV editing must be complemented by an investigation into the interaction among spectators' biological, psychological, cultural, and historical dispositions and the text. Whereas cultural reception theorists grasp such dispositions through analyzing cultural phenomena and discourse, I make use of psychological studies.

So how, then, is the relation between glance shot and object shot recognized, surmised, inferred, or understood by the spectator? Carroll (1993) presents a framework to explain these processes. The spectator understands POV editing, Carroll maintains, because it is a representation of an event that is basic to humans, namely, the habit of following and determining the object of another person's gaze, so-called deictic gaze. "[P]oint-of-view editing [. . .] works because it relies on depicting biologically innate information-gathering procedures" (Carroll, 1996a:129). Although Carroll is reluctant to go into details of the mental processes of understanding – an endeavor he may gladly pass on to psychologists – his basic idea is worth exploring, as it presents a way not only to describe mental processes of understanding, but also, as we will see, to explain stylistic features and changes of the POV convention. To this end, we must take a closer look at what deictic gaze is and how it is structured.

The Structure of Deictic-Gaze Behavior

Gazing in humans involves a wide set of behaviors with a similarly wide set of functions, for example, social, emotional, and information gathering (Kleinke, 1986). A simple distinction, though, can be made between mutual gaze, in which two persons look at each other, and deictic gaze, in which person A monitors the direction of person B's gaze and tries to establish the target of this gaze. *Deixis* is a linguistic term, denoting

a "reference by means of an expression whose interpretation is relative
to the (usually) extra-linguistic context of the utterance, such as who is
speaking, the time or place of speaking, the gestures of the speaker, or
the current location in the discourse" (Linguistic Glossary, 1997). English
examples would be *I*, *You*, *Now*, *There*, *That*, and *The following*. Deictic gaze
thus works as pointing and other indexical practices, which contextualize
and anchor linguistic utterance in space. Deictic gaze creates a "perceptual space" common to both participants and is thus often referred to as
joint visual attention (Butterworth, 1991). It is primarily this latter form
of gazing behavior that I discuss.

DEVELOPMENT. Because deictic gazing is a basic form of human behavior,
it is easily overlooked and taken for granted. To understand its fundamental importance in human life and to emphasize that it *is* an acquired
ability, psychologists have turned to toddlers. In the typical experimental setting, infant and parent are placed in a room with different target
objects, e.g. toys. The parent is instructed to interact naturally with the
child and then, at a signal, to turn, silently and without pointing, to in-
spect one of the objects. The reaction of the infant is recorded on video
and judged by two independent observers, who estimate the direction
and the accuracy of the infant's response relative to the objects of the parent's line of gaze. Results suggest that deictic-gaze competence develops
in three stages, with each stage introducing new abilities (Butterworth,
1991).

At the age of six months, babies apprehend and are quite sensitive
to the change in the parent's gazing behavior. They make clear efforts to
investigate the direction of the parent's attention. They also look at the correct side of the room for the target. When there are two identical targets on
the same side of the room, however, the six-month-old babies cannot differentiate between them, although the objects may be separated as much
as 60 degrees. When the correct target is the first one on the scanning path
from parent to target, babies are mostly accurate, but when the correct
target is second on this path, they perform only at chance level; that is,
these children cannot determine the right target on the basis of the parent's action alone, but the perceptual salience of the object and its setting
seem to play a part (e.g., differentiating color, movement, and shape).

At six months of age, the babies also fail to follow gaze if the parent
looks at an object outside the field of view, for instance, behind the baby.
These findings cannot be attributed to an inability to turn around, as
children at this age often react that way to noises and other events. Instead,
Butterworth (1991) suggests, the most likely explanation is that the child
lacks an awareness that it is surrounded by a continuous space. The adult's

expectation of a space existing outside the immediate field of view appears to be absent in the six-month-old child. This corresponds well to Piaget's theory about *object* and *space permanence* (recapitulated and scrutinized by Harris, 1983:715ff), a stance that a baby supposedly develops after the first year of life. Irrespective of the fact that six-month-old babies' inability to look for objects behind them can be attributed to a lack of space permanence, it is fair to assume that, for deictic gaze to function properly *in adults*, this spatial assumption has to be in place.

By the age of twelve months, the infant is beginning to localize targets correctly, whether first or second along the scan path. This suggests that some form of "geometric ability" is now definitely in place, independent of the perceptual salience of the target object. Butterworth observed in the experiments how the infant fixated on the mother while she was turning; only a second or so after her turning ended did the child turn its head to the target objects, indicating that some form of angular estimation process occurred. It is interesting to note that this geometric ability surfaces at the same time as index-finger pointing starts to be understood by the child (toward the end of the first year, a couple of months before production of the gesture). Both abilities seem to include the understanding of a projection or extension of a straight line in space[7] (perhaps connected to the act of throwing things and monitoring their trajectory). Still, however, twelve-month-old children failed to search for targets located behind them. Even though the visual field was emptied of targets, the children scanned only approximately 40 degrees of visual angle; when they encountered no object, they gave up the search (Butterworth, 1991:227).

By the time a child is eighteen months of age, geometrical ability is refined, although not complete. Adults can discriminate changes of visual angle as small as 1 minute of arc of visual angle (Bruce, Green & Georgeson, 1996:357). That ability is probably not in place at eighteen months of age. Moreover, an infant is reluctant to search behind itself unless the space in front contains no objects at all. Although the assumption of object permanence is gaining force in the child's spatial understanding, it is not as developed as that of adults.

Among children and adults, deictic-gaze behavior seems triggered by some sort of *change* in the gazer's behavior: The gazer makes a clear shift of direction of gaze, becomes quiet or still, or changes from a wandering gaze to a still one. When Butterworth's parents not only gazed but also pointed with arm and index finger, deictic-gaze behavior was triggered to a significantly larger extent in all age groups than with gaze only (Grover, 1988; retold in Butterworth, 1991). This indicates that some gazer-related *event* prototypically must be acknowledged in order to trigger deictic gaze behavior.

FUNCTIONS. Deictic gaze fulfills important social functions in humans and animals. First, joint visual attention creates among the participants a common "semantic–perceptual space," which enables and supports communication and language learning. Caretakers, for instance, are exceptionally sensitive to the direction of a child's gaze in order to establish what object, event, or situation catches the attention of the toddler at the moment. It has been shown that caretakers adapt and constrain their language use in order to "level" with the toddler and the object of attention, for instance, in labeling objects, activities, or situations (Bruner, 1983:67ff). From the child's perspective, this shared perceptual space makes language learning much easier and faster, as the reference of the adult's discourse is "right there in front of its eyes." In adults, shared visual attention often has crucial functions in everyday discourse. Indexical gazing and pointing provide the context in which verbal utterances or other behaviors are meaningful and understandable (the fluctuating reference of *this* and *that* are perhaps the clearest examples).

It is interesting to note that this shared perceptual–semantic space is somewhat different from Euclidian space. Two persons looking at the same object do not share the same angle and visual input. Nevertheless, object and event recognition processes work more or less the same way ("That's a cat"), thereby creating a "protosemantic" space in which labels, words, and utterances can easily acquire meaning. Of course, in some situations, the difference in visual angle may create different shared semantic spaces (e.g., in playing cards, one can see the opponent gazing down at the cards, but one cannot determine the exact object of this gaze). Alternatively, the terrain may block visual access (perhaps a pillar in the theater blocks one person's view, but not another's). Here, visual angle interferes with deictic gaze, creating difficulties for a shared semantic space. In these cases, people are mostly aware of the complications involved and either try to reposition themselves or take care with determining the object of attention. Thus joint visual attention refers to something more abstract than exact visual field or input. Although the sensory input of light and visual angle may differ, both persons in a deictic-gaze situation still achieve similar categorizations of objects, activities, and spatial features. It is these parameters that are shared, not visual angle.

It is crucial to determine and consolidate shared attention in a given situation. To this end, after following the direction of gaze to its target, we often return to the gazer to confirm the direction and the location of the target. This behavior becomes particularly apparent in cases in which we are unable to localize any target ("What is he looking at?"). If no shared semantic space can be established, we return to the gazer to either reestimate the direction of gaze or question whether the gazer is looking at anything at all ("Is he kidding me?").

Returning to the gazer's face, in conjunction with the shared per-ceptual–semantic space, creates the context within which nonverbal communication can take place, in adults as well as in children. After the shared object of attention has been established, it is common to return to the gazer's face in order to determine his or her *attitude* toward the object or event in question. In social psychology, this process is called social referencing (Klinnert et al., 1983). Here, the joint visual attention context, in combination with a facial or gestured expression, provides the basis for understanding the intentions or emotions of the person (e.g., "He really wants that cell phone," "She is really disgusted by the sight of that behavior"). As we shall see in Chapter 4, these processes seem particularly relevant for understanding characters in visual narratives. Social referencing may also create expectations about impending behavior toward an object ("I can see in his face that he is going to rise and grab that telephone"). Although such predictions may not always be correct, they provide a powerful everyday method for predicting behavior in other peo-ple or animals. Such a prediction ability must have had an evolutionary value.

In children, social referencing appears to have a clear pedagogical func-tion. In returning to the face of the caretaker, the child seeks vocal and non-vocal guidance and advice on how to behave vis-à-vis a new and unknown object or situation. In one set of experiments, Klinnert et al. (1983) sent in somewhat frightening remote-controlled toys (a spider, a dinosaur, or a model of a human head) into a room with a twelve- or eighteen-month-old infant and its mother. If the child turned to her, the mother was instructed to look alternately from the toy to the infant, displaying one of three facial expressions: joy, fear, or neutrality. Not only did referencing the mother prove to be a common behavior in the children (because the objects were indeed something new for the child), but the displayed facial expression also influenced the babies' subsequent behavior toward the toys. Babies moved closest to the mother when she expressed fear, moved closest to the toy when she smiled, and maintained an intermediate distance when she was neutral. The same consistent results have appeared in visual cliff studies (Sorce et al., 1981).

For infants, social referencing is an important preverbal method of seek-ing guidance or sense making of an event or object that is ambiguous or beyond the child's own intrinsic appraisal abilities. This is a simple way to create hierarchies of good and bad, safe and dangerous, thereby guiding and constraining behavior in appropriate ways. For children as well as for adults, social referencing demands a host of other abilities to work properly (e.g., knowledge of facial expressions, body language, FP, knowledge of the personality), but joint visual attention is one important component.

A third function of joint visual attention is deception. Once a person knows that other people tend to attend to his deictic gaze, he or she can use this fact to his advantage. Everybody is familiar with the practical joke of pretending to look in a direction, thereby inducing the belief in others that there is something worthy of attention ("Made you look!"). This may appear banal from a human perspective, but it can have useful functions among animals. Byrne (1995) reports an incident involving a baboon that apparently avoided punishment with this strategy. This young adult male had played too violently with an infant, who screamed. The mother subsequently arrived on the scene, and started to chase the male. Instead of running, however, he jumped to his hind legs and stared, as these baboons typically do if they have seen a distant predator. The pursuit stopped and was not resumed. There was, however, no sign of real danger (Byrne, 1995:125).

In another case, a gorilla traveling in a group detected some food up a tree. Instead of looking, however, she pretended to self-groom. Not until she was alone did she look at the food again and climb the tree (Whiten & Byrne, 1988:218). This case is perhaps not an obvious example of deception, but it shows the constant awareness of deictic gaze and its importance among animals. It is well known, for instance, that many primates have the ability to hide objects, events, and situations from other primates in the group if the detection of those objects has the potential to cause them harm. Subordinate males, for instance, will often attempt to copulate only after they have maneuvered their partner into a position out of sight of more dominant males. In one reported case, a female baboon groomed a subadult in the presence of another male. Because this behavior is generally not tolerated by adult males, the female had positioned herself and the subadult behind a rock, so that only the tail, back, and crown of the female were visible, but not her front, arms, and face (Whiten & Byrne, 1988:215).

It is worth noting that not only primates (Gómez, 1991) display deictic-gaze behavior. Ristau's (1991) fascinating studies of plovers' "injury-feigning" behavior following an intrusion into the nest, and the complex monitoring of the intruder's direction of gaze show that deictic gaze is a widespread behavior pattern among a number of species. In all of such cases, deception and *Machiavellian intelligence* (Byrne & Whiten, 1988) play a crucial role.

UNIVERSALITY AND THE QUESTION OF ORIGIN. All of the psychological studies cited in the preceding subsection were conducted on Western children and adults, which implies a lack of formal evidence of deictic-gaze behavior in other cultures.

However, in the light of ethological evidence, joint visual attention seems to be an interspecies behavior, encompassing humans as well as higher animals. Such universality seems intuitive. It is true that cultures have different rules and conventions about whom one may watch and that such rules often reflect and enforce power relations in a society. This situation does not, however, restrict the assertion that the *ability* for deictic gaze is universal. It is also true that social referencing includes other types of knowledge that may be cultural in character (e.g., facial expressions, folk psychology, body language). The claim being made here, however, pertains to only joint visual attention, which appears to be a universal pattern of behavior. Moreover, this universality makes sense in the light of the linguistic, sociocognitive, and deceptive functions that the deictic gaze fulfills; these functions are indeed vital and useful for all humans, regardless of cultural settings.

The question of the (individual) origins of deictic gaze is an interesting one. Although Carroll does not deny the value of the socialization process that a child undergoes, he seems to suggest that deictic gaze is a "biologically innate" propensity, "virtually preprogrammed," and "bred in the bone" (Carroll, 1996a:127–9). These terms are not clear, but Carroll points to some sort of genetic explanation. Such an explanation could be countered with a sociocultural framework, claiming that the ontogeny of deictic-gaze behavior is fundamentally dependent on other people's behavior and on the social context within which a child is brought up. A compromise position might postulate a genetic basis that provides us with some *predisposition* to develop patterns such as deictic gaze but whose actual development probably demands a rich physical and social environment.

These questions are as intriguing as they are difficult to answer. Fortunately for the theory I propose here, however, we do not have to decide in favor of nature or nurture. When I claim that deictic-gaze competence is *universal*, I make no claims about the *origins* of deictic-gaze behavior. I merely propose that deictic gaze is *geographically* universal, in the sense that it is universally spread in all cultures (and many species) on Earth. Whether this universality is caused by biology or social upbringing is an interesting, but separate, issue. In this sense, I think deictic-gaze behavior conforms well to the standards of Bordwell's notion of *contingent universals*:

Nonetheless, I propose that we can make some progress if we bypass the nature/culture couplet for the moment and concentrate upon some "contingent universals" of human life. They are contingent because they did not, for any metaphysical reasons, have to be the way they are; and they are universal insofar as we can find them to be widely present in human societies. They consist of practices and propensities which arise in and through human activities. The core assumption here is that given certain uniformities in the environment across cultures, humans have in their social activities faced comparable tasks in surviving and creating their ways of life. Neither wholly "natural" nor wholly "cultural," these sorts of contingent universals are good candidates for being at least partly responsible for the "naturalness" of artistic conventions. (Bordwell, 1996a:91)

In summary, then, deictic gaze is a behavioral pattern that involves the following prototypical structure:

- A geometric ability to estimate the angle of eye direction and to follow that trajectory through space. If that angle is zero, *mutual gaze* is said to exist, in which case deictic-gaze behavior is not triggered.
- Some perceptually or contextually salient event or object along the line of the gaze. If we cannot establish a target object, even after returning to the gazer to reconfirm, no joint visual attention is triggered. We assume that the person is simply staring out "into space" (perhaps occupied with mental tasks such as thinking or dreaming; see Baron-Cohen & Cross, 1992).
- An assumption about space permanence must apply, stating that searchable space continues outside the immediate visual field.
- Deictic-gaze behavior is triggered by some sort of *change* in the gazer's behavior (turning the head or eyes, moving a hand or the body).
- After we look for the object, we often return to the gazer, confirming ambiguous or uncertain joint visual attention or determining the attitude of the gazer vis-à-vis the object.
- On the basis of the reactions or nonreactions of the gazer, we try to infer the gazer's attitudes toward an object or event. These processes require a host of other forms of knowledge, but the basic point is that we are making some effort to understand why the gazer looks at the object and what the consequences of this gaze will be (possibly influencing our own behavior).

It is now time to turn to the details about how this extracinematic, everyday structure of knowledge or ability participates in spectators' understanding of POV editing, as well as influences the design of this convention.

How Does Point-of-View Editing Work?

Why has the POV convention persisted and prevailed through the past eighty years of cinema? Why has it maintained popularity, not only in Hollywood cinema, but in national cinemas and nonfiction genres as well? One part of this explanation, Carroll and I maintain, is that the convention exploits a basic form of human behavior and that the inferences spectators make during the understanding of this device are habitual and automatic. POV does not demand a high-level interpretation that varies across different (groups of) spectators. Because all viewers share a basic behavioral ability, POV inferences seldom cause dispute; when they do, the reasons for the ambiguity are generally agreed on. It is symptomatic that Gunning's critic (in the subsection on the Functions of POV Editing) talked about POV in terms of "trick effect," as tricks do not usually demand learning or interpretation to be appreciated. Because of the human's basic cognitive–perceptual makeup, the appearance of a trick is immediately evident. Of course, people will have different views of how the trick was accomplished, but the appearance is unlikely to be disputed. As with tricks, POV is more of an *effect*, in the sense that the POV inference happens quickly and more or less involuntarily. This does not, however, mean that the effect is all in the text. There is still an interaction between textual properties and spectators' dispositions. It is with the details of this "matching" between textual structure and the structure of the deictic-gaze behavior that I am concerned.

If understanding POV editing involves inferring a sight link between two shot spaces, under what circumstances is this inference likely to occur and what criteria does the spectator use to justify or appraise the probability of this inference? Because a cut can have many meanings, how does the spectator know that the object shot really *is* an object shot, and does not depict another scene, another place, another time, or simply another segment of a scene to which the character's visual attention is *not* directed? What cues in the context of the object shot guide the inference process?

If we presuppose that deictic-gaze ability has something to do with the way spectators make POV inferences in cinema and that this ability has a specific structure, then we can assume that POV inferences will be more likely and more certain if the structure of POV editing contains the important elements of everyday deictic-gaze experience; that is, if the design of POV editing is similar to the structure of deictic-gaze ability, then deictic-gaze ability is more likely to be activated and used by the spectator for understanding. Moreover, because we know the specific features of the deictic-gaze experience, my argument will generate a concrete and perhaps empirical set of hypotheses with which we can work. It is to those hypotheses that we now turn.

Eight Hypotheses

1. All other things being equal, a POV inference should be more certain and less ambiguous if there is some change in the character's gaze behavior just before the cut between glance shot and object shot. Because joint visual attention in real life is triggered by a change of behavior on the gazer's part, this should also happen in POV inferencing. If there is a change in gaze direction, a change from wandering to still gaze, manual

pointing, or use of binoculars, reading glasses, or other visual devices, one of these should compel the spectator to infer the POV status of the next shot, at least more so than if those changes did not occur.

For instance, let us consider the clearly visible changes of gaze direction in the first scene after the credits of *Rear Window* (1954), in which Jeff speaks on the phone with his boss and looks at his neighbors (Figure 14). These changes should generate more, and more certain, POV inferencing than if those changes did not occur. Of course, there are many other POV cues in this scene that make the POV inference probable anyway, but the occurrence of gaze change would, according to my theory, make the spectator consider the inference more certain. Intuitively, I think that such a case can be made.

If correct, this claim implies that an inference will be less certain if the spectator for some reason fails to perceive a change of direction or behavior. If a filmmaker wants to trigger a POV inference in the spectator, certain textual designs seem to meet the basic requirements better than others. For instance, relying on smallish movements of the gazer – such as changing the direction of the eyes only or a small shift in head direction – plus having the gazer in a long shot, is not an efficient strategy. In *The Lonedale Operator*, there is a POV situation in which the operator has just arrived at work. Through the office window, she waves goodbye to her fiancé, the engine driver, who departs aboard his machine. Although other features eventually assure the spectator that the operator is in fact looking at the engine (see hypothesis 3), the initial transfer from the operator (interior) to the train (exterior) is somewhat confusing. One reason for this is that the long-shot framing of the glance shot makes it virtually impossible to notice that the girl in fact turns to the (offscreen) window just before the cut, unless the spectator has a chance to examine the film more closely. In the tableau style of early cinema, often with bustling and crowded long shots, there is less chance for the spectator to appreciate changes in glance and thus infer POV status for the object shot. This may indeed explain the delayed introduction of the POV convention in early cinema (see the subsection on Editing between Adjacent Places).

Of course, if a filmmaker wants to trigger certain POV inferences and still prefers to stick to a long-shot style, he or she must rely on more obvious methods such as pantomime acting (pointing offscreen with arms and largish body movements) or using visual devices such as binoculars (e.g., as in Griffith's *The Redman and the Child*; see Gunning, 1994:71). In fact, the extensive use of such devices in early cinema POVs seems to suggest that they were important ways to make cuts more acceptable to the audience as well as to establish the POV convention despite the long-shot style (in a cinema of attraction, as well as in its narrative form; see Gunning, 1994).

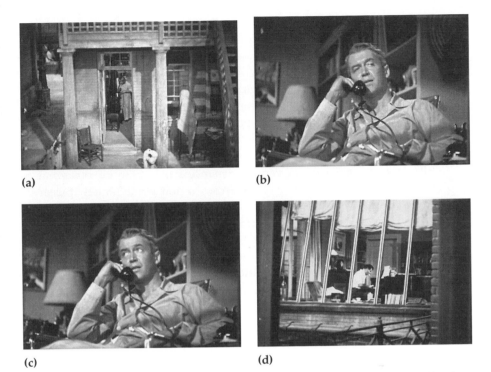

(a)   (b)

(c)   (d)

FIGURE 14. *Rear Window* (Alfred Hitchcock, 1954). In between shots of the yard and the piano player, Jeff makes a clear change of gaze direction, supporting POV inferences in the spectator. (Obtained from the Wisconsin Center for Film and Theater Research.)

However, if one rejects the pantomime acting style in favor for a more "naturalistic" and low-key mode, which many American directors started to do between 1909 and 1913 (Thompson, 1985:189), then POV editing becomes hazardous in long shots. From a psychological point of view, long shots, naturalistic acting, and POV editing are simply not compatible in a system that strives for clarity and disambiguity. If, at the same time, one acknowledges that gazing is a powerful mechanism for connecting different spaces as well as imbuing the characters with a simple form of psychology, then it is easy to assume that the long-shot norm must be discarded. We see here how a system of narrativity, a striving for clarity, visualization techniques, and psychological factors force a stylistic shift. The reasons why the camera crept closer to the actors are complex; we must take into account the economic, distributional, and narrative transformations of cinema and its industry. Within such a system, however, the psychological dispositions of the audience – such as the deictic-gaze ability – surely played a part.

2. A POV inference should be more certain and less ambiguous if the glance shot and the object shot are followed by another glance shot. If the object shot is sandwiched between two glance shots, the spectator should be more likely to make a POV inference than if it is not, as this is the same mechanism as the one used in everyday joint visual attention. Returning from the object to the gazer fulfills important functions and hence is a very common behavior in children and adults. Because the return to the glance shot imitates this experience, the POV inference should be more easily triggered and more certain. Can we make such a case?

Although the *The Lonedale Operator* sequence may initially be somewhat ambiguous (Is the exterior shot of the engine a new scene? A new place? A temporal ellipsis?), the confusion is probably resolved when we return from the train to the operator inside. The cut back triggers POV inferencing and *in retrospect* determines the status of the engine shot ("Oh, she is looking at that engine through a window!"). If the cut back to the operator had been absent, the object shot of the engine departing would have had a more ambivalent and ambiguous status (particularly because the glance change was difficult to distinguish).

This clarifying aspect of the returning glance shot is sometimes pointed out by critics and viewers. In the following review of Edison's *The Sales-lady's Matinee* (Edison, 1909) it is the lack of alternation between glance shot and object shot that is the subject of complaint:

A New York melodrama manager . . . hires a champion pugilist to star in a new "thriller." . . . Later the saleslady reads the billing and determines to go. We see her seated in the balcony when the curtain goes up. Then we are shown a scene from the "thriller," but we do not know it is a scene from the play, as we see no sign of arch or footlights. Dastardly deeds are being performed but the pugilist hero smashes his way in and rescues the girl. Then we are shown the balcony, with the audience, including the girl, exhibiting by their faces and action their interest in the play. Another climax of the play follows, and this is the capital burlesque of the lurid drama. We recognize the stage this time, and see the "heavy" bind the heroine to the railroad track, but again the pugilist jumps in, scatters the scoundrels right and left and rescues the girl just as the "lightning express," a car and an engine made of scenery, bump their way across the stage. Another view of the balcony is now presented and to understand the conduct of the audience we are obliged to imagine that they are witnessing the railroad scene previously exhibited. Here is where skill in preparing the film for exhibition would have made this picture a model of its kind. If short scenes had alternated back and forth between the stage and the balcony, showing the progress on the stage and the effect on the balcony audience concurrently, the effect would have been greatly increased. ("Reviews of New Films," *The New York Dramatic Mirror*, Vol. 61, No. 1574, February 20, 1909, p. 16. Reprinted in Pratt, 1973:59. See also Burch, 1990:135)

This account substantiates claims about the close association between returning glance shots and POV inferences, as do some scholars' reactions to a sequence from *The Birds* (1963). Melanie is seen waiting outside the Bodega Bay school playground. The sequence alternates between her sitting nervously smoking and looking off frame and shots of birds massing at the playground monkey bars. Both Carroll (1980:74) and Messaris (1994:75) assert that this alternation of glance and birds initially may be understood as a POV sequence, although the continuation of the scene makes it clear that it is not. (The birds are gathering *behind* Melanie.) Messaris even conducted an informal reception study of this scene on his students and "at least some of them did indeed experience uncertainty or discombobulation" (1994:75). It was probably not the filmmakers' intention to lead the spectator down the "wrong" inferential path ("Melanie sees the birds massing on the monkey bars"), but the fact that such ambiguities arise testifies to the tendency to interpret alternating glance shots and other shots as having a POV relation.[8]

There is a similar sequence later in *The Birds*. In the explosion scene at the gas station, shots of people (including Melanie) looking out the window of a diner are alternated with long shots of the gas station and a man being attacked by sea gulls. Then the alternation starts including inserts of gasoline flowing down the asphalt and eventually hitting the tire of a car. The alternation might lead the spectator to infer that the people are looking not only at the attacked man but also at the flowing gasoline when it hits the car. However, Melanie in the next moment turns her head in another direction than the other people do and then utters a warning about a man stepping out of the gasoline-surrounded car to light a cigarette. Not until here does the spectator become aware that people failed to notice the gasoline ("Nobody saw the gasoline flow down the street, but all were focused on the gas station accident"). Again, a "false" or misleading POV inference is cleared up later in the sequence.

In both of these examples, the alternation between shots of objects and shots of people looking off frame generates a propensity to infer a POV relation. This causes "uncertainty or discombobulation" because this conclusion later proves to be "wrong." This uncertainty acts as evidence for my hypothesis that alternation constitutes a key POV cue. Moreover, alternation constitutes an important POV cue because it mimics a crucial aspect of real-life deictic-gaze experience.

Contrarily, if the object shot is *not* followed by another glance shot; this will ambiguate or even obstruct the POV inference. In the very last moments of *Halloween* (1978), Dr. Loomis learns that Michael has risen and disappeared in spite of repeated gunshots and a three-meter fall from a balcony. Pondering this situation, Loomis changes his direction of gaze (turns his head), and then a shot of a hallway appears. This in fact looks much like an object shot; perhaps some spectators are inclined to make a POV inference. The sequence continues, however, not with a return to

Loomis, but with more empty interiors (and eventually exteriors) with a heavy voice-over breathing of Michael. There are, of course, no objective criteria to determine whether that hallway shot was indeed a POV of Loomis or if it belonged to the subsequent montage sequence. The status of that shot is only more or less probable. The central claim here, however, is that spectators consider the absence of a returning shot at Loomis when determining this probability. As in everyday life situations, the return to Loomis would have confirmed POV status, but because that element is missing, so will be the certainty of the POV inference.

3. A POV inference should be more certain and less ambiguous if there is some form of reaction on part of the gazer than if there is not. As we saw, returning to the gazer after an object is often associated with a need to find out the gazer's attitude toward the object; the gazer often gives such feedback in situations of joint visual attention. If this reaction is present in a real joint visual attention situation, then the spectator should be more inclined to make POV inferences in cases that contains the feature. I believe this is the case.

Reactions are tremendously essential in generating coherence in POV editing. Returning to the glance shot after the object shot may be a good indication of a POV, but if the character reacts in some way, the inference will be even more certain, as the reaction and the seen object form a coherent structure. One of the main cues that eventually makes clear the sequence from *The Lonedale Operator* is that the operator waves and throws kisses into offscreen space. She reacts to something the spectator cannot see in the frame, but the departing engine and its driver seem to be the best candidate. The link between reaction and target object triggers the POV inference (also, the engine driver seems to be waving, although much less clear).

The critic reviewing *The Saleslady's Matinee* in hypothesis 2 seems to have taken this coherence as an indication of the POV link. In spite of the fact that he "see[s] no sign of arch or footlights" in the shot of the stage, he still infers the POV relationship because the reaction of the audience makes sense in connection with the play. ("Then we are shown the balcony, with the audience, including the girl, exhibiting by their faces and action their interest in the play.")

Let us return to the sequence in *The Birds*; it is probably Melanie's reaction that eventually clarifies the ambiguous status of the alternation between her and the birds at the monkey bars. After this alternation, in which Melanie has stared off frame with a neutral face, she changes her direction of glance; then we cut to a bird flying in the sky and then cut back to Melanie as she turns her head and (presumably) follows the bird's trajectory. We cut to the bird again as it sits down on the overfilled monkey bars, and the final part shows Melanie reacting with a horrified face and running into the schoolhouse. It is difficult to avoid the inference that Melanie is reacting to the sight of the massed birds. If this is true, however, why did she not react during the initial alternation between her and the monkey bars? The most likely strategy for a spectator would be to deny the POV status of the initial alternating shots of the scene. It is the *absence* of reaction in that part – as well as the *presence* of reaction in the latter part – that makes this clarification possible. This was indeed what Messaris found in his informal study:

> However, this uncertainty [from the first part of the scene] was only momentary, and in no case did it result in the wrong interpretation. The reason may be evident even to someone who hasn't seen this movie. Because the woman's facial expression in the shots intercut with the shots of the bird doesn't contain anything that can be construed as a reaction to them (she already knows that birds have been attacking people in this area), she obviously can't be looking at them. Rather, she must just be gazing abstractedly into the distance. This interpretation is reinforced by the fact that, when she finally does turn around, she is clearly horrified. (Messaris, 1994:75ff)

The coherence constructed on the basis of the gazer–object–reaction triad is indeed very strong and often involves some form of character psychology.[9] The spectator attributes emotions, intentions, and beliefs to the reaction (Carroll, 1993; Gunning, 1994:71ff; Plantinga, 1999:241; see also Chapter 4, the subsection on The Minds of Cinematic Characters). For instance, "Melanie is *horrified* because she knows that the birds constitute a potential danger to her and the children in the school, and she enters the schoolhouse with the *intention* to warn or save the children." The POV inference triggers not only inferences about the mental lives of characters, but these attributions also act as psychological motivations and causes for the ensuing scene, in which she organizes the escape of the children from the schoolhouse.

Of course, the reactions could involve any change in behavior (facial expression, body or motor behavior, verbal reactions), the meanings of which are determined only in relation to the object seen, the narrative context, and a host of other kinds of knowledge in the spectator (facial expressions, folk psychology). The point, however, is that the reaction substantiates POV inferences and makes them more certain. Even if the meaning of the reaction is not fully understood by the spectator or seems to be contradictory, I believe the presence of the reaction *in itself* adds to the probability of the POV inference. The reason for this may be sought in the structure of our everyday life experiences and ability for joint visual attention.

4. A POV inference should be more certain and less ambiguous if the gazer *avoids* looking into the camera. Deictic-gaze behavior in everyday life is triggered only when the angle of the gazer's direction is more than

zero degrees, that is to say, *not* mutual gaze. If someone is looking *at* you, you do not turn around and look for a target object (which, in fact, happens to be yourself). If this theory is correct, the POV inference should be harder to trigger and definitely less certain if the character gazed into the camera instead of looking off frame. We can probably make such a case.

Perhaps the most convincing evidence for this is that POV efforts with characters looking into the camera are indeed difficult to find in the history of cinema. Gunning (1994:167ff) and Burch (1990:218) discuss a scene from Griffith's *A Drunkard's Reformation* (1909), which alternates between a theater stage and the gazing and reactions of the audience (in particular the father and daughter in the front row; see the subsection titled Spatial Immersion Begins). The medium-long-shot format of the glance shot, however, makes it difficult to establish whether the characters really gaze into the camera. Another case would be *Il Buono, il brutto, il cattivo* (1966), which opens with a deserted landscape with a head coming from the side into extreme close-up, looking into the camera. We cut to a long shot of a town and, after an extended period of time, cut back to the gazer, establishing the POV connection between the two shots. Then we return to the shot of the town, showing two riders entering its outskirts. Note how the alternation between glance and object shots makes clear the gaze into the camera, and creates a more or less stable POV inference.

Because clear and unambiguous POV editing and glances into the camera are incompatible from a psychological point of view, and because ambiguity is avoided within *The Movies* (Carroll, 1996a), this practice has never established itself as a convention. Although this study is not the right forum, I believe that the same argument can be applied to cases in which the object is another gazer, as in SRS sequences. If a filmmaker wants to create the impression that two characters in separate shots are looking at each other, the spectator will be confused if they look into the camera; this look seems to imply that the characters stare out at the *spectator* and not at *each other* (triggering mutual gaze instead of deictic gaze).[10] A filmmaker who wants to maintain clear and unambiguous POV editing and still allow characters' glances into the camera would eventually run into problems of understandability; the structure of the spectator's basic deictic-gaze ability seems to contradict such a technique. Because POV editing is a powerful trope within a system that tries to tell stories – because it creates spatial links between different shots, as well as psychologizing the characters and easily conveying their emotions and intentions – I believe that gaze into the camera was eventually sacrificed. Of course, if the film medium had not been narrativized or if it had joined a tradition of storytelling in which ambiguities were allowed and encouraged, maybe POV editing with glances into the camera would have become the dominant convention. As it turned out, this did not happen.

Explaining the abandonment of camera glances in this way, as an incompatibility with other representational techniques on the basis of spectator psychology, is a different approach than the voyeuristic and illusionist theories that dominate contemporary cinema studies. Burch, for instance, asserts that "[t]he solitary and ubiquitous voyeurism of the Institution demanded as its indispensable complement the spectator's *invulnerability*: the actors spied on must never return the spectator's look, must never seem aware of the spectator's presence in this auditorium, their looks must never pin the spectator down to that particular seat" (Burch, 1990:216). Burch proceeds to cite Frank Woods from an article in *The New York Dramatic Mirror* of 1910, which discusses actors' turning their faces on the audience: "Immediately the sense of reality is destroyed and the hypnotic illusion that has taken possession over the spectator's mind, holding him by the power of visual suggestion, is gone." It is quite possible that glances into the camera have such effects of antirealism or breaking of illusion, and this was one of the reasons for that this acting style was discontinued. My theory makes no claims about this deep psychological level. Thus, to a certain extent, the theory stands in complement to the voyeuristic and illusionistic ones (see also my discussion on voyeuristic close-ups in Chapter 3, the section on Voyeurism).

5. A POV inference should be more certain and less ambiguous if there is continuity between the apparent environment of the glance shot and the apparent environment of the object shot. A joint visual attention situation in real life involves two people and an object within visual range. This implies in most cases that the gazer and the object of the gaze will be in the same kind of environment (e.g., in a kitchen, at a café, in a street). If we experience a similar environmental continuity between the two shots in POV editing, then this experience should support a POV inference.

Occasionally there will be a shift in environment, even in real-life deictic situations, for instance when the gazer is inside a house and the object of the gaze is outside in the street. Our knowledge of houses, windows, and streets, however, makes such a shift fully understandable. If it is true that shifts in apparent environment in everyday deictic-gaze situations are rare, this rarity should influence the way spectators appraise the probability of a POV inference. That is, if the spectator experiences a shift in environment from the glance shot to the object shot, the spectator would, following this line of argument, be less inclined to make a POV. If the spectator did, the inference would be less certain. Can we make such a case?

First, in many POVs, it is simply impossible for the spectator to recognize whether the environment of the object shot is compatible with the environment of the glance shot. In these cases, the principle does not apply. The object or the glance may be presented against neutral backgrounds, with no real clues as to where they might have been taken; the shots may be close-ups that lack informative deep focus, or they may be presented so quickly that there is no time to guess the environment. It is only when the shift is *apparent* to the spectator that it is used as a criterion for the probability of POV inferencing.

Imagine, though, a glance shot that the spectator understands as being situated in a living room and an object shot obviously taking place on a fishing boat in the middle of the Atlantic Ocean; or consider a glance shot set in a dark cave with almost no light and an exterior object shot in full sunlight; or imagine a gazer standing in front of Big Ben and the object sitting beside the Eiffel Tower. In all these cases, it is likely that the spectator will experience a form of environment shift, and that this shift will be an "impossible" one. Even if all the other parameters discussed in the preceding paragraphs may have been present, a POV inference would be problematic: The transition would be ambiguous and much less confident. In fact, the spectator must construct a rather implausible or imaginary situation if such inferences are to maintain coherence: "Is there perhaps a living room on the boat, overlooking the deck?" Alternatively, such impossible situations may be related to genre-specific conventions, for example, fantasy or science fiction.

If a shift in apparent environments tends to make spectators' POV inferences ambiguous, a filmmaker who still must effect such a transfer and wants to maintain a clear POV structure can use other POV cues. A POV editing in *Halloween* (1973), for example, when Laurie from her classroom (interior) sees Michael standing by his car (exterior), uses a clear change in gazing behavior, returns to the glance shot twice, has a reactive character, and has a clear sound overlap. Moreover, the shades of the window are visible in the frame of the object shot. In spite of the fact that there is a break in environment recognition, these cues make it highly unlikely that the spectator would infer relations between shots other than POV.

6. A POV inference should be more confident and less ambiguous if the POV editing is situated within a context that promotes a spatial reading strategy.

Establishing spatial relations between objects and between objects and ourselves is perhaps one of the most fundamental aspects of everyday life. We consciously use such spatial intelligence when we navigate in cities and buildings, when we identify landmarks, and when we estimate our present position and destination goal in relation to landmarks. Not so conscious perhaps, are those moment-to-moment distance estimates we make when walking, running, or handling things with our hands and bodies. Think, for instance, about all kinds of ball games. Estimating distances between objects seems to be a basic *attitude* or *stance* we take toward the environment. This stance includes, I believe, an assumption of space permanence, that is, that space continues outside our immediate field of vision. It also involves object permanence: We assume that objects in space have identity and duration through time. We presuppose, for instance, that things do not simply appear and cease to exist without warning. We also assume that the movement of objects through space takes some time.

All these processes seem to be at work when we establish deictic gaze in real life. When we follow another person's gaze to an object, we not only create a joint sphere of attention, but we also relate to gazer, target object, and ourselves in spatial terms. We can estimate the distance among the object, ourselves, and the gazer, thus creating a spatial configuration of the bodies and objects involved. Adults expect things to persist and exist outside our field of vision. Young children do not seem to have developed such an expectation, and that was why Butterworth's toddlers failed to search for object targets behind them, despite being sensitive to the mother's direction of gaze (see the subsection on development). Spatial inferences and assumptions are always part of the package when we establish deictic gaze.

If deictic gaze in real life is associated with spatiality, it is fair to assume that this association holds for POV inferencing in cinema. Indeed, POV inferences are not only abstract "gaze connections" between two shot spaces, but always involve spatial relations. A POV inference includes at least a crude estimation of the spatial relations between the gazer and the object – "within visual range" – but the angle of the camera, the spatial surroundings of the scene (interior or exterior), and sound usually make a POV inference more precise (e.g., "three meters," "across the table"). In cinema as well as in real life, it is difficult to differentiate between POV inference and spatial inferences.

Hence, if a film generally encourages the spectator to establish spatial relationships between elements in the fictive world, then POV inference would be much more probable and confident than in a film that does not. In mainstream cinema, such spatial relationships often take on great importance for a spectator's understanding of the narrative, as well as in promoting emotional responses. In *Rear Window* (1954), for instance, it is important to establish relationships among the yard, the different apartments, and Jeff's and Lisa's positions. In addition, one aspect of the emotional excitement of the climax scene involves understanding the close distance between Jeff and the approaching Thorwald. Space and spatial relations here are of crucial importance; the spectator's efforts to create such spatial relations between shot segments are often "rewarded" by the film in the form of suspense and other emotional bonuses.

Other types of film seem less interested in the geography of the fictive world, but emphasize more abstract inferences. In *The Man With a Movie Camera* (1929), spatial relationships between shot segments are not the film's primary purpose. It does not matter where the tramway ride takes place in relation to the sport events, nor the spatial relations between the various sport events. Rather, the film seems to encourage associative, rhythmic, and conceptual connections between different shots, foremost within the frame. Space is not concrete, but rather is abstract and formal. Also, the frequent intellectual montage of the 1920s and 1930s – for instance, the juxtaposition of strikers being shot at and the bull being slaughtered in Eisenstein's *Strike* – encourages the spectator to establish metaphorical or propositional connections, rather than spatial ones, between shots. Today, the genre of visual commercials has taken over and developed this type of "conceptual" montage.

If spatial reading strategy goes hand in hand with POV inferencing, we should expect spectators to be more open for POV inferences in *Rear Window* than in *The Man With a Movie Camera*. Because the former encourages the spectator to construct relationships between objects onscreen and offscreen, POV inferences should be more probable and with a higher degree of confidence. As *The Man With a Movie Camera* is primarily concerned with other types of coherence, POV inferences may not be so important. This, of course, does not imply that POV is impossible in more abstract films, only that, *all other things being equal*, the POV inference will be more likely and confident in a spatial context than in a nonspatial one. Moreover, this is so because of the connection between spatiality and deictic gaze in real life.

Of course, the spectator might adopt a spatial reading strategy for *The Man With a Movie Camera*, but there would be few rewards as in *Rear Window*; this situation would make a spatial reading strategy less common. Alternatively, the spectator could adopt an abstract and conceptual reading strategy for *Rear Window*, but then that spectator would probably miss key narrative relationships as well as emotional payoffs. Had the same POV editing sequence appeared in both of these films, the POV inference in *Rear Window* would have been more common among spectators, more confident, and less ambiguous. So at least I claim.[11]

7. A POV inference should be more confident and less ambiguous if there is an overlap of assumed diegetic sound between the glance shot and the object shot. Even though many sounds in everyday life are ambient and appreciated below the threshold of consciousness, sounds are still present, supporting our sense of spatial permanence. This is true in all kinds of situations, including joint visual attention; turning from a person to the object of that person's gaze generally does not alter the sonic environment.

If the spectator uses the deictic-gaze experience as a guide in understanding POV in cinema, then we should expect that spectator to produce more – and more confident – POV inferences if sound overlaps between the glance and object shot. If there is no sound at all, if the sound is nondiegetic, or if there is a break in the diegetic sound over the cut, we can assume that the POV inference would not be as confident. Is this assumption valid?

Diegetic sounds are significant in promoting a spatial reading strategy and encouraging the spectator to build a continuous space. Consider the POV structure from *Rear Window* that we discussed earlier (Figure 14). In this sequence, shots of Jeff are intercut with shots of his neighbors while he is talking to his boss on the phone. The voice provides powerful reason to think of the relation between shots as a POV connection. It would be hard to reconcile this editing and sound with a temporal ellipsis or a spatial cutaway. If the voice had stopped and changed to piano playing or some other sound exactly at the cut, the POV inference would lose credence, and the spectator would perhaps start looking for other relationships between shots.

It seems as though nondiegetic sounds have a minor – if any – effect on POV inferencing, as the POV relation is diegetic. In early cinema, in which sound was mostly nondiegetic, POV inference was perhaps more problematic for the spectator. Of course, the musical accompaniment often emphasized scene changes and thus guided the spectator's appraisal of shot relations. Because POV inferences often take place within scenes, however, it is difficult to see how music could have provided any support for such inferences.

Of course, sounds are not diegetic in themselves, but their status is always a matter of judgment of and interpretation by the spectator. As the preceding formulation emphasizes, however, it is the *assumed* diegetic sound that creates the effect, not the sound itself.

8. The last point to focus on is perhaps the most complex and, for my theory, the most problematic: the apparent position of the camera. Let us start with a couple of clarifications.

First, I am still discussing only object shots that exclude body parts in the frame. As I have said, body parts – as in over-the-shoulder shots – are powerful cues to trigger POV inferences. I think that they override any camera position cue, or any other cue for that matter. Such images, however, are not my concern here.

I am discussing how spectators evaluate position and angle of the object-shot camera. The differences in location of the object-shot camera have been acknowledged, as mentioned, by cinema scholars insofar as they make distinctions between true POV and sight link or eyeline match. The latter terms designate a structure that triggers POV inferences, although the object-shot camera does not assume "the exact position of the character, or the shot being understood as the character's literal point of view" (Gunning, 1994:169). The sequence from *The Musketeers of Pig Alley* already discussed contains an instructive sight-link example (Figure 8).

For the purpose of my argument, however, it is important to make a further distinction *within* the sight-link category. Because I focus on deictic gaze, there may be a difference between sight links that are being shot from the position of the glance-shot camera (let us call this place *the monitor's*, as it is from this position that we monitor the gazer's glance behavior), and other camera positions. Let us call the first type of editing a *monitor sight link*, and the latter a *nonmonitor sight link*. The sight link from *The Musketeers of Pig Alley* is thus a nonmonitor sight link, because the camera of the object shot [Figure 8(d)] is placed neither at Snapper's location at the doorway nor at the glance-shot camera's position in the ballroom [Figure 8(c)]. The camera has clearly moved, but not to a true POV.

Moreover, by camera position, I do not mean the *actual* one, but the *apparent* one. It is the spectator's impression or judgment of camera position that we discuss here, not the physical or profilmic one. The apparent camera position can be shaped by many (actual) cinematic means, such as lens length, angle, or actual distance to the objects. These parameters, however, are not of interest here. Apparent camera position is thus a psychological construct in the mind of the spectator. Now, many types of framing and lens are spatially vague and admit a wide range of understanding by the spectator as to where the camera is placed. Long lenses are one example. This implies that the differences among true POV, monitor sight link, and nonmonitor sight link are rarely clear-cut, but drift and are subjectively judged by spectators. In many cases, the object shot contains little or no information about the angle from which it was taken and how this angle relates to the position of gazer. In the preceding *Rear Window* example (Figure 14), it is clear from the mise-en-scène and the actual camera position that the object shots of the woman in the yard and the composer in the neighboring apartment are shot from Jeff's apartment and not from down in the yard or up on the roof. It is impossible, though, to judge whether they are shot from Jeff's exact position or from the monitor's position. The distance between Jeff and the monitor is simply too small in the glance shot (medium shot) and the distances between the object-shot camera and the neighbors are simply too large (extreme long shot) to allow for distinction between Jeff's and the monitor's position.

In *The Lady and the Mouse* (1913), however, the glance shot and the object shot are clearly from the same position [Figures 15(b) and 15(c)]. The stationary camera of the glance shot [Figure 15(c)] just shifts attention from the gazer to the object [Figure 15(b)], thus creating a monitor sight link. The camera has not moved; it has merely shifted angle.

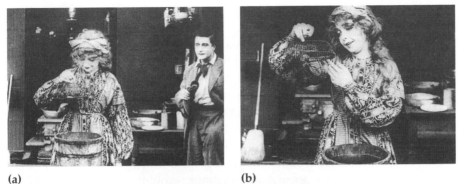

(a)   (b)

(c)

FIGURE 15. *The Lady and the Mouse* (Biograph, 1913), with Lillian Gish and Harry Hyde. From (a) Griffith cuts into (b) and then into (c), and then alternates between the last two shots in order to establish a sight link. (Stills are from Gunning [1994:266ff], who obtained them from the Museum of Modern Art.)

How then does camera position influence POV inference? Let us first recall what was previously said about angles and joint visual attention. In real-life deictic situations, we never share the exact angle or sensory input of the gazer: What we share is a perceptual–semantic space, which contains objects and events of different sorts. This space exists on a level of abstraction that is more or less independent of, for instance, differences in angles and light conditions between the positions of gazer and monitor.

Still, as monitors, we construct this semantic space from a specific position, which may vary from situation to situation. This position may have any relationship to the gazer's optical perspective, but it is always the same position from which we looked at the gazer. That is, because the monitor seldom moves between the time he or she sees the gazer and the time he or she sees the target object, those two entities are more or less always seen from the same position in space. Thus if POV inferences were based on and appraised by deictic-gaze experience, monitor sight links such as the one in *The Lady and the Mouse* would generate more and more confident POV inferences than would true POVs (as well as all other camera positions). According to this argument, monitor sight links would be more easily understood as POVs than would true POVs. Is this true?

One piece of evidence might be that monitor sight links were introduced before true POVs in the narrativization process of early cinema. Put aside for the moment those instances in which binoculars and magnifying glasses were represented in the object shot as irises – which are true POV on the basis of other visual techniques, and not primarily on camera position. Then it is fair to say that the classical scene breakdown, in which the camera became free to move around and take positions and angles within the scene space, was preceded by a more frontal and rigid camera style. Sideways camera movement was conventionalized earlier than drastic changes of angle contained within conventions like the SRS structure (see the subsection on Gazing). Both sequences from *The Lady and the Mouse* and *The Musketeers of Pig Alley*, for instance, use a space-beside style and typically refuse to show the object shot from the position of the gazer within the scene. The shot of Gish in Figure 15(b) is not shot from Hyde's position inside the scene, but at the position from where the scene as a whole is witnessed ("the theater seat"). As discussed, this frontal style was probably due to close affinities with the theater and vaudeville context, but this style also seems intuitive from a deictic-gaze perspective. The sensory input is similar to that of a real-world deictic situation – the position of the monitor has not moved across the cut.

Unfortunately for my theory, monitor sight links do not seem to trigger more and more confident POV inferences than do true POVs. Imagine the sequence from *The Lady and the Mouse* as a true POV, with Gish shot in the same shot scale as in the film but from the side and behind, from a position near the door (with kitchen utensils in the background). Although not certain, I think that spectators would consider this to be a more sure POV structure than the frontal editing now in the film. I must be specific about the claims being made here. When discussing POV inference, I mean something along the lines of "This is what Hyde sees." Let us call this a basic POV inference. Of course, true POV may give rise to more *specific* conclusions such as "In the very eyes of Hyde" or "We are literally inside Hyde's head." Such inferences may be connected to stronger experiences of subjectivity and possibly identification (Mulvey, 1975). The subjective character of the true POV shot may also be emphasized through other visual means, such as irises symbolizing binoculars or magnifying glasses or out-of-focus filming representing a drunk or poor-sighted person. These effects are, however, lying on top of basic POV inference, which is the focus here.

Nevertheless, I am afraid that basic POV inferences seem more confident and probable with true POV editing in comparison with monitor sight-link editing. Of course, as with all of the preceding features, such an assumption must be verified through research. Intuitively, however, I think this is the case. If true POVs generate more confident POV inferences than do monitor sight links, this cannot be accounted for by my theory of deictic gaze.

What the theory can explain, though, is the difference between monitor sight links and nonmonitor sight links. Consider a sequence from the first part of *Napoléon* (1927). In the snowball fight scene, one of the kitchen staff is standing by the wall of a building, obviously watching a game in the field in front of him (medium long shot). When he looks off frame left, there is a cut to an extreme close-up of someone putting rocks in snowballs (only the hands are visible). Cut back to the man at the wall, who turns his gaze off frame right and shouts warnings to Napoleon that his enemy is preparing to cheat. Of course, the context makes it certain that the close-up is a POV (i.e., change of gaze, return to the gazer, reaction of the gazer). However, spectators would consider the extreme close-up shot to be momentarily ambiguous, as it is *clearly* not shot from the perspective of the man at the wall, nor is it a monitor sight link. Here it is perhaps less the angle of the shot than the framing and distance vis-à-vis the object that marks displacement from the position of the gazer or monitor.

Pickpocket provides a similar example. At one point in the film, Michel manages to steal a watch from a man by bumping into him at a pedestrian crosswalk. In the beginning of the sequence – in a close-up glance shot – Michel makes a change in gaze direction to offscreen right; then we cut to a long shot of a man tying his shoelaces. The man gets up and *walks past the camera*. Then we cut back to Michel still looking in the same direction. From the subsequent shots, it is evident that Michel is still looking at the man offscreen right, although the man *passed* the camera of the object shot. Obviously the object shot was not taken near Michael's position, nor at the monitor's position, but on the *other* side of the crosswalk.

The ambiguous effects generated by these two sequences, I would argue, arise because they use the usual prototypic set of POV cues (it is more or less impossible to interpret these as other than POVs) and then radically displace the camera relative to the gazer and the monitor. I would argue that nonmonitor sight links of this sort generate less probable and confident POV inferences than do monitor sight links of the sort discussed for *The Lady and the Mouse*. *This* difference can be accounted for by my theory of deictic gaze. The monitor sight link is much closer to the everyday joint visual attention situation than is the nonmonitor sight link. As a monitor, one does not jump from one place to another when turning from gazer to target object.

In summary then, a theory of deictic-gaze ability may explain why clear monitor sight links generate more and less ambiguous POV inferences than do clear nonmonitor sight links. The theory fails, however, to account for the fact that clear true POVs seem to be more efficient than are clear monitor sight links. In the latter case, I suggest we seek explanation elsewhere.

Conclusions

POV inferences are always a matter of judgment, understanding, and probability. I have presented a set of cues to which spectators may be sensitive when determining whether two shots belong together under the scheme of POV. These cues are neither random nor primarily historical or arbitrary. They are chosen on the basis of the psychological and behavioral structure of deictic gazing. If the intuition about the connection between deictic gaze and POV inferencing is correct, these parameters should apply when real spectators make judgments about POV relations between shots. Together, these cues constitute a "prototypical" or "ideal" POV structure, which contains all the essential elements for provoking the most confident and unambiguous POV inference. Few actual POV structures contain all of these cues.

Thus, in making POV inferences, the spectator detects, appraises, and evaluates cues in a film. If enough cues are present, the POV inference is triggered. If the POV editing lacks a few cues or if there are inconsistencies between different cues, the POV inference may take place, but it will be less confident than in the prototypical case (e.g., *Napolèon*). If the POV editing lacks too many important features, it may be difficult to establish a POV at all, and spectators will disagree on interpretations (e.g., the hovering eyes of *The Man With a Movie Camera*, Figure 16). When cues are lacking or ambiguous, the spectator starts looking for other alternative relationships between shots. Perhaps the second shot is a new scene, at another place or time, or both. Maybe the second image is a character's dream rather than visual field. Perhaps the relationship between shots is conceptual or metaphorical instead of spatiotemporal. In these situations, the spectator must evaluate the importance of different cues and the way in which they are presented in a given sequence.

I do not claim that these are the only processes involved in experiencing POV editing. There may be other POV effects of subjectivity and deep psychology. Perhaps the basic POV inference has consequences for the ways in which the spectator morally allies with a given character.[12]

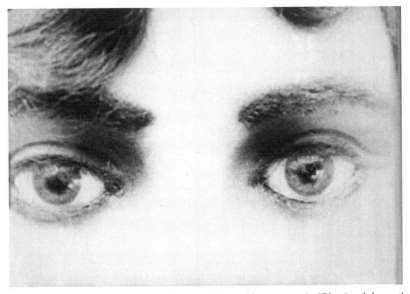

FIGURE 16. *The Man With a Movie Camera* (Dziga Vertov, 1929). (Obtained from the Wisconsin Center for Film and Theater Research.)

I have discussed only the general POV connection between shot spaces ("C looks at O"). The glance shot may contain many objects and events; how that object is chosen and recognized by the spectator depends on the composition of the shot, perceptual processes, and the context of the POV. In the opening scene from *The Birds*, for instance, Melanie is just about to enter the bird shop, when she turns around and glances offscreen. The glance shot contains a bustling street scene with a large monument in the center. What Melanie specifically looks at, however, is clarified by the soundtrack, which attracts the viewer's attention to the birds hovering in the sky. These processes of recognizing and selecting the "right" objects from among many in the glance shot are crucial to understanding POV, but have not been my concern here.

Furthermore, I do not claim that the cues presented here are the only ones used by spectators to infer POV relationships between shots. Although they are central, their placement in the narrative, genre, and historical context must be taken into consideration. For instance, the strategies of encouraging or discouraging general spatial inferences constitute such a context. In addition, the narrative may have established that two locations are diegetically distant and thus that a POV inference is impossible, although many essential POV cues are present. Historical conventions and modes of reception may also affect POV inferences and temporarily override them. Take, for instance the convention of "switchback," which appears to have been in effect in early cinema, here described by Griffith:

"The switch-back" is the only way of giving the action in two contemporaneous trains of events. Its psychological value is even greater. By the "switch-back" you show what a man is thinking of or what he is talking about. For instance, you see a scene shot showing a man musing. Then the picture "switches back" to his sweetheart and then back to the man again. Thus you know what the man was thinking of. ("Weak Spots in a Strong Business – XIV," *Motion Picture News*, Vol. 11, No. 18, May 8, 1915, p. 39; cited in Bordwell, 1981:129)

As Bordwell (1981:129) has already pointed out, Griffith here recognizes the fact that the switchback contained both a subjective element ("what the man is thinking of"), but also the objective diegetic occurrence of the event ("giving the action in two contemporaneous trains of events"). These cutaways, Gunning writes,

do not function simply as subjective images, but serve as omniscient revelations of actual events occurring simultaneously. The narrator never completely abdicates the authority of these images to the characters. They are not unequivocally marked as mental images. (Gunning, 1994:118)

Gunning provides a number of examples from Griffith's productions (e.g., Gunning, 1990b:344, 1994:113 & 294). *The Salvation Army Lass* (1908) is a story about Mary Wilson, a woman who becomes a member of the Salvation Army and tries to convert her gangster boyfriend Bob Walton. Mary physically tries to stop Bob from committing burglary with his gang, but is brutally knocked down. In the scene with the crime, Bob is handed a gun by his buddies but stops and looks offscreen [Figure 17(a)]. There is a cut to Mary still lying on the ground [Figure 17(b)]. When we return to Bob, he is standing in the same position as before [Figure 17(c)]. He turns to the gangsters, hands over the gun, and leaves (Gunning, 1994:121). This switchback contains both an objective element ("It is a cutaway to Mary still lying on the ground") and a subjective element ("Bob thinks about Mary lying on the ground, which makes him regretful and changes his mind about the burglary").

   In addition to the psychologizing function of this sequence with respect to the Walton character, it is interesting to note that the sequence contains many prototypical elements of POV editing that the location of the burglary and the place where Mary was knocked down. Because I have not seen the film, I do not know whether the narration establishes the distance between these locations at other points in the film, but Gunning (1994:121) suggests that the shot of Mary also can be read as "something Walton actually sees in his glance off-screen." To a modern spectator, the POV inference makes sense, as it accounts for Bob's gaze offscreen, his

(a)

(b)

(c)

FIGURE 17. *The Salvation Army Lass* (D.W. Griffith, 1908). (Reproduced from Gunning [1994:121ff], who obtained them from the Paper Print Collection, Library of Congress, Washington, D.C.)

reaction afterward, his emotions ("At the sight of Mary, he regretted what he had done") and his intentions ("At the sight of Mary, he decided to not go through with the burglary"). To an early viewer who was familiar with the switchback convention, such a POV connection would probably be weaker and less probable. Here the switchback interpretation, with its duality as both mental image and objective cutaway to another (distant) place in the diegesis, would suffice, without resorting to a glance–target relationship between shots. In a switchback interpretation, historical context and the spectator's awareness of certain discursive practices could interfere or even override the POV inference in favor of other understandings.

I have made a case for a prototypical or "ideal" POV structure. To avoid misunderstanding, I must point out that this case does not entail aesthetic commitments. I do not assert that prototypic POV editing is ideal in the sense of its being aesthetically better or more "filmic" than POV editing

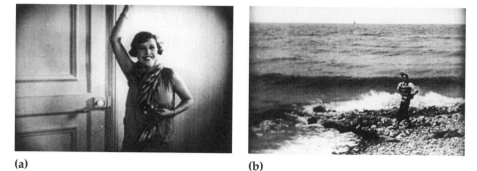

(a)   (b)

FIGURE 18. Surreal POV in *Un chien Andalou* (Luis Buñuel, 1929). (Obtained from the Wisconsin Center for Film and Theater Research.)

with fewer cues or than other forms of practices (in contrast to Carroll, 1980:71). A given representational technique is not good or bad in itself. Only in relation to the aesthetic, ideological, or other purpose, can we judge its value and strength. I *do* maintain that the prototypical POV is better than other alternatives if the purpose is to evoke clear, certain and unambiguous POV inferences in the spectator. It is better because of the specific structure of the spectator's deictic-gaze ability. However, not all films seem to have this ambition, and it remains an aesthetic choice on the part of the filmmakers. For instance, in the final scene of *Un chien Andalou* (1929), the open, inexplicable, and indeed surreal characteristic of the POV editing seems to be the very objective of the sequence (a woman exits a city apartment, turns around, and spots a friend on a beach; Figure 18). Here the atypical and conflicting features of the POV fulfill its purpose better than would a prototypic POV (although both instances draw on and base their effects on the spectator's deictic-gaze ability).

POV inferences seldom rise above the level of consciousness. When we are looking at a film or taking part in an intense café discussion, there is much going on, and we have no reason to believe that people will consciously think about the fact that they use deictic-gaze abilities to make sense of a situation. In explaining this *non*conscious dimension of POV inference, there is, however, no need to resort to Freudian or ideological concepts of the *un*conscious (see Chapter 1, the subsection on the Parameters of Dispositions). In POV inferences deictic-gaze behaviors are situated in the cognitive unconscious because they are so automated and habituated that adults no longer think about them:

Automatization provides a better explanation of what most theorists are driving at when they talk about ideology as 'unconscious'. Automated practices and beliefs are indeed 'beneath consciousness', but they are not repressed. (Smith, 1995:50)

The fact that an operation is automated does not mean that spectators are unable to make the process conscious if desired or requested, but only that in most cases spectators do not. POV inferences are good examples of this.

It is important to emphasize that deictic-gaze ability not only constrains POV inferences (evaluating the importance of different cues), but that it in fact *enables* the viewer to understand all forms of gazing behavior in cinematic discourse, including POV editing. If we imagine a creature with eyes and an object recognition system but *without* deictic-gaze ability (this is difficult, I know), I doubt it would be able to draw any form of POV inference. Even if gazer and object were placed in the same shot, such relations would be unnoticed by such a creature. It is in the collision between cinematic textual cues and abilities and dispositions of the spectator that understanding, meaning, and POV inference emerge. Without this psychological baggage, gaze in film would be meaningless. The point is that no processes in cinematic discourse take place in the text per se, but only in relation to the *Horizont* of biological, psychological, and cultural dispositions brought to the film by the spectator. Of course, because the ability that supports such inferences is basic and universal, many of these inferences are so clear and certain that they *appear* to be independent of spectator presence. That is indeed how we talk about these things: "It's there! She's looking at the door!." Such impressions, however, do not emerge because they are objectively in the text, but because all or most humans share a type of disposition.

Explaining the Presence of the Point-of-View Convention in Mainstream Cinema

The preceding investigation owes much to Carroll's (1993) basic idea of POV editing and deictic gaze. Whereas Carroll's proposition is fruitful and has opened up a field of inquiry, his claims, however, tend to be general and philosophically slanted. By studying the particular details of the structure of POV and deictic gaze and by focusing on the psychological and mental reception of POV editing, I may have produced an improved and more nuanced theory. In contrast to Carroll, I believe that a psychological investigation has a greater explanation value than a purely philosophical or theoretical one. If we focus on the processes of understanding involved in POV, then we may also be in a better position to explain stylistic features of POV editing and their transformations over time.

One reason why Carroll hesitates to delve into the psychological details of his theory may be because he has a specific objective, which points beyond the mere connection between POV editing and deictic gaze: He wants to explain the popularity of the POV convention in mainstream cinema. Carroll's argument goes something like this: The POV convention has proved to be a remarkable success in filmmaking. It has remained stylistically intact for over eighty years, in a wide range of genres, in a wide set of national cinemas. Why is this so? If we assume that *The Movies* is a mode of production that strives for a good return on invested money, this mode seeks a mass audience for its products. To obtain a mass audience, the representational system used must be clear and understandable, but also easy to learn. Because the understanding of POV editing exploits a psychological ability that is basic and probably universal, POV requires no extensive learning and generates a clear and coherent interpretation for large segments of the audience. This is why filmmakers and production modes have continued using the conventions for so long:

> Since movies are, by definition, aimed at mass markets, movie makers are apt to favor design elements that will render their narratives accessible to large audiences. That is, ideally, movies will exploit structures that make them susceptible to fast pick-ups by untutored audiences. (Carroll, 1996a:133)

In contrast to natural languages, POV editing requires no extensive cinema-specific knowledge, but can be picked up by force of a simple, everyday psychological disposition.

I am quite sympathetic toward this mode of reasoning, and I believe it has a strong bearing on the present discussion. To achieve a more complete explanation, however, Carroll's argument must be complemented with other levels of description. Although POV editing fulfills important functions in the dissemination and understanding of mass-produced movies, it also performs important functions within the narrative system. As was pointed out, in a representational system that tells stories, POV editing is a powerful device. Not only does POV inference relate different shot spaces in a clear and straightforward manner, it also psychologizes the characters involved (intentions, beliefs, and emotions toward the object). In a narrative system such as mainstream cinema, this psychologization is crucial. Perhaps the POV convention would not have achieved its popularity if early cinema had taken a route other than the narrative one (e.g., information, persuasion or nonfigurative art).

Yet another explanation for the popularity of POV editing might be sought in the concrete production circumstances, as POV editing often has a concrete production value and may in fact save money. POV editing enables the filmmaker to shoot the glance shot and the object shot at different places and times. In a mode of production in which the stars are paid by the hour, such a feature could help to reduce a budget. In addition, both the glance and the object can be shot in close-up, which demands less elaborate mise-en-scène (e.g., props and lighting), which in turn saves the filmmakers much time and money. Such economical advantages must surely contribute to mainstream cinema's continued use of the convention.[13]

All in all, the reasons why the POV editing convention is popular in mainstream cinema must be sought on economical, psychological, and narrative levels, as well as in concrete production circumstances. In all of these systems, the POV convention performs important functions that the system as a whole has difficulties doing without.

Such a multifaceted framework is equally important in trying to account for stylistic changes in film. Of course, studies of production modes and historical context of reception provide useful tools for investigating these matters. However, certain stable and semiuniversal processes and mental structures make some stylistic changes more plausible or even mutually exclusive. Because of the psychological dispositions of the spectator, some representational techniques and devices may simply not be compatible if understandability, clarity, and coherence are to be maintained. (These are important features for many modes of production.) For instance, as claimed, long shots and POV editing may not work well together, as the character's change of gaze is important to POV inference. POV editing and gaze in the camera may not be successful, as these will be associated with mutual gaze – not joint visual attention. These oppositions are directly related to the spectator's everyday deictic-gaze ability. In this way, I think the psychological perspective may provide a complement to historical frameworks for explaining stylistic features and transformations.

By now it should be clear that I do not take POV editing to be an *arbitrary* convention. It is not arbitrary in the sense that there are no external reasons for it to exist. It performs *functions*, and, as such, its presence within a given context can be explained and motivated by psychological, narrative, and economical frameworks. In the same way, the function of dissolves as markers for scene shifts is not arbitrary, because they perform a pivotal function within the narrative system.

Neither is POV editing arbitrary in the sense that its signifier is arbitrary and could have had another structure or feature. I have devoted much energy in this chapter to showing that the design of the POV editing convention is motivated by the fact that its parameters match the ability of deictic gaze. The convention triggers the same or similar processes or experience as would a real deictic-gaze situation. The surface of POV editing is not a matter of arbitrary choice, but is adapted to exploit, trigger, or "tap into" the structure of joint visual attention. Thus the dissolve differs from the POV in the sense that the dissolve can be replaced by a wipe or a fade-out/fade-in, and still perform the same function. Its signifier has no relation to a disposition structure in the spectator and is indeed subject to an arbitrary agreement in a given historical audience–production context. The POV editing convention is not arbitrary in this sense, as some of its features (the change of gaze, the returning glance shot, overlapping sound, and reaction of the gazer) overlap with those of real deictic-gaze stimuli. Thus we might say that the features of the prototypical POV are just as arbitrary as deictic-gaze ability. If everyday gaze ability were different, I suppose that the prototypical POV would be too.

CHAPTER THREE

Variable Framing and Personal Space

Intimate space . . . is the distance of both lovemaking *and* murder!
(Meyrowitz, 1986:261)

[W]e should be aware that, just like the language of poetry is dependent on natural language, so must cinema be related to in-set visual and kinesthetic patterns of cultural behaviour. (Tsivian, 1994:197)

Variable framing seems to be one of the crucial formal and discursive aspects of moving images in general and narrative cinema in particular. Changing the framing of the profilmic space is a powerful device for narration to create hierarchies within the image, direct the spectator's attention to important details, give spatial overviews of scenes, and affect the spectator emotionally. As we shall see, cut-ins, close-ups, and camera or character movement have had different functions within the history of film. I will argue that some of those functions work in relation to, and can be accounted for by, a theory of *personal space*. At the core of this argument lies the assumption that the spectator brings to the theater spatial and bodily "expectations" or "dispositions" with which the cinematic discourse interacts and thereby produces certain meanings and effects.

The idea is not new. The link between personal space and variable framing has been given some attention over the past fifteen years in media psychology (Messaris, 1994:89ff; Meyrowitz, 1986; Reeves, Lombard & Melwani, 1992) and in historical reception studies (Tsivian, 1994:196). Some of these may have appeared independent of each other, which suggests the feasibility of the connection. None of these accounts, however, has systematically tried to couple spatial behavior and film reception. Through a careful examination of personal-space behavior and its mechanisms, in this chapter we will try to gain insight into how close-ups and cut-ins function, both narratively and emotionally. Of course, such an investigation must be accompanied by historical awareness of the particular system within which the device works. Tsivian (1994:197) warns "against applying proxemic categories too simplistically to the history of film reception." Thus in the first section of the chapter I survey what sociologists, psychologists, and anthropologists know about personal-space behavior. I then discuss different historical functions of variable framing and try to explain their effects, reception, and "meaning" through a theory of personal space. I argue that the textual structure of many variable framing conventions – as well as spectators' reactions to them – makes sense if we assume that film interacts with specific sociopsychological dispositions in the spectator.

Personal Space

Space is a fundamental aspect of animals and humans. From an individual point of view, organisms are free to roam in space however they like. However, as members of a species, culture, or society, animals and humans have strictly regulated territorial behaviors. The ways in which species place such constraints on space are, of course, not arbitrary, but fulfill important biological, social, and communicative functions. Spatial behavior can in this respect be seen as an important bridge between the biological and the social.

All animals, from fishes to primates, display intraspecies territorial behavior of some sort (Watson, 1970). This behavior ensures, among other things, that individual members are spread evenly over a given biotope, thus not only securing food supplies, but also making it more difficult for diseases to spread. Individuals who lose or fail to establish territory are more likely to be vulnerable to predators. Territorial behavior is also closely linked with sexuality and reproduction. In general, territorial behavior (e.g., defending offspring) becomes more prominent during the breeding season; it has been shown that birds that do not establish territory do not reproduce (Watson, 1970:22). Animals expend much energy making clear or communicating such boundaries to other species members through olfactory, visual, or sonic means. The basic mechanisms holding the system in place are stress and aggression, which are triggered by invasions of territory. For many animals, continuous transgressions of territory boundaries, for example, through overcrowding, generate high levels of stress that may be lethal. Thus territoriality offers a dynamic stability and self-regulation that is favorable for a species' social welfare and survival.

The term proxemics has been coined for the general study of space structuring in humans; it covers a range of levels (Hall, 1966). Nations, cities, or tribes often define their identities in the form of spatial boundaries; so do ethnic minorities and "gangs" within those formations. The conception of "private property" often denotes a spatial limit beyond which only a few people have access. Through architecture and urban planning, we set up boundaries to ensure privacy and peace in crowded situations (e.g., churches, apartments, houses). Even within those territories (and similar to animals), we designate certain areas for specific activities (living room, dining room, bedroom, kitchen, and toilet). Such constraints are important means for the individual, family, or group to distribute the social and the private aspects of life. These means may also provide dominant groups in society the possibility of regulating or even excluding other groups from certain spaces. Spatial boundaries can be created to preventing "uncomfortable" interactions between social groups.

The term personal space, which is the focus of this chapter, refers to one specific level of proxemics, that is, the space surrounding every individual and following that person as he or she moves around the environment. This phenomenon is often described as a kind of boundary, "sphere," or "bubble," regulating distances in interpersonal interactions. It is a *personal* territory, somewhat different from the territories described in the preceding paragraph. Personal space is dynamic in character; its size changes across cultures, individuals, ages, gender, and, most important, situations. Failing to comply with codes of personal-space behavior generally leads to misunderstandings, unpleasantness, discomfort, or stress. Many of us have probably experienced such problems in contact with other cultures. The distance codes and frequency of touching in personal interactions in Mediterranean Europe and in Arab cultures may be considered offensive by Scandinavians or North Americans. Conversely, the lack of closeness in Northern Europe may be conceived of as cold and impersonal by Arabs, whose culture, for instance, prescribes that close male friends hold hands or arms in public. Likewise, many Caucasian Americans "are struck by the apparent shyness of the Navajo Indians, who speak in a voice so quiet to be barely audible and avoid direct eye contact" (Watson, 1970:15).

Personal space has attracted attention within psychology and cultural psychology; up until 1987, approximately 700 studies were conducted on the subject, mostly in the 1970s and 1980s (Aiello, 1987:389); I have found at least 200 more. Aiello (1987) offers the most comprehensive overview, and in this chapter I rely on his work for the most part.

One of the primary functions of interpersonal spatial behavior is to establish an "appropriate distance" vis-à-vis other people in conversations and other situations. The ability to estimate and behave according to those tacit "rules of appropriateness" constitutes a spatial ability that all people acquire during upbringing. What parameters influence our estimation of appropriate distance?

The perceived relationship with a conversation partner is one factor. Friends, lovers, business colleagues, and strangers will use different distances with each other. The anthropologist Edward Hall (1966) was the first to postulate different distance zones according to the relationship between interlocutors. Hall elaborated on the visual, olfactory, tactile, and auditory cues associated with each of these zones:

- *Intimate distance*, according to Hall, ranges from zero to eighteen inches and is characterized by strong sensory input. Sight is a bit distorted; heat and smell from the other person are inescapable; the voice is held at a low level or even a whisper. There is potential for tactile and physical involvement. This distance is generally reserved for intrafamiliar interactions (lovemaking, wrestling, playing).
- *Personal distance*, ranging from one-and-one-half to four feet, is within "arm's length." The voice level is moderate, vision is no longer distorted, and body heat and olfaction are only minimally perceptible. This distance is most likely used by friends and acquaintances.
- *Social distance* extends from four to twelve feet and is used in business transactions and in formal settings. No person touches or is expected to touch another person. Voice level is louder, and transactions are more formal.
- *Public distance* extends beyond twelve feet and is generally used to address an informal group or larger gatherings. This distance may also be used between the public and high-status officials. Voice and gestures must be exaggerated or amplified.

Although the measured distances are not to be taken in a rigid fashion, Hall's observation about the connection between relationship and distance seems to be relevant. The estimation of appropriate distance is thus a function of evaluating the relationship to the person with whom one interacts. If the other person perceives the status of the relationship differently than one does, this may lead to conflicts and spatial misunderstandings. In addition, if one dislikes, negatively values, or is unable to evaluate the other person, then the appropriate distance will be larger than if one assesses the person as likable, handsome, or attractive. Studies have shown that greater distance is maintained with individuals who are hostile, threatening, physically impaired, or smoking (Aiello, 1987:459). In evaluating personality types and appropriate distance vis-à-vis strangers, stereotypes, prejudices, and social bias are often invoked, as in all social cognition and behavior.

Often the relation to the conversation partner is not reducible to one type, but one may take different roles during the course of a conversation. The appropriate distance may thus vary according to the topic of conversation (Meyrowitz, 1986:255). Progressing from business matters to intimacy may stimulate people to move closer together (if the spatial infrastructure allows it). Speaking with someone about theoretical or business matters nose-to-nose may feel uncomfortable, even if speakers are close friends.

Appropriate distance is also affected by the perceived age of the other person. In general, adults allow themselves to touch and stay closer to children than to other adults. The conventions of distance behavior between adults do not seem to apply to children, who do not have a full-fledged spatial behavior until the age of twelve years. The transfer from child to adult is often acknowledged by adults, who clearly treat five year-old children spatially different than they treat ten-year-old children. In one study (Fry & Willis, 1971), adults waiting in line for a movie were approached as closely as possible (without touching) by five-, eight-, and ten-year-old children. Whereas the five-year-old children elicited positive reactions from the adults (e.g., smiles, pats on the head), eight-year-old children were ignored, and ten-year-old children received negative responses. Clearly children are expected to have learned proper spatial norms by the age of ten years, but are still considered "cute" when they have not learned these norms by the age of five years.

So far, we have talked about only how one's *assessment* of the other person influences spatial behavior. Individual and personality differences also appear influential (Aiello, 1987:458). People with high self-esteem and self-confidence, for instance, are more inclined both to approach others more closely and to allow others to approach them similarly. On the other hand, people with schizophrenic and neurotic tendencies are often more sensitive to invasions of personal space than are other adults.

Appropriate distance is related also to culture. As mentioned, different cultures have different spatial norms. A substantial number of studies have dealt with this issue, most of which have investigated immigrants' (e.g., foreign students) and natives' interactions. This research largely supports Hall's hypothesis about *contact* and *noncontact* cultures. (Aiello, 1987:434, 445).

Finally, there seem to be gender differences, although it is extremely difficult to isolate these from other factors. On the basis of a large number of studies, Aiello (1987:432) claims that although "women *are approached* much more closely than men and *allow* closer (nonthreatening) approaches, they are *less* likely than males to intrude on another person's space – unless it appears that the other is 'accepting' and relatively harmless." Many of the studies, however, show contradictory results.

Personal-Space Invasions
All of the factors mentioned in the preceding subsection interact when interlocutors establish appropriate mutual distance. Thus personal space

does not refer to a bubble of a certain size around every individual, but rather to a dynamic system that adapts to the situation at hand.

Now, the distance established may be perceived as inappropriate. One may *feel* that the other person is standing too far away or too close in relation to how one understands the situation. In particular, too close a distance generates clear sensations of unpleasantness and discomfort. Many people are stressed in crowded elevators or public transit, where personal-space violations by strangers cannot be avoided.

Many empirical methods used by psychologists to measure and investigate personal space behavior include the so-called stop-motion technique. In this experiment, subjects "are asked to approach or be approached by another person (often an experimenter or a confederate) and to stop the approach where the subject begins to feel uncomfortable" (Aiello, 1987:408). The physiologically and behavioristically inclined experimenter may also want to measure increased heart rate and elevated levels of skin conductance, which are clear stress symptoms (see Meyrowitz, 1986:256).

Invasions thus trigger stress mechanisms, which work as warning signals to the individual and force the individual to take appropriate action. Such *regulation mechanisms* might include physical responses such as leaning away, blocking, take a step backward, or, in some cases, departing (Aiello, 1987:485; Lombard, 1995:292).

Like animals, humans display a wide repertoire of signals to encourage, avert, or otherwise regulate personal-space invasion. Touching or nontouching, body posture, and vocal volume are some of these signals, although the primary one is undoubtedly gaze behavior.[1] It is often claimed that continuous mutual gaze in animals is invariably associated with aggression. To a certain extent this is also true of humans. Hughes and Goldman (1978) reported that men and women were less likely to violate the personal space of a man standing in front of elevator buttons when the man was staring at them. Men, but not women, were also less likely to violate the personal space of a staring woman.

However, although increased gaze can stop an invader, the same seems true of *reduced* gaze. By averting the gaze, turning the head in another direction, or visually blocking the invader's access to our face, we flag the desire for less involvement. Moreover, in many situations, increased mutual gaze means a wish for greater involvement and encourages "invasion" rather than stopping it (e.g., flirting).

In addition, the invader may use gaze to express intentions, apologize for an intrusion, or otherwise explain why a violation takes place. In crowded elevators, buses, and subways, for instance, people tend to avert the gaze by looking at the floor, ceiling, advertisements, or out the window. In this way, people signal to others that the invasion or potential invasion is nonintentional. The averted gaze marks submissiveness and asks the other person not to interpret the violation as an aggressive act. In summary, gaze offers a rich source of markers, but it can have different meanings depending on the situation.

Gaze is probably the first regulation mechanism we encounter if we violate the personal space of a stranger without apparent motivation. The stranger will acknowledge the intrusion by trying to catch our eye. Binoculars and long-lens devices are technologies by which we can invade personal space *without* the usually associated moral responsibilities. Binoculars may give us the same visually sensory input as Hall's *intimate zone*, even if we stand far away. The experience of voyeurism and "spying" associated with such occasions occurs because the invaded person does not acknowledge the invasion as he or she would under normal circumstances. Through binoculars, we can gain access to the intimate sphere of another without being "discovered." Perhaps the voyeurism embraced by psychoanalysis and exemplified by the child illicitly watching its parents making love can be clarified by personal-space theory. We will return to this.

The sophisticated system of stress symptoms and actions involved in unwanted invasions functions as a warning mechanism. Because this mechanism "switches on" before someone or something hits the body, one can easily see the evolutionary value of such a system. Early research on personal space emphasized this *protective* function of personal space. From this perspective, it is important to recognize that invasions are not necessarily just interpersonal affairs, but can also occur with objects and animals, that we consider dangerous or that we have no time or opportunity to evaluate. Some people experience stress when near snakes, spiders, or scorpions, as these are collectively considered "dangerous" or "frightening." Moving objects that suddenly break into the visual field are startling and trigger reflexive protection behavior such as backing up and raising the arms or hands for protection. Here, there is no time for evaluating the object before it is close to the body. The system thus "plays it safe" and reflexively puts up protection. The prank of jumping on somebody from behind or from a hiding place exploits these processes.

The protective function of personal space can also be seen in many people's fear of darkness. In the dark we are denied visual access and control over the personal space, which substantially reduces our ability to discern whether personal space is violated. For some people, this is a stressful situation.

However, invasions are not necessarily bad in themselves. Violations of space are experienced as good or bad, depending on how the invader is evaluated. This brings us to the communicative functions of personal-space behavior.

Personal-Space Behavior: A Vehicle for Communication
The ability to determine (non)appropriate interpersonal distance across
a wide range of situations also enables communication. People exploit
proxemic norms to express intentions, making space and spatial behavior
"speak" (Meyrowitz, 1986:256).

On the one hand, moving closer or farther than usual signals a desire
to change a relationship, situation, or subject. Generally, by moving closer
to someone, we flag a wish to establish closer contact (e.g., moving from
friend to lover status). By moving away, we indicate a desire to limit
accessibility and intimacy (e.g., moving from friend to colleague status).
Changing personal zones may also mark shifts in a conversational topic
(e.g., from business to intimate matters).

Invading personal space can be seen as an invitation to another to
reconsider the parameters of the situation (e.g., relationship status). This
invitation may then be rejected or accepted. By letting the interlocutor
violate personal space without reaction, we signal trust and confidence
vis-à-vis that person. We may even move closer in response to make things
clear. We may, however, also back up to reestablish original distance and
thereby show that we have no interest in greater involvement. The invader,
it is hoped, will notice this retreat and withdraw.

Manipulating interpersonal distance in combination with regulatory
mechanisms thus fulfills important social functions.

Conclusions
There are surely many sociocultural variations of personal-space behavior.
Contact versus noncontact cultures is one. Societies may also have different codes for invasion and gazing according to social hierarchies, gender,
and authority (Kleinke, 1986). All the same, there is reason to believe that
personal-space behavior *as such* is universal; or, as Bruner (1981:260) puts
it, "[s]o though there may be universals at the competence level, at the
level of performance, in the uses to which competence is put there will be
wide divergence." In this respect, personal space is similar to language,
which all human cultures display, although in different configurations.

Like natural language, it is impossible to say whether the development
of personal-space is driven by genetics or by social learning. Psychologists
know little about how personal-space behavior is developed and acquired
through childhood. Some studies suggest that babies are born with a notion of personal space and associated stress mechanisms. Ball and Tronich
(1971) had two- to eleven-week-old babies sit in front of a backprojected
white screen. They then produced a symmetrically expanding shadow
that appeared to be an object rushing toward the toddler. All babies re-
acted to the shadow and displayed some form of protective behavior. This

included widening of eyes, head withdrawal, raising of the arms towards the face, "stiffening" of the body, and later crying.

At the same time, children seem to display different personal-space norms from adults. Before children are five years old, results are unreliable, as the ability to evaluate interpersonal distances in infants and toddlers is rather limited. However, it is fair to say that small children seem to lack a substantial notion of personal space and that, through childhood, they develop increasingly larger interpersonal distances (Aiello, 1987:412). This finding suggests that personal-space behavior is learned through social interaction with other people.

To explain the causes of a particular behavior or disposition, the nature–nurture issue is not very fruitful. Although biologists and anthropologists someday may have to answer that question, it suffices for now to acknowledge that personal space fulfills important functions in humans' biological and social environment. Human culture has maintained, and continues to maintain, personal-space mechanisms because they make a valuable instrument for protecting the body from physical attacks, for communicating intentions, and for understanding the intentions of others.[2]

Visual Media and Personal Space

If personal-space behavior is active during everyday life, we could expect it to be active also in the reception of cinema. Because personal-space behavior is a rich system of norms, moving imagery may exploit this disposition to create cognitive, emotional, and narrative effects.

As noted in the preceding section, vision and hearing seem to be the major ways in which one's personal space is scanned and controlled. Invasions are detected by means of the eyes and the ears. The basis for my claims about the connection between cinema and personal space is that photography-based visual media *contain the potential to display the sensory properties we are accustomed to in personal-space situations*. Close-ups, for instance, can reproduce the "strong and intense sensory inputs" from Hall's intimate zone – low-level voice, clothes rustling, distorted sight, or being able to discern eyelashes and pores.[3] This sensory stimulation, I would argue, is strong enough to trigger in the spectator mental processes like those the spectator would execute in a real personal-space situation. Of course, moving images cannot reproduce smell and touch, which may be present in the intimate zone. The auditory and the visual inputs, however, seem to be sufficient to cross the sensory–psychological threshold.

Meyrowitz's theory of shot scale and the personal-space dispositions of the spectator is quite clear: "In a particular shot, therefore, the way in which a person is framed may suggest an interpersonal distance between that person and the viewer" (Meyrowitz, 1986:257). That is, shot scale and framing have the ability to suggest distance and thereby in what personal-space zone the "meeting" between character and spectator takes place. Thus, reasons Meyrowitz, every shot scale already has a "meaning," thanks to our real-world expectations of personal-space.

Although Meyrowitz's idea makes much sense – and I shall occasionally refer to it – it may be a bit simplified, insofar as it focuses on shot scales per se and not on *changes* of shot scale. In contrast to written media, moving images and variable framing have the capacity to "simulate" transfers between different zones (through cuts, tracking, zooming, and moving character or objects in relation to the camera). This encompasses cut-ins as well as "cut-outs" from and to any type of shot scale, enabling characters on the screen withdraw from and play with the personal-space dispositions of the spectator. It is in the *variable* framing that personal-space effects of visual media make themselves most forcibly known.

What makes the connection particularly pertinent is that variable framing seems to be understood by the audience in similar terms as those of real-life personal-space. As we have seen, depending on who is invading, a personal-space invasion creates sensations of *intimacy* (positive) or *threat* (negative). If invaded by someone we like, we feel intimacy. If invaded by someone or something undesirable, indefinable, or unknown, we feel threatened and stressed. As I try to show in the following analysis, spectators and scholars alike have talked about and conceptualized variable framing in precisely those terms.

Personal Space and Variable Framing

Early Cinema
The first ten to fifteen years of cinema displayed a radically different form of visual imagery from that of today's mainstream traditions. To understand the use and reception of variable framing in the earliest cinema, we have to return to the connection between film and other forms of contemporary stage arts. Vaudeville appears to have been the norm by which cinema was produced, received, and evaluated (see Chapter 2, the section on the Historical Context of Point-of View Editing). This becomes perhaps most apparent in the handling of space. In this system, long shots and long takes were norms:

The camera, conventionally, was understood to stand in for the eye of the spectator, static and frontal, presenting an ideal view of the entire filmic space with all the players visible in full figure. The audience was affiliated with the display through pro-filmic practices and enframing, but rarely through editing. (Olsson, 1998:240)

FIGURE 19. *The Great Train Robbery* (Edwin S. Porter, 1903). (Obtained from the Wisconsin Center for Film and Theater Research.)

Maintaining the spatial continuum of watching a vaudeville stage, one-shot films were standard until around 1905. There was a respect for the wholeness of the event depicted (what Burch, [1990:149] calls the "autarchy of the primitive shot"). The camera's static position was sacred to the degree that in situations in which the gag demanded another optical angle on the event, actors were transferred rather than the camera. *Ladies' Skirts Nailed to a Fence* (1900), for instance, simply reverses the positions of the boys and women, rather than moving the camera (Figure 11 in Chapter 2). Such a practice indicates the heavy inheritance from the stage arts, in which the only solution to changing the optical angle is to move the set in some way (see note 7 in Chapter 2).

This inheritance also favored the long shot as the dominant shot scale (Figure 19). Theatrical performances enabled the spectator to see the *whole* scene and the *whole* figures of the players. Likewise, film actors were not allowed to approach the camera so that body parts ended up outside the frame. In perfect analogy with the stage metaphor, everything was to be contained within the frame of the shot, and there was no or little offscreen space. When the *nine-foot line* (approximately 1910–11) became the American standard for the master shot, regulating the minimum distance between character and camera with a 50-mm lens (Salt, 1992:88), the change was symptomatically met with resistance:

Some time ago in the columns of the *World* there was voiced a light protest against the tendency of many motion picture makers to cut the feet of the actors out of the scene. . . . [But] instead of following that bit of wise counsel, the filmmakers straightaway began cutting off the figures at the *knees*. Nor did it end there. Things kept getting worse, until now it is a common sight to witness a photoplay the greater part of which is acted so close to the camera that the actors are seen only from the waist upwards. . . . Pictorial art is composition. A picture is a combination of several factors into a complete and harmonious whole. An arrangement with the feet cut off is not a whole and harmonious whole. There is something lacking. Most people cannot tell exactly what is wrong, but they feel it nevertheless. Neither can they analyze and tell why a composition is correct, but they realize it unconsciously because it satisfies.[4] (Hoffman, 1912:53)

The unwillingness to dissect bodies and space in combination with hanging painted backdrops created the extremely shallow playing area so characteristic of films until 1906. With a large, empty, and "useless" foreground and a painted backdrop effectively blocking receding movements, the space of action may have been as shallow as two meters. Of course, the backdrop could be moved farther back, but that would have made the players "objectionably" small (Thompson, 1985:216). In such a system, acting is preferably stretched horizontally rather then in depth, generating frontality.[5]

Variable framing not only involves body parts that end up in offscreen space; it also varies the absolute screen size of the actors from shot to shot in a way completely alien to the size changes of players on a vaudeville stage. These consequences of variable framing were the targets of some complaints. Here is a reviewer commenting on the shifts (cuts?) between different shot scales:

Now, here was a total lack of uniformity, due entirely to a want of intelligence on the part of the producer and the photographer, and the effects of the minds of the people who saw this picture was of extreme dissatisfaction. . . . Where the fault lay was in the disregard of uniformity of conditions evinced either by the photographer or by the producer, or both. If these figures had been photographed at equal distances from the camera, then they would have appeared of equal sizes on the screen, instead of varying between the dimensions of a Brobdignagian monstrosity and Lilliputian pygmies. It is curious to reflect that in an hour entertainment of a moving picture theater, the visitor sees an infinite variation in the apparent sizes of things as shown by the moving picture. This is absurd. On the vaudeville or talking stage, figures of human beings do not expand or contract irrationally or eccentrically; they remain the same size. Not so on the moving picture stage, where, as we have said, one film shows us giants and another manikins. ("The Factor of Uniformity," *The Moving Picture World*, Vol. 5, No. 4, July 24, 1909, pp. 115–16. Reprinted in Pratt, 1973:95)

Again, the film is conceived as a "moving-picture stage." The standards for this space are always calibrated vis-à-vis the norms of the vaudeville stage, in which no substantial change in size occurs. Tsivian (1994:131) notes

(a)   (b)

FIGURE 20. *L'Arrivée d'un train à la Ciotat* (Lumière, 1895–6). (Obtained from the Wisconsin Center for Film and Theater Research.)

that the "notion of 'life-size' that almost invariably figures in scale-related statements in film literature of the early years, probably corresponded to the writer's intuitive sense that the distance between actor and spectator in the theatre constituted a cultural norm, and that this cultural norm was felt to be at risk."

All in all, in the first ten to fifteen years of filmmaking, variable framing and the effect thereof were associated with problems and ambiguities. If they occurred at all, closer-ups basically had two functions: threatening images and emblematic shots. They were the earliest examples of personal-space invaders.

THREATENING IMAGERY OF EARLY CINEMA. Although the discourse of classical Hollywood cinema would be subordinated to narrative purposes, early cinema was

fascinated by other possibilities of cinema other than its storytelling potential. Such apparently different approaches as the trick film and actuality filmmaking unite in using cinema to present a series of views to the audience, views fascinating because of their illusory power (from the realistic illusion of motion offered to the first audiences by Lumière, to the magical illusions concocted by Méliès) and exoticism. The cinema of attractions, rather than telling stories, bases itself on film's ability to show something. (Gunning, 1994:41)

In this system, variable framing had no narrative function, but constituted an attraction in its own right. One of these attractions seems to have been having objects, people, and vehicles moving toward the camera. Lumière's *L'Arrivée d'un train à la Ciotat* (Figure 20) and its numerous remakes over the next few years, placed the camera next to the tracks and let a train approach and then pass the camera. *How It Feels to Be Run Over* (1900) is composed of one shot in which a motorcar is driving toward the camera

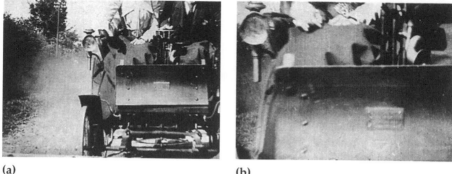

(a)   (b)

FIGURE 21. *How It Feels to Be Run Over* (Cecil M. Hepworth, 1900). (Reproduced from Burch, 1990:203.)

(Figure 21), ending in a close-up of the front followed by a black leader and the inscription "Oh. Mother will be pleased!"(*The Big Swallow*, 1900) is also a one-shot film that depicts a man approaching the camera so close that he is able to swallow the lens, camera, and the photographer (Figure 22). The final (or initial) shot of *The Great Train Robbery* (1903) features the outlaw pointing and then firing the gun toward the camera (Figure 23).

In all of these films, playing with and challenging the spectator's personal space seem to be the primary objective.

They seek to simulate a violation of personal space, triggering stress, fear, and threat associated with real personal-space invasions. Of course, picking objects and vehicles that – at the time – were associated with accidents and danger adds to the threat (e.g., motorcars and trains). Nevertheless, the basic mechanism by which these effects arise seem to originate in personal space, as here in Maxim Gorky's 1896 review of the

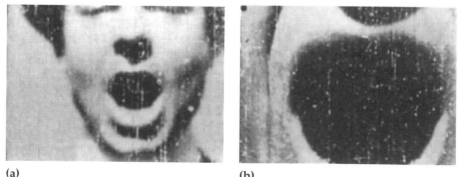

(a)   (b)

FIGURE 22. *The Big Swallow* (Williamson, 1900). (Reproduced from Burch, 1990:221.)

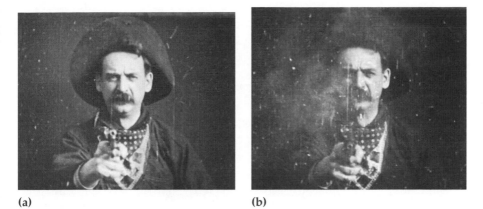

(a) (b)

FIGURE 23. *The Great Train Robbery* (Edwin S. Porter,1903). (Obtained from the Wisconsin Center for Film and Theater Research.)

Lumière programme:

Suddenly a strange flicker passes through the screen and the picture stirs to life. Carriages coming from somewhere in the perspective of the picture are moving straight at you, into the darkness in which you sit.... Suddenly something clicks, everything vanishes and a train appears on the screen. It speeds straight at you – watch out! It seems as though it will plunge into the darkness in which you sit, turning you into a ripped sack full of lacerated flesh and splintered bones, and crushing into dust and broken fragments this hall and this building, so full of women, wine, music and vice.... A boy enters, steps on the hose, and stops the stream. The gardener stares into the nozzle of the hose, whereupon the boy steps back and a stream of water hits the gardener in the face. You imagine the spray will reach you, and you want to shield yourself. (Gorky, 1896)

Many of the Gorky's experiences in this account are related personal-space invasions ("straight at you," "watch out!," "the spray will reach you"). In addition, there seems to be a propensity for body movement ("shielding" oneself), which points to the connection with personal-space behavior. These bodily reactions have the same structure as the babies described by Ball and Tronich, who were exposed to a symmetrically expanded shadow on a white backprojected screen and shielded themselves with arms and hands and by turning their heads (see the opening section on Personal Space). In addition, the babies' stiffening and agitation (e.g., crying) correspond well to the shock that Gorky appears to have experienced.

Although the similarity of body reactions in real personal-space invasions and in the theater seat makes their interconnection clear, we must be more specific about the nature of this "invasion." It was obviously not a

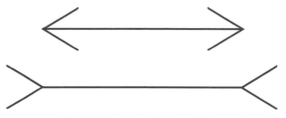

FIGURE 24. The Müller–Lyer illusion. (Diagram by author.)

complete illusion; the audience did not mistake the depiction of the train for a real train in the sense that they expected to be run over and physically hurt. Gunning (1989) and Tsivian (1994:Chap. 6) have spent much energy finding flaws in and tracing the genealogy of the myth about the panic-stricken first spectators of Lumière's film. Although Gorky may have "wanted to shield himself," he may not actually have put a hand before his face or risen from his seat.

The fact that people were not running about the theater, however, does not imply that there was no effect, but rather that we must distinguish between different forms of illusion. Allen (1993) makes a distinction between illusions that are dependent on context knowledge and those illusions that are not. Mirror images may at first sight (e.g., by a child) make one believe that what one sees is a real space and a real personal double; as one continues to experience mirror images, however, one starts to understand how they work. This understanding destroys the perceptual illusion. "Once we *know* that our visual array is an illusion produced by a mirror we no longer *see* it as an illusion" (Allen, 1993:36).

In the Müller–Lyer illusion, on the other hand, the illusion of the different arrow lengths will be unaffected by measuring them (Figure 24). Despite the observer's knowledge about their equal lengths, they will still appear different. Illusions of this kind

are always compelling because the sensory deception continues to exert force even when we know that what we see is contrary to fact. We experience a conflict between our judgment and our senses; the illusion drives a wedge between thought and perception. (Allen, 1993:36)

We may be able to describe the 'experience' of personal-space invasion in similar terms. Cinema spectators have throughout history been quite knowledgeable about the mechanisms of camera and projectors. Indeed, during the first couple of years, it was the machine itself that was on display, rather than the films (Gunning, 1994:42).

However, although we *know* that film is only twenty-four frames per second, we still *see* movement; although we know we look at only a 2D screen, we still see depth; and likewise, although we know that the train or person is coming toward the camera and not us, we still see it (and discuss it) in terms of a personal-space invasion.

Thus the illusion was not strong enough to make the audience believe that a real train was coming toward them – and thus they did not rise from their seats. It was strong enough, however, to trigger processes and feelings similar to those of a real personal-space invasion – thus Gorky's "wanting to shield" (and other expressions and metaphors in the account). When I previously claimed that the cinematic image has the potential to simulate personal-space behavior, it was this weaker form of illusion I had in mind. Simulations maintain some features of a real event but leave out others (cf. also Lombard's [1995] idea of "direct responses").

If the cinematic image gives the impression of a personal-space invasion, this illusion, however, differs from the Müller–Lyer diagram in one significant respect. Whereas the line-length experience involves only *perceptual–cognitive* factors, a simulated space invasion triggers *affect* (e.g., threat, intimacy, stress). Gorky's account was enlightening on this point; so is that of L. R. Kogan, who focuses on the threat the train poses, and the relief when it disappears into offscreen space:

[A] train appears in the distance coming with great speed right towards the auditorium. There is involuntary commotion in the audience, a cry of alarm, then laughter: the engine and the carriages have slipped away somewhere to the side. (L.R. Kogan (1894–7) *Vospominaniya* [Memoirs], Part 2, No. 1. GPB, 1035/35, p. 39. Cited in Tsivian, 1994:146)

We find this form of illusion – *emotional illusions* or, better, *illusions of sensations* – in today's visual culture as well. The immersive space of the IMAX format, virtual-reality systems, and flight simulators provide few spatial anchors and occasionally make people nauseated (Oman, 1993). One may recall the forerunner of IMAX (called *Cinema 2000* in Sweden and mostly shown in amusement parks), which was projected onto a vaulted screen with the audience standing on the floor. The films were produced with the explicit intention of manipulating the spectators' balance, for example, a camera placed on the bumper of emergency vehicles. Such films created amusing effects on a floor packed with standing people. Loss of balance, nausea, seasickness, and invasion stress are all basic sensations that can be triggered by the illusory properties of moving images. This does not imply that spectators think that they watch reality. It is just that psychological systems of perception, cognition, and sensation react to sensory input that is perceptually close to those in a real-world situation. This pertains not only to the threatening invasions described in this subsection, but to the kinds of personal-space effects discussed in the next subsection, for example, "intimate" invasions.

FIGURE 25. Title unknown (Mutoscope, 1904). (Obtained from the Wisconsin Center for Film and Theater Research.)

EMBLEMATIC SHOTS: MARKS OF INTIMACY AND EMOTIONAL REPOSE. In addition to threat, variable framing had another function in the earliest cinema, associated with *positive* invasions of personal space. *Emblematic shots* were "attached to the beginning or end of a film and were intended to betoken the gist of the story rather to present a part of it" (Tsivian, 1994:189). They were textual "appendages." In a Mutoscope production from 1904 (title unknown), a group of villains are involved in counterfeiting and kidnapping, but are discovered by the police. The emblematic shot displays three hands with money, gun, and handcuffs, symbolizing the three major themes of the film: the counterfeiter, the kidnapping, and the police rescue (Figure 25). In this case, there is also action in the scene (the gun fires), which was not common (see Gunning, 1994:74). This view summarizes the previous (or impending) plot and provides the theme and moral of the plot in an abstract way.

Thus these emblematic shots functioned similar to written titles, film titles, or even today's marketing slogans, for instance, "crime never pays," "love is stronger than death," or *Die Hard*. Like titles, the emblematic shots and their content were not part of the story world, but "hovered" at or outside the boundaries of diegesis (cf. Burch, 1990:198 and the first/last shot of *The Great Train Robbery*, Figure 23).

FIGURE 26. The emblematic shot of *Bangville Police* (Keystone, 1913). (Obtained from the Wisconsin Center for Film and Theater Research.)

Another form of emblematic shot focused on main characters of the film. In *Bangville Police* (1913), all players come together in the last scene to display their reaction to the story's outcome through gestures, for example, the furious police chief jumping up and down and pulling his beard in anger (Figure 26). The emblematic shot of *Rescued by Rover* (1904) contains the dog and the baby it has saved (see Burch, 1990:195). *Le Chien de Montargis* (1909) concludes with the dog hero who provided invaluable help in solving the murder of his master (Figure 27). In *The Redman and the Child* (Biograph, 1908) and *The Mended Lute* (1909), Griffith supplies a "coda" after the films.

The Indian appears in his canoe, paddling towards the camera with the recovered gold and rescued child. The boy leans back, secure in the Indian's protection, and falls asleep. The Indian smiles and paddles further, moving nearly into close-up. (Gunning, 1994:74)

The Mended Lute ends with a lyrical postscript which directly recalls the last shot of *The Redman and the Child*. As Little Bear paddles and Rising Moon leans back against her lover, the couple comes toward the camera in their canoe, moving almost into close-up. As in the earlier film, we draw near to the characters in a moment of repose and intimacy. (Gunning, 1994:210)

Again, notice the connection between the film titles and the content of the emblematic shot. Even as late as 1916, "ending a story with a close-up of

FIGURE 27. *Le Chien de Montargis* (SCAGL, 1909). (Obtained from the Wisconsin Center for Film and Theater Research.)

the protagonist's face was fairly common in Russian films . . . [and] may be seen as emblematic parallels to the title 'The End' " (Tsivian, 1994:192).

There are two important features of these emblematic shots that are relevant for the present discussion. First, emblematic shots were invariable connected with closer framings (Burch, 1990:193). *Le Chien de Montargis*, for instance, is shot in a typical long-shot style (see Figure 7), but in the final shot, the framing gets considerably tighter. Indians in the Griffith films almost paddle into a close-up; *Bangville Police* contains few cut-ins or inserts, but in the final scene the narration shifts from full shot to a medium long shot. Second, emblematic shots were associated with emotional repose and calm after narrative resolution. Jack Leyda has termed it a "lyrical postscript" that conveys an "emotional tone" (see Gunning, 1994:74).

Why were emblematic shots associated with an emotional regime? Tsivian (1994:189) suggests that by the time of cinema's emergence, this connection was already established by other forms of imagery, above all, by nineteenth-century theatre and slide show culture. Nevertheless, why was there a connection in the first place? Moreover, was it arbitrary?

The closer-up of the emblematic shot may contain several features that make it sensitive for emotions. First, it was (primarily) placed after the story's resolution, assuring the spectator that narrative equilibrium had been restored. The "emotional cleansing" of the narrative was probably invested in the last shot of the scene (in similar ways to "The End" title). Second, the closer shot enabled access to the faces and expressions of the characters. In a system that displayed players only in full length and in which access to facial activities was rare, the final closer shots psychologized characters through expressive faces (Gunning, 1994:74). This presumably provided audiences a psychological intimacy with the character, which was highly emotional in tone.

Third, however, I also think that personal space might have had some part in this. If framing gives the spectator a suggestion of distance to the character, then different framings may correspond to Hall's distance zones:

Hall's theory of proxemics, therefore, can be adapted to an analysis of television. The *framing variable* "places" the viewer within scenes or reveals spatial orientations of characters. Shots portray distances and therefore have a "meaning" which corresponds to the functioning of spatial cues in interpersonal interaction. (Meyrowitz, 1986:262)

If we assume that variable framing is able to simulate personal-space behavior, then moving toward a person "means" greater involvement. In this respect, it makes sense that closer emblematic shots – placed in an environment of nothing but tableaux, full shots, and extreme long shots – were associated with intimacy and greater emotional involvement. The convention of closer framing thus exploited the spatial dispositions of the spectator in order to promote and reinforce affective investments in the image. As we shall see, this technique still plays a similar role in contemporary mainstream cinema.

Variable Framing in Mainstream Narrative Cinema

Merely analyzing the textual surface of cinematic discourse will take us nowhere unless it is paired with a discussion of the system and context within which the device is used. Variable framing was present in both early cinema and the mainstream narrative tradition that developed through the 1910s and into our mainstream cinema. The functions of variable framing, however, changed along with this transformation. In the same way as chase films resurfaced as run-to-the-rescue scenes and tableau shots turned into establishing shots (Thompson, 1985:175, 195), variable framing became *narrativized* (Gunning, 1994). In this new system, variable framing came to serve a number of new functions.

"CLOSER-UPS". From 1909 onward, camera and players came closer to each other. In addition, variable framing within a scene was eventually allowed on a regular basis, either by bringing actors up to the camera or by cut-ins. Only a few of the 1910 films in Salt's corpus used cut-ins in the middle of a scene, but in 1911, 16 out of 124 American films and 28 out of 130 European films contained at least one such instance. In 1912 and 1913, approximately 40 out of 216 American films used cut-ins, and the European percentage seems to have been in the same quarter (Salt, 1992:92). Of Thompson's 1912 American sample,

only a third of the ES [Extended Sample] films from 1912 had cut-ins, and only one had two of them; of the 1913 films, slightly over half had cut-ins (several with two or three, and a couple with cut-ins involving a distinct change of angle); by 1914, every ES film had at least one cut in (Thompson, 1985:197).

These earliest forms of variable framing were almost invariably without change of angle and moved straight in (Thompson, 1985:200).

Although variable framing initially was met with resistance, as we saw, the new aesthetics of closer-ups contained too many valuable functions to be discarded. First, closer camera positions meant that characters could be recognized on the basis of their faces, a significant capacity in narratives with many characters in a series of scenes and shots – see Smith's (1995) notion of *character recognition*. In early cinema, recognition was relegated to costume as, for example, in *Le Voyage dans la lune*. Occasionally color and tinting techniques were used; the three main characters of the previously discussed *Le Chien de Montargis* are differentiated by their green, pinkish, and yellow capes. By introducing facial discrimination through closer framings, narrative cinema started to exploit the sophisticated face-recognition system of humans.

Second, tighter framings enabled not only face recognition across scenes, but also across *films*, with the Biograph girl as the earliest and most famous example. Reinforced by fan-magazine pictures, closer-ups of players in the films lay the foundation for the star system that was to reach full bloom during the 1920s. It is difficult to understate the importance of stars in a system of visual consumption and in the way in which films acquire commodity value (Gunning, 1994:219; deCordova, 1990). In this respect, facial discrimination of actors in films fulfilled – and continues to fulfill – essential functions in mainstream cinema.

Third, and perhaps most important, tighter framing was the primary means by which characters were isolated from the surrounding, thereby encouraging their psychologization. The cut-in was able to "bracket" (Carroll, 1988:202) a character from the rest of a scene:

Used for details, reactions, or intense emotions, the medium close-up often isolates the single figure from both the setting and from other figures. Depth, after all, implies that the spectator sees different objects in different planes. When only one item is dramatically relevant, a tight framing prevents our noticing the surrounding space, sometimes in combination with a mask at the edges of the frame to

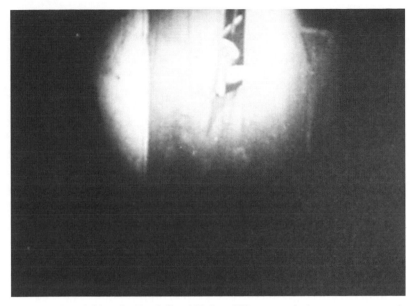

FIGURE 28. *Das Cabinet des Dr. Caligari* (Robert Wiene, 1920). A woman appears in a window crying for help, after having been attacked by a burglar. (Obtained from the Wisconsin Center for Film and Theater Research.)

cut down the prominence of the background. . . . Aware of the surroundings from the establishing shot, the viewer nevertheless sees the character filling most of the frame. (Thompson, 1985:216)

Interestingly, closer framings and masking occasionally appear together in the films of the 1910s and the 1920s, which indicates their shared isolating function. Sometimes this is a means to suggest a POV structure (see Chapter 2, the subsection on the functions of Point-of-View Editing), but often the masking appears in narratively objective shots, simply isolating an object from the background. A film such as *Das Cabinet des Dr. Caligari* (1920) persistently uses masking with closer and long-shot framing (see Figure 28).

Isolating a character with a cut-in is valuable for the psychologization of characters. Isolation encourages or "compels" spectators to direct their attention to a single item. This implies not only "directing the eyes," but most importantly, guiding the understanding processes. In contrast to a bustling long shot, the cut-in gives guidance and provides time for thinking, enabling spectators to attribute mental states, establish causal relations, and speculate about future events and their relevance to this character (see Chapter 4, the subsection on Textual Techniques).

The cut-in in *The Egyptian Mummy* (1914) performs precisely these functions (Figure 29). In order to collect a reward, a vagabond has agreed to act

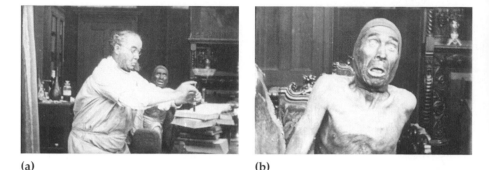

(a)   (b)

FIGURE 29. *The Egyptian Mummy* (Lee Beggo, 1914). The ignorant professor intends to inject a poisonous embalming liquid into the vagabond who fearfully realizes what is about to happen. (Obtained from the Wisconsin Center for Film and Theater Research.)

as a fake mummy and has been delivered to an Egyptologist. However, when the professor plans to inject a poisonous conservation liquid into "the mummy," the vagabond rises in the coffin [Figure 29(a)]. We then cut from the long shot to a medium shot that shows his reaction [Figure 29(b)]. The narration here isolates the vagabond from the energetic professor and encourages the spectator to concentrate on the vagabond, his cognitive and emotional experience, and the precautions he might take to prevent disaster. This function of cut-in is present in much contemporary visual media. Dramatic endings of television drama episodes, for instance, often present a close-up of a character who has just discovered important information about adultery, marriage, pregnancy, or a business transaction. The close-up is held for an extended period of time, giving the spectator an opportunity to ponder the consequences of this discovery (see Chapter 4, the subsection on Textual Techniques). SRS sequences, with the camera resting with either the speaker or listener, also give the filmmakers tools to regulate this "timing" of the narration.[6]

Isolating a character in a narrative situation is thus of great importance to a system of representation that has character psychology as one of its lynchpins. In contrast to its precursor, the emblematic shot, the cut-in is a definite part of the diegetic action and space and does not linger at the margins of the story world. At the same time, it retains the tie to emotional and intimate affects. In 1913, this connection was already established to the degree that it was an object of some disapproval:

The directors are clearly people with no idea of artistic taste: the slightest hint of emotion in a scene and for some reason they immediately shoot figures and faces enlarged almost to twice life-size. Imagine what it is like to see a huge nose, a vast mouth, monstrous whites of eye, unnaturally protruding lips, all leering down at you. And when all of these bits of a face belonging to a visitor from outer space begin to move, to express profound emotion – well, the sadder the scene is meant to be, the more grotesque and totally ridiculous is the effect. (Stark, E. (1913) "S nogami na stole" [Feet on the Table], *Teatr i Iskusstvo* [Theater and Art], No. 39, p. 770. Cited from Tsivian, 1994:131)

In the same way as emblematic shots were associated with the regime of intimacy, so were the new closer-ups. Of course, part of this effect can be explained by the fact that closer-ups occur in parts of the story that include emotional involvement with the characters. Ability to read facial expressions and to attribute emotions to characters creates a *psychological* involvement with the characters, for instance, Plantinga's (1999:243ff) affective mimicry. Closer framings, however, also seem connected with a visual or *spatial* intimacy, here described in an account by Jean Epstein:

The close-up modifies the drama by the impact of proximity. Pain is within reach. If I stretch out my arm I touch you, and that is intimacy. I can count the eyelashes of this suffering. I would be able to taste the tears. Never before has a face turned to mine in that way. (Epstein, 1921/1988:239)

Here the intimacy or "intensity" (Epstein, 1921/1988:235) is not psychological, but rather proxemic, with sensory impressions similar to those in Hall's intimate zone. There is a potential for touching and olfactory input (*If I stretch out my arm. . . . taste the tears . . .*), and the visual sensations are exclusive to intimate distance (*count the eyelashes . . .*). It is also interesting to note that Epstein uses *you* about the individual depicted, as if describing a personal encounter. This focus on effects of greater intimacy in closer framings continues in the works of modern commentators, "greater 'involvement'" (Branigan 1984:6) and "repose and intimacy" (Gunning, 1994:210). Although these critics and viewers are (presumably) not aware of any theory of personal space, their choice of formulations concurs with it and thus points to the relatedness of the two phenomena.

Another piece of evidence for the connection between closer-ups and personal space is found in the experience of "grotesqueness," "obscenity," and "vulgarity" reported among early cinema audiences in many countries (Gunning, 1994; Thompson, 1985:191; Tsivian, 1994). Here is one voice raising concerns about this:

There are many moving pictures made nowadays, even by reputable makers, in which the figures are too near the camera: that is to say, they assume unnecessarily large, and therefore, grotesque proportions. The reason for this is manifold. Film-makers have the idea that the public wants to see the faces of the figures large; consequently, the camera is placed too near the figures; or perhaps, it is an optical defect, the focus of the lens is too short. ("Too Near the Camera" in *The Moving Picture World*, Vol. 8, No. 12, March 25, 1911, pp. 633–34. Reprinted in Pratt, 1973:96ff).

Effects of "grotesqueness" may be caused by the absolute body size of the projected character on the screen. If we assume that cinema, with the exception of slide shows, was the first mode of representation that used big screens and large-scale projections, it seems natural for the audience to react to the oddity of enlarged bodies, faces, and things on the screen. This is especially true if the closer framing also cuts out portions of a body.

Nevertheless, why was this oddity specifically expressed in terms of "grotesqueness" and "vulgarity," and not just "difference" in general? Personal space may provide a fuller and more nuanced explanation, as suggested by Tsivian:

> [N]one of these refers to the insertion of a non-facial detail: the attack is aimed exclusively at facial close-ups. This leads me to think that the response may have been conditioned by proxemic norms. . . . We may assume that, by isolating a face or a part of the it, close-up framing created a kind of surrogate field of vision anthropologically associated with, say, 'intimate' distance, thus forcibly imposing intimacy on the unprepared viewer. . . . This may well be the norm responsible for facial close-ups being perceived as grotesquely out of proportion. (Tsivian, 1994:196ff)

Cinematic characters and actors were "strangers," and closer-ups simulated invasion of the personal space of the spectator. Whereas the train and vehicle films already discussed were "threatening," closer-ups seem to have generated a weaker form of inappropriate distance with people/characters unknown to the spectator, referred to as "grotesqueness" and "vulgarity." If we assume that the turn-of-the-century audience was less urbanized and less exposed to personal-space invasions by strangers in buses, metros, cinemas, and on sidewalks, this makes more sense. In addition, as society was then more divided by class, and fewer interclass encounters with strangers took place than in today's semiegalitarian Western society, cinema's depiction of people from all classes must have stirred social identity borders. The invasive character of the closer-up surely amplified those tendencies.

In addition, as Tsivian notes, these effects were directed toward closer-ups only of faces or bodies, not toward close-ups of objects (inserts). This also makes sense from the perspective of personal space, as this behavior is mainly related to interpersonal relations. We do not apply rules of appropriateness to objects and dead things, and they may be approached without proxemic constraints. Because inserts may involve fewer emotional effects than do facial close-ups, this can be taken as a confirmation that personal space is somehow involved in the reception of variable framing.[7]

Whereas effects of grotesqueness and vulgarity have died out in the context of facial close-ups in modern narrative film, they may still be seen

(a)

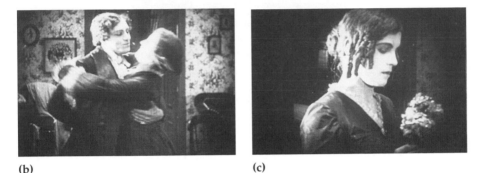

(b)   (c)

FIGURE 30. Analytical editing in *Nosferatu* (F.W. Murnau, 1922). (Obtained from the Wisconsin Center for Film and Theater Research.)

in other genres. The pornographic film, for instance, with its "vulgar" (and therefore exciting?) close-ups of body parts, still exploits these kinds of effects. Here the intimacy simulated is most inappropriate – sexual activities being perhaps the most private of human behavior – and tight framing intensifies this intimacy to the point of vulgarity and obscenity.

ANALYTICAL EDITING: EXPLOITING PERSONAL-SPACE INTIMACY. If closer framings simulate personal-space invasions, then we could expect cinematic discourse to exploit this simulation. For instance, the spatial intimacy of close-ups may reinforce the psychological intimacy generated on the narrative level. This may be most elegantly exemplified by *analytical editing*, which is the primary method for spatial articulation in mainstream cinema, continuing and extending the cut-in techniques of the 1910s. The typical procedure, here exemplified by *Nosferatu* (1922), is to establish the scene with a long shot [Figure 30(a)]. As the action and dialogue grow more intimate and dramatic, the camera creeps closer to medium [Figure 30(b)] and closer framings [Figure 30(c)]. Often a scene is rounded off with a reestablishing shot. This technique was more or less in place in the early

1920s (Salt, 1992:144) and is now standard in mainstream film, sitcoms, and soaps. Sometimes it would start with a close-up or insert in order to withhold the scene establishment and retard the narration[8] (Salt, 1992:141).

In this way, variable framing is able to exploit personal space for affective purposes. For instance, it is common in mainstream cinema and television to reserve the close-up for the most climactic intimate moment of the scene. By withholding the intimacy effect produced by close-up until exactly the right moment in the scene, the narration can enhance an already emotional tone. In *Nosferatu*, for instance, the close-up occurs when Anna receives Allan's flower. The gratitude and love she feels toward her fiancé are intensified by the close-shot scale. The *psychological* intimacy of her love and affection is reinforced and enhanced by the spectator's *spatial* intimacy with the character.

Another feature of analytical editing that points to its relationship with personal space is the way in which transgressions of shot scale often occur with progression in dialogue topics. Shifting from business to private discourse (and vice versa) is often accompanied by a shift from wider to tighter framings. In *Citizen Kane* (1941), for instance, Susan invites Kane into her apartment after his clothes have been drenched by a passing car (Figure 31). She does not know who he is, and they engage in small talk and jokes before Kane introduces the subject of his mother.

[*Medium two-shot of Kane and Susan – Figure 31(a)*]
KANE: Do you wanna know what I was gonna do tonight before I ruined my best Sunday clothes?
SUSAN: Oh, they are not your best Sunday clothes. You probably have a lot of clothes.
KANE: I was joking. [*Close-Up Susan smiling (c)*] [*CU Kane (b)*] I was on my way to the Western Manhattan Warehouse. In search of my youth. [*CU Susan*] You see, my mother died a long time ago [*CU Kane*] and her things were put in a storage out West; there wasn't any other place to put'em. Thought I'd send for them now and tonight I was gonna take a look at them. You know, a sentimental journey. [*CU Susan*] [*CU Kane*] I run a couple of newspapers. What do you do? [*Medium shot Susan and Kane (a)*]
SUSAN: Me?
KANE: How old did you say you were?
SUSAN: I didn't say.
KANE: I didn't think you did. If you had, I wouldn't have asked you because I would have remembered. How old?
SUSAN: Pretty old.
KANE: How old?
SUSAN: Twenty-two in August....
[...]
SUSAN: I wanted to be a singer, I guess. That is, I didn't. My mother did it for me.

(a)

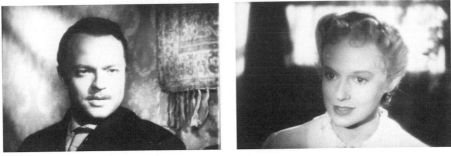

(b)   **(c)**

FIGURE 31. *Citizen Kane* (1941). (Obtained from the Wisconsin Center for Film and Theater Research.)

KANE: What happened to singing?
SUSAN: Well, mother always thought about grand opera for me. Imagine....
    But my voice isn't that kind....you know what mothers are like.... [*CU Kane*]
KANE: Yes.... Have you got a piano? [*CU Susan*]
SUSAN: A piano? Yes, there is one in the parlor. [*CU Kane*]
KANE: Would you sing to me?
SUSAN: Oh, you don't wanna hear me sing.
KANE: Yes, I would. [*CU Susan*]
SUSAN: Well....
KANE: Don't tell me your toothache is still bothering you?
SUSAN: That's all gone. [*CU Kane*]
KANE: All right. Let's go to the parlor.
[*Dissolve to parlor*]

The joking and the small talk take place in medium shot, but when Kane introduces the warehouse and his dead mother's things, the narration shifts to close-up. When Kane reintroduces the small-talk theme of his and Susan's occupations ("I run a couple of newspapers. What do you do?"), the camera returns to a less personal–intimate distance. This scheme

repeats itself later when Susan broaches the topic of mothers once again
("...you know what mothers are like...").

Certainly variable framing here *reflects* or simulates the progression of
zones that is associated with dialogues of this kind in real life. By introducing the intimate topic of his mother, Kane tries to redefine their roles
from acquaintances to friends and thus invites Susan and the camera to
come physically closer. The close-up is thus fully "appropriate" in respect
to the topic. Although the two characters are not moving closer to each
other in fictive space, the camera acts as a substitute for this movement
and enables the spectator to approach them.

The closer shots also *intensify* the change of topic for the spectator in
a different way than if the scene had been shot in a single medium shot.
Of course, the change of topics by Kane and Susan would probably have
been understood by the spectator as an invitation to greater involvement,
even if the camera had maintained medium shot. The close-up format,
however, intensifies this change (Messaris, 1994:91; see also Meyrowitz,
1986:261). The close-up's effect of intensifying content stems from its relationship to the personal space of the spectator. The close-up format means
greater involvement for the spectator, and this is exploited by the analytical editing to emphasize aspects of a scene or a dialogue.

THE IMPORTANT FOREGROUND. In addition to explaining effects of intimacy in closer-ups and analytical editing, a theory of personal space
may also provide the context for one of the most basic methods used by
cinema and theater to hierarchize discursive practices: When objects and
characters are placed in the *foreground*, they gain greater importance than
objects in the *background*. This is a fundamental principle or convention
in all stage arts. For instance, by embracing closer framings and discarding the painted backdrops, the cinema of the early 1910s was able to stage
scenes in depth, creating hierarchies of importance in this way[9] (Gunning,
1994:207ff; see also Thompson, 1985:215).

Is the important foreground convention arbitrary, in the sense that cinematic discourse could have chosen another convention that would have
worked just as well? Probably not. It seems to draw on basic cognitive–
perceptual dispositions in the spectator. Enlargement and object size seem
to be one factor: "Enlarging the screen size of an object generally has the
force of indicating that this object, or gestalt of objects, is the important
item to attend to at this moment in the movie" (Carroll, 1988:202 – see
also Münsterberg, 1916/1970:35). But why are large depictions of objects more "important" than small ones? Why has the screen size "the
force of indicating importance"? In real life, an enlargement of an object
perceptually implies that the object is closer. In combination with a theory of personal space, which states that objects in intimate-distance zones

generate stronger emotions of stress, discomfort, and pleasure than objects more distant, it makes perfect sense to talk about foreground objects as being more important than background ones. The convention of important foreground is specifically designed to exploit the zone warning system of personal space to create hierarchies of importance in visual discourse.

THREAT REVISITED. The threatening effects of *L'Arrivée d'un train à la Ciotat* (Figure 20) and of other films of the same genre were not one-time experiments; rather, they continued into the narrative mode of filmmaking. Action, horror, and drama are modern genres that exploit these effects to expand, extend, intensify, and deepen the emotional roller coaster of the narrative film.

Let us take a clear case. Many films of early cinema contain chases and fights. In the dominant long-shot style of the time, wrestling was represented in the long-shot style that dominated the first ten years of filmmaking (Figure 32[10]). A scene from the beginning of *Die Hard* (1988) contains more or less the same content, but chooses a radically different framing and mise-en-scène (Figure 33). Here the violent action takes place in medium shots or close-ups, with John McClane and Fritz falling, moving, and turning toward the camera. Often objects such as doors and aluminum bars are placed between the camera and fighters, so that they can fall upon the camera when the fighters run into them. In one case the camera moves sideways as bars and fighters threaten to fall toward it, simulating an evasion of physical impact. In all of these techniques, *Die Hard* – in stark contrast to early cinema – exploits the threat effect of closer framings in order to intensify an already intense scene. The closer framing is "threatening to transgress its frame, to burst the screen in order to invade the space of the spectator"[11] (Dubois, 1984:22).

In addition, the spatial threat of the *Die Hard* scene is narrativized in a way unlike, for instance, that of *L'Arrivée d'un train à la Ciotat*. The spatial violations take place within a context of psychologized characters (intentions, emotions, beliefs), a situation (hostages have been taken, including John's wife), and a moral continuum (Fritz is bad; John is good). Thus the variable framing in the fighting scene works within a system of already established hierarchies and emotions. Unlike *L'Arrivée d'un train à la Ciotat*, in *Die Hard* the invasions of the spectator's space are far from the primary purpose of the film.

The different effects in these two cases also raise questions about editing practices and personal space. These questions pertain to all kinds of personal-space effects, not just threat. Early cinema had a respect for the autonomy of the profilmic event and resisted manipulation and deconstruction of space. Assumptions that fictive space continued outside the frame seem to have been absent during the first ten years of cinema.

FIGURE 32. Title unknown (Mutoscope, 1904). (Obtained from the Wisconsin Center for Film and Theater Research.)

In the classical system, however, POV editing, SRS, the 180° convention, and movement across cuts constitute a tight system of cues on which the spectator bases his or her spatial inferences. By making spatial connections between different shot spaces (e.g., near, far, on the other side of the door), the spectator is able to create clear and elaborative expectations about offscreen space. In this way, the spectator constructs an imaginary or mental spatial layout by which – most important – the spectator seems to be encompassed:

> Primitive-period mise-en-scène created a flat playing area within a box-like space, seldom suggesting space behind the set or to the sides. But classical staging and sets suggested space receding into the distance, and cut-ins foster a sense of additional space on the sides, by showing only portions of the whole area. Space now apparently stretched out indefinitely, appearing to include the viewer. (Thompson, 1985:214)

The classical cinema spectator has clear expectations about offscreen space (left/right, up/down), as in computer-generated virtual-reality spaces and, for that matter, real space.[12] Continuity editing and the associated mental constructions construct an *immersive* space in which the spectator is situated.

This naturally has consequences for how personal-space effects are experienced. In *Die Hard*, not only do objects and characters fall or move toward the spectator, but they also come from offscreen space. The multiple

(a)

(b)

(c)

(d)

FIGURE 33.
Die Hard (John
McTiernan, 1988).
(Obtained from
the film archives of
Svenska Filminsti-
tutet, Stockholm.)

camera positions give the impression of a fight that takes place in front of,
at the side of, and occasionally even behind the spectator. This constantly
moving and shifting presence, in combination with closer framings, simulates invasions from different directions within short time intervals. The
same effect can be seen in the infamous shower scene from *Psycho* (1960)
(Figure 34). In Figure 32, on the other hand, the viewer has not only visual

FIGURE 34. *Psycho* (Alfred Hitchcock, 1960). (Obtained from the film archives of Svenska Filminstitutet, Stockholm.)

control of and a comfortable distance from the fight, but, there is no surround space from which attacks and intrusions can appear. If anything comes in at all, it comes from the front.

Modern horror films often exploit personal-space threats and invasions for emotional purposes. Sudden intrusions into the frame by a monster or an object – often with strong auditory accompaniment – are occasionally used to frighten the spectator. Such threats, which may trigger protective physical behavior by the spectator, are of the same type as real-world pranks, in which someone jumps on somebody from behind or from a hiding place (see the subsection on Personal-Space Invasions). The closer one gets to the victim before disclosing one's presence, the greater the effect. From this perspective, it would make sense if the burst-into-the-frame effects of horror films are more effective in closer framings than in wider ones. Intuitively speaking, this is probably true.

Again, the strength and the value of such effects depend on how the spectator evaluates the invader, which is determined by narration combined with the spectator's preferences. The stronger the emotional evaluation of the character (negatively or positively), the more emotionally the simulated invasion will be experienced. A real-world invasion, and presumably also the close-up format, will intensify an already negative evaluation of the invader. It is no coincidence that sudden appearances of killers and monsters, who are evaluated extremely negatively, often

FIGURE 35. *Friday the 13th: The Final Chapter* (Joseph Zito, 1984). (Obtained from a television broadcast on the Swedish channel TV4.)

use the close-up format, as these appearances perform specific affective functions.

If the purpose of the protective function of personal space is to keep people or objects at arm's length and thereby avoid the potential or threat of being struck, certain compositions within the horror genre exploit this fear. The killer in *Psycho* (1960) stabs repeatedly *at* the camera, and the close-up format makes this aggression more effective than would a long shot. The monster reaching for the camera and spectator in *Friday the 13th: The Final Chapter* (1984) (Figure 35) is considerably more stressful than the same incident in a long shot in *Nosferatu* (1922) (Figure 36). Again, the close-up format is not threatening per se, but it intensifies already disturbing visual content.

Threat effects are also exploited in nonfiction genres. In nature programs, close-ups of small dangerous animals may provoke dread in some viewers. Detecting small details of the physiology and motor activities of snakes, spiders, and scorpions (to mention just a few) is often accompanied by intimate auditory cues (e.g., a scorpion scratching in sand, a spider swallowing a fly, or a snake rustling in the leaves). Such image–sound combinations present similar sensory inputs to a real animal in our most intimate personal-space zone. If this study's theory about personal space and close-ups is correct, we could expect viewers to react more negatively to close-ups than to wider shots of the same content.

FIGURE 36. *Nosferatu* (F.W. Murnau, 1922). (Obtained from the Wisconsin Center for Film and Theater Research.)

Another interesting correlation between cinema and personal space is how physiological and motor behavior appears to overlap. This may be valid for variable framing in general, but gains particular significance for the threat function. It seems that viewers, especially in the horror and the action genres, lean or slide away, avert their gaze, use the arms and hands as visual or physical barriers, and occasionally even leave the situation, in ways similar to real, threatening personal-space invasions. The reaction and body postures of spectators in Williams' (1996) infrared photographs of first-time British spectators of *Psycho* and the promotional poster in Figure 37, may provide crude and informal evidence for this connection. The evidence is crude insofar as it is difficult to know how the close-up format contributes to experience and behavior and how much of these reactions are effects of "content" and narrative context. The evidence is informal in that the poster, of course, does not describe how spectators actually behave, but instead implies how they perhaps *should* behave according to horror film producers. The ways in which movies *move* (the body of) the spectator need much more investigation if we are to understand these processes.

Finally, I would like to mention that scholars' discussion of close-ups in fact imitate everyday talk about personal-space invasions. The terminology centers around "threat and anxiety"[13] (Dubois, 1984:14), "effect of horror"[14] (Dubois, 1984–85:18), "jolting and excessive" (Gunning, 1994:294), "aggressive"[15] (Olsson, 1996:34), "confrontation" (Gunning,

FIGURE 37. *House of Wax* (André De Toth, 1953).

1990a:101), or "shock" (Bordwell & Thompson, 1993:216). Eisenstein (1974:112) also focuses on the "terrible": "[A] cockroach/hypocrite filmed in close-up seems on the screen a hundred times more terrible than a hundred elephants captured in a long-shot."[16] Moreover, Martin (1984:37ff) describes the effects of close-up by means of a metaphor of being in an elevator with strangers.

These scholarly discourses on closer framings in cinema accord well with the connection to the spectator's personal space, although none of the scholars expands on this connection and makes it explicit. They *describe* effects of variable framing. They do not, however, try to *explain* them.

Voyeurism

Threat and intimacy, which have been discussed so far, are emotional effects that emerge from the impression that characters and objects of the image seem to "come out at" the spectator, simulating an invasion of personal space. There is, however, another emotional regime in which movement seems to be the opposite. Here it is the *spectator* who seems to invade the *characters'* personal space, rather than the other way around: The depicted world does not come out toward the spectator, but the spectator is brought closer to the fictive world and its inhabitants. The result of this movement, I argue, can be described in terms of *voyeurism*. In cinema studies, voyeurism (or occasionally *scopophilia*) refers to a spectatorial gratification obtained from vision and is usually associated with a hidden vantage point. The voyeur can see but is not himself or herself seen or acknowledged. Through psychoanalysis, this gratification has been analyzed in terms of sexuality, with Freud's "primal scene" as the model case. Mainstream cinema is exhibitionistic in this sense, as characters continue their lives and activities regardless of the presence of the spectator (Metz, 1982:58ff). Characters do not acknowledge the presence of the camera or spectator as they would in real life. Actions that people would not perform in the presence of strangers are performed by characters in the fictive space without consideration or second thought. The pornographic film thus presents an extreme case, in which people engage in activities that are utterly private in nature. Cinematic diegesis is an aquarium with one-way transparent glass (see Metz, 1982:96).

Modern mainstream cinema thus differs immensely from early practices, in which the mutual acknowledgement between stage and auditorium of the vaudeville was normal (Burch, 1990:251; Gunning, 1994:262ff). By looking and gesturing at the camera, early cinema characters sought empathy and shared jokes (an effect that is still practiced in the genre of comedy). Here, as in vaudeville, the voyeuristic barrier between fictive and auditorium space was terminated by the constant communal and interpersonal acknowledgements between spectator and characters or actors (e.g., laughter, improvisations for that laughter, glances, invitations onto the stage). It is no coincidence that some early cinema auditoriums – in accordance with the vaudeville tradition – appear to have been partially illuminated, enabling this kind of interaction between "stage" and audience (Gunning, 1994:147).

If we take voyeurism to be this play of public and private regimes (which may or may not be sexual in nature), then personal-space parameters will be one of the mechanisms by which this voyeurism is articulated. In real life, personal-space invasions are, as we have seen, acknowledged and regulated through many channels, gaze being perhaps the most useful. Approaching a stranger in public space will invariably *at some point* lead to visual acknowledgement from the person. Inappropriate distance will be noticed and dealt with, making the situation communal rather than private. Binoculars and other long-range devices are interesting to a voyeur, as they enable him or her to gain access to the intimate and most inappropriate personal-space zones without the moral responsibilities that such invasions would normally entail. The binoculars provide the voyeur with the same visual input as would the voyeur's real presence in the intimate zone, in spite of the fact that the distance may be great. In these cases, the "invader" is neither noticed nor acknowledged by gazing behavior. It is this inappropriate "presence" in the intimate zone that creates an experience of "being on forbidden ground" with which the use of binoculars are associated. This experience, I believe, is quite similar to the pleasure some people take in overcrowded metros and elevators, where they are temporarily allowed into the intimate sphere of others without the "questioning" of the acknowledging gaze.

Generally variable framing and close-ups in mainstream cinema seem to have effects similar to those of binoculars. Through the camera work's simulation of a personal-space behavior, the spectator enters a stranger's intimate zone (that of an actors or a characters). However, this situation differs from a real invasion insofar as it is not taken notice of through glances and acknowledgements. As with binoculars, the camera allows us to be on forbidden ground without this behavior's normal social implications. Therefore, if a character's behavior in fictive space is exhibitionistic *in general* (performing acts that he or she would not do in public), closer framings allow a specifically *spatial* kind of voyeurism. We might say again that closer framings *intensify* an already existing voyeurism. If variable framing triggers personal-space experiences, then the experience of an inappropriate and illicit presence must be somewhat proportional to the shot scale. The closer the shot, the more illicit the experience.

As we have seen, this situation may be a part of the explanation for the resistance to closer framings in the transfer from early to narrative cinema. It may also explain the late arrival of the over-the-shoulder shot, so ingrained in today's visual media (see Chapter 2, the subsection on Gazing). Until the 1930s SRS sequences were done in front of the shoulder rather than behind it, that is, with only one character in the visual field (Salt, 1992:94; Thompson, 1985:210). Having the camera linger over the shoulder of the character without the character's acknowledgment of its presence may have been too illicit and spatially provocative.[17]

Voyeurism is often accompanied by some degree of shame or guilt in doing or seeing something illicit. Hidden from view, the voyeur does not "play with an open hand." This shame effect may be present in the whole

(a)   (b)

(c)

FIGURE 38. *Sommaren med Monika* (Ingmar Bergman, 1953). (Obtained from the film archives of Svenska Filminstitutet, Stockholm.)

situation, but it becomes forcefully explicit when the voyeur is discovered by the person being looked at. For instance, Monika's notorious gaze into the camera in Bergman's *Sommaren med Monika* (1953) stands out from the rest of the film in which characters obediently remain in their aquarium (Figure 38). The emotional effect of this extended tracking shot is precisely this "being caught looking" at something illicit and private. If the depth of the illicitness is proportional to the shot scale, then the shame associated with discovery must reasonably be stronger in closer framings than in wider ones. That is, if a filmmaker wants to trigger shame effects by having characters gaze into the camera, such effects would be most successful in close-up. Bergman exploits precisely this feature by having the camera track in on Monika as she looks at the audience. In fact, this procedure is extremely unusual in real-world situations. We creep closer and closer, and even though Monika sees us and acknowledges us, we still keep on moving in on her. This scene simulates a real situation in which the spectator would be engaged in powerfully inappropriate spatial behavior, thus associated with extremely strong sociospatial taboos.

Of course, voyeurs are driven by some deep, psychological (perhaps even sexual) pleasure in watching others in private settings without being watched themselves. If we want to sketch out the specific *mechanisms* by which such pleasure arises, however, personal-space behavior and expectations may provide a rich path to follow. This, I think, will refine and perhaps strengthen the deep-psychological approach.

Conclusions

It is essential to be specific about the claims being made here. They are not aimed at a description of the whole experience, meaning, emotions, or what have you, of the images analyzed. My goal has not been to explain individual and unique understandings of my film examples. Rather, in this investigation I have tried to detect *one of many* parameters in the experience of variable framing and close-ups. Claims of experiencing threat, intimacy, and voyeurism naturally depend on other aspects, such as narrative context, space-construction editing, emotional and moral evaluations of characters and objects, and the spectator's emotional dispositions at the particular moment. Nevertheless, personal-space effects can be seen as a contributing factor or, again, as an *intensifier* of the vague notion of content.

Nor do I claim that variable framing *only* has personal-space effects. As was shown in the previous sections, variable framing fulfills crucial narrative functions in directing spectators' attention and inference processes, thereby clarifying, linearizing, and disambiguating the visual discourse of cinema.

Instead, the claims are made on a more abstract level: The general features of personal space interact in complex ways with the properties of visual media. To view it from the direction of the text or filmmaker: The conventions of visual media exploit the spectator's personal-space dispositions. Of course, it would be foolish to think that these phenomena have no flesh-and-blood validity in real, unique, and individual encounters with film (otherwise I would not have found the project interesting); but to describe all parameters involved in such cases is still impossible because of the enormous complexity involved. For now, we must resort to abstraction and simplification to understand at least *some* of the processes.

The claims presented in this chapter have been substantiated with different kinds of evidence. On the one hand, I have referred to verbal accounts of spectators and scholars, in which personal-space effects surface consciously or unconsciously. On the other hand, I have analyzed the textual features of certain conventions and their functions within a historical and discursive context and discussed how these match an assumption about the spectator's personal-space dispositions. The physical behavior of spectators in the theater constituted a third type of evidence.

However, a theory about variable framing and personal space needs more confirmation before it can be considered valid. When historical evidence has been used up, then more formal empirical reception studies remain a feasible alternative. This theory is rich enough to frame specific hypotheses, which may be tested in media–psychological studies. For instance, Reeves et al. (1992)[18] made video recordings of people with divergent framings, and then measured subjects' responses to them. People shown in close-ups were given less attention, but were remembered better and were evaluated both more positively on passive adjective pairs (e.g., happy/sad, interesting/boring) and more negatively on active adjective pairs (e.g., violent/gentle, competitive/cooperative). Such results suggest that different framings do indeed affect experience, and that this effect is double (both intimacy and threat). In a later study, Lombard (1995) kept the framing constant but tested different screen sizes and viewing distances. In this experiment, the recordings showed a person associated with a high reward valance (high status, credibility, competence, and physical attractiveness) telling a simple news story while addressing the camera. Starting from the personal-space theory, Lombard hypothesized that emotional responses to, and impressions of, the person depicted would be more positive when the viewing distance was close and the screen size was large, compared with a moderate distance and a small screen size. Results mostly confirmed this prediction. This study suggests that close-up effects are functions of personal-space ability and framing, but also of relative image size.

Another approach to validate the theory of personal space and variable framing would be to investigate reception in different audience groups. If personal space has a cultural, developmental, and gender variation, this should reasonably be reflected in the experience of cinematic close-ups. Are there differences in the reception of variable framing across cultures, ages, and gender (see Meyrowitz, 1986:269)?

Such media–psychological experiments raise the usual problems of empirical studies: How are we to sort out interesting parameters from the rest? How can we be sure that differences in experience are due specifically to shot scale, and not to narrative and pragmatic context with which shot-scale effects seem intimately connected? This, of course, places extreme demands on the design and the methodology of a potential experiment and on how cause and effect are established. It must be remembered, however, that such complexity is "business as usual" in experimental studies, regardless of the scientific domain; that is, complexity is not a valid reason for students of cinema studies to shy away from experimental inquiry.

CHAPTER FOUR

Character Psychology and Mental Attribution

Literature is written by, for and about people. (Bal, 1985:80)

Introduction

In the preceding chapters we were occupied with clear and fairly "small-scale" dispositions of the spectator (deictic gaze and personal space). These were intimately related to bodies and physical behavior. We now turn to a more general set of dispositions; namely, how people know or infer what others think or feel. This ability is much more "cognitive" and knowledge based than the two dispositions already discussed, involving sophisticated forms of reasoning. Eventually, it all comes down to *characters* and the strategies and competencies used by spectators to understand and make sense of the characters' screen behavior.

Characters have central functions in most narratives. In contrast to other modes of discourse, narratives focus on anthropomorphic creatures. In narratives, as in scientific descriptions of solar systems and molecules, events take place in a rule-based fashion. Unlike scientific descriptions, however, narrative occurrences have some form of *human significance*. They involve humanlike entities who act within and react to a social and physical environment. In fact, it seems that spectators' "'entry into' narrative structures are mediated by characters" (Smith, 1995:18). In this respect, characters (in the broadest sense) should occupy a central position not only in a theory of narrative texts (narratology), but also in a theory of the reception and understanding of narrative texts.

To put the present project in perspective, it is important to outline dominant approaches to characters within literature and cinema studies.

Textual Theories of Characters

The structuralist approaches narrative bypass stylistic or surface manifestations by claiming that a narrative is basically "a deep structure quite independent of its medium" (Chatman, 1990:117). The recurrent distinction between *text* and *style*, *syuzhet* and *plot*, and *fabula* and *story*, of course, acknowledges the surface level of description, but narratologists still expend most of their energy at the fabula and syuzhet levels. Bal, for instance, distinguishes between *actors*, who exist on the fabula level, and *characters*, who exist on the syuzhet level. Actors are not necessarily persons, but can also represent states aspired to by characters (e.g., being richer, possession of X, happiness, a place in heaven, or a just society). In this endeavor, there are *obstacles, helpers, opponents*, and *instruments*, which again do not necessarily have to be persons. Actors perform *functions* in the narrative on a deep level. An actor is a "structural position" (Bal, 1985:79). There have been quite a few proposals for the exact nature of these frameworks of actors or functions (Bal, 1985; Barthes, 1966; Greimas, 1966; Propp, 1928/1968).

Narratology also tries to specify different (preferably binary) opposites between actors and functions. Actors are seen as representing deep-level axes of meaning, for instance, feudalism/liberalism, liberalism/socialism, country/city, home/abroad, patriarchy/egalitarianism, marriageable/nonmarriageable, femininity/masculinity, or subversive/submissive. Such opposites are related to cultural setting, universal archetypes, or the Freudian unconscious, and may become manifest in narratives and other cultural practices. A psychoanalytical version of this approach deals with the analysis of narrative deep structures in terms of sexual and family relations; here characters stand in relation to each other as mother, father, and daughter/son do in Freudian theory. Bellour (1975), for instance, argues that Roger Thornhill's trip in *North by Northwest* (1959) is not only a trip from New York to Mount Rushmore, but, more importantly, is a trip from mother to wife, all in terms of the Oedipal theme (see Jacobs, 1993:140). Krutnik (1991) analyzes and explains recurrent male character types of *films noir* in terms of desire and law ("the father"). Here the textual system and the relations between characters in the plot are taken, quite literally, as a dream, whose deeper meaning needs to be excavated by the analyst (Metz, 1982:30).

On the level of syuzhet or plot,[1] Bal argues, we go from actor and function to *character* proper, which is seen as a "complex semantic unit" (Bal, 1985:79). In contrast to functions, characters are personages and can be analyzed primarily as bundles of *traits* (see Bordwell & Thompson, 1993:68). This notion is taken from psychology to denote a more or less enduring and stable disposition of a person (e.g., shyness, snobbishness), which can often be described in terms of opposites (e.g., extrovert/introvert, strong/weak, curious/prejudiced – see Chatman, 1978:119ff). *Traits* are not equivalent to *habits*, but can be seen as predispositions to *behave* in a certain manner in a specific situation. By extracting such traits or positioning the character on a trait scale, the structuralist can properly describe what a character is, how characters stand in relation to each other, and why a given character behaves the way she or he does in the plot (Chatman, 1978:134; Bal, 1985:86). From such an analysis of characters, a dramaturge such as Egri (1946:59ff) proposes that one of the most distinctive features of narratives is the way in which characters transform and "grow" through the story. Narratives tend to end when the main character has learned a lesson or has come to realize something. This process can often be described as the character's having changed from one end of a trait scale to another (e.g., from introvert to extrovert, from poor to rich, from insecure to self-assured).

Perhaps the most extensive issue of character in the narratological tradition, which also takes place on the plot level of analysis, is the question of *point-of-view*. Related to the issue of characters,[2] this term – somewhat simplified – refers to the way in which the narration chooses a character as the major or the only source of information about diegetic events (*perspective*) and the way characters distribute story information to the reader (*filtration*). Such an analysis may include the way in which characters "know" more or less than the spectator or other characters (Bal, 1985:114; Bordwell, 1985:57ff: Tan, 1996:186), how characters can be (un)reliable as sources of information about diegesis (Bordwell, 1985:60), and how story events are presented from the visual, cognitive, and moral perspectives of a certain character, creating hierarchies of perspectives within the text. In the end, it is often claimed, these processes more or less determine not only how characters are understood, but also how spectators emotionally, morally, and ideologically align with them:

> According to this approach, the control of point-of-view is the most powerful means of inducing a kind of imaginary response on the part of the spectator, "positioning" the spectator by addressing the viewer through visual devices such as the point-of-view shot and shot/reverse-shot cutting in order to fashion a very tight bond between spectator and text. In this way, the text may be said to "interpellate" the spectator into the fictional world so that its values, and its ideology, become one with the viewing subject. (Stam et al., 1992:86)

Through the mechanisms of POV, texts and discourse become important and powerful channels for ideology and moral influence of all kinds.

Somewhat related to the issue of POV, feminist writing has been preoccupied with describing structures of passive/active characters in different genres. Mulvey (1975) defines "active" both in visual terms (to be active is to look; to be passive is to be looked at) and on the level of plot: To be active is to be the cause or triggerer of plot events, making things happen, as opposed to passive, being an object of investigation or the end point of a quest. Active characters rely more on their cognitive and physical abilities to deal with situations, whereas passive characters rely more on other characters. Active characters create their own destinies, whereas passive characters are the objects of other's desires, or victims of coincidences, natural causes, and "fate." Such an analysis may reveal genre-distinct character types, for instance, the active and successful hero or heroine of action films and thrillers (like Thornhill in *North by Northwest*) and the active but unsuccessful hero or heroine of women's pictures (see Jacobs, 1993:140). Mulvey claims that the active/passive pair is correlated with gender and can be seen as manifesting underlying sociocultural hierarchies (although some genre characters undoubtedly contradict such social structures, for instance, the "final girl" of stalker films). When an active female character, such as the *femme fatale* of film noirs, "gets punished" by the narrative, this can be seen as an expression of patriarchy in our culture and can easily be mapped onto the psychoanalytical notion of the law of the father (see Krutnik, 1991).

Structural theories about characters are not primarily concerned with reception and the (real) spectator–reader. There are no claims made about how functions or actors appear and operate in reception; rather, they are considered to be textual structures, independent of a reader. Deep-level representations of character are abstractions of the analyst for properly describing "the object" we call narrative. For instance, to facilitate the scholar's determining which character is most important or which character performs what function, Bal (1985:86) presents appropriate criteria. Bal, however, makes no claims that semantic trait axes in fact play a role or are present in the understanding of readers other than literary scholars. The discussion about POV is another case in point, because for many narratologists there is a clear difference between the *implied reader* and the *real reader*, the former being a hypothetical construct on part of the analyst (Chatman, 1978:267). Although a narratological approach provides a detailed analysis of "the effects" of narration and POV on the implied reader, little effort has been made to extend this analysis to claims about real readers. In these ways, structuralist theories contrast with the psychological approach developed in this book, as well as with the reception-based theories of characters in general.

Reception-Based Theories of Characters
There is a large body of writing around the notion of *identification*, which – if we exclude Metz's "primary" identification – revolves mainly around the relation between real spectators and fictional-narrative characters.

Giving a concise overview of this debate, Smith opens the set of questions with Richard Wollheim's distinction between *central* and *acentral* *imagining*:

> While central imagining is expressed in the form 'I imagine . . .', acentral imagining is expressed in the form 'I imagine that . . .'. If we say, 'I imagine jumping from the top of a building', we imply that we represent this event to ourselves, as it were, from the 'inside': I imagine, for example, the view I would have as I fall, the nauseating sensation I experience as my body picks up speed, and so forth. Or again, in imagining being revolted by the smell of rotten eggs, I recall the characteristic sulphurous stench. . . . By contrast, in imagining *that* I am revolted by the smell, I need generate no such olfactory 'image'; in 'imagining *that* I jump from the building', I do not represent the event to myself with any of 'indexical' marks of the imagined action – for example, transporting myself imaginatively to the appropriate position. I do not place myself 'in' the scenario, so much as entertain an idea, but not from the perspective (in any sense of the term) of any character within the scenario. (Smith, 1995:76ff)

In contrast to acentral imagining, central imagining is a stronger form of "fusion" or "mind-meld" between spectator and character. Smith introduces this distinction because it enables him to discuss the different models of identification in cinema studies. Smith claims that psychoanalytical writers such as Mulvey, Cowie, and Clover tend to look on identification and the general relationship between spectator and character as a central imagining phenomenon, although this relation may shift across several characters during the story. Smith also claims that Carroll (1990), on the other hand, denies central imagining process any status in the reception of fictive characters. Spectators can understand characters' understanding of a given situation, but spectators need not *replicate* the mental state of the protagonist. This may be most evident when spectators are considering villains, whose emotions, intentions, beliefs, and sensations may be perfectly understood by the spectators, although a viewer's emotions may hardly overlap those of the character (e.g., taking pleasure in killing the hero).

Smith tries to strike a balance between central and acentral processes, claiming that both in fact take place and have structure: the structure of *sympathy* (acentral imagining) and structure of *empathy* (central imagining).[3] Processes of sympathy can be divided into three layers. First, there is a *recognition* or basic *construction* of a character, which refers to the way in which the spectator understands several bodily appearances as one and the same person, having stability, identity, and continuation over time. Recognition of faces and clothing and an impression of a stable body come into play here. Recognition also relates to the question of agency and the way in which spectators distinguish between intentional agents and unintentional objects. In addition, recognition involves recognition of character types and their traits.

Second, "*alignment* describes the process by which the spectators are placed in relation to characters in terms of access to their actions, and to what they know and feel" (Smith, 1995:83). Alignment involves those processes in which the spectator comes to understand how a character understands a situation and the character's emotional reaction to it. According to Smith, narration promotes alignment either through *spatiotemporal attachment* to a given character (following a character through fictive space and time) or through *subjective access* to the character's mind and emotions. Processes of alignment in fact lie close to narratology's idea of *POV* (Branigan, 1984, 1992; Stam et al., 1992:83ff), *mood* or *focalization* (Bal, 1985; Genette, 1980:Chap. 4), *filtration* (Chatman, 1990), and Bordwell's (1985:57ff) theory about *range* of knowledge (restricted/unrestricted and depth). All of these theories deal with the way in which narration generally distributes narrative information through and by characters, particularly information about characters' mental states.

Finally, on the level of *allegiance*, Smith argues, the spectator morally evaluates the character and the character's behavior on the basis of this understanding and responds emotionally to this evaluation:

Allegiance depends upon the spectator having what she takes to be reliable access to the character's state of mind, on understanding the context of the character's actions, and having morally evaluated the character on the basis of this knowledge. Evaluation, in this sense, has both cognitive and affective dimensions; for example, being angry or outraged at an action involves categorizing it as undesirable of harmful to someone or something, and being affected – affectively aroused – by this categorization. On the basis of such evaluations, spectators construct moral structures, in which characters are organized and ranked in a system of preference. (Smith, 1995:84)

In this way, allegiance depends on alignment (and recognition) and lies perhaps closest to the everyday notion of "identification." Above all, the relation between the character's and the spectator's view of justice and morals determines the allegiance process (see Tan, 1996:168ff). Smith is also careful to point out that all of these processes are acentral in nature:

Neither recognition nor alignment nor allegiance entails that the spectator replicate the traits, or experience the thoughts or emotions of a character. Recognition and alignment require only that the spectator understand that these traits and mental states make up the character. With allegiance we go beyond understanding, by evaluating and responding emotionally to the traits and emotions of the character, in the context of the narrative situation. Again, though, we respond emotionally without replicating the emotions of the character.[4] (Smith, 1995:85)

If sympathy has a structure, so does empathy. Smith and others recognize three processes here. *Emotional simulation* is a voluntary act by which we not only recognize and understand an emotion of another individual, but also act it out in our imagination, trying to revive the way in which the character feels or senses. We are able to simulate the smell of rotten eggs or the act of jumping off buildings. Such processes may occasionally take place in the reception of cinema (Smith gives a couple of examples of where this *may* happen, but provides no evidence that it actually happened). Another process is *affective mimicry*, which refers to the involuntary reaction and "reflexive simulation of emotion of another person via facial and bodily cues" (Smith, 1995:99). The author gives an example of flipping on the television set after a day at work and being confronted with a middle-aged man crying. "Without any knowledge of the character, or what is at stake in the larger framework of the narrative, before I know it, a lump forms at the back of my throat" (Smith, 1995:98). Here, mere physiology tends to provoke emotion simulation and affective mimicry (Plantinga, 1999:243). A third process of empathy is autonomic responses, such as "startle" responses to sharp, loud noise and unexpected movement inside and into the frame (see Chapter 3, the section on Variable Framing in Mainstream Narrative Cinema). According to Smith, such reactions

bind spectator and character together in a qualitatively different manner to that which we find in the structure of sympathy. We experience an identical shock to the character, and in this sense the response is central or empathic. (Smith, 1995:102)

Although Smith recognizes central and acentral imagination in the experience of fictive cinematic characters, the amount of attention given to acentral processes suggests that those are more prevalent, at least in classical cinema (Smith, 1995:98).

Smith's account is seminal because it takes a broad view of spectators' engagement with characters – cognitive as well as emotional, mental as well as embodied – while still providing a detailed framework within which we can describe all of these processes without resorting to a notion of general *identification*. Smith's account demonstrates that the concept of identification actually contains so many different processes and layers that the applicability and the explanatory value of this term overall are close to zero. It is simply too crude and abstract to be useful (see also Bordwell, 1996b:16ff; Carroll, 1990:88ff; Tan, 1996:189ff).

The Psychology of Recognition and Alignment

I am now in a better position to sketch what I seek to accomplish in this chapter. I do not elucidate textual structures, in contrast to textual theories, or provide an analyst with tools with which to describe characters in a text; rather, I describe processes of understanding and reception. The focus is on real, everyday processes for real, everyday spectators. I do this by bringing psychological and anthropological research into the reception process. Focusing on both textual structures and spectator dispositions, I question the structuralist's propensity to consider texts as "objects out there," describable independent of any observer, "comprehender," or understander. I hope that this generates a better account of how texts and fictive characters work.

Smith's framework also enables us to avoid the general notion of identification and focus on some of its subprocesses. While acknowledging that other processes of engagement are important, we may nevertheless start investigating the specifics of each level. In this chapter we do not deal, for instance, with central imagining processes. Neither do we address allegiance and the moral–emotive evaluation of characters. Emotional reactions are crucial parameters of the relationship between characters and spectators, but, because of space constraints, those processes must be left aside (see, instead, Tan, 1996). Here the center of attention is on the more cognitive aspects of character comprehension, that is, what Smith refers to as *recognition* and *alignment*.

My account, however, diverges from Smith's in two ways. On the one hand, my emphasis is on the *psychology* of alignment rather than its textual manifestations. I argue that the spectator is equipped with certain psychological dispositions, obtained from everyday physical, social, and cultural life, whose structure may illuminate cognitive appraisals of cinematic characters. Smith does mention such schemas in his argument, although not in a systematic manner.

On the other hand, I emphasize the spectator's strive for coherence. Within a psychological framework of reception, spectators (and animals in general) are organisms that actively use knowledge and dispositions to create coherence to sensory input. In Chapter 1 we discussed the layers of coherence making in which the spectator may be involved (levels 0–5). If this is true of cinematic texts in general, it is also relevant for viewers' understanding of characters. The processes of understanding characters take place on many levels, and each level may give coherence to a scene or an action (Zacks & Tversky, 2001:7).

Levels of Meaning

A scene from *Seven Samurai* (1954) will make the argument a bit more concrete and manageable. Threatened by pillagers, the farmers of a village hire seven Samurai for protection. Fearing the charm of the Samurai who might take advantage of his beautiful daughter, a farmer cuts his

(a)　　　　　　　　　　(b)

(c)　　　　　　　　　　(d)

(e)　　　　　　　　　　(f)

FIGURE 39. *Seven Samurai* (Akira Kurosawa, 1954).

daughter's hair and dresses her in boys' clothes. In this sequence, the youngest Samurai meets the girl for the first time in the forest (Figure 39). She tells him that she is a boy [Figures 39(a) and 39(b)], and the Samurai orders "him" to return to the practice military drill in the village. A chase ensues [Figure 39(c)], and they start to fight [Figure 39(d)]. Suddenly he backs away from her [Figure 39(e)] and sits watching her while she adjusts her clothes [Figure 39(f)].

In relation to the characters, what levels of cognition, understanding, meaning, and coherence might be in play in this scene?

LEVEL 0. On a nonrepresentational level, the spectator can disconnect his or her recognition abilities, and see events only as changes in color and shape. The chase, for instance, can be seen as regions of shades expanding, contracting, and taking new forms as the film rolls on. Movements and events are understood on a formal or abstract level only. This is an extreme reading, but most spectators are probably capable of achieving it, even in films such as *Seven Samurai*, which are representational in nature.

LEVEL 1. On a representational stratum, we can think of characters and actions in a purely behaviorist mode: "The girl lowers her arm," "She turns her head in direction of the Samurai," "She moves her lips and shakes her head," "She places one foot in front of the other at a fast pace." Descriptions and experiences of this sort are almost anatomical or physiological in nature. They are surely representational in the sense that they require recognition of body parts and their spatial displacement, but there is still no notion of a unified body. These are just simple fragments of behavior. The coherence making remains at the level of body parts rather than proceeding to the level of the body.

LEVEL 2. When behavioral fragments are put together, they may form more abstract coherent structures such as "She runs," "The Samurai stands up," "They wrestle." These are more holistic units, consisting of *sets* of physiological behavior. We may call them *simple actions*, i.e., patterns of movement involving whole bodies, attributes, and instruments whose identity and relationships must be recognized (e.g., "She opens the door"). Physiological behavior and simple actions are behaviors without intentionality, but merely sophisticated movement. Movements of plants ("The leaves are rustling"), insects ("The crab grabs his prey"), and machines ("The piston moves up and down") are probably understood on this level of coherence. Physiological behavior and physical action demand complex processes of object and movement recognition.

LEVEL 3. Simple actions can also be understood within a broader framework if the action is placed in a *situation* (see Chapter 1, the section on Psychology: Understanding and Dispositions). It is a bit difficult to find this level of understanding in the scene from *Seven Samurai*, but perhaps "picking flowers" or "chasing each other" might be seen as situations in this sense.

LEVEL 4. Another fundamental way of understanding verbal and physical behavior is to place it in a framework of *character psychology*. By ascribing a mental life to characters, spectators can make sense of what is going on in the scene, and thus construct a coherent model of understanding:

- The Samurai *believes* the girl is a boy.
- The Samurai chases the presumed boy, because he *wants* all boys to be drilling in the village for the upcoming attack of the pillagers. She runs because she is *afraid* that her real gender will be revealed.
- In the fight, Samurai touches her breasts and *realizes* that "he" is actually a she.
- The Samurai backs away because he is *surprised*.
- The girl is *frightened* and *guilt stricken*, and she is *frightened* because she *understands* that her secret has been revealed and *expects* punishment.

Understanding the *emotions, beliefs, goals,* and *sensations* of characters enables the spectator to subsume a set of complex physiological movements and actions under one description; the psychology of the characters provides a "conceptual glue" through which large amounts of simple actions and behaviors become coherent. Ascribing psychology to characters also creates a causality between different sections of the scene ("The Samurai chases the girl *because* he wants all the boys down in the village," "The Samurai is surprised *because* he believed that the girl is a boy," "The girl is frightened *because* she understands that her secret has been revealed"). Spectators do not ascribe to people or characters a random psychology. *Folk psychology* is a coherent system of a finite number of mental states and their causal relations, which – as we shall see – has been studied by cognitive anthropologists. This level of understanding lies very close to Smith's notion of *alignment*.

LEVEL 5. Characters can also be understood in terms of *personality traits*. Traits – in real life as well as in fictions – are enduring features of people, their stable predispositions to behave a certain way in a certain situation. Traits differ from moods and mental states of characters insofar as they are more permanent (Chatman, 1978:126). Traits change only with great time and effort. Trait terms are handy ways of summarizing our impression of a person, and we use such terms extensively in everyday life, for example, shy, optimistic, thoughtless, stupid, aggressive, curious, selfish, pragmatic, nervous, idealistic, or self-confident. *Trait* or *personality psychology* is a scientific version of this, which collects facts about a person and then abstracts those facts into different kinds of personality types (Brody, 1994). This analysis ends up in a series of trait scale characterizations, for example, *extroverted* (sociable, talkative), *agreeable* (sympathetic, kind), *conscientious* (organized, planning), *neurotic* (tense, anxious), *open to experience* (imaginative). *Types*, in the scientific sense of the word, are understood as bundles and constellations of traits and predispositions.

Psychological research has shown that people possess intersubjective criteria for attributing traits to other people and that such knowledge is cognitively real. Cantor and Mischel (1979), for instance, presented subjects with four equal-length descriptions of persons: a prototypical extrovert, a prototypical introvert, and two control cases in which neither the extrovert nor the introvert word was used. The subjects then had to do two things. First, they were to judge a person in each description according to six trait scales, one of which included the extroversion/introversion dimension. As expected, the prototypic descriptions were highly rated on the extroversion/introversion scale, whereas the control cases were not. Then the subjects were asked to indicate from a list of sixty-four randomly presented words which of these they remembered from the character descriptions. Words from the prototypic descriptions were better recalled than words from the nonprototypic control cases. In fact, often the subjects would indicate having recognized prototypic words (such as outgoing or spirited for the extrovert case and quiet and shy for the introvert case), although these were *not included* in the description. This tendency was much greater in the prototypic descriptions than in the nonprototypic, which suggests that a person schema of extroversion/introversion was used as a basis for the recall, supplying missing features for a subject when his or her memory failed.

Furthermore, because traits are fundamental parameters in forming impression of other people in the real world, there is reason to believe that spectators use similar strategies in comprehending narrative characters. In the reception of cinema, spectators probably bring a knowledge of traits and apply it to characters, for example, "The young Samurai is nervous, but tries to be authoritative; he is also open to new experiences." "This form of coherence around a character often lasts through many scenes. A change of a trait in the main character often marks the end of a story (see the subsection on Textual Theories of Characters). Traits can also be use to describe the difference between "flat" and "round" characters. For Chatman, "a flat character is endowed with a single trait – or very few" whereas "[r]ound characters, on the contrary, possess a variety of traits, some of them conflicting or even contradictory" (Chatman, 1978:132; see also Bal, 1985:81).

LEVEL 6. Finally, characters can be categorized and understood in terms of their *social role* (for references, see Chapter 1, the section on Psychology: Understanding and Dispositions). This relates not only to occupancy roles (doctors, waiters, police officers, scholars, chefs, farmers, and bus drivers) and family roles (mother, son, daughter, cousin, uncle, mistress), but also to social stereotypes (relating to ethnicity, gender, nationality, disability, etc.). Spectators are equipped with structured expectations and prejudices about such roles and stereotypes, and once a character has been categorized, these background assumptions provide the mental frameworks within which spectators can place the behavior of a given character. Evaluating and categorizing people (so-called *impression formation*) is a common process in everyday life and has been extensively studied in social psychology. We should expect that similar processes apply to our understanding of fictional characters (Gerrig & Allbritton, 1990; Tan, 1996:163ff). For instance, in understanding the Samurai character in *Seven Samurai*, the spectator may assume that the Samurai warriors are honorable men with fighting skills who can be hired for missions. Through such schematic expectations, the authoritative attitude of the young Samurai, as well as his efforts to force "the boy" back to drilling in the village, makes sense. In addition, stereotyped notions of Japanese men and women will guide our understanding of the actions performed. As stereotypes may shift between individuals and sociocultural groups, different spectra of reception may arise.

Social roles often link up with clear, visual body cues: skin color, hair color, body size, gender, clothing, age (Augoustinos & Walker, 1995:39ff). In the initial categorization of another person, this visuality or iconography acts to trigger social role expectations. With increased familiarity with a person, visual cues become less important.

Literary practices often develop their own character types that are based on everyday social roles. Stock characters, such as the hero, the villain, the princess, the mad scientist, the femme fatale, the Mafioso, the intellectual, the housewife, the detective, the hypocrite, the Bolshevik, are highly complex mixtures of the social schemas already described. Understanding these characters requires expectations of occupancy, family role, specific traits (e.g., good/bad, intelligent, naive, aggressive), as well as social stereotypes. The appearance and iconography of characters within film, opera, theater, and literature often play on and trigger such character models – see Smith's (1995:198) analysis of the iconography of types in Eisenstein's *Strike*. The stock characters of Commedia del'Arte might provide the clearest example, but all historical genres develop their own character galleries. *The Warning* (1914), for instance, is introduced with the intertitle "wilful, indolent country girl" (Thompson, 1985:178), which was a recurring type in early cinema (as well as in vaudeville and popular literature). This example plays on exactly the social schemas under discussion. The film here "assumes" the spectator's familiarity with this type of character. Returning to our Japanese film example, to many audiences all over the world, the Samurai warrior is a well-known character type, although details may shift between cultural and historical audiences.

Finally, characters may be understood in terms of the spectator's expectations about specific individuals whose characteristics may be known to the spectator. The spectator's assumptions about historical figures (Napoleon, Hitler, Karen Blixen) and cultural characters (the Lone Ranger, Santa Claus, Odysseus) influence the understanding of those characters in a given fiction. Bringing in extratextual expectations, the spectator can develop specific predictions about the behavior of that character (Bal, 1985:82; Tan, 1996:165). In addition, knowledge and assumptions about the actor may enrich the experience of character. Switching attention and understanding between actor and character can provide different interpretations and understandings of actions and behavior, in which the diegetic and the extradiegetic blend (deCordova, 1990). It is difficult to imagine how this level of understanding would be present in the scene from *Seven Samurai*, although some (historic, Japanese) spectators may be equipped with specific knowledge of the actors.

There is no reason to assume that levels 0–6 are exhaustive,[5] but they may be the most common ways in which spectators understand and make sense of characters and their behavior. It is important to stress that all of these are *cognitive* processes – not emotional – although they surely lay the foundation for allegiance and other more affective processes. In Smith's terms, these levels would make up recognition and alignment. As my analysis shows, it is problematic to draw clear boundaries between the two. Instead, it may be more productive to speak of different levels of cognition or understanding.

Processes at levels 0–6 strive to construct coherence for the events and occurrences in the film. There is no objective way to determine which one of these is the "correct" one, and different spectators, reception situations, and texts will promote some and downplay others. Perhaps the spectator "uses" the level of abstraction that is most appropriate – that is, the one that gives "maximum" coherence. Going to too high a level might oversimplify things by excluding or ignoring information in the text; going too low might prevent coherence and understanding of important relationships between textual units. This relates, of course, to the purpose of the viewing (e.g., Friday entertainment, scholarly investigations). Levels 0–6 are not mutually exclusive levels of understanding, but may occur in parallel during viewing. It is also likely that a given spectator shifts levels of understanding during the course of a film.

Each level also requires particular dispositions on the part of the spectator. This claim holds even on the lowest levels, which depend on cognitive–perceptual abilities (e.g., recognition of behavior and physical action). As discussed, some of this knowledge may be universal; some may be locally determined. Some may have its origin in specific media practices (such as the viewer's foreknowledge about fictional character types). For the most part, however, such knowledge probably comes from everyday sociocultural life. Spectators seem to use the same kind of impression-forming processes and social cognition on cinematic characters as they do on people in everyday lifes.

There is reason to believe that our comprehension of fictional characters takes place in the same way as our comprehension of people in the everyday world or in that of the psychological laboratory. (Tan, 1996:156)

In a variety of circumstances we are called upon to create mental representations for individuals for whom we have no direct evidence. We expect to find equivalent cognitive processes operating when we hear a story about a colleague's distant cousin, read a biography of a historical figure, or encounter a new character in a novel. (Gerrig & Allbritton, 1990:380)

Claiming that the spectator uses the same ability in real-life understanding as in the reception of cinema does not imply that real-life and fictional characters behave in the same way. Fictional characters of all sorts are usually more extreme and stereotyped than real persons, and often end up in situations that are rare in reality.[6] The claim that fictional characters are portrayed in a somewhat "unrealistic" manner, however, is different from the claim that spectators use everyday-life abilities in the reception process:

The distinctive aspects of a cognitive theory of literary character reside not in the special psychological structures, but in the operations of ordinary processes on extraordinary literary input. (Gerrig & Allbritton, 1990:389)

It is not the abilities and the processes of a spectator that are extraordinary, literary, narrative, fantastic, genre specific, and media specific: it is the diegetic world, presented by the narrative and constructed by the spectator. Although narrative films and literature are more "semiotically dense" than reality, the understanding of both fictional and real characters makes use of a similar set of dispositions and processes.

The levels of understanding also comprise a list with increasing abstraction. Traits, mental states, social stereotypes, situations, and simple actions are not literally *visible* or *observable* in the text or image, but constitute abstract inferences. There are, of course, cues and external manifestations (e.g., clothing, facial expression, physical behavior), but these are extensively expanded on by the knowledgeable spectator. Levels of coherence are thus foremost mental entities, existing not so much in the text as in the mind of the reader. There is nothing strange about this "mental space" of abstractions or going beyond what is "perceptually present": understanding real-life situations naturally involves the same processes.

Why Mental States?

We may now narrow down the focus further: In this chapter we deal with the spectator's understanding of cinematic characters' mental states (level 4), which we may call *character psychology*. First, the spectator knowledge contributing to this process is specified, and then the coherence established by means of this knowledge is described. We also look at some specific techniques used by cinema to trigger these processes.

Why mental states? First, mental states seem to be a quite common level of coherence in the reception of mainstream film and television for many spectators. Although spectators *in theory* can choose any level of coherence (levels 0–6), *in practice* character psychology may be the most common. It is therefore surprising that narratology and other theories of character have been so preoccupied with traits, more or less ignoring character psychology (or reducing it to a matter of intentions and desires). Few scholars have given systematic attention to character mental states.

Second, the understanding of mental states is interesting, as these states tend to fluctuate during the course of a narrative. In contrast to traits or types, mental states change rapidly from scene to scene, pushing the spectator to refresh continually the mental model of those states. If one believes that cinema in general, and mainstream cinema in particular, is a roller coaster that takes the spectator on a cognitive–emotive ride – and that it is because of the effectiveness of this ride most spectators consume films – then characters' mental states become much more prominent than traits.

"Subjective Access" versus "Mental Attribution"

In a sense, my interest here is similar to Smith's notion of *alignment*, that is, the ways in which spectators gain access to characters' minds, feelings, and subjectivity. Of course, this can be analyzed from the perspective of the text. Smith's notion of *spatiotemporal attachment* – with a narration restricting itself to the actions of one character – is a case in point. Within narratology, there have also been typologies of range and depth of subjective access and whether the narration is *restricted* to one character or *omnipresent* and "peering into" the minds of many characters (see Bordwell, 1985:57; Genette, 1980:189). For these scholars, subjective access to characters' minds is seen as something that the narration "apportions" or "distributes" to the spectator. In this approach, the force of the alignment process lies *inside* the text (in the form of a "narrator" or "narration"), and not with the spectator.

From a psychological and reception point of view, such textual emphasis gives only half the story in that the process of alignment – along with most processes of communication – also takes place in the spectator's mind. It is an *understanding*, thus involving mental processes. Smith seems to acknowledge this: "In a fuller sense, then, the concepts of recognition, alignment, and allegiance denote not just inert textual systems, but responses, neither solely in the text nor solely in the spectator" (Smith, 1995:82). However, he never really follows up the response theme.

In this chapter we investigate alignment processes from the perspective of spectator psychology and thus stand in a somewhat complementary position to use more textual approaches. An active spectator is not *apportioned* access to character psychology, but *achieves* it on the basis of cues in the text and expectations about how such psychology works (see Currie, 1995:235 for a similar stance). In our present investigation the emphasis shifts from *access* to mental states (in which the narration is the active force) to *mental attribution* of subjective states (in which the spectator is the active force).[7] Mental attribution emphasizes the fact that ascribing mental states to another person – whether that person is fictional or real – involves *inferential* activities by the observer. The notion of mental attribution refers to the ways in which the active spectator, striving for coherence, constantly uses everyday knowledge about mental states and their relations to understand character behavior. Mental attribution also stresses the constructive and the cognitively active role of the spectator's engagement in and reception of characters. Although both narratological and psychological approaches are legitimate paths of investigation, I think that the spectator's psychological activities have been pushed aside by mainstream narrative theory. It is this lack that I try to address here.

Mental Attribution in Everyday Life

Before we discuss mental attribution processes in cinema, let us look at mental attribution processes in everyday life. Mental states are notoriously firsthand experiences, and there is no *direct* access to the minds and moods of others. Still, most of us seem to have some understanding – or elaborated hypotheses – about the mental life of others. How, then, do we go about inferring people's mental states? What type of knowledge structures are involved?

Ability with Body and Gesture Cues
The most obvious answer to this question is simply that we observe other people's bodies, gestures, and behaviors. Proverbs such as "The face is the window to the soul" suggest a widespread assumption that face and

body are the primary gateways to the minds and emotions of other people. In Western cultures and languages – and possibly all over the world – the body is conceptualized as a "container," "inside" which mental life take place (Lakoff, 1987:383; see also Johnson, 1987:21). We also assume some connection between "the outer life" of bodies and gestures and "the inner life" of feelings, thoughts, beliefs, sensations, intentions, and desires. Mental states can be "externalized" on the surface of the body, through mimicry, gesture, or noise. We tend to experience this as a *causal* relation, which can be seen in the way we provide everyday explanations for such surface phenomena:

(1) PAUL CRIED *BECAUSE* HE WAS SAD.

The behavior is understood as an indication or effect of what is going on "inside" the person. In this way, we establish the "meaning" of a given expression by referring to a mental state of some type, which is assumed to be the cause of the expression (Currie, 1995:235ff). From social and personal experience, we presuppose that certain expressions are more likely to be caused by certain mental states. Certain expressions tend to be correlated with specific mental states. Such *body-cue ability* is a fundamental part of social life and has been studied intensively in nonverbal communication research. Some of this competence may be universal, whereas many aspects appear to be culturally determined (i.e., different cultures have different "body languages"). This variation is one of the reasons why it is impossible to give a complete "dictionary" of body expressions.

However, just to give some notion of how rich and diversified these expressions are, let me give a tentative list of "channels" used by humans.

Verbal content. One function of verbal language is that we can talk about (presumed) mental states and processes:

(2) I *WANT* ICE CREAM.
(3) I *FEEL* PAIN.
(4) I CAN *SEE* HIM.
(5) DO YOU *BELIEVE* IN GOD? *YES*.
(6) MY *EMOTIONS INFLUENCE MY THINKING*.

Verbal form. Prosodic features, such as pitch (level, range, and variability), loudness, and tempo of voice are informative indicators of emotions and mental states. (Think of *nervousness, excitement, anger, happiness* – for a review, see Pittam & Scherer, 1993.) At least in Western cultures, a soft volume is archetypically more connected with *boredom* than with *happiness* or *anger*. In addition, slips of the tongue may be cues to some mental states (e.g., *nervousness* or *excitement*).

The face is a prime passageway for emotions and other internal processes. First, there are what we ordinarily consider to be facial "expressions," that is contractions and expansions of facial muscles and parts: lips or mouth, eyebrows, eyes, nose or upper lip, cheek, and chin. Fear, surprise, happiness, disgust, anger, and sensations of pain are often connected to facial behavior of this sort (as are many other types of feeling).[8] Blushing and tears are examples of other, more temporal and extended, behaviors. Also, consider yawning and laughing. As we have seen, gaze behavior is a useful channel through which intentional states may be conveyed. In our culture, for instance, sadness, anxiety, boredom, and shame are archetypically connected with reduced mutual gazing (see Bull, 1984:44), whereas increased gazing might indicate happiness, fascination, or interest (see Rutter, 1984:56). Attention and perceptions are often indicated through turning heads, eyes, and ears to the objects perceived.

Bodily gestures and *movements* constitute, evidently, substantial conduits between the inner and the outer landscapes. Think of such cues as drumming one's fingers on table (perhaps indicating nervousness or impatience), heavy swallowing (anxiety, fear), bowing one's head (sadness), erect posture (pride, stubbornness), covering the mouth with the hand (disgust), covering the face with the hands and sobbing (sadness, sorrow), jumping and jerking (surprise), exhalation (relief), inhalation through the nose (perceiving smell, anger), heartbeat (fear, anxiety), advancing movements (aggression), or withdrawal movements (fear).

Personal-space behavior (see Chapter 3) is another pattern of behavior that may indicate mental states of another person. Having a person closing in on your personal space may indicate that the person has an *intention* of becoming more socially intimate. Conversely, if your interlocutor backs or tilts away, you might conclude that this person is afraid or desires to end the conversation.

Folk Psychology: Reasoning about Mental States

There is yet another aspect that makes it impossible to write a dictionary of body-gesture expressions: body cues take on different "meanings" – that is, they refer to different mental states – depending on context (Currie, 1995:235ff). Although some basic facial expressions may have strong direct correlations with mental states (for instance, smiling = happy), in most cases a host of other parameters influences the attribution process. For instance, crying may be a good indication of sadness, but it may also signify joy or other positive emotions; that is, few expressions have a definite meaning independent of situation (see Messaris, 1994:88). The body-cue ability never works alone, but the mental attribution process has to take into consideration contextual factors.

For instance, knowledge about the person under observation may influence the process (Planalp, DeFrancisco & Rutherford, 1996:143). Individuals may have idiosyncratic manners and mental predispositions of which the observer is aware. Spouses and close friends are most likely to have personal knowledge of each other's behavioral cues. Second, external cues can be manipulated. We not only display certain gestures, in most cases, we also *know* that we behave a certain way; we can thus simulate a facial expression without being in the corresponding mental state. This ability can be used for deception, lying, social dominance, or hiding mental states. In attributing mental states to others, "the attributor" must detect and consider the honesty of the displayer. Third, and most significantly, the *situation* around the expression may be just as important as the cue itself (DeConti & Dickerson, 1994; Planalp et al., 1996):

(7) – WHY IS ALBERT CRYING? – HE IS *HAPPY*. – HOW DO YOU KNOW? – WELL, HE
     WAS JUST REUNITED WITH HIS BOYFRIEND AFTER SIX MONTHS ABROAD.

Here, the understanding of Albert's mental state is influenced not only by his crying, but also by an understanding of the situation. If crying can mean many things, understanding the situation makes clear what Albert is experiencing. In fact, we may predict and attribute mental states even *without* information about the person's external reaction. Most people expect that reuniting with a partner after six months abroad would *prototypically* cause some form of happiness and opening a present may cause surprise and enjoyment. The point is that we possess an ability to *reason* about situations and the typical reactions or mental states connected to those, even in the absence of body and gesture behavior. By what kind of knowledge are we able to do so, and how is this knowledge represented and structured?

For one thing, the knowledge is not a "list" of concrete situations with corresponding emotions or states of mind. Although "opening a present" *often* generates (positive) surprise and joy, the same situation can evoke different sorts of emotions. For instance, if the birthday child *hoped* for a watch, but received only a pair of socks, then opening the present would cause sadness or disappointment (negative surprise). If Albert, during the last six months, had come to *hate* his partner, then emotions other than *happiness* would have been more likely during the reunion. This observation suggests that understanding another person's mental states is not directly tied to the concrete situation or event, but rather emerges out of understanding the relation to *other* mental states of that person: Does opening the present satisfy the hopes of the person (happiness versus disappointment)? In fact, mental terms seem to stand in certain relations to each other, irrespective of the concrete situation, enabling abstract reasoning of the following type: "*Disappointment* typically follows if an event fails to satisfy a *hope*." In this way, we have expectations on how mental terms are causally related, and these expectations are systematic.

Thus mental terms make up a system or network of interrelations. We refer to this systematic body of assumptions as *folk psychology* (FP).[9] This is a naive, common-sense "theory" about the constituents and common processes of the psyche and how these are related to actions and behavior. FP is reflected in consistencies in everyday discourse of mental states. By presenting examples of such informal talk and reasoning, we may demonstrate the underlying structure of FP.

FP is a schema for the individual to use in attributing mental states to others. FP is, however, also a cultural or social schema circulating in a given society. This is the reason why it has attracted such interest within the field of anthropology (see Holland & Quinn, 1987). It is crucial to stress the cultural aspect, as FP's structure and organization may vary between societies. Although it is fair to assume that all cultures have some form of FP and that some of the constituents and causal relations are universal, our knowledge about other FPs is indeed meager (Kirkpatrick & White, 1985; Lutz, 1985, 1987, 1996; Russell et al., 1995). For this reason, in this chapter we deal only with Western FP.

According to Western FP, the psyche consists of different types of mental states and processes. Research on an "everyday theory of mind" has studied conceptions of relations among perceptions, thinking, beliefs, feelings, desires, intentions, and sensations, and how we reason about these (Astington, Harris & Olson, 1988; Bartsch & Wellman, 1995; D'Andrade, 1987; Frye & Moore, 1991; Perner, Leekham & Wimmer, 1987; Wellman, 1990, 1995; White, 1995; Whiten, 1991). Emotion theories in general and appraisal theories in particular have focused on emotions and how we assess the causal value of events and actions preceding an emotion (DeConti & Dickerson, 1994; Harré & Parrott, 1996 – for an overview, see Omdahl, 1995; Harris, 1993; Orthony, Clore & Collins, 1988; Planalp et al., 1996; Roseman et al., 1996.) Although the schema of mind and the schema of emotions have been studied in separate research fields, we will see that they naturally overlap to a considerable degree.[10] However, we start with the folk theory of mind.

THE MIND AND ITS PARTS. By referring to mental states such as intentions, desires/goals, beliefs, perceptions, and feelings, we try to explain and predict external, observable actions. Knowledge about these terms and their interrelations is acquired during childhood and provides a schema for reasoning about them (Figure 40).

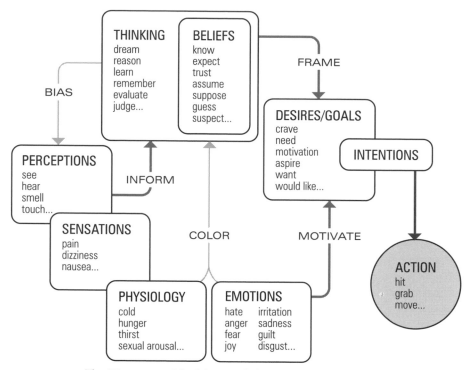

FIGURE 40. The Western model of the mind. (Diagram by Younghee Jung from an extended version of Wellman [1990] and D'Andrade [1987].)

Actions are Caused by Desires and Beliefs. At the core of Western FP lies the trinity of *action*, *beliefs*, and *desires/goals* (henceforth I use goals and desires interchangeably). Action is thought to be caused – and therefore explained by – the joint cooperation of beliefs and desires. In Western FP, people act because they *believe* that the action can accomplish a *goal* of some sort. It is this underlying logic that makes the following statements "explanationlike":

(8) – WHY DID ANNA GO TO THE SHOP? – SHE *WANTED* TO BUY SOME ICE CREAM AND *THOUGHT* THE STORE WAS OPEN.

(9) – WHY DID MARIA BEGIN FILM STUDIES? – SHE *LIKED* FILM STARS AND *IMAGINED* THAT SHE WOULD LEARN EVERYTHING ABOUT INGRID BERGMAN.

(10) – WHAT IS ANDERS DOING ON THE ROOF? – HE *SUSPECTS* THAT THERE IS SOMETHING WRONG WITH THE ANTENNA. HE *LOVES* WATCHING TELEVISION, YOU KNOW.

It is FP that enables us to make sense of these explanations. In all of these examples, the desire works as a motivation for the action whereas the belief frames and constrains the ways to achieve that goal. Goals and beliefs thus perform different functions in explanations of this sort.

Beliefs and goals are to be taken in quite a broad sense. They are both *about* something in the world (compare with what philosophers are prone to call propositional attitudes – see, e.g., Churchland, 1988:63ff). According to this model, we cannot just desire or believe in general: we must desire or believe in *something*.

When beliefs and goals are used to explain actions, one of them may be more important and informative than the other. Perhaps one of them can be inferred from the context and thus omitted from the explicit discourse:

(11) – WHAT WAS OLAV DOING IN THE ATTIC? – WELL, HE THOUGHT HIS KITTEN WAS THERE.

In example (11), Olav's goal (to find his kitten) is not mentioned explicitly, but may be inferred from the probability that kitten owners love their pets and want to find them if they are lost. To explain Olav's behavior, it is more informative to mention his belief than his goal. This everyday explanation is thus not *full*, but is still *acceptable* (Wellman, 1990:101).

Goals come in different strengths: desire, lust, will, craving, need, motivation, aspiration, want, preference, would like (in a tentative order of strength). Other goal terms express an evaluation of the prospects of the desire being fulfilled, for instance, wish, hope, or dream. Some goal terms imply some sort of duty or involuntary obligation, for example, ought or should. Goals can also be *appetitive* (wanting to obtain or keep something pleasurable) or *aversive* (wanting to get rid of or avoid something painful).

Goals can be very idiosyncratic and specific to a situation or an individual ("David wants to crush white shells from Northern India"), but there seem to be some sorts of goals that are more general. Schank and Abelson (1977:111ff) suggest such a (nonexhaustive) taxonomy of goals:

- *Satisfaction goals* are often tied to our biological makeup: hunger, sleep, sex, and the addictive consumption of drugs are examples. There is often a consumptive dimension to these goals, and they seem to recur with some frequency: If one has not eaten in while, one will soon be hungry again. Because goals of this type are basic to life preservation, blocking them often has serious consequences.
- *Enjoyment goals* are pursued for relaxation, for example, travel, entertainment, exercise, or competition. These goals are often weaker than satisfaction goals and generate only mild or moderate expressions of disappointment or boredom on failure.
- *Achievement goals* involve acquiring a cherished object or social position, for example, valuable property, power, a good job, a social

relationship, a skill, or complex or precious knowledge. These goals are realized over extended periods of time, often with a great amount of planning. Achievement goals and their realization often connect beginnings and endings of stories.

- *Preservation goals* include preserving or improving people's health, safety, well-being, possession, or property. Preservation goals often follow on the realization of achievement goals: When one has achieved something of value, one acts to keep it and preserve it from outside threats.
- *Crisis goals* are related to situations in which there are serious and immediate threats to valued persons or objects, for example, health emergencies, fires, storms, and falling down from heights. These goals are similar to preservation goals, but crisis goals arise more suddenly and usually have high priority.
- *Instrumental goals* realize a precondition of another goal, but do not in and of themselves produce satisfaction. The enjoyment goal of going to the movies and the preservation goal of protecting one's children suggest the instrumental goal of hiring a babysitter. These goals can be seen as subgoals of an overlapping goal and often require planning.

By taxonomies of this sort we can start to discuss why and how goals change over time and develop a hierarchy of importance between goals (Schank & Abelson, 1977:117). Crisis goals, for instance, take precedence over all other goals; enjoyment goals tend to be set only when other goals are of no great importance. According to FP, some goals are connected to all people (such as crisis goals and satisfaction goals), others to social types and stereotypes (e.g., doctors want to cure patients; waiters want to serve the customer; parents want to protect their children). Literary and media character types are often imbued with specific goals (e.g., dragons want to abduct the princess; detectives want to track down criminals).

Irrespective of type, goals tend to lie between intentions and emotions, often overlapping both (Figure 40). For instance, *hoping X* or *wishing X* can be seen as emotionally "colored" goals. The major difference between *goals* and *intentions* seems to be that the latter include some form of *decision* to take action. One may have a *desire* or *goal* to go to China but because practical circumstances one does not have the time, and thus does not have the *intention*. Even if a person does not have the *intention* to do X, that person can still have the *desire*. (*Daydreams* and *fantasies* provide perhaps the clearest examples of this.) In many cases, however, this distinction is not clear, mixing desires and intentions (D'Andrade, 1987:121).

When actions are explained within FP, the intention is seldom explicitly mentioned as a cause:

(12) – WHY DID JOHN GO TO CHINA? – BECAUSE HE *INTENDED* TO.

Example (12) sounds rather odd just because it is taken for granted that the action is preceded and caused by John's intention or decision to act. Because it is already assumed that action is caused by an intention, one never *explains* action in terms of intention. If the action is not preceded by an intention, it is not considered an action; rather it is just an *accident* or just *behavior*:

(13) – DID YOU DRIVE INTO THE GARAGE DOOR? – YES, I DID, BUT I DIDN'T *MEAN* TO. IT JUST HAPPENED.

Here the action is believed to be caused by circumstances and not by a decision to act. This part of FP is reflected in legal distinctions between deliberate and nondeliberate action, which is crucial in determining moral and legal responsibility (cf., for instance, the distinction between manslaughter and murder).

Like goals, *beliefs* are also attitudes toward some state of affairs in the world. Belief terms can express more or less certainty about this state of affairs: know, expect, trust, understand, believe, assume, suppose, presume, think, gather, guess, postulate, infer, conjecture, speculate, doubt, suspect, or question (in a tentative order of strength). As with goals, beliefs are often linked with social roles and stereotypes: We assume that certain groups of people embrace default beliefs about the world.

Goals and beliefs stand in intimate relationship to each other: Beliefs frame and solidify goals and enable people to formulate subgoals and instrumental goals. "Getting a babysitter," for instance, requires some everyday knowledge about the world and other people. Beliefs constrain (or enable) the formulation of goals, and can thus be seen as the crucial factor in *planning*.

The tight relationship among goals, beliefs, and action provides an inferential structure. We explain actions (retrospectively) in terms of goals and beliefs, but the causal connections may also reinforce predictions about impending action:

(14) – MARIA REALLY LIKES INGRID BERGMAN, AND SHE HAS HEARD THAT THE STUDY OF FILM STARS IS A BIG THING WITHIN FILM STUDIES. I THINK SHE WILL APPLY TO UNIVERSITY NEXT YEAR.

This kind of belief–desire reasoning is actually quite valuable in creating expectations about how people will act and react in specific situations, relative to assumed mental states.

Beliefs and Thinking are Informed by Perceptions. According to FP, *beliefs* are part of a more general process that might be called *thinking*. These processes include inferring, evaluating, judging, reasoning, learning, imagining, remembering, understanding, and daydreaming. Thinking might be considered as a process of handling different kinds of belief, comparing them, and negotiating contradictions. Thinking is, for instance, considered important when one is formulating and *planning* (complex) actions (D'Andrade, 1987:126; Wellman, 1990:112).

The major influence on thinking and beliefs is *perception*. Typically, seeing, hearing, smelling, reading, and touching inform us of what we believe and suspect about the states of the world. In everyday discourse, we explain and are motivated by beliefs with perceptions:

(15) – WHY DID OLAV *THINK* THE KITTEN WAS IN THE ATTIC (WHEN IN FACT IT WASN'T)? – WELL, HE *SAW* IT SNEAK IN THERE (AND FAILED TO *NOTICE* WHEN IT LEFT).

(16) – ARE YOU *SURE* HE WAS IN THERE? – YES, I COULD *HEAR* HIM BREATHING.

(17) – WHY DID YOU *BELIEVE* NORTHERN CHINA TO BE SO BEAUTIFUL? – A FRIEND *TOLD* ME ABOUT IT.

The flow from perception to belief is the dominant direction of causation (Figure 40). However, according to FP, belief is not considered to be just a reflex of perception. What one thinks and believes also affects and biases what one perceives. Proverbs such as "One sees only what one believes" reflect this part of the FP (cf. debates about observations of UFOs and angels).

Beliefs are formed not only through direct perception, but also through communication with other people. Moreover, because beliefs place powerful constraints on action, by manipulating other peoples' beliefs, we can affect their behavior. Concepts such as teaching and persuasion can be understood in this sense of deliberately trying to impose beliefs on another person and thereby indirectly changing that person's actions. In the case of lying or deceiving, a person intentionally tries to induce false beliefs in another person, often for selfish purposes. As we shall see, the landscape of thrillers and detective stories is filled with characters intentionally trying to impose false beliefs on other people in order to make them behave in a certain way.

Emotions and Physiology Motivate Desires. Whereas perception informs belief, emotion and physiology fuel goals (Figure 40):

(18) – DON'T YOU *WANT* YOUR STEAK? – NO, I AM *DISGUSTED* BY MEAT.

(19) – WHY DO YOU *NEED* TO BUY THIS BOOK, WHEN IT'S SO EXPENSIVE? – BECAUSE I *LIKE* INGRID BERGMAN.

(20) – DON'T YOU *WANT* TO SEE JACK? – NO, I'M *AFRAID* OF HIM.

According to the model, emotions such as disgust, hate, anger, fear, sadness, guilt, pride, amusement, joy, happiness, nervousness, and general liking are important motivators in forming goals. This is implicitly assumed in the preceding examples. In addition, physiological states such as cold, hunger, thirst, sexual arousal, and fatigue may also give rise to goals:

(21) – I *WANT* TO GET INSIDE BECAUSE I'M *COLD*.
(22) – COULD I *HAVE* A CHICKEN? – WHY? – BECAUSE I'M *HUNGRY*, THAT'S WHY!

Other close affinities to emotions and physiology are sensations of pain, dizziness, or nausea. Sensations are intermediates between perceptions and physiology. The boundaries among sensations, physiology, and emotions are important but imprecise, as is evident in the broad scope of the generic term feeling. Moreover, as already noted, the distinction between emotions and goals may often be undetermined.

EMOTIONS AND THEIR CAUSES. The basic assumption in appraisal theory (for an overview, see Omdahl, 1995) is that real emotions are preceded by some form of cognitive assessment or understanding of a given situation. The purpose there is to investigate what parameters of appraisals lead to certain emotions. What parameters of a situation do people take into consideration when they become angry or sad or feel guilty?

The goal in this investigation is somewhat different as emotions of the spectator are not the primary interest (see the preceding section). Rather, in this chapter I try to describe how the spectator *assesses* the mental states and emotions of *others*, in this case fictional characters.

The insights of appraisal theory may, however, serve our purposes, because the mechanisms for assessing situations for ourselves overlap the mechanisms for assessing them for other people. Being in a situation ourselves or observing someone else in a situation, we still use the same kind of appraisal criteria to describe the situation.

So then, how do we understand emotions in other people? As we have seen, emotions are considered to influence action and desire in significant ways. Nevertheless, how do emotions enter the inferential system in the first place? And how are emotions differentiated?

Emotions tend to be caused by events and actions outside the individual. Fear, surprise, hope, relief, joy, anger, and frustration are all reactions to something happening in the environment. However, as already noted, the same situation can evoke different sorts of emotion, depending on other mental states. If there are causal relations, these must be described on a more abstract level than that between emotions and concrete situations. To assess, for instance, happiness in a particular situation (e.g., "opening a present") we have to know the person's goals and expectations. It is the investigation of the systematics of these relations that is the primary research goal for appraisal theory. This can be said to constitute the emotional part of FP.

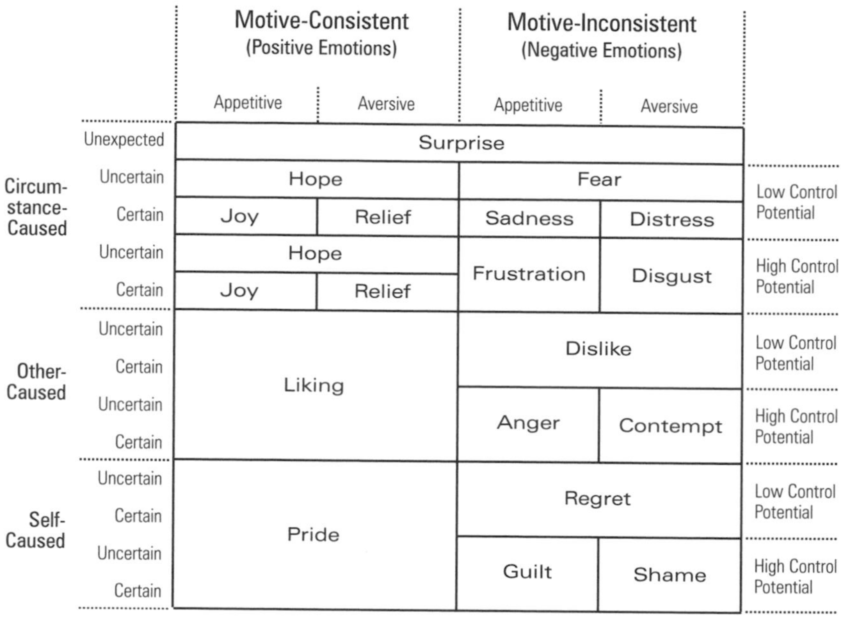

Circumstance-Caused / Other-Caused / Self-Caused		Motive-Consistent (Positive Emotions)		Motive-Inconsistent (Negative Emotions)		
		Appetitive	Aversive	Appetitive	Aversive	
	Unexpected	Surprise				
Circumstance-Caused	Uncertain	Hope		Fear		Low Control Potential
	Certain	Joy	Relief	Sadness	Distress	
	Uncertain	Hope		Frustration	Disgust	High Control Potential
	Certain	Joy	Relief			
Other-Caused	Uncertain	Liking		Dislike		Low Control Potential
	Certain					
	Uncertain			Anger	Contempt	High Control Potential
	Certain					
Self-Caused	Uncertain	Pride		Regret		Low Control Potential
	Certain					
	Uncertain			Guilt	Shame	High Control Potential
	Certain					

FIGURE 41. Model of appraisal parameters. (Based on Roseman et al. [1996].) Diagram by Younghee Jung.

As Omdahl's (1995) elegant overview shows, there are a number of appraisal theories. They are similar in many respects, but emphasize different parameters. I have chosen Roseman's model because its structure is simple and manageable and it appears to have good empirical support (e.g., Roseman et al., 1996). The basic idea behind Roseman's model is that people appraise six different parameters in a given situation in order to determine what type of emotion the other person is experiencing. Figure 41 shows these and corresponding emotions in schematic form. Let us discuss them individually.

Motive-Consistent versus Motive-Inconsistent Events. In most emotional systems around the world, there is a clear distinction between positive and negative emotions. In Western FP, emotions are considered positive when the situational event, action, or occurrence is consistent with the person's goals, desires, intentions, or motives and negative when inconsistent. Hope, joy, relief, liking, and pride are caused by events working toward a person's goals ([see example (7)], whereas fear, sadness, distress, frustration, anger, dislike, disappointment, and guilt tend to be evoked by events that are goal inconsistent. This seems to be in line with observations from researchers on the model of the mind (Wellman, 1990:106). Note here that *motive* in Roseman's theory is quite similar to the earlier definition of *goals*. In the following subsections, these terms are used interchangeably.

Expectedness versus Unexpectedness of the Event. Surprise holds a special position because, in contrast to all other emotions, it does not necessarily take positive or negative valence, but can be neither or both (Figure 41). The cardinal sign of *surprise* is that it is understood and appraised not in relation to the motives of the person, but to that person's *beliefs*. An event elicits surprise if it is incongruent with the beliefs and expectations of the person, the latter of which must be appraised on their own or inferred from context. If a person *expects* it to rain the next day, that person will not be *surprised* if it is raining cats and dogs when he pulls up the curtain. However, if the weather forecast promised sunshine, and the person has faith in weather predictions, then a rainy morning will typically generate *surprise*. The fact that surprise can be appraised independently of motives places it in between positive and negative emotions. If the forecast promised sunshine and the morning comes with heavy showers, you may be surprised, but because you are going to work inside all day anyway, it does not really matter. This, however, does not imply that surprises cannot be negatively or positively valenced (cf., e.g., happy surprises and disappointments).

Unexpectedness is closely related to novelty and unfamiliarity. Novel and unfamiliar events are mostly unexpected, but not necessarily so. A person might *expect* novel things to happen in a particular situation (e.g., traveling in other countries), and then the level of surprise might be limited. It would seem that only when novel and unfamiliar events are unexpected will they produce surprise.

Circumstance-Caused versus Other-Caused or Self-Caused Events. In appraising a situation and attributing emotion to a character in that situation, the agent causing the situation to emerge seems to be critical. Hope, surprise, relief, sadness, and frustration are emotions emerging out of situations and events that are due to "circumstances" and for which no particular person is responsible. For instance, if Jackie's car breaks down every other month for no particular reason, she will typically be *frustrated*. In contrast, anger, contempt, or general liking are connected to intentional acts by other people. If Jackie found out that the breakdowns were due to sabotage by a mean neighbor, then her *frustration* might well become *anger*. Furthermore, Jackie herself could be responsible for the event eliciting the emotion. Such cases will generate emotions such as pride (positive), guilt, shame, and regret (negative). To continue our hypothetical case, if the breakdown of the car was due to Jackie's deliberate carelessness in driving, she may experience some form of *regret*.

The same case can be made about emotions on the positive side of the schema, e.g., joy (circumstance caused), liking (caused by another person), and pride (self-caused) – see Figure 41.

Believed Certainty versus Uncertainty of the Event. Another important parameter is whether the person *believes* the event to be certain. The believed *probability* of an upcoming event explains the difference between joy and relief versus hope. If an event is consistent with a person's desires and is believed to have happened with partial or complete certainty, then joy and relief are inferred. On the other hand, if the person has reasons to doubt whether the event actually took place or will take place, then hope will typically follow. The same distinction can be made for events that contradict a person's desires: *Sadness* and *distress* depend on certainty, *fear* depends on uncertainty.

Often, of course, the negative and the positive emotions go hand in hand. If one is gliding down the roof of a cathedral, one *fears* a fall. At the same time, however, one also *hopes* to be stopped by a gargoyle. As we will see, dramatic situations – in which the outcome is uncertain – tend to present both (potentially) positive and negative emotions, which make the situations strong and distinct.

Some emotions are immune to the certainty/uncertainty distinction. In the case of anger, for instance, it does not really matter if one knows that the event actually took place or if one only has reason to believe that it happened (or will happen) – all other things being equal. The same holds for contempt, dislike, and other emotions (see Figure 41).

Appetitive versus Aversive. As mentioned, goals seem to have two basic characteristics (see the subsection on The Mind and Its Parts). On the one hand, a person may want to obtain or keep something pleasurable (*appetitive*) and, on the other hand, get rid of or avoid something painful (*aversive*). This distinction clarifies the difference between *joy* and *relief.* If an event is certain and consistent with a person's desire and if this desire is appetitive, then the event will elicit joy (success in obtaining something pleasurable). In the aversive case, relief will be evoked (success in avoiding something nonpleasurable).

The same distinction can be made for the negative emotions of *sadness* versus *frustration* and *distress* versus *disgust.* If an event is inconsistent with the desire and the person *failed* to obtain or keep something plea-surable, then sadness or frustration will follow. However, if the person failed to avoid something nonpleasurable, then distress or disgust might be evoked. There seems to be a similar distinction between anger and contempt, as well as between guilt and shame (in the other-caused and self-caused spectra). On both the positive and the negative sides of the schema, the distinction between appetitive and aversive motives is im-portant for several emotions, although not for all.

High versus Low Control Potential. Among negative emotions, it also makes a difference whether a person believes that he or she can change the course of events, and restore or undo an event (Figure 41). If a person has high control potential in a situation, then a motive-inconsistent event will trigger, for instance, frustration/disgust rather than sadness/distress. In the former case, the person thinks that he or she could act to avoid or even undo the unpleasantness of the situation. Sadness and distress, on the other hand, imply helplessness or surrender. The way a person apprehends his or her own power and potential will affect the emotion elicited. One subject in the study of Roseman et al. (1996) reported on his emotions in an exam situation. On receiving the results, he felt frustrated rather than sad because he knew that he could have passed if only he had made some effort. It was precisely because his control over the outcome was high that the results made him feel frustrated rather than sad.

Often, as Roseman et al. note, high control is connected to perceived legitimacy or "moral power." For instance, if a person thinks an other-caused event is not only motive inconsistent, but also morally wrong, then anger is more likely to follow than just general dislike, or frustration rather than sadness. The same seems to apply to regret and guilt/shame. One may *regret* choosing the wrong career, but one does not feel *guilty* about it (unless crime is the chosen line of business). Guilt and regret also appear to differ in whether an event harms other people or just oneself.

This is not a complete list of either appraisal parameters or emotions (e.g., think of jealousy, envy, empathy, admiration, melancholy). Furthermore, emotions seldom come in the pure states as discussed here, but often blend and mix (Omdahl, 1995:17). Nevertheless, the six dimensions presented provide a reasonable basis for appraising most emotions within Western FP.

DEEP PSYCHOLOGY. As Freudian, Jungian, and other deep psychological frameworks become more popular in accounts of the psyche, these tenets may be incorporated into the FP, merging with models of mind and emotions. Since the beginning of the twentieth century, Western FP has been under the influence of these deep models, and they are occasionally referred to in everyday explanations and understandings of other people. In relation to the models presented here, however, deep psychology occupies a marginal position in everyday thinking and is primarily used in medical, scholarly, and scientific contexts. Therefore I do not believe that they are primary parts of FP. Hence they are not the focus of this chapter.

Additional Remarks

The model of mind and the model of emotions overlap to a considerable degree. Appraised emotions (Figure 41) operate within the general architecture of the model of the mind, motivating goals (Figure 40). Goals and beliefs play important roles when the identity of a given emotion is to be appraised. Although understandings of mind and emotion have been studied in separate fields of inquiry, they merge in everyday mental attribution. In combination, they constitute the complex but coherent system of relations between mental states that is referred to as folk psychology. These relations enable inference making and reasoning about the psyche and its parts. In combination with body-cue ability, FP thus constitutes a powerful mental tool for attributing mental states to another person.

Emerging from this discussion is a FP that is not merely discrete and isolated bits of folk wisdom or common sense. Rather it is an organized and structured body of understanding, underpinning much of everyday discourse and reasoning about other people and their behavior. As with many other types of schema, FP contains elements causally connected in a systematic way. These connections are not "true" or certain, but probable and prototypical, providing an idealized or simplified model of the psyche. These connections are causal enough to enable reasoning, but loose enough to provide dynamics and adaptation in the attribution process.

The causal network provides possibilities for everyday reasonings of many types. If we know that a man *wants* a book, we can assume that he will be *happy* when given one, and possibly express it by a smile or some other body response (predictive inference). If we see a man get a book and then smile, we can infer that he is not only *happy* about the book, but also that he *wanted* it in the first place (retrospective inference). If we know that the man *wanted* the book very badly and starts to cry, we can infer that the body cue in fact is expressing *happiness* rather than *sadness* (disambiguating or clarifying the inference). In these ways, the causal structure of FP makes it possible to enrich the situation at hand and the displayed behavior, thus enabling and supporting *cognitive creativity* in understanding other people's behavior. This form of constructive reasoning is extremely common in everyday life and – as I shall argue – in understanding the discourse of cinema.

FOLK PSYCHOLOGY IS A CULTURAL UNDERSTANDING. It must be emphasized that FP is an everyday cultural *conception* of human behavior and psychological processes; it should not to be confused with scientific theories about mental states in psychology, neuroscience, or philosophy. It is a common-sense *folk theory* or a *cultural model* (see the first section of Chapter 1). People and cultures use and have used such naive theories in many areas of everyday life, for instance, physics, nature, psychology, energy, morality, causality, time, and space (for numerous examples, see Holland & Quinn, 1987; Lakoff & Johnson, 1999). The early Greeks had a folk theory about the elements (Earth, Water, Air, and Fire). These were made up of cold versus hot and dry versus wet binaries (Earth = cold and dry, Water = cold and wet, Air = hot and wet, Fire = hot and dry). This system of interrelationships can be called a folk theory, as it constituted a basic model of explanation for the Greeks (and for many other Europeans until the sixteenth century).

The FP just described is a folk theory for the same reasons: It is a widespread and popular frame of reference, and it is complex and causally structured enough to generate explanations of behavior and action. Insofar as it is a cultural understanding, it also has a history, and we can sketch its development. For instance, there seems to have been a surge of interest in the psyche and "soul" in Greek culture (see, e.g., Bremmer, 1983; Snell, 1953). By analyzing documents of the ancient world and the Middle Ages, Olson and Astington (1990) showed how the English language during 1150–1350 started to develop a much richer and nuanced set of terms to describe speech acts and mental states. Olson and Astington focus on only the theory of mind, but their method could be applied to a study of overall Western FP, including emotions.

Folk theories are different from scientific theories. A dedicated behaviorist professor, denying any *scientific* explanatory value in referring to mental states, will still use these mental terms in *everyday* explanations of human behavior. By describing a folk theory such as FP, I make no claims regarding mental states' *real* nature or how they *actually* relate and affect behavior. Rather, the preceding discussion describes how Western people make sense of behavioral phenomena in everyday situations. Thus the preceding description of FP makes no psychological claims, only anthropological.

Of course, scientific theories have always been heavily influenced by folk theories. The analysis of Lakoff and Johnson (1999) of the use of folk theories and everyday metaphors in philosophy, physics, and (first-generation) cognitive science is an impressive case in point. Science and the humanities, in discussing abstract and complex matters, often draw on cultural forms of thinking and understanding in order to be understood:

When philosophers construct their theories of being, knowledge, mind, and morality, they employ the very same conceptual resources and the same basic conceptual system shared by ordinary people in their culture. Philosophical theories may refine and transform some of the basic concepts, making the ideas consistent, seeing new connections and drawing novel implications, but they work with the conceptual material available to them within their particular historical context. (Lakoff & Johnson, 1999:338)

What is said about philosophy here also applies to psychology and other sciences, as well as to the humanities.[11] FP as a *cultural understanding*, has influenced the way institutionalized psychology postulates mental states, their interrelationships, and their causal relations to behavior. Then again, scientific theories and folk theories are different in scope and can be studied separately.

Furthermore, there is no intended derogation in calling these folk theories. They can be just as complex as scientific theories, often with a strong inferential structure, as in the case of FP. They are used for explaining and making sense of phenomena around us, albeit situated in everyday life rather than with in a context of scientific pursuit.

PEOPLE WITH DIFFERENT FOLK PSYCHOLOGIES. Like most schemas and cultural models, FP is automatized, transparent, habituated, and "natural" to the extent that one no longer thinks about it when applying it (see the first section of Chapter 1). However, when "the apparently natural" is contrasted with something "other," the model or habit becomes defamiliarized or alienated (Smith, 1995:50). This "other" might be another culture or individuals who have different notions of FP or seem to lack such a schema.

Children are interesting in this regard. In a wide range of studies in developmental psychology, the first linguistic use of intentional words such as *know*, *mean*, *feel*, and *see* has been studied. One of the most discussed and replicated tests of belief–desire reasoning has been the *false-belief test* (Astington et al., 1988; Perner et al., 1987; Wellman, 1990, 1995; Whiten, 1991). In a typical version of this test, the experimenter sits in front of the child. The child is shown a scenario involving two dolls, Sally and Anne. The first doll, Sally, hides her favorite marble in a box, and then goes away for a walk. While she is away, Anne transfers Sally's marble from the box to a bag and hides it there. Sally returns home wanting her marble. The child is asked some control questions to make sure that he or she has followed the events. Then the child is asked, "Where will Sally look for the marble?" If the child is able to understand that Sally *believes* the marble is still in the box (and not in the bag), then the infant should point at the box.

The interesting thing about these experiments is that three-year-old toddlers typically do not point to the box (where Sally *believes* the marble to be), but rather to the bag (where the marble *actually is*). Children four years old and older do markedly better on these tests. These results are taken to support the hypothesis that the child lacks a basic conception of beliefs. This seems to involve a failure to understand that beliefs about a situation are separate from the situation itself, and that these beliefs may be more or less truthful. Alternatively, the child fails to understand that beliefs in fact influence and constrain (Sally's) action. Even though the scientific interpretations of the results are still debated, they display a striking gap between adults' and children's conceptions of beliefs and actions.

Another group of people who seem to have impaired conceptions of the mind of others are autistic people (Baron-Cohen, 1991a; Leslie, 1991). Autism is a complex phenomenon, and diagnoses are based on a wide range of symptoms, but many autistic children appear to have severe difficulties in attributing mental states to other people. Autistic children accomplish the false-belief test, for instance, at a much later age than do normal children (or even mentally disabled children). Baron-Cohen (1991b) found that autistic children showed severe deficits in appraisal of emotions, particularly those emotions related to beliefs. In addition, Baron-Cohen (1991a) investigated autistic children's inability to infer beliefs from perceptions and gazing behavior. Autistic children were just as skilled in deictic gaze (see Chapter 2) behavior as normal children, but they failed to attribute an *interest* to the gazer and to understand that the gazing could in fact influence his beliefs and knowledge. They failed to see the mental and attentional implications of the perceptual act. The fundamental problem with beliefs, as displayed throughout these studies, has led some researchers to propose that autistic children have a *desire* FP only, failing to understand the ways in which beliefs constrain and narrow down actions and behavior.

RELATIVISM VERSUS UNIVERSALITY. Is the FP described here universal, or is it only the Western conception of psyche, and, as such, incompatible with other cultural FPs? Even though evidence is scarce, probably all cultures share some form of universal core or structure. This core, however, is probably extended and expanded on by cultural context. What this core might consist of can at this time only be a subject for speculation. A study by Avis and Harris (1991) may, however, provide some hints. They studied children of a pygmy group in southeast Cameroon with the false-belief test described in the preceding subsection. The subjects, a group of 5-year-old children and a group of 3-year-old children, were invited to move a desirable food item from its container to a hiding place and then predict whether an adult would approach the empty container. Mirroring the results of similar Western studies, the older children managed to predict the adult's behavior and to predict that the adult would feel *happy* rather than *sad before* lifting the cover of the container and *sad* rather than *happy after* lifting the cover. Only a minority of the younger children were successful on all parameters. These results may be taken as support for the claim that some parts of FP, such as belief–desire reasoning and some simple positive–negative emotion appraisal, are universally acquired. Then again, it would take a much more systematic effort to verify this. The point of this discussion, however, is that the dispute of relativism–universality in a given domain is not a question for armchair philosophizing or speculation: It is an empirical matter (see Lakoff & Johnson, 1999).

It is also worth noting that the question of universality and relativism is overlapping *but different* from the question of biological or cultural origin of FP (see Chapter 2, the subsection on Universality and the Question of Origin). Whereas the relativism–universality issue can be resolved by empirical investigation, the influence of *nature* versus *nurture* in the shaping of FP is virtually impossible to determine, at least with the scientific knowledge of today. As suggested by Bordwell (1996a), it might be more fruitful to explain the presence of a given phenomenon by looking at its *function*. Why do we try to attribute mental states to other people and creatures, and why have cultures around the globe developed powerful sociocognitive structures to guide individuals in this endeavor?

One part of the answer is that mental attributions *explain* and *make sense* of complex external behavior. Explaining something in everyday discourse involves attributing a cause–effect structure to different phenomena, and the complex network of causal relations between mental states supports exactly this. By understanding an event or situation on a mental level, FP is able to impose a cause–effect architecture on human behavior, making it meaningful or coherent.

In this way, attributing mental states to a given set of behaviors is cognitively *economical* because the mind does not have to pay attention to all details of the behavior. Subsuming a complex set of behaviors under a mental state (e.g., "being angry") simplifies the situation and makes it cognitively manageable. Thus mental attribution works in the same ways as general cognition, categorization, and pattern recognition do, in the sense that it is occupied with abstraction processes, bringing coherence and meaning to a given set of chaotic stimuli (see the first section of Chapter 1). Categorizing a complex set of situational factors, behaviors, and body cues such as "Jackie is angry" is working with the same principle of economy and abstraction as when the mind categorizes an extremely complex retinal pattern of colors, patches, lines, shapes, and movements as "a tree."

ANTHROPOMORPHISM: INTENTIONAL STANCE AND PSYCHOLOGICAL CAUSALITY. This sense-making and economical function also manifests itself in the way FP is attributed to nonhuman or even nonliving entities. Anthropomorphism and animism are processes in which the FP framework is attributed to animals, objects, and organizations:

(23) THE UNIVERSITY *THINKS* THIS IS A GOOD IDEA, AND *WANTS* US TO GO AHEAD.
(24) THE COMPUTER DOESN'T *WANT* YOU TO DO THAT.
(25) THAT BIRD LOOKS VERY *SAD* AND *LONELY*.[12]

In a now-classic experiment, Heider and Simmel (1944) showed subjects a film with 2D black triangles and squares moving around on a white surface. When asked to describe what happened in the film, many subjects tended to use FP terms and reasoning to interpret (and thereby perhaps better remember?) the events in the film. For instance, the large triangle was described as *chasing* and then *fighting* the smaller one, while the small triangle was *trying to get away*. The same type of "animistic" stance has been found in people's interaction with computers, which people often conceptualize and make sense of by invoking mental state terms and sociopsychological processes (Persson, Laaksolahti, & Lönnqvist, 2001; Reeves & Nass, 1996).

These studies suggest that FP reasoning has a meaning-creating function in encounters with new, complex, and difficult "behavior situations," regardless of whether these are of a human nature. FP reasoning and mental attribution bring new and unknown phenomena into a known context within which the phenomena can be understood. In this sense, anthropomorphism and FP reasoning work very much like metaphoric understanding: they map a known domain of knowledge (source domain) onto an unknown or abstract domain (target domain), and thus enable us to form a structured understanding of the abstract thing (Lakoff & Johnson, 1980, 1999). Universities are indeed abstract organizations, but by thinking of them in terms of intentions and mental states, we make this abstract domain understandable and graspable.[13]

Applying FP reasoning and mental attribution explanations to phenomena in the world – human or not – is thus a "stance" or an "attitude" of the observer. This *psychological, anthropomorphic, animistic,* or *human* perspective on reality differs greatly from a *physical* or a *mechanistic* stance, which does not deal with the relationship between mental states and behavior, but only with behavior and action. Both stances, I believe, are folk theory stances, and both deal with explanation and causality. Whereas anthropomorphism deals with *psychological* causality, the mechanistic explanations of the natural sciences deal exclusively with *physical* causality. The latter deal with causality between billiard balls, falling apples, and inclined planes, whereas the former uses causality between FP terms and sees phenomena as psychological entities inhabiting a world with other likewise complex psychological entities. A number of scholars in different fields have acknowledged these two stances or attitudes toward reality and causality and have argued that they involve completely different sets of terms and standards of causality. Bruner (1986:14) argues that human thought can be divided into *paradigmatic* and *narrative* modes, of which the former is engaged in "the landscape of action" and the latter "is the landscape of consciousness: what those involved in the action know, think, or feel, or do not know, think or feel." In analytical philosophy, Dennett (1987) makes a fundamental distinction between *the physical* and *the intentional stance*, of which the latter considerably overlaps my notion of mental attribution:

> This sort of interpretation calls for us to adopt what I call the *intentional stance* . . . : we must treat the noise-emitter as an agent, indeed a rational agent, who harbors beliefs and desires and other mental states that exhibit *intentionality* or "aboutness," and whose actions can be explained (or predicted) on the basis of the content of these states. (Dennett, 1991a:76)

> Here is how it works: first you decide to treat the object whose behavior is to be predicted as a rational agent; then you figure out what beliefs that agent ought to have, given its place in the world and its purpose. Then you figure out what desires it ought to have, on the same considerations, and finally you predict that this rational agent will act to further its goals in the light of its beliefs. (Dennett, 1991b:341)

The physical stance, on the other hand, involves no such intentionality:

> Consider the physical strategy, or physical stance: if you want to predict the behavior of a system, determine its physical constitution (perhaps all the way down to the micro-physical level) and the physical nature of the impingements upon it, and use your knowledge of the laws of physics to predict the outcome for any input. This is the grand and impractical strategy of Laplace for predicting the entire future of everything in the universe, but it has more modest, local, actually usable versions. The chemist or physicist in the laboratory can use this strategy to predict the behavior of exotic materials, but equally the cook in the kitchen can predict the effect of leaving the pot on the burner too long. (Dennett, 1991b:340ff)

In investigating how causal conceptions arise in children, developmental psychology also seems to acknowledge this distinction:

> Events can be related in many different ways. Perhaps the most important to our understanding of the world and for deciding on how to interact with the world are causal relations. Knowledge of causal relations between physical events, for example between something falling and it breaking, allows us to bring about desirable events and prevent undesirable ones. Likewise, knowledge of causal relations between people's motivations and their actions, for example, between a person's mood and his or her behavior, allows us to successfully negotiate our social world. (van den Broek, 1997:323)

In the anthropomorphic mode, we use the intentional stance vis-à-vis phenomena that are usually not treated as agents. However, there are also cases in which the physical stance seems to be applied to a sociopsychological world. Mention has already been made of autistic children, who appear to have a *behavioral* notion of humans and their actions. (Just like physical objects, humans are conceived of as only more or less unpredictable patterns of behavior without mental activities.) In Gómez's (1991) laboratory studies of gorillas, the same basic difference of attitude could be observed. Here, some desirable food item was stored behind a door, but the hatch was placed too high for the animal to manipulate by itself. Instead, one of the human experimenters – who could easily reach the hatch – was placed in the room. All gorillas tried to use the experimenter to reach the hatch, but they did so in different fashions. The young gorillas tried to *push* the human toward the door, without ever having eye contact. The elder animals, on the other hand, displayed extensive eye contact with the experimenter (plus deictic-gaze behavior). These animals tried to *lead* him towards the door, placing his hand on the knob of the door. The young animals treated the experimenter as any other physical object – which could be pushed to the door and then perhaps be climbed upon. The elder gorillas seemed to have developed some intentional stance and tried to *convince* the experimenter to *understand* the animal's desire. This example shows the fundamental difference between physical and intentional stance and the different forms of causality they imply. In our discussion of understanding narrative causality, we will come back to this distinction.

INSTRUMENTAL VALUE OF FOLK PSYCHOLOGY. Another reason why FP and mental attribution have arisen and persisted in different cultures is that FP's coherent set of relations enables not only inference making in general, but *predictive* inferences in particular. By attributing desires, beliefs, and emotions to a person, it is possible to anticipate what that person will do next – see example (14). These predictions are surely often misguided, but seem to present a better probability than the more physical stance displayed by the gorillas or no attributions at all. Dennett (1991b) argues that intentional stance explanations of complex behavior and systems (such as machines, computers, humans, societies) are often more instrumental and useful than physical stance explanations. In most everyday situations, descending to the concreteness of human anatomy is a less effective way to describe human behavior then trying to attribute FP mental states. In humans' complex sociopsychological environment, the abstract and primitive architecture of FP and the intentional stance may have had a clear evolutionary value. This *predictive value* of mental attribution and FP might be the reason why possibly all human cultures – and those of some primates – have developed some type of it (Byrne, 1995:Chap. 8; Byrne & Whiten, 1988; Whiten & Byrne, 1997; see also Graesser et al., 1994:372).

FOLK PSYCHOLOGY = NORMALITY. FP also appears to be the yardstick by which we measure normality. FP is considered to be the "normal" way a person functions psychologically. If the schema does not seem to apply, we take the person to be "other" in some sense. Children or "foreigners" may have other forms of FP, and mental attribution must take that into account. Individuals are judged to be mentally ill if they substantially deviate from FP norms: a "mean" person seems to lack emotions of *regret/guilt* and *shame*; a "depressed" person seem to be obsessed with *regret/guilt* and *shame*. "Psychopaths" are considered to be *irrational* with dysfunctional FP, and their behavior and mental life are therefore difficult to understand and predict. (In these cases we may use deep psychology frameworks instead.) Other groups of people may display minor and specific dysfunctions. Blind and deaf people, for instance, lack some channels from *perception* to *beliefs*, which often, however, can be compensated for by other sensory flows. Because FPs, like all schemas, act as prototypes, they give rise to such "abnormality effects." Because the nature of the FP is basic, such conceptions of "otherness" (as well as ethical judgments of it) are often hard to alter. This may hold true for FPs in all cultures.

Mental Attribution Processes in Reception of Cinema

Characters do not have "lives"; we endow them with "personality" only to the extent that personality is a structure familiar to us in life and art. To deny that seems to deny an absolutely fundamental aesthetic experience. Even fantastic narratives require inferences, guesses, and expectations according to one's sense of what normal persons are like. . . . I am arguing simply that the character-interpretative behavior of audiences is structured. (Chatman, 1978:138)

If we assume that FP is a fundamental framework within which to explain and make sense of other people in daily life, there is little reason to doubt that these mental attribution abilities are employed by spectators in encountering cinematic characters. The basic assumption in the following discussion is that characters' appearances in cinema trigger similar abilities and mental attribution processes as do live performances and live people.

Some scholars seemingly take issue with these assumptions. Kristin Thompson, for instance, makes the following claim:

Since characters are not people, we do not necessarily judge them by the standards of everyday behavior and psychology. Rather, as all devices and collections of devices, characters must be analyzed in terms of their functions in the work as a whole. Some characters may be fairly neutral, existing primarily to hold together a series of picaresque imbedded narratives. . . . Even in a more unified, psychologically oriented narrative we can find various functions of characters: providing information, providing the means for withholding information, creating parallels, embodying shapes and colors that participate in shot compositions, moving about to motivate tracking shots, and any number of others. (Thompson, 1988:40ff)

On one level Thompson is right: Cinematic characters need not *necessarily* be understood in terms of common-sense theories of behavior and psyche. As discussed, characters can be understood, described, and interpreted on many different levels. The narrational and the textual functions that characters perform in a given film (described in Thompson's passage) constitute one of these levels, although it was not explicitly mentioned. More important, however, many types of spectator probably *do* judge characters within their everyday frameworks of understanding (such as FP). For the type of spectator and the type of reception situation focused on in this study (some form of "everyday consumption" of visual media) the spectator hardly notices, consciously or unconsciously, the ways in which characters' movements motivate tracking shots and shapes and colors participate in shot compositions. If Thompson had been keener on defining and specifying the reference of "we" on the first line of the preceding extract, the apparent discrepancies between our positions might have evaporated. Thompson aims at providing cinema scholars with methods with which to analyze and evaluate films; my purpose is to describe general psychological processes of understanding in everyday cinema spectators. Mental attribution processes are not random or idiosyncratic, but highly and intersubjectively *structured* by the common FP shared by most spectators in a given cultural setting. Applying the structure of FP to the behaviors and actions of characters in a film is part of the general striving for coherence and sense making in discourse understanding. "The comprehension of characters is a major strategy for lending coherence to the film text" (Tan, 1996:159). For instance, by attributing *surprise* to the Samurai in Figure 39, the spectator creates coherence for many movements, behavior, and events in the scene. Mental attributions make the diegetic situation – and thus the discourse – understandable. In striving for textual meaning, the spectator will in FP find a strong and important mental tool. Below I try to show how this system of interrelatedness might be applied by spectators in order to understand film sequences.

Some General Principles

On the basis of the preceding presentation of mental attribution, what can be said about these processes in cinema? For one thing – as will recur in the following discussion – mental attribution of fictional characters is not solely a question of face and body-cue ability and the ways in which the film gives access to acting faces and bodies. As noted in the preceding section, face and body cues do provide valuable information in the attribution process, but only when they are placed within a context of mental states.

The ways in which the spectators' naive theories about psychology contribute to understanding characters have often been ignored by cinema scholars. Textually oriented theories usually remain content with observing that the cinematic medium is "deemed" to give us only the external appearances of characters:

The visible body is our only evidence for the invisible mind. . . . The necessity of films is to deal with exteriors, in objects and people; to separate and objectify, and pause in wonder at what is hidden. (Braudy, 1976:184f)

This is why human expressivity can be so striking in the cinema; the cinema does not give us people's thoughts, as the novel has long done; instead, it gives us their behavior, their special way of being in the world, their manner of dealing with things and with each other. (Merleau-Ponty, 1966:104[14])

From a textual point of view, this claim is of course true: The mental lives of other people are not "directly observable." This is true in staged situations and scenes as well as in real situations in everyday life. However, if we look at this situation from the perspective of reception and understanding, the visible body is *not* "our only evidence." The complex network of FP provides a strong inferential structure, greatly supporting the spectator in inferring mental states of characters. The only "textual evidence," of course, is the external appearance of the actors. This evidence, however, is greatly expanded on by FP reasoning. FP enables the spectator to go beyond the explicit information given in a text. Mental attribution not only decodes facial and bodily expressions, but also assumes underlying mental states and processes that are correlated in structured ways. This process disambiguates and makes coherent the external appearances of the actors. If we assume that the understanding of mental states predominantly depends on significant background knowledge and cognition on the part of the spectator, it is not surprising that cinema scholars, who tend to avoid spectator cognition, to a large extent have refused to describe the ways in which character psychology emerges in the reception process. Carroll (1988:210ff), for instance, sees the step from the text's "depiction of human action" to the spectator's understanding of characters' intentions, beliefs, and desires as unproblematic and naturally given. It is this gap that I will try to fill in in the following paragraphs.

There are additional "requirements" before mental attribution processes can start to operate. A pivotal one is that the spectator has to *recognize* a given figure in the text as a specific character, a process in which several body appearances in different shots, scenes, and parts of a film are understood as being one and the same *person* (see Smith, 1995). In literature, such continuity is often achieved through proper names. In cinema, it has to be inferred by the spectator through recognition of face, clothing, and voice. It is only when such continuity has been established that the spectator can use *former* mental states in the attribution process. If the spectator fails to recognize a given character, then all the attributions made earlier in the film will become "useless"; in these cases the spectator will treat the person as a "new" character. In most films, the processes of recognition are not problematic, as film producers usually make great efforts to mark their characters with distinctive features. Closer-ups of faces provide useful individuality, as do unusual and unique articles of clothing (e.g., in color and design). In the long-shot style of early cinema, in which face individuality was impossible because of the prohibition against closer framings, clothing was the only way to achieve this marking. In French filmmaking, which often contrasted with the American by frequent use of color (Abel, 1994:47), tinting was often used to perform this function. *Le Chien de Montargis* (1909), with the mantles of the three protagonists distinguishably colored in green, yellow, and pink, is a nice example of this (see Chapter 2, the section on Historical Context of Point-of-View Editing).

In other films, however, filmmakers play with and obstruct the character recognition process. In Godard's *Weekend* (1967), Roland and Corinne ride to her mother's home to sort things out after her father's death. However, just before they leave, there is a scene in which a man talks on the phone to a possible mistress about "fixing" Corrine after she has got the money. Because the man is shot in an underexposed medium long shot, it is difficult to recognize his face, and the continuity between the man and Roland remains problematic. Because Godard, in this way, obstructs the recognition process, it is likely that the intentions established in the telephone scene ("fixing Corrine"), are not transferred to Roland when he shows up later in the film. If the recognition is ambiguous, so are the mental attributions.

Another form of recognition obstruction occurs in *That Obscure Object of Desire* (1977), discussed by Smith (1995). Here Buñuel casts two actors in one of the central roles and provides no motivation whatsoever to explain the discontinuity. In this case, the obstruction does not involve a *lack* of salient cues, as in *Weekend*, but rather provides *false* or *misleading* cues.

It is important to point out that there is no normative or aesthetic hierarchy between supporting versus obstructing recognition processes. If the filmmaker wants to establish clear mental attributions and unambiguous continuity between different body appearances in a film, then providing salient cues are surely more effective. That, however, is an aesthetic choice made by the filmmaker. The artistic objective of Buñuel's film is presumably different: In fact, it is precisely the process of recognition that he wants to problematize and make the spectator aware of.

In the next sections, some films and particular scenes from films are discussed. If we assume that that the spectator actively uses FP in the reception of these scenes, we can start reconstructing the processes of understanding for a spectator who has "chosen" character psychology as the level of coherence. My focus is on the ways in which FP "guides" the spectator in mental attributions, and specifically how these attributions bring coherence to the behavior and events in a scene. Finally, the textual aspect of these processes is discussed: the different techniques, conventions, and practices that cinematic discourse makes use of to trigger, guide, and constrain mental attribution processes.

The Minds of Cinematic Characters

GOALS BRING COHERENCE TO EVENTS. Narrative theorists often acknowledge the importance of character goals. Often the discussion concerns the way in which goals and desire propel the plot (e.g., Propp, 1928/1968:35). In psychoanalytical approaches, these needs and goals are often identified in Freudian terms (e.g., lack or pursuit of a phallus). In addition, there have been efforts to create narrative taxonomies on the basis of the kind of goal pursued. Bal (1985:26ff), for instance, argues that detective stories are driven by a detective who *wants to know* (the identity of the murderer), and that nineteenth-century novels often involve a woman who *wants to become independent*. Villains, such as Gruber in *Die Hard* (1988) and Batala in *Le Crime de Monsieur Lange* (1935), are often driven by greed, vanity, and the craving for power. Positive characters, on the other hand, often strive for possession of valuable objects, establish social relationships (such as marriage), or project a demeanor of general happiness. Note here that most of these goals are achievement goals (as defined in the preceding section), extending over some period of time, often involving threats and obstacles to be overcome. Tragedies end with goals unfulfilled, whereas most other genres end with the realization of the main character's goal. Although some genres or modes of production, such as art film, seem less focused on character goals, others pay particular attention to them, for example, the classical Hollywood cinema (Bordwell, 1985:157; Bordwell et al., 1985:12).

Although narrative theory deals with goals that span the whole narrative, it is less concerned with how the overall goal generates subgoals, which change and transform during the story. That is, although there may be a general goal pursued by the character, it is necessary for the spectator to understand the specific and often short-term goals that fluctuate to the same extent that emotions and other mental states do. For instance, the overall achievement goals may generate instrumental goals (planning subgoals). In melodramatic and action narratives, crisis goals (such as catastrophes) often arise from a situation, placing the hero or heroine in situations that involve conflicting goals and in which one goal must take precedence over the other.

These ongoing processes involve a constant evaluation and "updating" of a character's goal. For instance, to understand the actions of Gruber in *Die Hard*, it is not enough to comprehend his overall goal of obtaining $600 million in bonds in the vault of the Nakatomi building. The spectator must also constantly make temporary subgoal attributions that are compatible with the superordinate goal. Late in the film, for instance, Gruber, Karl, and John McClane are involved in a shoot-out in an office space. Gruber orders Karl to shoot through the glass of the office interior. Gruber's intent can be understood only in the context of other overall goals: He wants the bonds in the vault and poses as a terrorist to mislead the police. To do so, he needs to blow off the roof of the building. In this endeavor, he requires a bag of detonators, which happens to be in the hands of John McClane. Therefore Gruber wants McClane. He also knows that McClane is barefoot; by shooting through the glass, Gruber hopes to subdue him.

This subgoal attribution is made possible by a complex system of superordinate and subordinate goals. It is only within this system that Gruber's and Karl's shooting of the glass can be understood by the spectator.

Neither does narrative theory address the fundamental coherence-making function of character goal attribution, which is the primary focus here. Local or global attributions of goals serve the purpose of lending coherence to actions in the text. What is the common denominator for all the events presented in *Die Hard*? Why do Hans Gruber and his colleagues, as well as John McClane, go to all that trouble? It is because Hans et al. *want* to steal the $600 million in bonds in the vault (and McClane and the police *want* to prevent them from doing so). Almost all the events and situations in the text can be interpreted as attempts to achieve these goals (or subgoals thereof), failures or success in doing so, or reactions to the outcomes of those attempts. Failing to make such a mental attribution to Gruber would render the events random and disconnected and would generate only superficial understanding by the viewer.

Discourse psychology has a rather extended body of studies dealing with the coherence-making function of goal attributions and the ways in which these create a "holistic" experience of a text (e.g., Bourg & Stephenson, 1997; Graesser, et al., 1994; Long & Golding, 1993; Stein & Liwag, 1997; Trabasso, 1991; Trabasso et al., 1995). Trabasso et al. (1995), for instance, examined the correlation between the holistic experience of a narrative text and the quantity of goal attributions performed by the reader. The experimenters asked a group of subjects to read short narratives and then to rate them on a scale of coherence. Another group of subjects read the same stories and were asked tell the experimenter about their understanding after each sentence (a so-called think-aloud method – see Trabasso & Suh, 1993). These subjects were instructed to try to understand the sentences in the context of the story. In the data analysis, the experimenters looked at inferences of character goals (called motivational inferences) and how the subjects made efforts to explain the events and information in the current sentence in terms of these intentions. The results showed that the number of motivational inferences actually could predict the degree of coherence experienced by the other subject group.

If we assume that coherent stories are recalled better and can thus be retold with more accuracy, then we may also suppose that texts that promote character goal inferences should be better *recalled* than similar stories that do not. Trabasso et al. (1994) found that this was indeed the case.

Both of these studies suggest that narrative coherence is in fact strongly related to the reader's understanding of character goals.

This situation becomes apparent when we look at children's comprehension and generation of narratives, which often tend to be less focused on character goals and hence on coherence. In contrast to adults, children seem to have problems with inferring the goals of fictional characters, even though the superordinate goal is explicitly mentioned in the text (Trabasso, 1991:298). This can perhaps be attributed to an "underdeveloped" FP (see the subsection on People with Different Folk Psychologies).[15]

Experience of coherence is of course not the same as the aesthetic or the emotional quality of those stories. The studies suggest, however, that if a filmmaker wants to create textual coherence, then enabling the spectator to attribute clear-cut character goals is a good strategy. Redundancy and other techniques of mainstream cinema try to accomplish precisely this.

Other genres, however, intentionally seek to obstruct or make ambiguous spectators' goal attributions. This can be done in a number of ways. First, some characters are driven by strong goals, other by weak ones. Satisfaction, achievement, and crisis goals are strong goals, whereas enjoyment goals are weaker (see the subsection on The Mind and Its Parts). In *Die Hard*, McClane and Gruber et al. are driven by strong goals. The main characters in *My Life as a Dog* (1985), *Les Vacances de Monsieur Hulot* (1953), and *Play Time* (1968), on the other hand, are not trying to realize strong goals. Instead, they tend to "drift along" in the fictive world, at best reacting to the situations in which they end up. In these cases, the coherence of the text is less related to character goals and more to a theme or situation (e.g., vacation) or place (e.g., a resort).

Although Hulot can be said to have weak goals, some modernistic filmmaking blocks goal attribution to the extent that it is difficult to infer any goals whatsoever. At the end of Godard's *Weekend*, Roland and Corinne are kidnapped by the *Front de Libération de Seine et Oise* (FLSO). Although the name suggests a clear goal for this group, it is extremely difficult to establish coherence for their actions. They walk around with guns and speak on the radio with (possibly) other resistance groups. Ernest the chef cracks eggs over the bodies of Corinne and Roland, and places a fish in between the legs of a younger female hostage. The leader plays the drums. Pigs and ducks are slaughtered. Naked women are painted on. The group makes a failed hostage exchange. Eventually we see the leader and Corinne eating the meat of slaughtered English tourists (and possibly also of Roland).

The text blatantly resists any attempts by the spectator to infer intention on the part of FLSO members and hence to create coherence among textual elements. Just after the brutal killing of Roland, a male voice says to a female voice that "to overcome the horror of the bourgeoisie, you need still more horror." This might suggest some intentions of the FLSO: making Corinne a true revolutionary. However, because we see only the feet of the persons talking, it is never established to whom the sentence is addressed and who the speaker is. Moreover, many of the events are difficult to fit with this intention anyway. The experience of fragmentation so prevalent in art films, including many of Godard's works, may have many causes. The effective obstruction of the spectator's efforts to make goal attributions, however, is a contributing one.

Moreover, if the spectator does succeed in this endeavor, actions may often be unrelated to that intention. What gives many a Godard film its special atmosphere is that there may be a character goal – e.g., Corinne and Roland in *Weekend* driving to her mother to settle her father's inheritance. The narration may even be spatiotemporally attached to some main characters – we follow them on their trip. The majority of the events presented, however, are simply not related to this goal. Witnessing car accidents on country roads and in villages, walking along a field with a French revolutionary, the garbage truck scene with voice-over politics, and the concert at the farm are simply unrelated to the goal of arriving at the house of Corinne's mother. It seems that the radical denial of character goals as the foundation for textual coherence lies at the core of Godard's aesthetic objectives.

Another way to problematize character goal as the unifying principle in textual understanding is to provide strong goals, but have them shift abruptly and seemingly without reason. In the latter part of *Blowup* (1966), for instance, the main character Thomas drifts into a pop concert, which degenerates into a turmoil in which the players destroy their instruments. The audience surges onto the stage in order to obtain parts from the mistreated instruments, and our photographer manages – after great effort – to get hold of a broken guitar neck. Here the spectator is presumably led to believe that obtaining the guitar neck, for some reason, is important to the character or related to the (supposed) crime, which he is in the act of uncovering. This inference, however, is immediately thwarted in the next scene. The photographer leaves the concert with the guitar neck. In the alley he looks at it and, without further ado, throws it away. Here, a strong character goal of possessing the guitar neck at once becomes irrelevant and is disposed of. Such unmotivated shifts of strong character goal are often understood as "irrational" behavior. According to FP, people do not pick up and leave strong goals and desires randomly and without motivations. Of course, goals may shift, but seldom with the abruptness of *Blowup*.

Thus films and filmmakers can – for aesthetic, narrative and other reasons – choose to promote clear and unambiguous goal attributions by a spectator or to block such inference making. What are the specific techniques, channels, and conventions for doing either of these? By which means can a film encourage goal attributions? There do not seem to be particular conventions, but methods vary across a range of "channels." Dialogue and intertitles are perhaps the most explicit ones. In *Die Hard*, the spectator learns about Gruber's goals through his conversation with Takagi (by means of an emphasizing track-in shot). When the Doctor at the beginning of *Das Cabinet des Dr. Caligari* (1920) enters a rather anonymous white room with people at desks, the spectator is informed through the intertitle that the Doctor *wants* permission from the town clerk to put up his show.

Less explicit than dialogue and intertitles is the physical behavior of characters (e.g., the fight over the guitar neck in *Blowup*). In the pantomime acting style of early cinema, with its system of gestures, this behavior probably played a crucial role. Often body cues are used in combination with other information. At the very end of *Le Crime de Monsieur Lange*, Batala reappears after a long absence, and the scene ends with Batala leaving and Lange looking at the gun placed on his desk. On the basis of that gaze, the spectator infers Lange's desire and intention to kill Batala, in combination with other situational parameters (e.g., Batala suggests that Lange ought to kill him for his behavior; Lange is angry and full of contempt for Batala). In *Meet Me In St. Louis* (1944), the protagonist's goals are presented through a song (*"The Boy Next Door"*). In *Die Hard*, the goals of the main characters may even have been revealed in advance through posters, trailers, and public relations material.

All of these methods are quite "textual" in nature in the sense that they are text driven and need little engagement on the spectators' part. The most substantial way to infer goals in characters, however, deals more with the social and cultural expectations brought to the film by a spectator. For instance, all human beings have satisfaction goals; parents want to protect their children; waiters must be helpful and make customers happy; detectives want to discover the identity of criminals. Event schemas, occupancy roles, family roles, traits, social types, social stereotypes, and the aggregation of all of these into fictional character types deal with "default" goals of specific characters (see the first section of Chapter 1 and the subsection on Levels of Meaning in this chapter). The film needs only to trigger the correct recognition of a given character type. Then the mentally represented, sociocultural dispositions of the spectator take over and attribute implicit goals to the character. In understanding villains, monsters, psychopaths, and heroes, there is already an expectation about their main goals (e.g., getting the loot, killing people, saving a princess, stopping the villain). By using iconographic codes, which circulate in society and are known to many spectators, visual media trigger these expectations and exploit them in the unfolding narrative. Once the spectator has identified the villains in *The Girl and Her Trust* (1912) – through change of musical accompaniment, makeup, costume, and stylized acting – it is relatively unproblematic to infer goals. Fictional traditions and everyday social experience have equipped the spectator with sophisticated assumptions about such people or characters.

These goals need not be stated explicitly by dialogue, intertitles, or acting. Instead, the main function of the text becomes *specifying* the goal of a given character. Spectators know that villains generally are greedy, want to possess valuable things, and are prepared to use illegal means to accomplish this goal. Through the focus on money delivery (in the title and in the narration), *The Girl and Her Trust* enables the spectator to solidify the goals of these particular villains: they want the strongbox that is guarded by the female operator. Here we see how text and spectator dispositions interact in intimate ways to generate understanding and coherence: Neither can be described on its own.

From the point of view of narration, the timing of when to trigger goal attribution can be used to create certain effects. Occasionally the disclosure of character goals is retarded by the narrative in order to arouse curiosity, anticipation, suspense, or surprise. A common pattern in thrillers and detective stories is to wait until the end to reveal the goals of the character gallery, thereby making the spectator reconsider plot events on a new basis (Bordwell, 1985:64). In *Die Hard*, the real superordinate intentions of Gruber et al. are revealed approximately fifteen minutes into the film; by then we have seen several well-organized activities of the villains without fully understanding their specific goals. Such deferral creates curiosity and suspense. In mainstream cinema, such indeterminacies will for the most part be resolved at some point in the narrative, but in other genres, they will not (e.g., *Weekend*).

EMOTIONS ARE IMPORTANT MOTIVATORS FOR GOALS AND ACTIONS. According to FP, goals and actions are often motivated by emotions. Desires and goals can be formed on their own, but, by appealing to emotions, the spectator establishes a broader, more fundamental understanding. Emotions provide *motivations* for goals (see Figure 40).[16] Emotions do not necessarily have to give rise to goals, but when the two appear together, it is FP that provides the causal connection. FP provides the framework within which the causal connection between emotions and goals appears so natural.

In *Le Crime de Monsieur Lange,* there is no explicit, textually represented causality between Batala's return and Lange's killing him. Nevertheless the spectator infers this causality on the basis of mental attributions and FP. Because Batala's return is an intentional act and inconsistent with Lange's goals, Lange becomes *angry* and full of *contempt* for Batala. Because FP contains a strong causal connection between emotions and actions (by means of goals and intentions), the causal relationship between the return and the killing of Batala is constructed by the spectator. Such coherence and motivational reasoning is supported by the underlying FP structure.[17] The notion of *revenge,* which is a common pattern in narrative films, can be understood in terms of a standardized chain of actions and mental states of this sort.

In Kieslowski's *Trois couleurs: Bleu* (1993), the main protagonist's emotion of grief after her family's death, functions as the basic motivator for all of the actions and her reactions throughout the film. Here her apparently disparate behaviors are not primarily centered around goals, but rather around the complex emotions associated with periods of mourning. Both *Trois couleurs: Bleu* and the example from *Le Crime de Monsieur Lange* deal with negative emotions, but we could have provided a similar argument at the positive end of spectrum.

Some narratives provide little emotional contextualization of goals and action. In *Pickpocket* (1959), Michel obviously has an intention of stealing, which is clear throughout the film. However, the spectator is never given any hints as to *why* Michel has this obsession, that is, what emotions fuel his behavior. Toward the end, Jeanne asks him about motives, but they are only vaguely referred to and provide no substantial reason ("I couldn't achieve anything. It drove me mad"). Such opacity gives Bresson's characters a "flatness" and superficiality (see Bordwell, 1985:290). The same can be said about many monsters, stalkers, and psychopaths, whose reasons to kill and pillage are seldom explained other than hastily and stereotypically and appear to be subordinate to the main objective of the genre. (Occasionally, the emotions invoked are Freudian in character rather than folk psychological, e.g., childhood memories.)

The claim here is not simply that the understanding of character goals becomes richer with emotional motivation, but that this richness stems from the structure of FP, which postulates a strong causal connection between emotions and goals–intentions–actions.

It is difficult to discuss emotions under a single category, as there are many different types of emotions. Some of them appear to have a greater influence on goals than others. I return to this theme in the subsequent subsections.

PERCEPTIONS INFORM BELIEFS THAT CONSTRAIN GOALS AND ACTIONS. In FP, perceptions imprint beliefs in the mind, which in turn frame and specify goals and actions. This basic architecture underlies many scenes in mainstream cinema. Take, for instance, the scene at the beginning of *Die Hard*, when Karl hunts John McClane from the roof into the ventilation shaft (Figure 42). After almost falling down the big vertical shaft, McClane succeeds in entering a smaller horizontal one, in which he uses his cigarette lighter to see better [Figure 42(a)]. Through a POV tilt, Karl sees this light from the top of the vertical shaft [Figures 42(b) and 42(c)], whereupon he rushes down the stairs into a room and starts looking, eventually shooting randomly at the ventilation shaft along the ceiling [Figure 42(d)]. This is intercut with McClane in the shaft, preparing his gun for a potential shoot-out. Karl, however, must leave, because the police arrive downstairs.

There are no explicit or textual causal connections between these events. They make sense first when the spectator infers that Karl shoots at the shaft because he *suspects* that McClane is there, and he *suspects* McClane is there because he *saw* the light from the top of the vertical shaft. Note how the perception motivates the suspicion and the suspicion motivates why Karl chose the specific room in which McClane happens to be hiding (beliefs constrain action). Such motivations are not in the text 'itself', but depend on the spectator's mental attributions and reasoning.

Sometimes reasoning of this sort can motivate character behavior through the whole of a film. In *North by Northwest* (1959), Roger Thornhill is falsely recognized by the villains as Mr. Kaplan, because he coincidentally raises his arm when the name of Kaplan is called in a hotel lobby (Figure 43). This act of perception and its accompanying belief motivate the behavior of the villains for the rest of the film. It thus operates as the hub around which the global narrative revolves. It is the attributions at this point that make the following narrative events understandable. Such erroneous beliefs, while still granting the spectator omniscient access to the "truth" of the fictive world, often create dramatic tension (de Vega, Díaz & León, 1997; Bordwell, 1985). Romeo's ignorance of Juliet's and

(a)

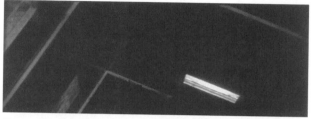

(b)

(c)

(d)

FIGURE 42. *Die Hard* (John McTiernan, 1988). (Obtained from the film archives of Svenska Filminstitutet, Stockholm.)

(a)

(b)

(c)

FIGURE 43. *North by Northwest*. Villains falsely recognize Thornhill as Mr. Kaplan, after which they kidnap him. (Alfred Hitchcock, 1959.) (Obtained from the Wisconsin Center for Film and Theater Research.)

Friar Laurence's drug experimentations may be the most classic example of this.

These examples are *mistakes*, which can in fact be described in FP terms as action based on erroneous beliefs. For instance, in the scene from *Seven Samurai* of Figure 39 – given in a new format in Figure 44 – the Samurai chases the girl because he assumes that "she" is a "he." The Samurai is led to believe so because she has cut her hair and lied to him. Not until he happens to move into a close encounter with her does he tactilely perceive her physical attributes: The mistake is resolved and leads their story in new directions. Mistakes often constitute the core of comedies in general, and love comedies in particular – for example, *Some Like It Hot* (1959). In *Les Vacances de Monsieur Hulot*, the comic effects of perceptual mistakes are exploited to the maximum, for instance, in the train scene at the beginning. Here, the vacation party mistakenly enters and exits train platforms a number of times, as they are led to believe (through different perceptual channels) that their train is approaching that platform. In order to cash in on the joke, the spectator needs understand

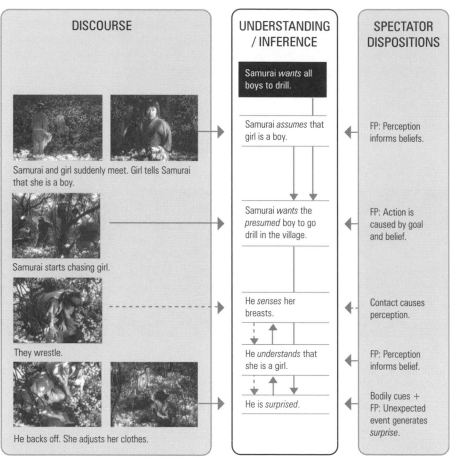

FIGURE 44. *Seven Samurai* (Akira Kurosawa, 1954). The left-hand column shows the textual surface of the discourse; the right-hand column specifies the spectator dispositions contributing to the construction of meaning (in this case, different aspects of FP and body-cue ability); the middle column states the understanding, i.e., the emergent meaning, arising from the confrontation between text and spectator. The black box represents attributions made earlier in the film. Italics indicate mental state terms. (Diagram designed by Younghee Jung.)

the underlying chain of perception–beliefs–goals–actions–reactions–new perception–goals. Tati exploits FP reasoning for comical purposes.

A similar case can be made for a scene from *Steamboat Bill, Jr.* (1928) in which Senior and Junior – who have not met since Junior's childhood – try to find each other in a train station. Whereas the spectator has full visual access to the scene, the view of Senior and his assistant is partially blocked by a wall, which leads them to false, and hence comical, beliefs about Junior (Figure 45). To understand the misunderstanding (and hence

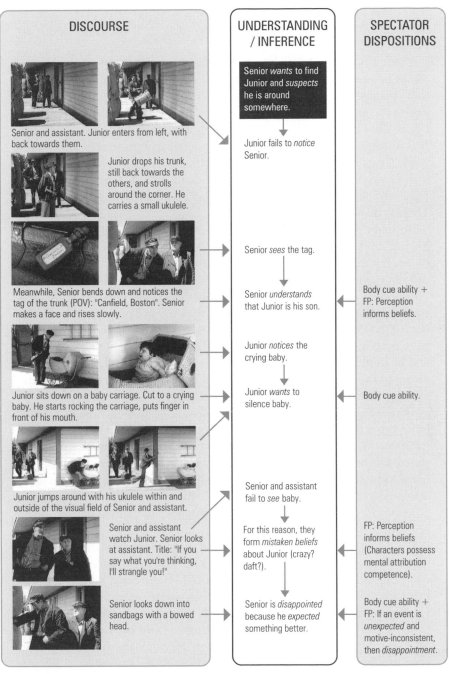

the humor of the sequence), the spectator has to make causal connections between failed perceptions and mistaken beliefs. These connections are provided by FP.

From a filmmaker's point of view, the structure of FP implies that if she or he wants to trigger attributions of clear and well-motivated beliefs to a character, then the perceptions of this character must also be clear. Take a scene in *Pickpocket*, for example. Michel – picking pockets as never before – has been confronted by one of his victims in the Metro, a situation that induces some caution in Michel and causes him to stay home for a week. The first time he leaves the apartment, he stops on his stairs and sees a man (Kassagi) standing on the sidewalk outside the house (through POV editing). Then Michel turns around and climbs back up the stairs. There is no dialogue in this scene.

To make sense of this scene, the spectator must reason along the following lines: After the incident in the Metro, Michel is cautious. When he *sees* the man on the sidewalk, he *believes* the man to be a policeman or detective, which makes him *afraid*. This is why he returns to the apartment.

The clear and unambiguous POV shot is a crucial element in this reasoning. If the spectator were not able to attribute this perception to Michel (e.g., if the POV editing had been left out of the film), his behavior would have been indeterminate: Had he forgotten something in the apartment? Did he think it was too cold outside? Bresson and his colleagues are well aware of the importance of establishing characters' perceptions in order to trigger attributions of determinate beliefs.

Because attributions of perception have an important role in making other types of mental attributions unambiguous, it is not surprising that mainstream cinema developed conventions for conveying this. Acting styles, for instance, were crucial in early cinema (see Figure 46), and continue to be so today. The understanding of characters' gaze behavior is also pivotal. In a long-shot tableaux style like that of early cinema, line of gaze may have to be emphasized by binoculars and manual pointing (Figure 13 in Chapter 2), as well as lighting and mise-en-scène. In addition, POV editing – as we saw in Chapter 2 – is perhaps the most common technique. Here, gazer and perceived object appear in separate shots. What was not touched on in Chapter 2, and should be stressed here, is the way in which POV inference ("X looks at O") in combination with the gazer's reaction enables mental attributions. POV editing supports attributions of beliefs, but also emotions. The POV editing convention, with its structure of "perception and then (re)action," is a primary means of bringing character psychology to the fore. The POV in *Pickpocket* works in precisely this way: It infuses Michel with beliefs about the man in the street, which in combination with the fear of being caught, explains why he turns around and returns to his apartment. In a similar way, Karl's tilt POV of the light in

FIGURE 46. *Der Letzte Mann* (F.W. Murnau, 1924). The woman *hears* what goes on behind the door.

the ventilation shaft makes him *suspect* that McClane is there (Figure 42). This is why he turns around and descends the stairs to the floor below. Note also the reaction of the professor in *The Egyptian Mummy* (Figure 10, Chapter 2).

Another clear example of how perceptions, reactions, and beliefs depend on and reinforce each other is provided by *Rear Window*. In one particular scene, Jeff looks at the newlyweds next door by means of a rhythmic alternation between shots of Jeff and the couple (Figure 47). Here, the spectator must infer a number of mental activities on Jeff's part in order make sense of his reactions.[18] First, we see him looking curiously at the couple as they are being handed a key by the landlord [Figure 47(a)]. After an interlude with the couple kissing [Figure 47(b)], we see Jeff smile, and the spectator probably infer that he feels some sort of *sympathy* and *happiness* for the lovebirds [Figure 47(c)]. Cut back to the couple with the man reopening the door and leaving the room with his wife [Figure 47(d)]. Cut to Jeff lowering his eyebrows, indicating some *puzzlement* about the behavior of the neighbors [Figure 47(e)]. Cut back to the couple reentering the room with the husband carrying his wife [Figure 47(f)]. This is followed by a reaction shot of Jeff moving his mouth and leaning backward in his wheelchair, which must be interpreted as some *understanding* or *mild surprise* [Figure 47(g)]. We return to the couple, now kissing and embracing with renewed intensity [Figure 47(h)], followed by a shot of Jeff looking away from the window with some *shame* at intruding on the neighbors' privacy [Figure 47(i)].

This sequence is a perfect example of Hitchcock's idea about the articulatory power of POV editing:

You have an immobilized man looking out. That's one part of the film. The second part shows what he sees and the third part how he reacts. This is actually the purest expression of a cinematic idea.[19] (Truffaut, 1966:161)

 (a)

 (b)

 (c)

 (d)

 (e)

 (f)

 (g)

 (h)

(i)

(j)

FIGURE 47. *Rear Window* (Alfred Hitchcock, 1954). (Obtained from the Wisconsin Center for Film and Theater Research.)

What is interesting in these examples is that objects, gaze, reactions, and mental attributions motivate and reinforce each other, forming a causally tight and coherent inference structure. Discussing a POV editing device from Griffith's *The Redman and the Child*, in which an Indian witnesses the abduction of a child by means of the typical gaze–object–reaction scheme (see Chapter 2, the subsection on Functions of Point-of-View Editing), Gunning describes this structure in terms of "narrative sandwiching":

> The meaning of each shot is dependent on its place within a three-shot editing pattern. The cause of the Indian's alarm in the first shot is revealed by the shot through the telescope. The circular matte of the point-of-view shot is only explained by the look through the telescope. The reason for the Indian rushing off in the last shot is given by what he sees in the shot before. A narrative sandwiching occurs in which none of the shots can be fully understood independently. This narrative unit is not centered around physical movement of a character, but around his perception and emotional reaction. (Gunning, 1994:73f)

Although Gunning does not describe it in terms of inference processes and spectator psychology, the POV editing convention allows perceptions to enter characters' psychology clearly and disambiguously. In itself, this provides little psychologization, but in combination with situational parameters and other mental attributions, POV editing enables the spectator to infer complex mental activities in characters (see Carroll, 1996a:129ff). For instance, it is not only that Michel observes a man in the street that explains his turning around: The spectator must relate this to other mental attributions such as *cautiousness* and *fear* of being caught by the police. Likewise, the Indian's reaction is not only a product of some neutral observation, but rather that he happens to see the brutal kidnapping of one of his best friends (triggering a protection and crisis goal). POV editing, however, provides the channel by which characters appraise situations. With perceptions "in the system," the spectator has a richer set of psychological terms to play with, reason about, and create coherence from; this promotes the psychologization of character that was so central for the new narrative cinema emerging between 1905 and 1915. Gunning's (1994:116ff) analysis of Griffith provides excellent examples of this.

The Emotions of Cinematic Characters

One area of discourse psychology has been concerned with the ways in which readers represent emotions of fictional characters in narrative comprehension, incorporate them into the mental text model, and continuously update that representation while reading (de Vega, León & Díaz, 1996). The basic assumption, again, is that the mental process of "representing characters' emotions in stories is a cognitive phenomenon that deserves attention itself," independent of the emotional responses of the reader or spectator (de Vega et al., 1996:305). de Vega et al. reconstitute and justify Smith's distinction between allegiance and alignment, on which my scheme is also based.

Moreover, those mental representations of emotion, constructed by the spectator,

> serve as a 'glue' that integrates contents that are relatively distant in the text. By tracking the characters' emotional states, readers are in a privileged position to integrate pieces of information widely distributed throughout the text. Emotions, therefore, may contribute in providing global coherence to stories. (de Vega et al., 1996:304)

In both verbal and cinematic texts, these emotions may be explicitly mentioned, or their tacitness may require inference making. If appraisal theory has laid out the parameters by which we judge emotions in daily life, it is fair to assume that we resort to this ability in comprehending cinema. Hence, in the following subsection, we investigate how appraisal parameters are manipulated by the filmmakers, triggering an appropriate emotional attribution. We could also consider it from a reception perspective: How does the spectator use appraisal parameters in emotional attribution? How does such appraisal create textual coherence? Throughout this subsection, explicit and implicit references will be made to Roseman's figure of appraisal parameters (Figure 41).

POSITIVE/NEGATIVE EMOTIONS. If goals are important tools for helping spectators create coherence out of a given character's behavior, goals are equally central in establishing the distinction between positive and negative emotions. As we have seen, the negative/positive value of an emotion is dependent on whether the event or situation works for or against the character's goals. The clearer and stronger that goal is, the easier it is to distinguish between positive and negative emotions.

Let us consider McClane in *Die Hard*. Given that his top priority is to stop Gruber from getting away with theft, many events seem to work in his favor (e.g., discovering the fire alarm and witnessing the fire department hurrying toward the building; being able to eliminate Gruber's men and steal their weapons and equipment; Al's trust in what he is doing; revealing Gruber's trick when McClane meets him under the roof). On the other hand, some events work against this goal (e.g., the fire department turning around at the last minute; the SOS assistant refusing to take McClane's emergency call seriously; Argyle failing to hear the shots and call the police; getting glass in feet; fighting with Karl). All of these events generate emotions with clear positive/negative value, as they reinforce or repress McClane's goal.

In addition, the strong preservation and crisis goals appearing through-out the film (e.g., avoiding falling off the building; avoiding being shot or injured; avoiding detection) generate emotions that oscillate abruptly be-tween negative and positive (e.g., between *fear* of falling over the edge of the roof and *relief* when it is avoided). The action genre, in general, seems to be particularly aware of the basic and powerful instinct for survival, as well as how to use it to create impressions of definite positive or negative emotions in the characters (and in the end, of course, also the emotional reactions of the spectator).

In characters with weak or nonexistent goals, such emotional attribu-tions become increasingly difficult, indeterminate, and unresolved. The main characters of *My Life as a Dog* or *Les Vacances de Monsieur Hulot* possess precisely this openness, as their goals are less clear-cut than McClane's. In *Weekend*, this openness becomes even more problematic. Even if the spectator in the first scene manages to ascribe goals to Corinne and Roland (e.g., "driving to mother," "fixing Corinne"), the events of the film seem unrelated to these goals. This also implies fewer cues by which the spectator can judge the emotional valance of these events. Witnessing a piano concert at a farm may be pleasurable in general, but because this has little to do with the character's trip (it is neither obstructing nor helping them), it is difficult for the spectator to determine how Roland and Corinne feel in relation to it. This may be one reason why Godard's characters often seem flat and superficial. Again, this is not to say that superficial characters or emotionally "irrelevant events" are filmic flaws that lead to "bad film." In this I am merely trying to explain why and how these effects arise, not to judge their aesthetic value. Emotionally "numb" characters – such as those in *Weekend* – may appear in mainstream films too, although mainly in transient situations. For instance, McClane's air-port encounter with Argyle at the beginning of *Die Hard* may generate a small *surprise* for him (he was not *expecting* a car to pick him up). How-ever, because the spectator at this point in the narrative is unaware of definite goals on McClane's part, the event does not give rise to emotions of either positive or negative valence. Thus far in the film, McClane has not been attributed the forceful goals that mark his later appearances in the film.

If the filmmaker wants to trigger positive or negative emotional attri-butions, then he or she has to plant some form of character goal *before* a relevant event is depicted. For instance, how could the spectator un-derstand the *hope* and *joy* of McClane's watching the fire department hurrying down the street toward his building (and his *disappointment* when they turn around) if the film had not already established that he *wanted* to attract the attention of the police in order to stop the Gruber gang? If the filmmaker wants positive- or negative-valenced attributions to arise on the spectator's first viewing of a film, then such temporal ordering of information is essential. Moreover, the *reason* for this can be found in the structure of FP: It is not a conventional or arbitrary feature, but is based on the structure of our conceptual network of mental states.

As with all appraisal parameters, the goal (in)consistency of a given event must be perceived and understood by the character in order for emotion to emerge. There are, for instance, many events in *Die Hard* that fall outside John McClane's attention and knowledge, and hence do not contribute to his mental life (although they may to other characters'). It is the realm of narration that determines the spatiotemporal attachment to characters (Smith, 1995), and the way knowledge and emotional reactions in the fictive world are restricted to one character or distributed over many (see the subsection on Textual Theories).

The distinct difference between happy and sad endings of narratives seems to be strongly connected with positive or negative emotions of characters. In happy endings, for instance, there is a fulfillment of the overall character goal. Perhaps the character realizes that the goals he had adopted were vain or inappropriate, which generates a positive emotion in him. Although this situation often relates to a positive emotion in the spectator as well, it is not necessarily so. Goal fulfillments, minimally, also have to be *morally good*: The fulfillment of Gruber's intentions in *Die Hard* would surely generate positive emotions in *him*, but would hardly be experienced as a happy ending by the *spectator*. The relation between character and spectator emotion is not one of identity.

SURPRISE. Surprise is the only emotion that does not have a clear position on the positive/negative spectrum. Rather than relating to the goals of a character, surprise emerges when expectations are flouted. In *Le Crime de Monsieur Lange*, Lange and the other people in the house are led to believe that Batala is dead, because of the radio announcement of the train accident. This firm belief of Lange's is later disconfirmed by Batala's "return from the dead" in Lange's office. Here, surprise is attributed to Lange, who did not expect Batala to be alive and well. Note that the understanding of the relation between Lange's *surprise* and *beliefs* in fact creates a connection between scenes of the film: Lange's *surprise* on Batala's return is consistent with the scene in which Lange *learns* about Batala's death. It is coherent, because such relations between beliefs and surprises are innate in FP.

Surprise is primarily appraised in relation to beliefs and expectations; this does not mean that surprises cannot be negative or positive. For Lange, Batala's return is surely negative, as this event threatens all the valued things Lange and the cooperative have built up during Batala's absence. To understand this negative surprise, the narrative has to establish the satisfaction and pride Lange feels over the work done by the cooperative (e.g., the success of *Arizona Jim*; the scene in which Lange tells the concierge about the improvements to the house since the cooperative was initiated; and of course, the party celebrating the filmatization of *Arizona Jim*).

On the other hand, when Batala early in the film agrees to publish *Arizona Jim*, this generates a *positive* surprise in Lange by working in favor of Lange's general achievement goal to become a famous writer.

Finally, some surprises may fall between positive and negative extremes. Lange's reaction to the radio announcement is of this type: the event is not really related to a goal of Lange at that moment. Batala was not his best friend. As far as Lange's job at the company is concerned, Batala was not the most responsible employer anyway. Therefore the spectator can expect neutral surprise from Lange.

The major point to be gained from these examples is that, in order for the spectator to attribute the emotion of surprise, the narrative somehow must establish what expectations the character holds. The radio announcement scene establishes Lange's belief that Batala is dead. Expectations can also be inferred from common-sense knowledge about the world, for example, that train accidents involving acquaintances are fairly rare (which motivates Lange's surprise upon hearing the radio announcement). Again, the temporal ordering of relevant narrative information is of crucial importance if mental attributions are to emerge and be definite.

The tight connection among surprise, body or facial expression, and failed expectations provides a tight inferential structure. This structure enables not only appraisals of emotions but, in reverse, also inferences about the nature of the expectation. For instance, if someone opens a package of books and is surprised, then we assume that the person believed the contents to be something other than books. In the beginning of *The Wind* (1928), the leading female character – Letty Mason – disembarks from a train and embraces a man (Lige), whose back is turned toward her. Immediately afterward, she steps back and displays a surprised expression. From this behavior, the spectator understands that Mason *thought* the man was somebody else (probably the relative she is supposed to be visiting). Here, body cues and FP-based reasoning about surprises combine in attributing beliefs that would otherwise have to be expressed in dialogue or titles.

In reverse, if a character does not show signs of surprise, then the spectator may infer that the event was in fact expected or normal for the character. This is one reason why characters in many Godard films appear so baffling. In *Weekend*, for instance, Roland and Corinne encounter a number of situations that – at least to a modern Western spectator – would run counter to everyday beliefs and expectations: burning cars everywhere, dead and bloody bodies on the roads, dressed-up French revolutionaries walking around reading aloud from books, cars transforming into sheep, kidnappings, women raped in ditches, and cannibalism. Yet neither Roland nor Corinne displays body or facial cues that indicate surprise: In fact, there are no reactions at all. If the mental lives of Roland and Corinne follow those of FP, the absence of reaction seems to indicate that the events are *expected* to be as commonplace as smoking a cigarette. If this can be expected in the fictive world of Roland and Corinne, then this world is indeed different from the one the spectator inhabits. This disjunction may make the fictive world difficult to relate to. (The same can be said of the diegesis in the *Monty Python's Flying Circus* series [1972]. In this case, however, the apparent lack of character surprise, despite the most bizarre situations, becomes a comical gag.)

Another possible account of Roland and Corinne's behavior is that these events *are* unexpected, but neither of them displays nor experiences any form of surprise. In this case, the spectator would have to assume extremely dysfunctional mental lives in these characters (at least according to the standards of FP), perhaps classifying them as "emotionally cold" or "robotlike" (see Grodal, 1997:chap. 5).

EVENTS CAUSED BY CIRCUMSTANCE, OTHER, OR SELF. To differentiate between emotions in the range of events caused by circumstance, other, or self, these parameters must first be explicit and appraised; the spectator must have some notion of the agency that is causing an event. Let us return to the example of Batala's return: It is clear to Lange that this situation, which seriously threatens his goals and happiness (and thus evokes negative emotion), is caused by an intentional act on Batala's part. Batala's return cannot be ascribed to circumstances (despite what he says, he is not "just passing by"); hence no *sadness* or *distress*. Neither can Lange be held responsible for the situation; hence no *regret* or *guilt*. Rather, Batala has *intentionally* returned with the specific goal of retaining command of the company. It is therefore likely that Lange experiences some *dislike* or *anger* vis-à-vis Batala. As we have discussed, it is this *anger* that then transforms into, and hence motivates, Batala's shooting.[20]

Of course, in many cases, the agency behind an event is not clear to the character in question. Let us examine Lange's reactions when *Arizona Jim* is first published. Of course, Batala had some part in this (he made the decision), but circumstances also seem to have worked in Lange's favor (Batala happened to catch a glimpse of *Arizona Jim* in the editing room).

Moreover, the publication would not have occurred if Lange himself had not written the piece. Therefore, although Lange's emotion is clearly positive, the particular nature of this emotion becomes rather vague, transgressing the boundaries of circumstance-, other- and self-caused (*joy*, *like*, and *pride*).

An analogous negative case appears in *The Big Parade* (1925). Jim has been swept away by nationalistic spirit (and love for a girl) and has finally enlisted with the Yankees during the American Civil War (Figure 48). Because he knows that his mother strongly disapproves of his enlistment, he has to decide whether to lie or to make her sad. Having chosen the former, he probably experiences a mixture of *distress* and *regret*, as his lie was caused both by himself (enlistment was ultimately his decision) and circumstances (he *had* to enlist in order to win the heart of his girl; he *had* to lie in order not to hurt his mother).

Weekend once again provides a case in which such mental ascriptions become problematic or blocked, creating an impression that characters are acting strangely or nonsensically. At one moment in the film, Roland sits smoking at the side of the road waiting for a lift, and Corinne lies down to rest in a ditch nearby. An unknown man passes, enters the ditch, and, judging from Corinne's screams, apparently tries to rape her. A few meters away, Roland continues smoking, with no sign of surprise or disapproval. Afterwards, Corinne has nothing to say about the incident and acts as if it were the most natural thing in the world.

Rapes in general – and rapes of family members in particular – often trigger strong preservation and crisis goals in the victim, the family of the victim, or passersby. Because rapes are intentional acts on another's part, *anger* and *dislike* are emotions strongly associated with these kinds of situations. Nothing of this sort seems to be present in either Roland or Corinne. Roland's continued smoking and apparent lack of interest make *surprise* toward the situation and *anger* toward the stranger a low probability.

There are, of course, several different ways of understanding the mental processes at work here (see Omdahl, 1995:19). If one assumes that Roland in fact *wants* to kill his wife (which is indicated in his [?] initial phone conversation with his mistress), then complicity in the rape (and potential murder?) makes perfect sense. Such an attribution would make Roland a very cold character indeed, which correlates badly with his other behavior toward Corinne. In any case, after the rape, some sort of *dislike* or *contempt* over Roland's failure to interfere would be an understandable reaction on Corinne's part. Nothing of the sort, however, seems to occur. They continue their trip as if nothing had happened. Of course, the spectator may assume that Corinne in fact *approved of* the rape. Such attributions seem

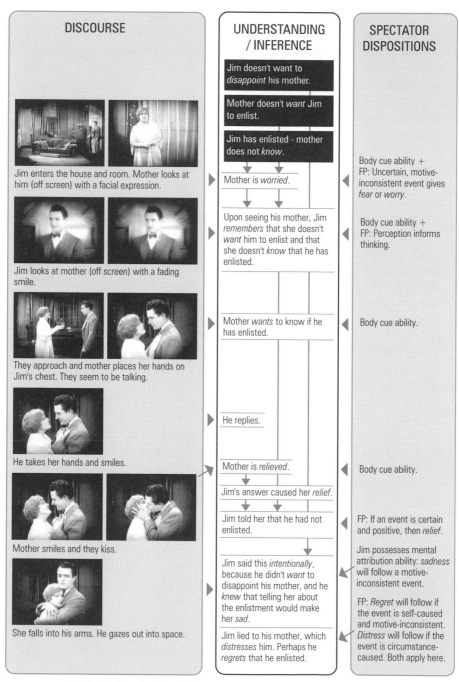

DISCOURSE	UNDERSTANDING / INFERENCE	SPECTATOR DISPOSITIONS
	Jim doesn't want to *disappoint* his mother.	
	Mother doesn't *want* Jim to enlist.	
	Jim has enlisted - mother does not *know*.	
Jim enters the house and room. Mother looks at him (off screen) with a facial expression.	Mother is *worried*.	Body cue ability + FP: Uncertain, motive-inconsistent event gives *fear* or *worry*.
Jim looks at mother (off screen) with a fading smile.	Upon seeing his mother, Jim *remembers* that she doesn't *want* him to enlist and that she doesn't *know* that he has enlisted.	Body cue ability + FP: Perception informs thinking.
They approach and mother places her hands on Jim's chest. They seem to be talking.	Mother *wants* to know if he has enlisted.	Body cue ability.
	He replies.	
He takes her hands and smiles.	Mother is *relieved*.	Body cue ability.
	Jim's answer caused her *relief*.	
Mother smiles and they kiss.	Jim told her that he had not enlisted.	FP: If an event is certain and positive, then *relief*.
	Jim said this *intentionally*, because he didn't *want* to disappoint his mother, and he *knew* that telling her about the enlistment would make her *sad*.	Jim possesses mental attribution ability: *sadness* will follow a motive-inconsistent event.
She falls into his arms. He gazes out into space.	Jim lied to his mother, which *distresses* him. Perhaps he *regrets* that he enlisted.	FP: *Regret* will follow if the event is self-caused and motive-inconsistent. *Distress* will follow if the event is circumstance-caused. Both apply here.

FIGURE 48. *The Big Parade* (King Vidor, 1925). (Diagram designed by Younghee Jung.)

quite far-fetched and are at odds with her screams (expressing genuine horror).

All of these attributions, in fact, seem to contradict either the behaviors of Roland and Corinne or the structure of FP reasoning. From the perspective of FP, their behavior is *incomprehensible*. The main point here is that such "strangeness" effects are possible only if there is a schema of "normality," in our case FP. Godard breaks, and thereby exploits, this schema to generate those effects.

Naturally it might be argued that the scene is not supposed to be understood in terms of character goals and emotions, but only on a symbolic or abstract level. This is precisely the point. Because the scene so obtrusively defies any FP explanation, the spectator may well move on to other frameworks of understanding (e.g., Roland's ignorance of the rape is a symbol of society's ignorance of rape victims and its major focus is on the perpetrator). Character psychology is only one of many levels of coherence and meaning making. Having said that, however, I suspect a spectator in general *first* tries a FP explanation, and, only when such efforts have failed, does the spectator move on to other stances toward the text. Godard's filmmaking provides instructive examples of these processes.

APPETITIVE/AVERSIVE EMOTIONS. The distinction between *joy* and *relief* versus *anger* and *contempt* depends on whether the motive is primarily possessive or repellent (see the subsection on Emotions and Their Causes). When McClane manages to hang onto an edge of the ventilation shaft, thereby avoiding certain death, the emotion attributed to him is probably *relief* rather than *joy*. The same holds true some minutes later, when Karl suspects McClane's whereabouts in the shaft, shoots randomly, but eventually leaves the room (Figure 42). In both of these cases, McClane succeeds, through circumstances, in *avoiding* death rather than accomplishing a goal. In fact, the whole narrative focuses on how McClane tries to avoid theft and human catastrophe, which often leaves his emotions on the aversive side of the spectrum. In contrast, Gruber is driven more by a possessive goal. When he finally enters the vault with the bonds, the spectator probably infers some form of *joy* on his part (although this delight will be proved as premature). Again, it needs to be emphasized that these character emotions are not to be confused with spectator emotions. In McClane's case, the spectator may also experience *relief* (together with McClane), but how and why such emotions arise in the spectator is a different and much more complex story.

Some film genres seem to deal with characters who have clearly aversive or appetitive emotions. In horror, stalker, and monster films, the victims have strong aversive goals (e.g., avoiding a monster rather than attaining some goal). The opposite is true of course of the monster itself.

The difference between appetitive and aversive emotions is not always clear. Let us take again Lange's reaction to Batala's return in *Le Crime de Monsieur Lange*. On the one hand, Lange is probably *angry* because Batala is trying to take something valuable from him. On the other hand, Lange probably feels *contempt* for Batala because he wants to avoid him as much as possible. Here the situation can be seen from several perspectives, thereby causing different mental attributions or a mixture of them.

Some emotions are immune to the appetitive/aversive distinction. In the case of *hope*, for instance, for which the outcome of the event is uncertain, it does not really matter if the goal is possessive or repellant.

CERTAIN/UNCERTAIN EVENTS. One crucial aspect of mainstream narration is the constant shift between uncertainty and certainty in events and outcomes. The convention of last-minute rescue is perhaps the most obvious case, in which the outcome of the situation is held uncertain until the very end, for spectators as well as for characters. Such uncertain events archetypically generate *hope* (positive) or *fear* (negative) in the characters involved. When the outcome of a situation is finally known, then *joy* and *relief* (positive) or *sadness, frustration,* and *disgust* (negative) will emerge.

The uncertainty/certainty parameter is not exclusive to last-minute rescues, but can be found in smaller-scale examples as well. In *The Big Parade*, after having enlisted in the army for the Civil War, Jim arrives home and must tell his mother about it (Figure 48). On the basis of body cues and information given earlier in the film, the spectator attributes to the mother some mixture of *hope* and *fear* (worry): she seems to *suspect* what has happened, but is not quite certain. When Jim successfully lies to her, she is probably *relieved* because she trusts the received information. However, later in the scene (not included in the figure), when she finally finds out about his enlistment, mother's *relief* turns into genuine *sadness*.

Here, the character moves back and forth between uncertainty and certainty about a strongly motive-inconsistent event, thereby generating emotional turbulence. It is only through assessing the (un)certainty parameter that the spectator can appreciate the differences between emotions such as *hope* and *relief*. The same holds true when McClane, at the beginning of *Die Hard*, slides down the sloping roof and at the last moment is saved by a railing. Judging from McClane's screams, he does not seem to be in control of the situation; for a fraction of a second, he *fears* that he will fall off the building. By the sudden appearance of the railing, however, this *fear* is transformed into *relief*. It is clear to the spectator that McClane has gone from uncertainty to certainty.

Sometimes the same event may generate both certainty and uncertainty on different levels. Take McClane's killing of Fritz at the beginning of the film (Figure 33). McClane no doubt feels *relieved* at having avoided death (certainty). On the other hand, the killing probably makes him realize the seriousness and professionalism of the Gruber gang, and that there will be dangerous impending fights (negative uncertainty generates *fear*). Like many situations, this one triggers attributions of mixed emotions.

LOW/HIGH CONTROL POTENTIAL. The way in which a person understands his or her control potential and moral power in an event makes distinctions between certain emotions. In *Le Crime de Monsieur Lange*, the first time *Arizona Jim* is published, Valentine informs Lange that Batala has manipulated his story through an extensive product placement for Ranimax Pills. Lange becomes physically agitated; because the event runs counter to his intentions, the event is planned and executed by another person, and the product placement is perceived by Lange as something that he could have stopped, the attribution is likely to be *anger*. Moreover, he believes that he has moral right on his side. *Dislike* would have been more probable if he had signed away all rights and had no power to influence publication.

Additional Remarks
On the basis of the structure of FP, in the preceding paragraphs I tried to reconstruct (some of) the mental attribution processes and understandings of character psychology in a number of film scenes. The discussion demonstrated that spectators' appraisals of character minds and emotions are heavily interwoven and can be understood only in relation to each other. The model of the mind and the parameters of emotion appraisal jointly constitute FP. The understanding of the scene from *The Big Parade*, for instance, in which beliefs, goals, and emotions of different kinds interact in complex but structured ways, is a good example.

INTRADIEGETIC ATTRIBUTIONS. I should point out that, in order to understand the mental states of characters, the spectator must assume that characters *themselves* possess mental attribution abilities. Characters are not diegetic islands. What goes on in the mental landscape of a given character is often directly related to the mental states of *other* characters. Just as the spectator is engaged in mental attribution, so are the characters themselves, and this social ability must be taken into account in the mental attribution process.

An instructive example of this is a scene from *Die Hard*, in which Karl, after an unsuccessful chase after McClane, returns to the room in which the hostage is being held. Using his gun, he violently tears down a shelf. This act is observed by McClane's wife (Holly), who thereby infers that McClane must be alive: "Only John would make someone that mad." To understand what goes on in Holly's mind, the spectator has to assume that she possesses FP and mental reasoning abilities: "Karl is *angry* because John has evaded him again, which means that John must be alive." We might call such processes *intradiegetic mental attribution*, as mental attribution takes place within the fictional world. In *Steamboat Bill, Jr.* (Figure 45) it is the *mistaken* intradiegetic mental attribution that constitutes the humorous core of the scene. Whereas the spectator understands that Junior jumps around and plays his ukulele in order to comfort the baby, Senior fails to attribute this motive to his son. Since Senior's view is blocked, he thinks that Junior is crazily fooling around. To understand the joke in this scene, the spectator not only must make goal attributions to Junior, but also must understand Senior's mistaken understanding of Junior and the situation. It is from this discrepancy that the humor emerges.

Moreover, in many genres, it is essential to expect not only that characters attribute mental states to each other, but also that they try to influence these mental states somehow. *Lying* and *deception*, which are common phenomena in detective stories, soaps, and (psychological) thrillers, are perhaps the clearest examples. To understand that character A is lying to character B, the spectator must infer an *intention* in A to change the *beliefs* of B in a direction favorable to A's *purposes*. Such mental attributions often involve a complex web of intentions and beliefs, including beliefs about another person's beliefs and intentions. Throughout *Die Hard*, we see Gruber and McClane talking on the radio with each other, although never face-to-face. Later in the film, when Gruber inspects explosives under the roof – having left his pistol somewhere else – he unexpectedly finds McClane's gun pointed at his chin [Figure 49(a)]. After a pause, Gruber suddenly falls down on his knees, screaming, "You are one of them, aren't you?," begging for his life. At this, McClane urges him to calm down and hands him a cigarette. Gruber introduces himself as Bill Clay, whereupon McClane asks if he knows how to use a gun and hands one to him [Figure 49(b)]. When McClane turns his back, Gruber aims the gun at him and calls Karl on the radio [Figure 49(c)].

To understand this set of events, the spectator must make a series of mental attributions: Neither Gruber nor McClane recognizes each other's faces; by getting down on his knees and *playing* subordinate, Gruber's *intention* is to make McClane *believe* that he is in fact one of the hostages in order not to get killed. His deception succeeds, as McClane hands him the gun and only when Gruber calls Karl on the radio does McClane understand that he has been fooled.

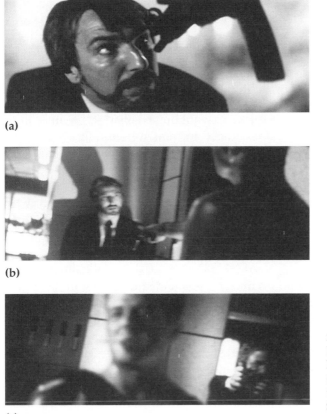

(a)

(b)

FIGURE 49.
Die Hard (John
McTiernan, 1988).
(Obtained from
the film archives of
Svenska Filminsti-
(c) tutet, Stockholm.)

Of course, these mental attributions must be revised in the next sequence: McClane provocatively approaches Gruber's aimed gun, whereupon Gruber fires and (surprisingly) finds that the gun is unloaded.
McClane *suspected* Gruber's real identity all along ("Do you think I am
stupid, Hans?"), but he made Gruber *believe* that his deception was successful. McClane *intentionally* handed Gruber the unloaded gun in order to
test his *real* intentions. To construct coherence in the dialogue and behavior in this scene, the spectator must engage in complex mental attributions
of deception and counterdeception.

MENTAL ATTRIBUTIONS AND TIME. Mental attribution is not a linear process, like the running reel of a film. It is true that a mental model of a given
character's psychology is continually updated by the spectator as the film
runs. This updating, however, involves parameters that were established

earlier or will be established later. It has been repeatedly emphasized that previous attributions are crucial in the mental attribution process: The more cues available, and the richer a situation is, the more precise and certain the attribution can be. Attributions must be remembered for future situations, in which they may become central to *those* attribution processes. In the schematic reconstructions presented in the preceding subsections, these previous attributions were indicated with black squares in the figures (e.g., "Mother doesn't want Jim to enlist" in Figure 48).

Such attributions are often crucial for making sense of a scene. It is no surprise that film scholars and lecturers, when showing or analyzing short film excerpts, often supply the reader or audience with precisely such mental attributions before the analysis starts. Here, the scholar verbally "supplies the memory" of earlier attributions, thereby creating the situational context within which the lecture audience can construct coherence. Understanding a scene requires context: One important part of that context is information about the mental states of the characters on entering the scene.

Some mental attributions must be suspended until later in the film or scene, as there are simply not enough cues present to warrant attribution. Although we see the Gruber gang execute a number of well-prepared actions at the beginning of *Die Hard*, it is not until the brutal interrogation of Mr. Takagi, that the (first time) spectator grasps their goal of opening the vault. It is only at that moment that those former scenes and actions make sense (on this level of meaning).

Such suspension can also be present within scenes and situations, for instance, in the previously discussed scene in which Gruber orders Karl to shoot the glass interior of the office in order to hurt the barefooted McClane. This goal is never explicitly stated, but is alluded to throughout the scene: First we see Gruber look at glass on the floor which is mixed with the blood of one of his crew members [Figures 50(a) and 50(b)]; then Gruber orders Karl to shoot twice through the glass; eventually we see McClane's feet on a floor filled with glass [Figure 50(c)], as he looks at the exit door; and finally – after an intervening scene – McClane is seen picking bits of glass from his feet [Figure 50(d)].

At what particular instance does Gruber's intention becomes clear to the spectator? Well, this depends on the amount of attention and constructive energy expended by the spectator: Some may have guessed it already at Gruber's POV of the blood and glass, others may not understand it until they finally see McClane hurt on the toilet. The point here is not to determine which of these timings is the most common one, but to state that mental attributions do not necessarily take place at the same time the mental state is formed in the character. It can be suspended to a later time – compare with Bordwell's (1985:55) notion of retardation.

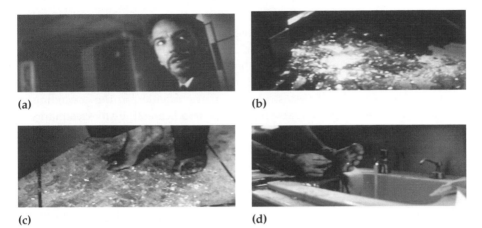

(a)   (b)

(c)   (d)

FIGURE 50. *Die Hard* (John McTiernan, 1988). Gruber shoots the glass, thereby taking advantage of the barefooted McClane. (Obtained from the film archives of the Svenska Filminstitutet, Stockholm.)

Such *retrospective* attributions may not only fill in mental states left unattributed in previous sections of the film; they may also *revise* earlier attributions that later in the narrative prove to be incorrect. This happened in the scene of Gruber's and McClane's meeting under the roof (Figure 49): McClane gave the unloaded gun to Gruber, not because he *believed* him to be one of the hostages, but because he *wanted* to test his credibility. McClane was more cunning than the spectator first expected.

Mental reasoning may also fill in gaps that were simply missed by the filmmakers or the spectators, but that "must have happened" in order for events to make sense. In the wrestling scene of *Seven Samurai* (Figure 44), the Samurai's touching the torso of the girl happens very fast and in a bustling shot. Most spectators will probably miss it (unless they have a VCR to rewind and pause). The dashed arrows in Figure 44 mark this lapse. However, through FP reasoning the spectator probably fills in the gap in retrospect in order to make sense of the Samurai's backing away. This line of reasoning – represented by the full arrows in Figure 44 – "goes backwards" and reconstructs what "must have happened" on the basis of FP and the situation. The filmmakers seem to be aware of this underdetermination on the film's part, because the last shot, with the Samurai and the girl sitting next to each other, gets ample screen time so that the spectator has time to fill in those necessary retrospective gaps. The so-called rhythm and timing of editing is intimately related to the cognitive activities the spectator is expected to perform in order to make sense of a given scene.

With respect to time, mental attribution processes not only pick up on previous actions and mental attributions, but also point forward to future ones. Because FP forms a strong inferential structure, it provides a potent mental tool for *predictive* inferences (see the subsection on the Instrumental Value of Folk Psychology). Several of the preceding examples contain such inferences, for instance, predicting that Lange will kill Batala after Batala's return to Lange's office. This prediction is, of course, influenced by the title of the film (*Le Crime de Monsieur Lange*). The mental attributions made during the scene, however, also play a vital role in creating an expectation of the killing ("Lange is angry with Batala; he *sees* the gun; *anger* fuels *intentions* and *actions*; Lange intends to shoot Batala").

Mental attribution is a process in which the spectator is forced to jump back and forth between "present" and "past," as well as into the possible "future." Understanding in general and mental attribution in particular are thus fundamentally temporal in nature, involving complex processes of memory, attention, and cognitive creativity by the spectator. Understanding, even on this rather simple level of description, presupposes an active spectator.

WHAT IS A ROUND/FLAT CHARACTER? On the basis of the preceding examples, we are in a position to complement Chatman's and Smith's definitions of flat and round characters, which were based on the notions of traits and stereotypes (see the subsection on Levels of Meaning). We may now define a flat character as a character that defies or makes difficult mental attribution processes. *Weekend*'s Roland and Corinne provide prototypical examples of this. The parameters blocking the understanding of the mental lives of these characters have already been given in detail. Flatness – in my definition of the term – also pertains to minor roles, as short acquaintance with these characters is unable to provide enough cues and appraisal parameters for clear and unambiguous attributions. Take, for instance, Gruber's henchmen. Some of these stick it out and are given more attention by the narration (e.g., Karl and his brother Fritz). Most of them, however, are reduced to shooting machines without mental lives: They do not belong to any particular social type (e.g., husbands or waiters); they are not equipped with traits (e.g., extrovert, talkative, curious); there is no time to attribute to them any beliefs or goals other than the most rudimentary (*wanting* to shoot McClane or the police and to *avoid* being shot at); and they are devoid of any feelings other than pain when shot at. Whereas *Weekend* "intentionally" seems to block the attribution process concerning the major protagonists, the minor roles of *Die Hard* are flat as there is no time for the narration to pay them any further attention. It is this lack of spatiotemporal attachment that resists mental attributions and hence gives these characters their flat nature.

A round character, on the other hand, is one that not only allows mental attributions, but also presents a wide range of cues and appraisal parameters with which to reason and "play around with." "The characters in quality films are round, in the sense that they display more emotion, and that emotion is more developed than that of the heroes in the popular genres" (Tan, 1996:173). I have returned again and again to the scene in which Batala returns to Lange's office, as this situation is so full of different ways to appraise Lange's emotions, goals, and beliefs. Lange's mental life in this and other scenes can be approached from a number of perspectives, taking up different events and circumstances that all contribute to the emotional blend of Lange's mental landscape. The roundness is thus a result of the interaction among the way in which the narration places the character in rich situations, the powerful inferential structure of FP, and the viewer's cognitive creativity.

This reconceptualization of round versus flat characters in no way opposes Chatman's and Smith's accounts, but can be seen as complementing them.

NARRATIVE CAUSALITY IS PRIMARILY A PSYCHOLOGICAL CAUSALITY. A far more important issue evoked by these examples is *causality*. Mental attribution and FP reasoning bind events, situations, and actions together and thereby create coherence and a holistic sense in discourse. It is essential to point out that these relations and connections are primarily *causal* in nature. The network of FP is basically a system of mental states interrelated through prototypical causality: for example, emotions *cause* body and facial expressions; beliefs plus goals *cause* actions; emotions *cause* goals; a motive-inconsistent event brought about by the intentional act of another person *causes* anger toward that person. FP and the mental level understanding of other people (as well as fictional characters) are the core constructions of causal relationships between phenomena. This is *psychological causality*, as it involves the relationship between hypothesized mental states and behavior.

Causality in narratives – often discussed in terms of "logic" (e.g., Bordwell, 1985:51) – has of course been investigated by many scholars. White (1990) argues that the notion of causality is the feature that distinguishes a list of events (e.g., in annals) from narratives. Branigan (1992: 19ff) expands on this notion and gives a list of different forms of relationships of varying causal strength (heap, catalogue, episode, unfocused chain, focused chain, simple narrative). In his *Aspects of the Novel* from 1927, Forster makes the following claim:

A plot is [. . .] a narrative of events, the emphasis falling on causality. "The king died and then the queen died" is a story. "The king died and then the queen died of grief" is a plot. (Cited in Murray, 1997:185)

Bordwell (1985:51) postulates time, space, and causality as the three basic patterns constructed by the reader or spectator.

None of these claims, however, is followed up by a systematic approach as to how spectators and text establish causal relations in narratives. Bordwell, for instance, spends a chapter each on time and space, but causality is undiscussed (see also Chatman, 1978; Genette, 1980). This lack is symptomatic for narrative theory, probably because causality is much more elusive than the fabula–syuzhet discussions of time and space.

In contrast to text-oriented theories, the reception-based approach used in this study is in a better position to discuss these matters. Causality is not a textual feature, but fundamentally involves inferential activities by the spectator on the basis of textual cues and models of causality. FP – as we have seen – is one such model, specifying and supporting causal inference processes in narrative discourse understanding.[21] By sketching the structure of those models – which are being investigated in the fields of psychology, anthropology, and cultural studies – as well as by describing textual techniques and structures, we can begin to think about general ways in which spectators construct causality and coherence. In this chapter I present a first effort in this direction.

In accordance with many scholars, I believe that causality in narratives primarily centers on *psychological* causality, rather than on other types (see Astington, 1990; Bordwell et al., 1985:13 & 174ff; Trabasso, 1991). Whereas the discourses of natural science use the *physical stance* (in e.g., research reports, studies, science television, everyday explanations of the physical, chemical, and biological world), narrative understanding revolves around the *intentional stance*. Narratives deal with intentional agents[22] interacting with other intentional agents in complex ways: "In almost every work of literature, 'something happens': and the cause of whatever takes place is attributed to either human or non-human agents" (Gerrig & Allbritton, 1990:381). This is not to say that physical causality is lacking in narrative landscapes (e.g., nature catastrophes, storms, lava eruptions, car crashes), but it does seem to take on marginal importance in most narratives: "I do not wish to argue that human agents are the only agents of causality in narratives, but I do want to argue that human agency has a centrality to our comprehension of narratives" (Smith, 1995:20). Narratives can be told about animals, planets, rocks, or molecules, but then these entities are often given anthropomorphic features that encourage the reader or spectator to use FP understanding. Even though nonanthropomorphic events and situations may arise – such as natural disasters – it is not these events per se that are in narrative focus. Rather, it is the cognitive, emotional, and behavioral *reactions* of anthropomorphic agents and the *human significance* vis-à-vis the events that become central in narratives. In these respects, I believe that FP reasoning becomes central to investigating how causality is constructed and experienced in narrative discourse.

Let me give an example. As noted, young children seem to have difficulties with FP reasoning in real life and in narrative understanding. This is obviously reflected in the genre system of children's stories, which often are tightly adapted to a specific age group. Astington (1990) recounts her two-year-old child's favorite story:

Here is a farm. Here is a stable. The horse lives here with one little foal. Here is the cowshed. The cow lives here with two little calves. Here is the barn. The cat lives here with three little kittens. Here is the pigsty. The pig lives here with four little pigs. Here is the duckpond. The duck lives here with five little ducklings. Here is the orchard. The hen lives here with six little chicks. Here is the field. The sheep live here with all the little lambs. Here is the farmer with all his animals. (From *The Farm*, Gagg, 1958)

Only two years later, the favorite story is something completely different:

The emperor thought he would like to see it while it was still on the loom. So, accompanied by a number of selected courtiers, among whom were the two faithful officials who had already seen the imaginary stuff, he went to see the crafty imposters, who were working away as hard as ever they could at the empty loom. "It is magnificent!" said both the officials. "Only see, Your majesty, what a design! What colours!" And they pointed to the empty loom, for they thought no doubt that the others could see the stuff. "What!" thought the emperor; "I see nothing at all! This is terrible! Am I a fool? Am I not fit to be emperor? Why, nothing worse could happen to me!" "Oh it is beautiful!" said the emperor. "It has my highest approval!" and he nodded his satisfaction as he gazed at the empty loom. Nothing would induce him to say that he could not see anything. (From Hans Christian Andersen's "The Emperor's New Clothes," in Briggs & Haviland, 1974:176ff.)

The younger child prefers a fictional landscape focused around space and characters without action and psychology. Hans Christian Andersen's narrative, on the other hand, revolves around the psychology of characters and the ways in which perceptions, beliefs, goals, and emotions interact in complex ways. Here the active use of FP reasoning seems to take center stage. This observation was confirmed by Trabasso & Stein (1997), who showed seven pictures of a frog narrative to three-, four-, five-, and nine-year-old children and asked them to narrate the events in the pictures. The youngest children were preoccupied with naming, identifying, and describing animate and inanimate beings and things. The four-year-old children tended to add action verbs to this, whereas reasons for actions, character goals, and initiating events and emotional reactions were part of the five-year-old children's narrative. The nine-year-old children elaborated on the scenes with even more character goals, as well as more action outcomes that indicated obstacles and failures.

This transgression from the *outer* landscape of action and behavior to the *inner* landscape of FP (Bruner, 1986:14) reflects the expansion of FP competence that takes place during these years of development. Mainstream narratives and narrative understanding, I believe, are specifically focused around the second type of stance.[23]

Psychological causality is, of course, a matter of degree, not of principle. Some narratives choose to emphasize character psychology (*Le Crime de Monsieur Lange*); others subdue or even block it (*The Farm, Play Time, Weekend*). These strategies do not only make differences between individual films, but also between genres. Mainstream narratives tend to be more focused on character psychology and psychological causality than art films are. Melodrama, soaps, and detective stories tend to be more focused on character psychology than action, adventure, and special-effects films are. In addition (as we shall see), early mainstream cinema was less focused on character psychology than modern mainstream cinema is. It is to the stylistic or textual ways in which a given film can accomplish these different emphases that we now turn.

Text and Mental Attribution

So far, I have discussed character psychology from the perspective of the spectator: What knowledge structures are used and what processes do they give rise to? We must not, however, forget that the text regulates, molds, and directs these processes (see Bourg & Stephenson, 1997:299; Omdahl, 1995:33 & 97). Thus my spectator account needs to be complemented with a textual one: If some texts encourage and others block effective mental attribution and coherence, what textual techniques, figures, strategies, and structures are used (or not used) by the narration? What conventions are at the filmmakers' disposal to trigger or discourage character psychology? How are psychologically rich or poor situations created? To explain such effects on the mental attribution process, we must investigate the textual side of the matter.

Textual Techniques
In presenting and discussing these techniques and their development, in this section I make explicit reference to the nature of FP reasoning and mental attribution. As I have tried to show throughout this study, discursive practices are seldom random, but rather are strongly *motivated* by how mental attribution works in everyday life. That is, in light of the preceding psychological investigation of FP, we can start investigating not only which techniques support mental attribution, but also *why* a given technique has gained popularity.

ACTING VERSUS SITUATION. Acting seems to be the first and most obvious technique for promoting mental attribution. As already discussed, however, the meaning of a given body or facial expression cannot be determined on its own, but is intimately interwoven with the situation in which it appears.

Imagine that we perceived the smile of the mother in Figure 48 totally out of context. In this hypothetical case, the spectator would perhaps be able to infer some general "positive emotion," but how this arose and its exact nature would be beyond substantiated reasoning. On its own, the smile warrants only a very abstract – and for the narrative virtually useless – attribution. To get at a more precise and nuanced understanding of the smile and the mother's mental state (e.g., *relief* rather than positive emotion), her goals, beliefs, and other mental states must be taken into account. Thus acting and physical behavior are not *expressions* correlating with a mental state: they are *cues*, which the spectators must expand on and reason about.

In fact, if the situation is psychologically rich enough, few acting cues may be necessary in order to convey the psychology of characters. Films such as Hirokazu Koreeda's *Maboroshi no hikari* (1995) or Hou Hsiao-hsien's *City of Sadness* (1989) deal with deeply psychologized characters, but acting is reduced to a minimum. The characters' behavior is subdued, and the extreme long-shot style makes it virtually impossible to detect (facial) acting even if there were any. Here – as in much of Bresson's corpus – FP reasoning, rather than reliance on acting cues, seems to play a stronger role in constructing characters' mental landscapes.

This, of course, does not imply that acting is superfluous for mental attribution. On the contrary, acting often provides important cues for determining the mental state. We must, however, formulate its importance in more nuanced terms. A tentative answer is to claim that FP reasoning and body behavior work in tandem to maximize the determinacy of mental attribution. If FP and situational understanding constitute the major sources of information in a scene, body behavior *confirms* the attribution. On the other hand, if we encounter a physical behavior with a more general meaning (e.g., positive emotion), then knowledge of the situation supports and constrains this attribution. In this latter case, the external cue works as a "range finder" and FP reasoning as a "focuser."

This constant interaction between FP and body cues was clear in the scene from *Seven Samurai*, in which the backing-away reaction of the Samurai was understood in conjunction with FP reasoning (Figure 44). The scene from *The Big Parade* (Figure 48) offers another instructive example, as it contains no dialogue or intertitles, but relies solely on the spectator's attributions earlier in the film and on the physical behavior of

Jim and his mother. Thus the understanding of the scene is based on how "situation" and acting dialectically support each other. For instance, on the basis of previous scenes and attributions, the spectator could expect Jim to have trouble telling his mother about enlistment (FP reasoning), but it is Jim's fading smile on seeing his mother that triggers this attribution and makes it pertinent to the present scene.

Of course, some texts aim to create *conflict* between FP reasoning and body cues when they cast doubt on each other. A clear example of this is Roland's (non) reaction when his wife is raped in *Weekend* (see the subsection on Events Caused by Circumstance, Other, or Self). Here, different FP reasonings try in vain to come to grips with his and his wife's external behavior.

Between these two extremes – FP reasoning and body cues confirming or conflicting with each other – there are probably cases in which the body cues are in harmony with FP reasoning, although these cues do not actively trigger or propel the mental attribution process. When Batala returns in *Le Crime de Monsieur Lange*, FP reasoning can easily predict Lange's emotional reaction (*surprise, anger*). The situation appears to be the major source of information. The small portions of Lange's body that the spectator gets to see are, of course, compatible with those mental attributions ("stricken by surprise"). In contrast to the scene mentioned from the *The Big Parade*, however, in the scene of Batala's return in *Le Crime de Monsieur Lange* Lange's body and face do not forcefully drive the mental attribution process, nor do they send this process in new and unexpected directions. The way in which acting cues in fact launch or drive the mental attribution process is a matter of degree.

CREATING PSYCHOLOGICALLY RICH SITUATIONS. If acting on its own may not be decisive for mental attribution, then what is? A lesson learned from our survey of everyday mental attribution and the structure of FP is that the understanding of most mental states is dependent on a number of *other* mental states and *situational parameters*. That is, the more parameters present at the time of mental attribution, the more sophisticated and nuanced the FP reasoning can be and the more specific and nuanced the attribution. From a textual point of view, this implies that, if a filmmaker wants to promote mental attribution and character psychology, then the filmmaker has to present those parameters to the spectator or assume that the viewer is able to infer them (see Omdahl, 1995:97). Mental attribution presupposes the situation to be "psychologically rich" from the outset. If those parameters are not present, then finer discriminations between mental states are impossible to work out (unless the spectator starts to "make up" those parameters that are absent from the film).

Spatiotemporal Attachment. How, then, are psychologically rich situations created? One of the most central means, which encompasses a range of conventions and practices, is the way in which the narration "follows" a given character through time and space. Smith (1995) calls this *spatiotemporal attachment.* I argue that this strategy is a direct consequence of how FP and mental attribution work in everyday life. If we assume that mental attribution is heavily based on many parameters, and even on previous mental attributions, then we may conclude that establishing psychologically rich situations takes time. The viewer must follow a character over time, picking up aspects of situations, before beginning to differentiate between different mental states. From the perspective of narration, presenting those situational parameters takes screen time (or page space). Even though this is a straightforward observation, it is fundamental.

The narration in mainstream cinema, for instance, tends to restrict itself to a small gallery of characters and to follow them for an extensive period of screen time. This makes it possible for the spectator to speculate about their mental states and appraise the emotional importance of the events taking place. In contrast, early cinema provided only brief access to characters, whereas in any Soviet films of the 1930s contained such a large gallery of characters that spatiotemporal attachment to individual characters became transient (e.g., in *Strike*). In these cases, mental attribution is more difficult to achieve, an effect the Soviets probably were aware of (promoting "identification" with a collective rather than with individuals). The point here is that spatiotemporal attachment to a character facilitates mental attribution, and it does so *because* mental attribution primarily relies on earlier mental attributions to a given character.

Mental attribution and FP reasoning take time in another sense. The process of collecting the appraisal parameters and other mental states from memory at a given point in the narrative takes cognitive processing. That is, pondering the consequences of a given situation for the characters involved – and perhaps even revisiting earlier attributions – are time-consuming activities. For those processes to work properly, the narration must allow them time, by presenting little new story information. In visual media, such passages are often characterized by "stopping of time" sequences in which nothing new or informative actually occurs. We have already touched on one such example when discussing the last shot of the scene from *Seven Samurai* (Figure 44). This shot shows the Samurai and the girl sitting some distance apart with little character movement. Instead, this "narrative pause" gives the spectator time to understand the psychologically complex and tense situation preceding this shot (what was the Samurai surprised at or afraid of?). Alternatively, this pause allows more specific and nuanced attributions by considering other appraisal parameters (e.g., in blended emotions). Narrative pausing is an important tool for filmmakers to create rhythm and timing and can be deployed through both acting and editing. Scenes and situations often end with pauses, for example, the clichéd final close-up in soaps and melodramas (often with heightened music), which is held for some time with no action at all (see Chapter 3, the subsection on "Closer-Ups"). This enables the spectator not only to make mental attributions for the preceding situation or event, but also to generate predictive inferences about future episodes or scenes.

Early cinema, as well as early classical cinema, appears to have indulged in such pauses to a much larger degree than contemporary mainstream cinema. In either case, the practice was probably adopted from narrative theater:

All of the sources we have seen suggest that poses were held for a considerable length of time in the theatre. There are some accounts of actors holding poses for five minutes, which seems implausible, but we would be less inclined to dismiss claims for a length of 20–30 seconds. We have never seen a film actor pause for more than a few seconds (Asta Nielsen holds the record with 18 seconds). (Brewster & Jacobs, 1998:259)

Actor's pausing in early cinema was probably influenced by the tableaux regime of the vaudeville, which indulged in poses and "staged paintings" in which narrative dimensions were peripheral. One may also, however, assume that film producers accommodated their discourse according to an (assumed) cinematically "uneducated" audience, giving it enough time to apply FP reasoning and to process the images.

Irrespective of historical period, the point here is that pausing in narrative theater and cinema is not a matter of arbitrary punctuation; it is a direct consequence of the structure and temporal nature of the mental attribution process and of understanding processes in general. Pauses fulfill important functions, but these functions can be described only if we consider the processes of cognition and understanding.

We may also ponder the primary importance of spatiotemporal attachment from another perspective. It is fair to assume that the spectator's ability to make mental attribution to more than one character at a time is rather limited. There may be more than one person in a given situation, but we seem to speculate about the mental landscapes of the participants one at a time. Perhaps we shift our mental attribution efforts between them in a back-and-forth movement, but it is difficult to imagine how the mental attribution process could work when attending to both at the same time. By spatiotemporal attachment, the narration partially determines to which character the spectator devotes attribution efforts at a given moment in the story. This process works on a general plot level through the choice of scenes in which a particular character is involved. It also works on the level of scene, in which the narration, through different mise-en-scène techniques "concentrates" on one of the participating characters. These techniques all aim at creating hierarchies of importance within the scene and between characters, and include a wide range of common practices.

- Framing may be used to isolate one and exclude other characters. In *The Big Parade*, for instance, the initial long shot of Jim and his mother is followed by a cut-in to the mother, guiding the spectator's efforts to her (instead of to Jim). The same technique lies at the core of one of the most widely used conventions in all visual media, namely SRS editing.[24]
- All sorts of physical and verbal behavior by one character may draw attention, at another character's expense. In sound film, verbal behavior may be one of the most attention-drawing techniques. A common device in preclassical cinema was to let the important character(s) break loose from the background group and step closer to the camera (Thompson, 1985:200). Here, movement and foreground/background relations, rather than isolation, create hierarchies of importance. We may also think of turn-taking and the temporal dimension of acting as regulating spectators' attention. Brewster and Jacobs discuss a scene from the Danish production *Klovnen* (1917), in which both actors are visible in the shot, but the timing of the acting between the two makes clear on which character the spectator should concentrate at a given moment:

> With this kind of acting one often finds alternations of poses as in this instance, in which Houlberg, although in the foreground, remains very still to allow attention to be focused on Psilander in the background. Then when he [Psilander] gets to the foreground it is her [Houlberg's] turn to pose and react. This kind of alteration of poses continues throughout the scene. It is just one illustration of the way that the acting ensemble could direct the spectator's attention, a function which is typically handled by editing or staging in later classical filmmaking

- We may also think of other mise-en-scène techniques such as color, lighting, and blocking of characters with sets.

Although these techniques may operate individually, they are often combined, for example, in the typical SRS structure (in which editing and framing follow the speaker). These techniques are often discussed under the heading of "directing attention" (e.g., Thompson, 1985:Chap. 17), but it is seldom spelled out what this notion involves *psychologically*. We are now in a better position to do so: As far as characters are concerned, these techniques choose on which character the spectator should spend his or her mental attributions efforts. Through spatiotemporal attachment, the narration channels the FP reasoning of the spectator.

Such focusing is, of course, a matter of degree. Some narratives channel the mental attribution process tightly and efficiently, whereas others leave the choice to the spectator. Analytical editing and SRS techniques regulate these processes clearly and unambiguously, as does turn-taking in dialogues. At the other end of the spectrum, a crowded long shot of early cinema, in which no character is more visually important than another, the "responsibility" of spatiotemporal attachment is transferred from text to spectator (see *The Musketeers of Pig Alley*, Figure 8). Here, it is more or less up to the spectator to "choose" the character of interest.

It is sometimes observed by early cinema spectators and reviewers, as well as modern cinema scholars, how this narrational refusal to promote hierarchies in the image becomes problematic when one is trying to convey a coherent story. On the basis of a one-shot scene from an early Griffith production (*The Greaser's Gauntlet*, 1908), Gunning discusses the consequences of the long-shot style for the understanding process:

Several narratively important actions happen in this barroom shot. The heroine, Mildred (Marion Leonard), is introduced and encounters Jose. They show a mutual interest. However, the distant camera position cannot stress the moment. During the crucial meeting only the gestures of the actors draw our attention, competing with the cowboys playing cards on the left, or the Chinese waiter (George Gebhardt) scurrying about. This lack of a clear dramatic hierarchy within the shot becomes a problem during the key action of the shot: the Chinese waiter picks a cowboy's pocket and plants a bandanna which had contained the money on Jose. Other than the actors' frantic gestures, nothing cues the audience that the Chinese waiter, previously an incidental character, has become the center of the drama. Present-day audiences frequently miss this essential action, which nothing in the filmic discourse (such as a cut to a closer shot isolating the theft) emphasizes. Through the lack of compositional hierarchy the film risks illegibility. (Gunning, 1994:76)

Although the complaints in 1908–9 about films' incomprehensibility (for examples, see Gunning, 1994:91f) cannot explicitly be tied to lack of spatiotemporal attachment, this must have been part of the problem. Of course, this lack of channeling mental attribution may have been compensated for by the increasing use of both lecturers and intertitles (a fact Gunning seems to disregard).

If mainstream cinema can be said to clearly channel attribution to one character at a time, a more open style occasionally appears. Take again the last shot of the *Seven Samurai* scene (Figure 44). Perhaps the girl's foreground position directs the spectator's attribution efforts more on her than on the Samurai; perhaps the earlier narrative focus on the Samurai makes him more interesting, but basically it is up to the spectator to make a choice. (The inferences in Figure 44 give only *his* reactions to the situation.) Here, the narration's channeling of mental attribution effort is kept minimal, delegating most responsibility for choice to the spectator.[25]

Three Other Techniques. Spatiotemporal attachment is a general principle by which psychologically rich situations can be created, but we may also think of other practices. All forms of subjective imagery – in which the ontological status of the visual information is given a degree of subjectivity – also strive to present cues for the mental attribution process. Such images are useful because they can be seen as external representations of what occurs in the psyche of the character. Visualizing dreams, hallucinations, flashbacks, and visions were important ways by which early cinema introduced character psychology. Until 1906, the different trick techniques that rendered subjectivity often presented "subjective images as self-contained attractions, of interest in themselves, rather than giving psychological dimensions to an extended narrative" (Gunning, 1994:117). Soon, however, such practices were integrated into and placed within a narrative context. Both Gunning (1994:116) and Thompson (1985:179) mention the frequent use of dreams and visions in films throughout the period 1908–15.

Another subjectivizing technique, whose history I have already traced in Chapter 2, is POV editing. In a mass discourse that promotes character psychology, POV editing enables perceptions of characters to enter the FP reasoning process (see the preceding section). Moreover, because POV editing depends on basic, universally spread spectator dispositions (following other people's gaze), it requires no learning and sophisticated cultural knowledge. This situation fits in with commercialized mass medium superbly.

Between objective and subjective images hover semisubjective ones. Art cinema makes frequent use of such ambiguous imagery (e.g., *L'Année dernière à Marienbad*, 1961). Early cinema also seems to have embraced this in the *switchback* convention (discussed in Chapter 2). The importance of this convention for promoting character psychology in early cinema cannot be overestimated (see Gunning, 1994:116ff).

Whether "arty" scholars like it or not, verbal discourse has always accompanied visual imagery to a great extent and has provided a set of rich inferential cues for mental attribution. Text in any form – catalogue descriptions, lecturers, posters, reviews, titles, intertitles, and, perhaps most important, dialogue – often gives invaluable support for FP reasoning. It is difficult to reconstruct the discourse of early cinema lecturers, but many seem to have used catalogue descriptions from production companies (see Gunning, 1994:91ff). Lecturers seem to have been in use around 1908, as well as in earlier vaudeville, museum, and fair exhibition modes. Lecturers probably had many functions in the mental attribution process. They pointed out, recognized, and named characters; they revealed characters' identities and relationships; they described actions and setting in a given situation; and they directed the spectator's attention to the temporarily important character. Studying some of these discourses more closely also reveals the frequent use of FP terms that compensated for mental attribution problems of early film. In *Lubin's Complete Catalogue* from 1903, we find a detailed description of *A Trip to Mars* (1903), which probably was stolen from Méliès' English catalogue text for *Le Voyage dans la lune* (1902), as there is no mention of Mars (reprinted in Pratt, 1973:25ff). Here we find a number of different terms for goals, beliefs, and emotions that make sense of the actions in the film. The frequent use of lecturers is often forgotten in scholars' claims for narrative (non)intelligibility in early cinema. This example shows that character psychology may have been more present in reception of early cinema than archival film material lead us to believe.

As Gunning (1994:91ff) eloquently describes them, the different narrational techniques developed and conventionalized during this transition period soon made the external narrator unnecessary.

Visual means – analytical editing and image composition – replaced some of the lecturer's functions. Above all, intertitles took on great responsibility. In her historical survey, Thompson traces two kinds of intertitles: *expository* and *dialogue*. Expository titles were used in the early period for summarizing events of the next scene and provided "the spectator with an explicit hypothesis for upcoming action, rather than guiding him or her to form hypotheses on the basis of the actions themselves" (Thompson, 1985:183). Later, such expository titles were used to set up a situation, and then the action presented causes and effects.

The main point here is that such expository titles often contained explicit reference to FP terms and relationships. Thompson provides the example of a title from *The Fatal Opal* (1914):

The title ['Not wishing to further antagonize his uncle, Frank says nothing of his marriage'] suggests the increasing use of expository titles to aid the presentation of psychological material, rather than simply summarizing action. In 1914 a scenario guide commented: 'Captions are not labels, but means of suggesting beyond the visible action and of furnishing deeper motives than those on the surface.' (Thompson, 1985:186)

One function of intertitles was thus to enforce and propel mental attribution processes, thereby supporting the spectator's striving for psychological coherence in the discourse.

Until the introduction of sound, expository titles were gradually limited, at the expense of dialogue titles:

Almost every film would use at least a couple at the beginning to introduce characters and situations. But frequently later scenes would contain one or no expository
titles. By the middle and late twenties, the predominance of dialogue titles com-
bines with the general handling of scenes to create films which were prepared for
the introduction of sound. (Thompson, 1985:188)

Whether in written or spoken form, dialogue content is, naturally, one of
the richest sources of cues for mental attribution. Dialogue can explicitly
refer to a mental state, for example, "I *know* you are betraying me" or
"I am *angry*." These are direct cues, leaving little cognitive work for the
spectator. Still, the situation in which they appear must be considered.
(There may, for instance, be reason to believe that the character wants to
mislead.)

Most of the time, however, dialogue merely *hints* at possible mental attributions that often require sophisticated FP reasonings.[26] *Die Hard* again
provides an example of this (Figure 51). In the first part of the scene, we
have a laconic dialogue ("You don't like flying, do you?" and "What gives
you that idea?"), which makes sense only if we consider a number of sophisticated mental attributions (which involve McClane's hand, perceptions, beliefs, and intradiegetic mental attributions). Note that dialogue
not only provides cues for the mental attribution process, but also that
mental attributions provide the context within which the dialogue is understood and made sense of. Understanding the meaning of the utterances
and understanding the mental landscape of the characters are reciprocally
and dynamically interrelated.[27]

Finally, if mental attribution is to be successful, the characters' behavior
must in some way conform to the relations and principles of FP. Consider
again Godard's *Weekend*. Here the narration is spatiotemporally attached
to Corinne and Roland, uses dialogue and acting in expressive ways, and
is not afraid to use POV editing and subjective imagery. Yet mental attribution appears to be rather difficult. For the FP architecture to apply to
a given situation, the behavior and actions of characters to a minimal extent must "map" to this structure. Of course, human behavior is open and
allows different attributions, but most of the time alternative attributions
are contained within the "normality" of FP. Nevertheless, when Roland
and Corinne blatantly and obviously contradict the FP structure, then
coherent mental attributions will become problematic. This, of course,
does not mean that Roland and Corinne are necessarily incomprehensible, only that understanding must take place on another level. The point
is that there must be some "normality" in the characters, in the sense that
there is a limit to how open and random given behaviors can be before FP
reasoning becomes irrelevant. Most (Western) spectators, despite every

DISCOURSE	UNDERSTANDING / INFERENCE	SPECTATOR DISPOSITIONS
Exterior: A jet lands.		
Interior, aircraft. CU hand holding arm-rest.	? (Hand expressed *fear*.)	
	X *sees* the hand.	Deictic gaze ability (POV).
Tilt to face of man (X) looking at hand (off screen).	X *suspects* McClane doesn't *like* flying.	
Camera moves back, revealing face of McClane.	X *suspects* McClane doesn't *like* flying because he *saw* McClane's hand.	FP: Perception informs beliefs.
X: You don't like flying, do you?	X *thinks* McClane's hand expresses *fear*.	Characters possess mental attribution ability (body cues).
McClane: What gives you that idea?		
X: Do you wanna know the secret to surviving air travel? After you get where you're going, take off your shoes and your socks, then you walk around on the rug barefoot and make fists with your toes.	McClane *understands* that X *saw* the hand and *thought* it expressed *fear* because McClane probably *saw* when X *saw* the hand.	Characters possess mental attribution ability (FP), and deictic gaze ability.
CU McClane: Fist with your toes?	X *thinks* he *knows* the secret to surviving air travel.	
MS X and McClane: X: I know, I know it sounds crazy. Trust me! I've been doing it for nine years. Yes sir, better than a shower and a hot cup of coffee!	McClane is *skeptical* of X's *beliefs*.	Facial cues ability + prosody ability (question).
	X *understands* McClane is *skeptical*.	Characters possess mental attribution ability.
McClane: OK.	McClane is still *skeptical*, but does not *want* to argue with X.	
People start to disembark. McClane rises and starts to take his things down from the overhead cabin.		
X sees a gun inside McClane's jacket (POV).		
X's smile fades. X looks at McClane (off screen).	X *realizes* McClane is carrying a gun, which makes him *feel scared*.	Body cue ability + FP: Perception informs beliefs and emotions.
McClane looks at X (off screen).		
McClane: It's ok. I'm a cop. X nods. McClane: Trust me, I've been doing it for eleven years.	McClane *understands* X *saw* the gun and was *scared*.	Characters possess mental attribution ability.

FIGURE 51. *Die Hard* (John McTiernan, 1988). (Diagram designed by Younghee Jung). The photographic material is obtained from the film archives of Svenska Filminstitutet.)

effort to understand their actions in terms of character psychology, probably believe that Roland and Corinne have transgressed that limit. This, of course, does not make the film less interesting from a media–psychological perspective. Quite the contrary.

NONARBITRARY CONVENTIONS. Acting, spatiotemporal attachment, POV editing, and dialogue are media conventions. They have been developed within the visual arts in order to provide narratives of both fictional and nonfictional nature, and they are often copied or adopted among different media and discourse types through history. These conventions, however, are far from just intramedia codes, developed solely within the context of mass discourse; they also make use of the *everyday* assumptions of spectators. Given that a spectator or consumer of discourse is equipped with rich FP expectations about behavior, we can expect that conventions of mass discourse exploit these dispositions (or this "context") to create certain effects. If filmmakers, studios, or modes of production want to promote character psychology and the mental attribution process, then the conventions must be designed in accordance with how such processes work in everyday life.

For instance, spatiotemporal attachment (with all of its subtechniques) is motivated by the observation that spectators can only mentally attribute to one person at a time. Creating hierarchies of importance between characters in a scene thus fulfills important functions (provided of course that one wants to promote mental attribution). Also, staying with a character over an extended period of time enables the discourse to present appraisal parameters and use earlier mental attributions in new and creative ways, thereby creating psychologically rich situations. If a filmmaker wants the spectator to make a distinction between positive or negative emotions, then a goal must be ascribed to that character (preferably before the attribution is made). If a filmmaker wants the spectator to understand the complex and blended emotion of a character in a particular situation, then the narrative must present the spectator with enough appraisal parameters to support this. Such rules of thumb are direct consequences of the fact that mental attributions rely on *other* mental attributions and appraisal parameters in order to work properly. In addition, subjective images and conventions such as POV editing can be quite useful for promoting mental attribution, as they fuel FP reasoning process with *perceptions*. And adding dialogue is important for the attribution process, as it complements acting and other body cues.

All of these techniques are thus *not* arbitrary, in the sense that they are only a matter of social agreement (*dog* vs. *chien*): They are designed and conventionalized in relation to and through careful consideration of spectators' FP. If FP had been different, these techniques probably would have been too. That is, these conventions are just as "arbitrary" as FP is.

GOOD/BAD CONVENTIONS. Given the structure of FP and everyday mental attribution, some techniques are *better* or more effective ("economic") than others. Because spectators' dispositions are structured in certain ways, techniques that adapt to that structure will be better equipped to trigger and support character psychology than others.

Of course, those techniques are "better" only in relation to the purposes of the cinematic discourse. Not all films or narratives strive for character psychology. *Strike*, for instance, with its large character gallery, seems to have been experimenting with other and more collective forms of "character." *Weekend* seems to be occupied with an explicit *critique* of character psychology, by creating indeterminate and contradictory mental attributions in very "flat" characters. In both of these cases, character psychology does not seem to be the main objective, and the techniques just surveyed would in fact be counterproductive for these aesthetic objectives. In all of this we find a pertinent observation to which we have returned throughout this study: cinematic techniques and conventions have no inherent value in and of themselves, but only in relation to the functions or purpose they are said to perform. Claiming that some techniques promote mental attribution more efficiently than others is a strictly psychological argument: If a filmmaker wants to promote mental attribution, some techniques are better because the psychology of the spectator is structured in a certain way. The argument will, however, have nothing to say about the strategies of promoting versus not promoting character psychology.

The Narrativization and Psychologization of Early Cinema

With these arguments fairly well anchored, I return to the question of the explanatory value of psychology in terms of history. Can a psychological investigation of mental attribution inform explanations of historical change, specifically in relation to style and textual devices? The focus of the argument here is the transition from early cinema to its classical mode, circa 1905–15. How are we as cinema scholars to explain the radical metamorphosis of styles, practices and techniques during those years of changeover?

One extreme position is that filmmakers during those years "discovered" some sort of inherent language of film; the "correct" and "right" methods to make films. Although I know of no proponent of this position (with the possible exception of some hardcore semioticians in the 1960s), it is often invoked by modern cinema scholars as a punching bag, in contrast to which they make their own claims.

Another crucial explanatory framework is the socioeconomical, which has occupied cinema studies for quite some years (Abel, 1994; Bordwell et al., 1985; Elsaesser, 1990; Fullerton, 1998; Gunning, 1994; Hansen, 1991; Musser, 1990a; Tsivian, 1994; Uricchio & Pearson, 1993). One recurrent argument is that cinema – initially a working-class form of entertainment focusing on the aesthetics of attraction – turned to established and "respected" art forms such as narrative theater and the novel in a striving for higher attendance, a more affluent audience, economic stability, and greater social, moral, and aesthetic respectability:

> [T]he desire for middle-class respectability, which arose soon after the first crest of the nickelodeon explosion, ultimately provoked the narrative discourse of film. . . . The techniques of the narrator system responded to the industry's desire to attract a new audience through a narrative discourse that could supply the ideological and psychological values the middle class expected. (Gunning, 1994:89)

The cinema of attraction aimed for "spectacular" experiences of shock and wonder, often "punctual" in nature rather than spanning an extended period of time (see Gunning, 1986). This form of entertainment was preoccupied with travelogues, actualities, electrocuting elephants, comical gags, illegitimate kisses in tunnels, wild chases through landscapes, magic and visual tricks, dances, and boxing fights, and had the clear connotation of "cheap" and "a poor man's" entertainment. In contrast to the narratives told in novels and "legitimate" theater, early cinema did not revolve around characters and had much less causal structure. For instance, the individual acts in a vaudeville program were not related and coherent in these manners. Also, the tableaux tradition of early cinema did not aspire to coherence and causal connections between tableaux, but wanted to show climaxes of the story, often relying on the spectator's prior acquaintance with the plot to fill in the intervening scenes[28] (Gunning, 1994:38ff).

Storytelling practices, on the other hand, populated novels, short stories, and legitimate theater. Whereas the aesthetic of attraction – permeating entertainment forms such as circus, carnivals, burlesque, vaudeville, traveling fairs, and amusement parks – was associated with low status, narrative practices enjoyed high respectability among the middle class. Hierarchies of taste were probably just as pertinent then as they are today. Cinema, however, destabilized these hierarchies. Narrative cinema not only tried to attract a new middle-class audience, but also introduced narratives to an audience that associated cinema with attractions. This transfer is eloquently reflected in the following newspaper article "Nickelodeons: The Poor Man's Elementary Course in Drama":

> Sometimes in a nickelodeon you can see on the screen a building completely wrecked in five minutes. Such a film was obtained by focusing the camera at the

building, and taking every salient move of the wreckers for the space, perhaps, of a fortnight. . . . Such eccentric pictures were in high demand a couple of years ago, but now the straight-story show is running them out. . . . Today a consistent plot is demanded. There must be, as in the drama, exposition, development, climax, dénouement. The most popular films run from fifteen to twenty minutes and are from five hundred to eight hundred feet long. One studio manager said: "The people want a story. We run to comics generally; they seem to take best. So-and-so, however, lean more to melodrama. When we started we used to give just flashes – an engine chasing to a fire, a base runner sliding home, a charge of cavalry. Now, for instance, if we want to work in a horse race it has to be as a scene in the life of the jockey, who is the hero of the piece – we've got to give them a story; they won't take anything else." (Patterson, 1907)

As this citation shows, there was an awareness of the difference between the "eccentric pictures" or "flashes" of the early days and the newly adopted narrative form ("drama"), which integrated the "flashes" into a causal whole, often with a small set of characters at its center ("the life of the jockey"). The attractions did not disappear, but they were *narrativized*. The low costs of mass-produced visual stories, in combination with an increasingly moneyed working class, enabled storytelling practices to spread into the cinematic medium.

What makes this transfer from attraction to narrative cinema pertinent to our discussion of mental attribution is that character psychology seems to lie at the core of the difference between these two traditions:

[T]he narrator system centers filmic discourse and narrative development much more strongly on to the psychological motivation of characters that early cinema. (Gunning, 1994:27)

Character psychology, then, forms the basis of numerous changes that distinguish the classical from the primitive cinema. It serves both to structure the causal chain in a new fashion and to make the narration integral to that chain. (Thompson, 1985:177)

The *narrativization* of (American) cinema, so elegantly accounted for by Gunning (1994), was intimately tied to the *psychologization* of characters:

The work that Griffith undertook on all levels of filmic discourse to develop character was tied to the new narrative forms in which character motivation and psychology were essential. Film stories which relied increasingly on a character's decisions and emotions made portrayal of psychological states a narrative necessity. Communicating these psychological states was a basic impetus for the development of the narrator system and of cinema of narrative integration generally. (Gunning, 1994:116)

One typical example of early cinema's disinterest in character psychology is the shooting of one of the train passengers in *The Great Train Robbery*[29]

(a)   (b)

FIGURE 52. *The Great Train Robbery* (Edwin S. Porter, 1903). Obtained from the Wisconsin Center for Film and Theater Research.

(Figure 52). In an extended long shot, the robbers loot the passengers, who are lined up along the train. Suddenly, and without warning, one of the passengers liberates himself from the group and runs toward the camera, but is shot down before he is able to escape. The robbers continue their plundering, and when they eventually exit to the right, the group rushes forward to the man lying on the ground. All of this takes place in one long shot: There is no special attention given to the escaping man, neither before the attempt (nervousness or estimating the risks of being killed?) nor after (is he in pain or will he survive?). Neither does the spectator get any opportunity to ponder how robbers and passengers perceive, feel, or think about the event and each other. Things "just happen" and the psychological consequences of those events are not relevant, which makes the situation psychologically poor. "The stories are simple because causality occurs on the level of external action; we usually need not infer characters' motives in order to understand what is happening" (Thompson, 1985:177).

Thus the socioeconomical framework explains the transfer from attraction style to narrative style by studying how cinema as a social and economical institution strived for greater respectability. To study the specific stylistic transformations, the socioeconomist describes how the low-status cinema picked up practices, conventions, and techniques from other more respectable texts, entertainment forms, media, and technologies (Elsaesser, 1990; Fullerton, 1998; Thompson, 1985; Tsivian, 1994; Uricchio & Pearson, 1993). This might include themes, motifs, plot structures, and well-known characters and stories, but also formal devices such as editing, composition, acting, and mise-en-scène. Such reconstructions of the media context often included phenomena that are forgotten and marginalized by the modern spectator, for instance the magic-lantern

culture (Musser, 1990b; Rossell, 1998), vaudeville (Allen, 1980) and museums (Griffiths, 1998), while also recognizing that cinema at the time
fulfilled discursive functions that are today relegated to other forums
(news, travelogues, educational film, etc.). Gunning nicely summarizes
the socioeconomical explanation:

> [I]n defining the change of filmic discourse in which Griffith participates, recourse
> to arguments about the essential nature of film are not very helpful. Although the
> narrator system did develop an approach to narrative without exact equivalent
> in any other medium, the influence of theater and literature played an important
> role. And over Biograph's rush to the classics, loom a series of social pressures:
> the economic policies of the MPPC designed to attract a larger and higher paying
> audience and the assaults of genteel reformers. The desire to imitate respectable
> forms of art and to counter allegations of obscenity provided a spur for the creating
> of a filmic rhetoric that could convey the mental life of characters and preach a
> sermon of morality. The narrator system took shape from this interweave of factors,
> rather than a single-handed discovery of the essential language of film. (Gunning,
> 1994:183)

I do not disagree with this line of argument. As a way of explaining,
defining, and understanding the stylistic changes of cinema during those
years, it provides a strong and powerful frame of reference. Yet – as already
indicated – psychology could complement and improve the precision of
the theory.

Psychology as Complement?

If we assume that spectators are psychologically predisposed in certain ways and if we assume that filmmaking traditions and individual
filmmakers exploit these dispositions for aesthetic, narrative, commercial, or other purposes, then we should expect that psychology influences or informs the ways in which visual and other discursive practices
are designed, developed, and stabilized. Socioeconomic and intermedial
changes and transformations seem to occur against a backdrop of certain
basic and culturally widespread psychological dispositions. FP and mental attributions are good examples of such relatively stable and structured
expectations, playing fundamental roles in the reception of fictional characters and narrative discourse. I would argue that, once socioeconomic
factors pushed cinema into the narrative and character psychology stream,
some stylistic changes can be explained by the way these styles appealed
to the psychological process of mental attribution. Of course, devices were
"borrowed" from other narrative art forms but, irrespective of medium,
these devices fulfilled valuable functions that can be described only in
relation to the psychology of mental attribution and the structure of FP.
These functions have little to do with historical context, other than the
long-term history of FP and mental attribution.

Let me give a couple of examples in which the psychological approach thus could complement the socioeconomic framework.

Considering that character *recognition* is an important prerequisite for mental attribution, it is no coincidence that the new narrative cinema conventionalized techniques to facilitate such processes. In previous chapters we discussed, for instance, how closer views make facial recognition possible (Chapter 3, the subsection on "Closer-Ups" and this chapter, the section on Mental Attribution in Everyday Life), and from around 1909 onward, characters were given names (Thompson, 1985:179). If the spectator is unable to infer the identity of a character and make connections between different body appearances in a film, then that spectator cannot use previous situational parameters or mental attributions. Because of the structure of mental attribution and FP reasoning, it is of vital importance for filmmakers who want to promote character psychology to also promote character recognition.

Considering the central role of spatiotemporal attachment in the attribution process, it comes as no surprise that the transition period saw the implementation of all devices discussed in the preceding section. The narrative cinema started to focus on a limited set of characters, which were followed for an increasing amount of time. Because mental attribution requires other situational parameters – and thus takes screen time – it is consequential that the length of film increased from three minutes to feature length during the transition years. In a one- or two-minute format, character psychology runs the risk of being superficial, as there are few appraisal parameters from which a spectator can attribute complex, blended, and deep mental states. The short format stands in stark opposition to the striving for character psychology (and the spectator emotions following in its wake).

In addition, the fact that mental attribution is limited to one person at a time must have been a contributing factor when cinema developed its different techniques for directing spectator attention. In American cinema, editing was to become the main instrument for isolating characters from each other, whereas European cinemas relied more on acting, timing, and composition to direct the spectator's attention. All national cinemas started to use lighting, dialogue, and other mise-en-scène devices. The ways in which such techniques signal which character is momentarily most important are invaluable for channeling the mental attribution process.

The FP structure also informs overall plot structures. It has often been remarked that narrativized and psychologized cinema centers around characters with strong goals, goals that are then hindered (by others) throughout the narrative. Classical storytelling deals with "psychologically defined individuals who struggle to solve clear-cut problem or attain specific goals" (Bordwell, 1985:157). In fact, the clear presentation of character goals seems to be one of the ultimate dividing lines between early and classical cinema. Why is this so?

Well, if we investigate the structure of FP, we see that goals take center stage in the model of mind (Figure 40), as well as in appraising emotions (Figure 41). For instance, goals must be considered in order for the spectator to appreciate the fundamental difference between positive and negative emotions (see Figure 41). That is, clear goals "open up" a mental landscape more effectively than any other mental state. The early scenarists seem to have been aware of this. In a 1913 guidebook, cited by Kristin Thompson, we read the following comment:

> It should be remembered that 'want,' whether it be wanting the love of a woman, of a man, of power, of money, or of food, is the steam of the dramatic engine. The fight to satisfy this 'want' is the movement of the engine through the play. The denouncement is the satisfaction or the deprivation of this desire which must be in the nature of dramatic and artistic justice. (cited in Thompson, 1985:180)

The ways in which goals inform the understanding of actions, as well as appraisal of emotions, make them specifically suited to giving the spectator access to a rich and extended character psychology. This instrumentality is directly related to the inherent structure of FP.

Let us now turn to a more complex case. The most visible change during the transitional years was the change of acting style (for contrasting examples, see Thompson, 1985:189ff). Why did the "crude" pantomime disappear from all major fictive genres in the 1910s and 1920s (with the possible exception of comedy)? Why did the highly codified and gestured sign language associated with vaudeville give way to a more restrained and "naturalistic" style of acting that we associate with the silent era and, in extension, also with contemporary mainstream cinema? In this case, the argument that cinema adopted techniques from neighboring arts or entertainment forms loses power, as there does not seem to have been any other medium that used naturalistic acting. Although the legitimate theater was probably not as pantomime driven as vaudeville, it surely did not restrain acting as classical cinema later would.

Another explanation would be to postulate that in order to be *believable*, cinema had to "imitate" reality in a naturalistic way. This argument often shows up in early commentaries, trying to promote and justify the transition, here expressed by Griffith in connection with the introduction of "the close-up":

> "There is no secret," he says. "I did not 'teach' the players with whom my name has been linked. We developed together, we found ourselves in a new art and as we discovered the possibilities of that art we learned together. It is this

learning, step by step, that brought about the 'close-up.' We were striving for real acting. When you saw only the small full-length figures it was necessary to have exaggerated acting, what might be called 'physical' acting, the waving of the hands and so on. The close-up enabled us to reach real acting, restraint, acting that is a duplicate of real life." (From "David W. Griffith Speaks," Robert E. Welsh, *The New York Dramatic Mirror*, Vol. 71, No. 1830, January 14, 1914, pp. 49, 54. Reprinted in Pratt, 1973:110–11)

Such naturalist claims – "real acting," "a duplicate of real life" – have of course been placed in larger contexts by cinema scholars. Realism, it is claimed, is not a property that all "realist" art works have in common, but an effect on the spectator whose conditions change over the course of time. Naturalist conventions are still conventions whose emergence and development can be described historically (Thompson, 1988:197). Such lines of argument can then be coupled to ideological frameworks: If we assume that the striving for naturalism is a bourgeoisie ideology, then we can explain Griffith's interest in naturalistic acting and the stylistic transition in terms of ideology (see Burch, 1990). Such explanations, however, seem much too abstract and apparently miss many functions of acting.

A third approach for accounting for the change in acting style addresses exactly this shortcoming. The standard answer to why acting changed is that the camera moved closer to make facial expressions available to the spectator. The close-up enabled the spectator to detect small details in facial expressions, which made large pantomime gestures unnecessary. The face alone could express what the pantomime bodily gestures had done before. This argument was used by filmmakers to motivate new visual practices (for examples, see Tsivian, 1994:194 and the preceding Griffith citation), as well as by other observers:

In the old days we would have 'shot' a struggle scene in 'long shot', showing, perhaps, two men fighting on the floor with a woman at one side. In the long shot we could get only a suggestion of the emotions being experienced. The physical action, yes, but the soul action, the reactions of the mentalities concerned, the surging of love, hate, fear, up from the heart and into the expressive muscles of the face, the light of the eyes, that, indeed, is something you can only get by a flash to a close-up or semi-close-up. And it is these flashes, short but telling, that have caused some scenario writers to increase scene numbers. (DeMille, 1923:380; also cited in Thompson, 1985:201)

This line of reasoning has been taken over in modern cinema studies. Here it is assumed that access to faces not only took on the expressive responsibilities that bodily gestures had earlier, but that the face in fact was a *better* and more articulate gateway to the psychology of characters: "The face was the main vehicle for narrative psychology" (Tsivian, 1994:191). And Thompson (1985:192) makes the following claim: "If the camera could linger on the mobile face of a Lillian Gish or a Blanche Sweet, individual incidents, and especially psychological states, could now provide major causes and sustain whole segments of the film."[30] Because the face was so expressive, the large and obtrusive pantomime was no longer needed to create psychologized characters.

Although I am not totally unsympathetic to this argument, there seem to be some problems with it. If we compare expressivity in faces and in pantomimes per se, without any "situational" context, gestures of pantomime in fact seem to have *greater* articulation potential than faces. It is true that facial expressions, on their own, can convey emotions of *anger, fear, disgust* (see the section on Mental Attribution in Everyday Life), but pantomime could also express all these emotions and, moreover, complex beliefs, intentions, and contents of dialogue (Brewster & Jacobs, 1998). Body pantomime was (and still is) a rich system of meanings. It seems unlikely that the face in itself could shoulder this responsibility, especially when acting in the new style was so restrained (and even more so in the sound era). One could even venture that facial close-ups *excluded* body parts that could act and behave in expressive ways.

Admittedly the close-up account is sound to a certain extent, but if we want to describe the value of faces and facial close-ups for the psychologization process, this framework needs to be paired with other transitions taking place at the same time. Mental attribution requires not only acting, but also a "situation" and appraisal parameters for the spectator to process. If the appraisal parameters are rich enough, then little acting is needed, neither as pantomime nor as facial expressions. Instead, the increased ability of the cinema of the early 1910s to create such "situations" is a much more important reason for the eventual abandonment of obtrusive style of acting:

During the transitional years of 1912 and 1913, the pantomime style was in the process of modifying into a more naturalistic approach to gestures. Still framed in long shot or *plan américain*, the actor used facial expression and non-conventionalized gestures, but with enough exaggeration that they would be visible. The increasing dependence on dialogue inter-titles aided in the formulation of this new acting style by taking over some of the informational functions of the codified gestures. The feature film would also promote it, by allowing, even encouraging, more time for character development. (Thompson, 1985:190)

The introduction of the new acting style is, as Thompson suggests, correlated in time with the increasing length of films – enabling greater spatiotemporal attachment to a small set of characters – as well as increased use of dialogue intertitles. Dialogue intertitles not only conveyed general story information, but also mental states of characters, forming the basis for mental attributions. The longer film format, in conjunction with all the techniques already discussed, created richly psychologicalized situations that were impossible in a shorter format. Because mental attribution processes and FP reasoning rely heavily on situations, by becoming more efficient in planting appraisal parameters in a story, films needed no longer to rely on highly codified acting such as pantomime. The restrained facial acting style, in itself rather uninformative or vague, could in conjunction with a rich situation trigger nuanced and distinctive mental attributions beyond the pantomime. If the situation was developed enough, even the smallest physical reactions gained great expressivity. Yes, faces became more expressive, but this was not due to an inherent expressivity in the face, but rather that faces were placed in psychologically rich situations. There is thus a connection between the disappearance of the pantomime acting style and the greater emphasis on presenting character goals and beliefs and other appraisal parameters (rather than facial close-ups). It is a theory about mental attribution processes and the structure of FP reasoning that suggests such a connection.

This connection between situation and acting is evidently expressed in the following review of *In the Days of '49* from 1911:

But the outdoor scenery is beautiful, the photography exquisite right straight along, and if the interiors are somewhat crowded and the action broken by too many changes of scene, the action itself is well done, and the acting first-class all the way through, albeit this leading lady, capable as she is, has still the absurd habit of jumping up and down to express delight as a child of ten might jump. Of course, the present scribe never saw the wife of a miner receive a letter saying her husband is doing well and asking her to join him, but his idea is that such news, while good, is not so frantically entrancing as to make the recipient behave like an inspired idiot. Perhaps the stage manager cautioned her, for she then proceeded to give a convincing presentation of a dissatisfied wife who, later disillusioned, comes to her senses. (Freelance, 1911)

Here the writer attributes mental states to the character on the basis of the situation, rather than the acting. Although "he has never seen a miner's wife receive a letter from her husband in real life," he understands the happiness on the basis of FP reasoning. Thus, as far as the understanding of the scene goes, there needs to be little acting to confirm this inference. It is the establishment of clear appraisal parameters that makes pantomime expressivity unnecessary. It is here that the genuine reasons for the transformation of acting are to be sought.

In this section, we have investigated several cases in which the formation and structure of mental attribution and FP reasoning informed the ways in which discourse techniques were designed and conventionalized. This does not, of course, minimize the socioeconomic and intermedial frameworks of explanation, but it proposes certain psychological and implicit constancies in which the socioeconomic reorganization of early cinema operated. We may say that industry during this period "discovered" certain ways to trigger and exploit mental attribution abilities in the spectator – in a similar manner as projector and camera entrepreneurs discovered ways in which they could exploit features of the visual–perceptual system to convey movement. In this way, the psychological and socioeconomic explanations complement rather than oppose each other: The socioeconomic level explains why cinema took a narrative turn and started to explore character psychology, whereas the psychological approach seeks to explain the specific details and strategies with which this new cinema tried to invoke mental attribution abilities in the spectator.

This does not mark a return to the position that transitional cinema discovered "the (true) language of cinema." There is nothing inherent in the medium that makes it more "suitable" for narratives or this or that convention. It is simply that once the social and economic context pushed the cinema into the narrative stream, there were certain sociopsychological constancies in Western culture (or universally?) that were efficiently exploited. Conventions cannot be appreciated or valued per se ("the language of cinema"), but only in relation to the functions they perform. The conventions of the new narrative cinema emerging around 1905–1915 performed not only *socioeconomic* functions (gaining respectability; attracting higher-paying audiences, etc.), but also *psychological* ones (triggering and exploiting FP reasoning).

The psychological framework may also, I believe, apply to children's films. Here we encounter themes, plot structures, characters, and discursive styles that are fundamentally different than mainstream cinema. Considering the fact that the psychology and understanding processes in children often diverge from adults in critical respects, this must of course influence the style and discourse strategies used in children's' films. It would be fascinating to investigate the specific structure of FP at different ages and then compare with the ways in which children's films try to establish character psychology. Studying how children's films adapt to the psychological abilities of its audience and reconstructing "childish" comprehension processes would perhaps clarify why and in what ways adult's and children's genres vary.

Concluding Comments

In this chapter I have sketched a theory of how character psychology emerges and works in fiction films.[31] It was argued that a structured and causally rich FP guides the spectator's mental attribution processes and striving for coherence. Of course, in the examples discussed, mental attribution processes is only one of many types of understanding. Perceptual processes of motion, depth, object recognition, and POV editing take place below this level; thematic, moral and interpretative processes occur above. Emotions take part in all levels. All levels interact. The mental attribution processes described in the figures capture only a slice of the spectator's experience.

Nor do I wish to maintain that these mental attributions are objectively "right" or "best" for the scenes discussed. By now, I hope it is clear that meaning, interpretation, and coherence are not "objectively" in the text, but are achieved through the spectator's active application of knowledge and disposition to the textual material. Mental attributions will be strongly affected by the structure of these dispositions; if the structure changes, so will the understanding. We could imagine other cultures or creatures (e.g., children) with different FPs coming up with radically different mental attributions for the very same text. It must be remembered that discussions about the "probability" or "correctness" of this or that interpretation take place only against a shared, often implicit, background of understanding, in our case a cultural model of how the human psyche works and relates to behavior. There is always some yardstick with which to judge interpretation. However, if spectators share such a ruler or paradigm, which most Westerners seem to do, we can well talk about "probable" or "improbable" interpretations. In this sense, the attributions described are not *objectively* probable, but are probable in the relation to Western FP.

However, even within Western FP, spectators may emphasize issues different from those in the preceding reconstructions. For instance, they may focus mental attribution on other characters (e.g., the girl instead of the boy in *Seven Samurai*), or they may find certain appraisal parameters more central than the ones proposed here. For instance, the understanding of complex and blended emotions requires the appraisal of many parameters. Different spectators may choose to emphasize some parameters and diminish the importance of others, thereby attributing a somewhat different blend of emotions. The specific nature of an attribution depends on what parameters a spectator detects and remembers.

Throughout this chapter, it has been argued that the spectator represents the mental states of characters and continuously updates that mental model during the narrative. It is the FP that gives structure to that understanding. In addition, establishing, maintaining, and updating a mental model of the inner lives of characters inform other impressions or experiences of a character higher in the processing hierarchy. On the basis of mental attributions during a story or scene, a spectator or critic is able to make more abstract evaluations and categorizations of characters, for instance to infer character traits. In fact, many trait stereotypes can be described in terms of FP. An optimist or a self-confident person, for example, has a high control potential and is thus associated with emotions such as frustration or disgust rather than sadness or distress or anger rather than dislike (see Figure 41). Heroes typically believe that they possess high control potential (in contrast to victims or princesses). An impulsive or thoughtless person downplays thinking and beliefs in constraining action and acts primarily on the basis of desires (see Figure 40). A dreamer revels in desires, but seldom forms intentions or actions. A curious person is open to perceptions to change beliefs, whereas a prejudiced individual lets his beliefs bias perception. Villains and monsters seem to be without the emotions of regret, guilt, and shame, which enables them to continue doing bad things to other people.

If character traits are not established by iconographic codes such as clothes, gestures, and appearance, the understanding of the characters' mental processes may provide the basis for such generalizations and characterizations. The distinction between active and passive characters, which is often invoked in feminist writing, is not textually given, but is informed by mental attribution processes. Determining which characters are active or passive involves, among other things, an understanding of the goals, beliefs, and emotions and the ways in which characters act on the basis of those mental states:

The concept of the situation necessitates a reconsideration of the grounds on which characters are classed as passive or active. This distinction is not simply a function of character traits – for example in *Beyond the Forest*, Rosa is strong-willed and active – which are then rewarded or punished by the plot – for example, the film makes Rosa pay for her active desire by her grotesque death. Rather the sense of activity or passivity is produced through quite complex narrative mechanisms. The distinction depends, in part, on how film handles coincidence, and hence the relation between chance and necessity; it also depends on the representation of character psychology, and the motivations, whether "internal" or "external," of situations and the events that resolve them (Jacobs, 1993:141)

Rather than taking the distinction between passive and active characters in a given narrative as objectively given, Jacobs here acknowledges that such a categorization has its root in mental attributions and FP reasoning ("complex narrative mechanisms").

In addition, perhaps the primary area in which mental attribution informs and partly determines higher-level processes is spectator emotion. To begin with, and as Ed Tan points out, the cognitive understanding of character provides pleasure in itself:

[U]nderstanding a character is in itself pleasurable, not least when the complexity of the narrative film is rooted in the development of the character, as in psychological film drama. But characterization of even the simplest kind is often a source of pleasure and not exclusively in a genre like the farce. (Tan, 1996:191)

Most of all, however, understanding of character psychology gives rise to higher-level emotions. Along with Smith (1995), Omdahl (1995), Cupchik and Laszlo (1994), Bourg and Stephenson (1997:296), and Tan (1996), I argue that many types of *spectator* emotion depend on an understanding or cognitive appraisal of the psychological significance of a given event for a specific character. Tan (1996:172), for instance, defines empathy along similar lines as my notion of mental attribution: "By empathy we mean all the cognitive operations on part of the viewer that lead to a more complete understanding of the situational meaning for the character." These processes then lay the foundation for empathic *emotions*: "By an empathic emotion we mean an emotion which is characterized by the fact that the situational meaning structure of the situation for a character is part of the meaning for the viewer" (Tan, 1996:174). That is, spectator emotions such as hope and fear, anxiety, sympathy, pity, relief, gratitude, admiration, shame, anger, terror, joy, sorrow, and suspense are all tied to the characters of the diegesis and the ways in which these characters understand and emotionally relate to fictive events. The mental attributions inform and influence those affective reactions. Of course, the understanding of character goals, beliefs, and emotions is not the only factor in this process – spectator emotions do not directly mirror those of the character (see the subsection on Emotions and Their Causes) – but this understanding does constitute a substantial factor. Narrativization and psychologization open up a completely different range of spectator emotion than does the attraction film or spectacle (Tan, 1996:175, 83).

A final point relates to the relationship between narrative practices and FP. In this chapter we have been occupied with the ways in which FP and mental attribution processes influence the understanding of narratives. We must, however, also acknowledge that narratives and narrative understanding influence the structure of FP. Although FP is a stable cultural model, it is not permanent, and it does not operate unaffected by discursive practices. On the contrary, both discourse generation and the understanding of that discourse maintain and uphold the structure of FP. As cultural studies have tried to show over the past thirty years, discursive practices are crucial for establishing, maintaining, and habituating cultural knowledge. In this respect, FP is no exception. The ways in which psychologized stories are told in documentaries, fiction films, novels, short stories, everyday discourse, news, and tabloid papers stimulate the circulation and practical application of mental attribution and FP in a given culture, and thus reinforce its structure (see Figure 5).

It has long been acknowledged that narratives and stories are perhaps the major ways in which children get to know the world and in particular how interpersonal relations are understood, regulated, and managed (Britton & Pellegrini, 1990; van den Broek et al., 1997). Perhaps children's seemingly endless fascination with even the simplest story (over and over again) may arise because narratives open up a "psychological landscape" of goals, beliefs, perceptions, and emotions whose complex and intricate relations are yet to be discovered and learned. In fact, the study of children's development of narrative preferences suggests that throughout childhood there is a striving for psychologically more elaborate and complex narratives (e.g., Trabasso, 1991). The first stories told are series of unrelated, descriptive states of affairs, but these protonarratives soon develop into coherent structures kept together by characters' goals, actions, and emotions. The understanding and generation of narrative in childhood seem to be pivotal for the individual development of FP and may provide an explanation for children's' obsessions with narratives.

In this way, fictional narrative discourse may be seen as the primary "playground" for FP reasoning, in which we can test our mental attribution abilities outside real situations, thereby avoiding the risk of losing social capital or making fools of ourselves:

There is a price to pay in real life when the bad guys win, even if we learn from the experience. Make-believe provides the experience – something like it anyway – for free. Catastrophes don't really occur (usually) when it is fictional that they do. The divergence between fictionality and truth spares us pain and suffering we would have to expect in the real world. We realize some of the benefits of hard experience without having to undergo it. (Walton, 1990:68:)

Through fictional narratives, we can learn things about the social and interpersonal world without really being in that world. The ways in which FP reasoning takes place in narrative thinking is like shooting blanks: we acquire qualitative training for the real thing, but nobody gets hurt. In this respect, narrative discourse constitutes an effective way to maintain FP competence within a cultural setting. The circulation of narratives within a social group confirms shared beliefs about the world (Bruner, 1986, 1990), for instance, models of FP. This may be one of the reasons why narratives can be found in all cultures on Earth. In a society such as ours – which is packed with narratives – perhaps "real" interpersonal situations will become less important for the ways in which people "learn" FP competence. The precise importance of mass-distributed narratives in this context, however, is yet to be determined.

CHAPTER FIVE

The Case for a Psychological Theory of Cinema

Illusionist theorists usually insist that only avant-garde texts make the viewer perform an 'active' reading, or force the viewer to 'work to produce meaning.' The Hollywood spectator, it is claimed, is little more than a receptacle; few skills of attention, memory, discrimination, inference-drawing, or hypothesis-testing are required. Now this is clearly too simple. Classical films call forth activities on part of the spectator. These activities may be highly standardized and comparatively easy to learn, but we cannot assume that they are simple. (Bordwell et al., 1985:7)

I hope that this study has presented a reasonably coherent psychological theory of cinema. I believe that this theory constitutes a somewhat new approach to the phenomenon of cinema, at least as far as cinema studies goes. Theories often acquire identity and motivation from the question they pose and seek to answer. A psychological theory of cinema poses the following questions:

1. In what way do textual structures and the mentally represented dispositions of the spectator interact, and how does meaning and coherence arise out of this?

This question has different variations according to perspective:

2. From the standpoint of the spectator: What dispositions in the spectator are used to make sense of a given convention, device, or film, and what mental processes are involved?
3. From the standpoint of the text: How does the text (convention, film, or genre) trigger, and thus make use of, the dispositions in the spectator in order to create a specific effect of meaning, emotion, or aesthetics?
4. From a communicational standpoint: How does the communicator manage to trigger the "right" dispositions and constructive processes in the receiver in order to convey the intended "message" and avoid

misunderstandings? How does the communicator know what dispositions to take for granted in a given audience?

5. From a historical standpoint: How can we explain changes in discursive practices by looking at the dispositions and constructive processes in the spectator?

6. From a standpoint of critical theory: In what way do discursive practices create, maintain, and manipulate the spectator's dispositions and thus indirectly affect his or her meaning construction processes?

This study has dealt with questions 1–3 and, to some extent, 5. The other questions, however, are just as legitimate to ask and pursue. They all fit into a psychological theory of cinema.

Throughout the book, I have postulated a spectator equipped with certain dispositions and then reconstructed how this spectator extracts meaning from a text. There has been no ambition to reconstruct the full experience, only segments of it. This spectator is not me. The reconstructions are not my own, but they belong – I argue – to a larger group of situated, flesh-and-blood spectators out there in the world. If we want to explain a process such as the reception of films, we must make general claims about the audience, whether we like it or not. We must venture onto thin ice and take intellectual risks. Although comfortable, the solipsism of poststructuralist interpretations ("I read this as . . . but other readings are just as legitimate") is not a fruitful position.

In some respects, we might argue that the spectator presented here was abstract and not historically situated. I equipped him or her with dispositions, which have been psychologically–anthropologically evaluated and studied, and investigated how these dispositions affected the construction of meaning.

If my analysis had stopped there – combining psychology with textual analysis – the spectator would have been too abstract and too near reductionistic. To obtain a fuller understanding of the interaction between text and spectator psychology, we have to place text and spectator in historical context – a mode of production, a genre, or a historical system of discourse. The surface "visuality" of the device or convention is not sufficient: We must also describe what *functions* that visuality takes on in a given system of representation. That is why the transition between "attractionist" and narrative cinema is so fascinating and fruitful; that is why I tried to anchor the discussion of spectator psychology in this historical context. As Miriam Hansen writes in somewhat different language,

We seem to be faced with a gap between film theory and film history, between the spectator as a term of cinematic discourse and the empirical moviegoer in his or her demographic contingency. The question, then, is whether the two levels of inquiry can be mediated at all; whether and how the methodologies and insights of each can be brought to bear upon the other. There is no doubt that the theoretical concepts of spectatorship need to be historicized so as to include empirical formations of reception. By the same token, however, a reception-oriented film history cannot be written without a theoretical framework that conceptualizes the possible relations between films and viewers. (Hansen, 1991:5ff)

This book has been an effort toward establishing this interaction between historical/situated viewers and a more general, abstract (psychological) framework.

In addition, the psychological theory presented here has made some efforts in a establishing a relationship with the academic discipline of psychology and its neighboring social psychology, cognitive anthropology, and psycholinguistics. With few exceptions, cognitivist scholars within cinema studies never systematically apply ontologies, results, and methodologies from these other disciplines in describing the cognitive reception of cinema. For instance, although Bordwell (1985, 1989a, 1989b) acknowledges that common-sense knowledge and everyday dispositions take a crucial part in the reception of cinema, he continues to deal with literary and formal schemas rather than connecting the psychological reception of movies to a larger sociocultural context. Few of his examples systematically take into consideration studies of social psychology, emotion theory, event schemas, and discourse processing, and he does not apply such studies on the cinematic spectator of a given film or convention. Grodal amply criticizes this kind of formalism that lingers on, not only in cognitivist cinema studies, but also in other traditions:

Some would argue that the phenomenon of film is a specific one, so that film research could study this specificity, this *filmnost*, without reducing it to other areas of scientific research, such as psychology or sociology. The idea that each aesthetic field has its own exclusive object of analysis and its own methods was especially popular in the 1950s and 1960s. But such a conception of specificity leads to a much larger 'reduction'; a narrow definition would leave out most of the viewer's film experience. The experience does not take place in a vacuum; it is connected to broad cultural and social types of practices, and to psychosomatic phenomena. (Grodal, 1997:12)

In addition, the discipline of psychology has great experience in experimental methodologies, which could be useful within cinema studies. The turn to historical evidence within the history of cinema and reception studies in the mid-1980s points to a driving urge, not to vaporize theory, but to strike a more nuanced balance between theory and empirical work than has been the case in cinema studies so far. The next logical step in this direction is to start setting up experiments in similar ways to those of discourse psychology and communication studies, although – of course – with a more clearly defined focus on historical, cultural, and critical conditions. Here both psychology and cinema studies are in for an unmistakable win–win situation.

This also involves the ways in which cinema scholars formulate their theories and the level of abstraction in their theories. To substantiate and verify them, theories have to come down a couple of steps on the abstraction ladder than most contemporary theories of cinema. Although this study did not devote itself to experimentation, it did seek to formulate its historical and psychological hypotheses and explanations on a concrete enough level to be testable.

Like any other theory, a psychological theory of reception seeks to explain phenomena – reception and understanding of moving images – by postulating a number of parameters involved and the basic structure of the processes (e.g., dispositions, meaning, construction, and striving for meaning). The theory aims at describing general processes of understanding. It aims at explaining why some understandings overlap or differ. Like any other scientific theory, it also aspires to *predict* understandings if enough conditions and dispositions are known. As it stands, the parameters are still admittedly vague, unspecified and not well substantiated, but the framework is there. The point is that the psychological theory presented in this book is not so different from the theories presented in the natural sciences. In contrast to a theory dealing with systems of planets, molecules, or atoms, a theory of discourse reception deals with a human, social, and communicatory system. It is probably true that human systems involve higher degree of complexity and more parameters. This, however, should not refrain scholars from explaining phenomenal worlds of humans (including that of moving imagery). We just have to work harder, sharpen our arguments better, and be more open to sound objections and refutations. That – I am afraid – is what scientific work is like.

Notes

Chapter 1. Understanding and Dispositions

1 This cultural–critical approach has dominated cinema studies for quite some time now. In this line of research, cinema is studied through its functions in society, for instance, the ways in which films are received by a specific social group; the ways in which films produce, maintain, and change knowledge, values, and ideals in a given social group; cinema's role as a commodity in a consumer society; and the economical, industrial, and social conditions underlying the production, distribution, and reception of cinema in a given historical context.

2 This argument will recur in the subsequent chapters.

3 Perceptual gestalts are also examples of perceptual mental structures (see Figure 2, in the subsection on Discourse and Meaning).

4 I agree with Shore that an integrated account of culture needs "a cognitive view of culture and a cultural view of the mind" (Shore, 1996:39).

5 See Smith, 1995:51.

6 See also Hoffman, 1998:48.

7 "[I]f specific knowledge or other beliefs are said to be presupposed and shared by speech participants, we need to make such knowledge and beliefs explicit in order to be able to specify how such presuppositions affect the structures of discourse." (van Dijk, 1994:108)

8 See also Johnson's (1987) image schemas.

9 See Cole (1996:117) for a similar broad definition of artifacts and cultural environments.

10 Compare the notion of "search for coherence" with Barthes' *proairetic* and *hermeneutic* codes (cf. discussion in Scholes, 1981:207).

11 I disagree with Bordwell, however, when he later seems to suggest that this fabula can be "embodied in a verbal synopsis." Mental representations and models of texts, whether coherent or not, are not the same thing as external ones.

12 In this respect, level 0 meanings and Tan's (1996:64) *A-emotions* are not too different.

13 In his examples, however, he refers to content-related meanings that belong to level 1 or 2 rather than to level 0.

14 "[W]e prefer to use the term *perception of layout* rather than perception of depth or of space. Strictly speaking, observers do not perceive depth but objects in depth, and they do not perceive space but objects in space." (Cutting & Vishton, 1995:69)

15 "Presented with two narrative events, we look for casual or spatial or temporal links. The imaginary construct we create, progressively and retroactively, was termed by Formalists the fabula (sometimes translated as "story"). More specifically, the fabula embodies the action as a chronological, cause-and-effect chain of events within a given duration and a spatial field." (Bordwell, 1985:49)

There is, however, also a tendency within the structuralist camp to treat the fabula as a deep structure, existing more or less independent of the reader's construction of meaning. Here I agree with Herrnstein Smith's critique of the concept of fabula:

"It is clear from the foregoing discussion that an adequate account of the phenomenon of nonlinear sequence must turn that phenomena around: that is, what must be described and explained is not how (or within what limits) a narrator can *re*arrange the chronology of a given set of events but rather how, on what bases, and sometimes whether his audience will infer from his narrative the chronology of some set of events that is not given." (Herrnstein Smith, 1981:225ff)

For a discussion of the similarities and the differences between discourse psychology and structuralism on these issues, see Zwaan 1993:163. Zwaan suggests that *plot* overlaps psychology's *surface* and *textbase* models, whereas *fabula* overlaps the *situation model*.

16 See Brewer and Lichtenstein (1982).

17 Some levels of meaning may be more functional in relation to the viewing purposes. For example, if a Friday-night spectator strives to identify with characters, to be entertained, and to be emotionally aroused (e.g., experience suspense), then it is probably more effective for the spectator to focus on levels 1–4, rather than on level 0 or level 5. A film reviewer with short publishing space will probably do better by looking for level 4 or level 5 meanings, rather than getting into details about levels 0 and 1. A film scholar interested in editing techniques had better focus on levels 1–3, rather than on level 0 or levels 4 and 5. The choice of level has an *instrumental* value for the purpose at hand. Some meanings and levels thus are "better" or "more to the point" than others, but only in relation to a given spectator, function, or purpose – not objectively so.

18 Because cinema studies have long taken a critical perspective, wanting to disclose the mechanisms by which the media shape the worldview of their audiences, reception studies have often focused on media-specific dispositions and understanding.

19 "Many film theories are implicitly or explicitly normative. It is, however, mandatory that the fictions are described without interference from normative criteria of dictating the way in which a film, the world, or the human subject should ideally be." (Grodal, 1997:9)

20 Initiating, maintaining, and fomenting trench warfare are also natural mechanisms within the academic institution. Preserving academic territory

and painting threats are key strategies to motivate research funding and publications.

Chapter 2. Understanding Point-of-View Editing

1   See also Walton, 1990:32ff.

2   In this perspective, the black, abstract background of the close-up of the poison bottle in *Dr. Jekyll and Mr Hyde* makes good sense (see the preceding discussion of the film).

3   For instance, the extensive verbal commentary of Méliès' *Le Voyage dans la lune* (1902) (reprinted in Pratt, 1973:25ff) provides valuable cues to understanding not only the action in the different tableaux, but also the shot transitions.

4   Also known as *A Narrow Escape*.

5   Interestingly enough, instead of the camera moving to the other side of the fence, the reverse angle is shot from the same place but with the ladies moved to the back and the boys to the front. Again, such a practice indicates the strong tendency to treat the camera as an immobile and literal stand-in for the spectator in the theater seat. Rather than the camera or spectator moving, the set or players are repositioned, which happens to be the only way for the theater to show spectators other perspectives of a given situation or set (moving sets or stage).

6   The affinities between (true) POV editing and the SRS schema are close and intricate, but I do not go into detail here. Suffice it to say that, if *one* single eyeline provides a strong spatial cue between two spaces, having a *second* one on the other side of the cut creates an even stronger one. In contrast to POV editing and eyeline matches, scene direction and 180° convention play a much stronger role here (cf. "looking at each other" or "looking away from each other").

7   See Johnson's (1987:113ff) *path schema*, involving "(1) a source, or starting point; (2) a goal or end point; and (3) a sequence of contiguous locations connecting the source with the goal. Paths are thus routes for moving from one point to another."

8   Hitchcock rarely embraces such ambiguities in his POVs (which often have a very prototypical character), but I suppose he had to make this compromise for production reasons. The problem of having the birds shown behind Melanie in the same shot were probably too significant.

9   "The performance of an actor linked with an object and built upon it will always be one of the most powerful methods of filmic construction. It is, as it were, a filmic monologue without words. An object, linked to an actor, can bring shades of his state of emotion to external expression so subtly and deeply as no gesture or mimicry could ever express them conditionally." (Pudovkin, 1970:143)

10 Such an explanation would complement that of Bordwell (1996a).

11 If we assume that a spatial reading strategy is the stance most people take in understanding everyday reality, this might explain why most spectators have considered *Man With a Movie Camera* to be less "realistic" than *Rear Window*, as the latter encourages more of a spatial reading strategy.

12   In respect to the question of subjectivity and general POV in cinema, the terms
      POV and subjectivity seem to contain quite a few different processes. It might
      be valuable to sort out different levels of possible POV relationships between
      character and spectator. Such a schema would perhaps differentiate among
      the following POVs:

      • Sensory POV. Spectator and characters share the same angle and light con-
        ditions – cf. true POV.
      • Perceptual POV. Spectator and character "share" the same object or event,
        but not the same angle – cf. sight link.
      • Psychological POV. Spectator understands the mental states and processes
        of the character and infers intentions, beliefs, emotions, and sensations of
        the character on the basis of gaze, object, facial expression, and situation –
        see Chapter 3 and Smith's (1995) *alignment*.
      • Emotional POV. The spectator not only understands, but also shares, the
        character's emotions – cf. Smith's (1995) *allegiance*.
      • Moral POV. The spectator not only shares the emotions, but also thinks the
        actions and emotions are morally just – cf. Smith's (1995) *allegiance*.

      Just like meaning, POV is a term too broad a term to discuss in one breath.
13   On the other hand, in a system that for some reason does not favor close-ups
      and is not too particular about lighting and mise-en-scène, having the ob-
      ject and the gaze within the same frame might in fact be less expensive and
      time demanding than POV editing. In an aesthetics of an Edward Yang or
      a Hou Hsiao-Hsien – or, for that matter, early cinema – there are extremely
      few camera setups and they are almost exclusively in long-shot format. POV
      editing here would require additional camera setups and may cost more pro-
      duction time and money. We saw how early cinema avoided change of angle
      and repositioning of the camera because it would demand more elaborate
      set building, in particular if the long-shot format were maintained (see the
      subsection on Gazing).

Chapter 3. Variable Framing and Personal Space

1   For an overview of different functions of gazing, see Kleinke (1986).
2   Although not related to the concerns of this study, it is fascinating to specu-
     late about the relationship between the human species' development of lan-
     guage and personal space. Personal-space norms, regulatory mechanisms,
     and experience of invasion stress probably constituted a prelinguistic system
     of "meaning" and interpersonal communication. It is easy to imagine that oral
     language, which appeared later, in personal-space behavior had a nonverbal
     and relatively sophisticated system of meanings with which it was lenient to
     "hook up" – and later expand. Indeed, personal space, in combination with
     other types of nonverbal communication, may have constituted a system of
     protocommunication.
3   I will reserve the term *close-up* for shots of people's faces (from the neck up)
     and *insert* for shots of "smallish" things (Salt, 1992:51). In this way, close-ups
     are relatively easy to define, whereas inserts may present the whole of an
     object or just a detail. Although the difference between *close-up* and *medium*

shot is easily drawn when we are dealing with human bodies (neck up versus waist up), these distinctions are impossible with regard to shots of objects. There are no criteria for the difference between a telephone in medium shot, in close-up, or in insert format. Detailed shots of body parts such as a hand or a foot fall somewhere in between the close-up and the insert. I will refer to these as *body close-ups*. Griffith's celebrated "close-up" was thus in our terminology rather a medium shot or medium long shot.

4 At the same time, however, it was acknowledged that focusing on body parts fulfilled important functions in the interaction between spectator and image. Here is an 1887 comment on Impressionist painting:

> Another marked peculiarity of the Impressionists is the truncated composition, the placing in the foreground of the picture of fragments of figures and objects, half a ballet-girl, for instance, or the hind-quarters of a dog sliced off from the rest of his body.... The composition is certainly strange, but it has a definite aim: it concentrates attention on the very parts where the painter wishes it to fall. There is thought and purpose in all this apparent oddness, and in all the good work of M. Degas it will be found that the strangeness of the composition is invariably subordinated to some particular detail, some curious study of movement or pose where he brings into play his astonishing skill in drawing and his exact observation of attitude, pantomime, and light. For that matter, the truncated composition is no longer looked upon as a singularity. (Child, 1887)

5 Although the painted backdrops were unrealistic, for a touring vaudeville troop they were handy; painted and portable backdrops provided a universal solution to the varying conditions presented by different provincial theater stages (Thompson, 1985:217).

6 Inserts of objects perform similar functions. Inserts explain, clarify, and specify relations between different story events and thus act as important guides in the spectator's sense making of the plot. Inserts of letters, for instance, seemed to hold specific significance in early cinema because of their powerful roles as conveyors of story information (Tsivian, 1994:189ff; Thompson, 1985:188). Generally, inserts and cut-ins are two of the most important means to *linearize* cinematic discourse in the sense of "blocking out" ambiguities and other possible misunderstandings and mis-interpretations. In this respect, narrativized inserts worked quite differently than the ones in early cinema, e.g., the POV inserts in *Grandma's Reading Glass* (1900), which fulfilled no narrative purpose but constituted the main attraction of the film (see Chapter 1, the subsection titled Some Specifications of the Model).

7 The fact that inserts seem to contain few of the strong effects of facial close-ups, is also reflected in cinema scholars theories of variable framing. Deleuze's (1983:125f) theory of close-ups, for instance, practically equates the close-up shot scale with close-ups of faces, ignoring inserts altogether.

8 Here, the tableau shot of the early cinema reappears in the narrative system, but this time as a part of a larger system of shot scales and hence has the specific function of establishing the spatial layout of the scene (see Thompson, 1985:196f).

9 Of course, the convention of "important foreground" could sometimes be inverted and played with. The bar scene in *The Best Years of Our Lives* (1946), for instance, has a narratively important phone call inaudibly in the background and Homer's piano playing in the foreground.

10 I have been unable to identify the title of this film. According to the notes at the Wisconsin Center for Film and Theater Research, the film is produced by Mutoscope and is catalogued as No. 59-84 in the Library of Congress Paper Print Collection.

11 "Il menace d'exceder son cadre, de crever l'écran pour envahir l'espace du spectateur."

12 See the discussion on the assumptions of space permanence, (Chapter 2, the subsection on Movement). See also Persson, 2001.

13 "de la menace et de l'angiosse"

14 "effet de frayeur"

15 "aggressiva"

16 "[Un] cafard filmé en gros plan paraît sur l'écran cent fois plus redoutable qu'une centaine d'éléphants pris en plan d'ensemble."

17 Although over-the-shoulder shots were absent, some films of the 1910s used entrances and exits close to the camera, e.g., *The Musketeers of Pig Alley* (1912).

18 Retold in Lombard (1995:295).

Chapter 4. Character Psychology and Mental Attribution

1 Bal uses the term story here.

2 Point-of-view also pertains to other factors of narration and narrators (see, e.g., Stam et al., 1992), but my focus here is on different frameworks within which to approach the phenomena of characters.

3 For an overview of various definitions of *sympathy* and *empathy*, see Omdahl (1995:14ff).

4 See Tan:

[T]he emotion that a situation evokes in a character does not necessarily coincide with the empathetic emotion of the viewer. . . . The emotion supposedly felt by the antagonist contrasts most clearly with the empathetic emotion of the viewer. When the antagonist coolly deals the hero a blow, this calls up anger on the part of the viewer – empathetic anger – because it is clear that the blow was deliberate and that the antagonist is enjoying her success. Conversely, schadenfreude [malicious pleasure] is evoked when the bad guy has to take his knocks. (Tan, 1996:174)

See also Münsterberg, 1916/1970:53ff.

5 Think, for instance, of a psychoanalytical understanding or interpretation of a character.

6 If we assume that most narratives seek to evoke strong emotions in spectators (narrative as "a cognitive–emotional roller coaster"), then extreme situations and characters are often important ways to accomplish this.

7 Mental attribution is my own term and should not be confused with attribution theory in social psychology (although they have overlapping emphases).

8 Fortunately for this discussion, I do not have to take sides in the tricky question of the universality of basic emotions and the universality of correlating facial expressions (see Ekman, 1982, 1993; Ekman & Friesen, 1975).

9 For a somewhat different approach to FP, see Bruner (1990).

10 For a somewhat different approach to a folk theory of mind, self, and emotions, see Lakoff and Johnson (1999:Chaps. 12 and 13).

11 It would be fascinating to make a metaphor analysis of the field of cinema studies along the same lines as Lakoff and Johnson do with philosophy and cognitive science: What metaphors have been used by scholars to make sense of and explain the phenomenon of film? How have these changed through the history of film theory, and how can these metaphors be embodied in the way Lakoff and Johnson suggest?

12 Bazin writes,

> As we know, the naive ambition of Jean Tourane is to make Disney pictures with live animals. Now it is quite obvious that the human feelings we attribute to animals are, essentially at any rate, a projection of our own awareness. We simply read into their looks or into their behavior those states of mind that we claim they possess because of certain outward resemblances to us, or certain patterns of behavior which seem to resemble our own. We should not disregard or underestimate this perfectly natural tendency of the human mind. (Bazin, 1967:43)

13 It is difficult to imagine how universities could be understood at all, without such metaphoric thinking. How could we understand what a university is and does unless we think of it in terms of *acts*, *intentions*, *aspirations*, *beliefs*, *planning*, or *allowing*? As Lakoff and Johnson (1999) repeatedly emphasize, it is only through metaphoric thinking that we are able to talk and reason and understand abstract phenomena such as love, time, space, arguments, causality, and anger. Because such abstract thinking also takes place in philosophical, scientific, and scholarly endeavors, metaphoric thinking is invariably a part of these discourses.

14 The passage appears in English translation in Livingstone (1996:155).

15 All of these studies have been conducted with printed or oral texts, but should be valid for narratives regardless of medium.

16 Compare with Thompson's (1988:198) definition of motivation in general and realistic motivation in particular.

17 Note that Lange's anger and his *right* to be angry not only motivate but also *justify* Lange's killing of Batala. Such moral evaluations are often conducted in relation to mental states and the current situation. Nevertheless, these processes again belong to *allegiance* and its emotionality rather than to *alignment* and the cognitive understanding of characters' mental landscapes.

18 Assuming, of course, that the spectator knows about the custom of a groom carrying his new bride across the threshold.

19 "Vous avez l'homme immobile qui regarde au-dehors. C'est un premier morceau de film. Le deuxième morceau fait apparaître ce qu'il voit et le troisième montre sa rèaction. Cela représente ce que nous connaissons comme la plus pure expression de l'idée cinématographique."

20 It is interesting to note that this anger is primarily inferred from the situation and FP reasoning, as the face and body of Lange are hidden from view during long sections of this scene (an over-the-shoulder shot and, at the end, a long shot of Lange looking at the pistol on the desk). The fact that mental attribution of Lange is possible in spite of this suggests that acting and body cues may have less important roles in mental attribution and character psychology than one might think.

21 For other cultural conceptions of causality, see Lakoff, 1987:54; Lakoff & Johnson, 1999.

22 In Dennett's sense – see previously p. 180.

23 Claiming that understanding of narratives often involves FP and the intentional stance is not to say that narratives *should* encourage the spectator to construct a tight causal structure. Whether "good narratives" promote or discourage construction of causality is an aesthetic question. Instead, I want to account for the spectator's use of FP models of causality, whether this is "premiered" by the text or not.

24 Framing not only isolates, but it also seems that closer framings generate *more* mental attribution efforts than wider ones. A SRS sequence, in which X and Y are framed in the same shot scale, may generate an equal amount of mental attribution process on each of them (given that the camera spends an equal amount of time on them). However, if the shot scale is tighter on X than on Y, then it appears that the spectator spends more mental attribution efforts on that character. If this is taken to its extreme, with a close-up of X and a full shot of Y, we no longer have a SRS ("X and Y see each other"), but rather a POV shot ("X sees Y"). In the latter case, the viewer seems to have forgotten Y's perceptions and mental landscape, and totally concentrates on X and X's perceptions. For instance, the sequence from *Pickpocket* (described previously on page 195) in which Michel turns around on the stairs is presumably understood as "Michel sees Kassagi" rather than "Kassagi sees Michel" or "Michel and Kassagi see each other." It is the much tighter framing on Michel that causes this is effect. The attribution processes appear to align with the character *along* with the camera.

25 In this way, the film also becomes more "open" and "hypertextlike" in the sense that increasingly more responsibility for meaning construction is transferred from narration to the spectator. This implies that the author or the filmmaker will have more difficulties in predicting how an audience will understand, interpret, and emotionally react to a given narrative (Persson, 1999b). If we assume that one of the basic motivations of consuming narratives in our culture is to be touched emotionally, this may explain why the commercial success of hypertexts (as well as other "open texts") has failed to appear (with the possible exception of computer games).

26 Actors and dramaturges often use *subtext* to describe this hinted-at dimension of the text.

27 There is a clear moral structure to this scene that is not reflected in the figure. Initially, when discussing air travel and toe fisting, X is authority and McClane is subordinate. At the end, this hierarchy is inverted: X is scared and McClane is the authority ("Trust me, I've been doing it for *eleven* years"). This level of understanding is fundamental in describing the humor of the scene, as well as establishing personality for McClane. Likewise, this moral level of understanding is emotional, leaving the sphere of *alignment* and entering that of *allegiance*.

28 Early cinema's disinterest in causality as well as the growing attention to causality in the transition period, is reflected in the following 1913 review of Hepworth's *David Copperfield*.

Readers of Dickens and particularly those who love the great author's favorite book, David Copperfield, will be entertained and edified in seeing the pictured version of that story recently produced by the Hepworth Company of London, now being marketed in America by Albert Blinkhorn. American companies have given us, in a small way, some excellent motion pictures dealing with the life of David Copperfield, but those have been brief character studies in the main, not attempting to cover the entire story. The Hepworth picture is in six parts beginning with the childhood life of David at the Rookery, Blunderstone, and depicting the more important incidents up to the time of his marriage with Agnes, terminating with the Yuletide dinner. . . . Rare discrimination has been exercised in the choice of events so that we have been given a story in pictures that holds together and does not tax the imagination of the observer or require a profound knowledge of the story itself in order to obtain the fullest enjoyment from the seeing of it. (From "David Copperfield," *The Moving Picture World*, Vol. 18, No. 1, October 4, 1913, p. 29. Reprinted in Pratt, 1973:118)

29 This scene was pointed out to me by Tom Gunning in personal conversation.

30 It should be pointed out that Thompson acknowledges other sources of the psychologicalization, e.g., the greater length of films (Thompson, 1985:161).

31 I have not explicitly dealt with nonfiction film, but there is no reason to assume that mental attribution and character psychology are restricted only to fiction film, although they may work differently and with different emphasis.

References

Abbott, Valerie, Black, John B. & Smith, Edward E. (1985). "The Representation of Scripts in Memory," *Journal of Memory and Language* (Vol. 24), 179–99.

Abel, Richard (1994). *The Ciné Goes to Town. French Cinema 1896–1914*, Berkeley: University of California Press.

Aiello, John R. (1987). "Human Spatial Behavior" in Altman, Irwin & Stokols, Daniel (eds.), *Handbook of Environmental Psychology*, New York: Wiley, Vol. 1, pp. 389–504.

Allen, Richard (1993). "Representation, Illusion, and the Cinema," *Cinema Journal*, Vol. 32, No. 2, 21–48.

Allen, Richard & Smith, Murray (eds.) (1997). *Film Theory and Philosophy*, New York: Oxford University Press.

Allen, Robert (1980). *Vaudeville and Film 1895–1915: A Study in Media Interaction*, New York: Arno.

Allen, Robert & Gomery, Douglas (1985). *Film History: Theory and Practice*, New York: Knopf.

Andersen, S. & Klatzky, R. (1987). "Traits and Social Stereotypes: Levels of Categorization in Person Perception," *Journal of Personality and Social Psychology*, Vol. 53, 235–46.

Anderson, Joseph (1996). *The Reality of Illusion: An Ecological Approach to Cognitive Film Theory*, Carbondale: Southern Illinois University Press.

Anderson, Joseph & Anderson, Barbara (1993). "The Myth of Persistence of Vision Revisited," *Journal of Film and Video*, Vol. 45, No. 1, 3–12.

Arnheim, Rudolf (1974). *Art and Visual Perception. A Psychology of the Creative Eye*, Berkeley: University of California Press. Originally published 1954.

Astington, Janet (1990). "Narrative and the Child's Theory of Mind," in Britton, B. & Pellegrini, A.D. (eds.), *Narrative Thought and Narrative Language*, Hillsdale, NJ: Lawrence Erlbaum Associates, pp. 151–71.

Astington, Janet W., Harris, Paul L. & Olson, David R. (eds.) (1988). *Developing Theories of Mind*, Cambridge: Cambridge University Press.

Augoustinos, Martha & Walker, Ian (1995). *Social Cognition. An Integrated Introduction*, London: Sage.

Avis, Jeremy & Harris, Paul (1991). "Belief–Desire Reasoning among Baka Children: Evidence for a Universal Conception of the Mind," *Child Development*, Vol. 62, 460–7.

Bal, Mieke (1985). *Narratology. Introduction to the Theory of Narrative*, van Boheemen, Christine (trans.), Toronto: University of Toronto Press.

Ball, William & Tronich, Edward (1971). "Infant Responses to Impending Collision: Optical and Real," *Science*, Vol. 171, 818–20.

Barkow, J., Cosmides, L. & Tooby, J. (eds.) (1992). *The Adapted Mind. Evolutionary Psychology and the Generation of Culture*, New York: Oxford University Press.

Baron-Cohen, Simon (1991a). "Precursors to a Theory of Mind: Understanding Attention in Others," in Whiten, Andrew (ed.), *Natural Theories of Mind. Evolution, Development and Simulation of Everyday Mindreading*, Oxford: Blackwell, pp. 233–51.

Baron-Cohen, Simon (1991b). "Do People with Autism Understand What Causes Emotion?" *Child Development*, Vol. 62, 385–95.

Baron-Cohen, Simon & Cross, Pippa (1992). "Reading the Eyes: Evidence for the Role of Perception in the Development of a Theory of Mind," *Mind & Language*, Vol. 7, No. 1–2, 172–86.

Barthes, Roland (1966). "Introduction à l'analyse structurale des récits," *Communications*, Vol. 8. Translated as "Introduction to the Structural Analysis of Narratives" by Heath, Stephen (ed.), and reprinted in *Image Music Text*, London: Fontana, 1977, pp. 79–124.

Barthes, Roland (1977). *Image Music Text*, London: Fontana. Essays selected and translated by Stephen Heath.

Bartsch, Karen & Wellman, Henry M. (1995). *Children Talk about the Mind*, Oxford: Oxford University Press.

Bazin, André (1967). *What is Cinema?*, Berkeley: University of California Press. Essays selected and translated by Hugh Gray.

Bellour, Raymond (1975). "Le blocage symbolique," *Communications*, Vol. 23, 235–350.

Biederman, I. (1987). "Recognition-by-Components: A Theory of Human Image Understanding," *Psychological Review*, Vol. 94, No. 2, 115–47.

Biederman, I., Mezzanotte, R. & Rabinowitz, J. (1982). "Scene Perception: Detecting and Judging Objects Undergoing Relational Violations," *Cognitive Psychology*, Vol. 14, 143–77.

Bordwell, David (1981). "Textual Analysis, etc.," *Enclitic*, Vol. 10–11, Fall 1981/Spring 1982, 125–36.

Bordwell, David (1985). *Narration in the Fiction Film*, London: Methuen.

Bordwell, David (1989a). "A Case for Cognitivism," *Iris*, No. 9 (Spring), 11–40.

Bordwell, David (1989b). *Making Meaning. Inference and Rhetoric in the Interpretation of Cinema*, Cambridge, MA: Harvard University Press.

Bordwell, David (1996a). "Convention, Construction, and Cinematic Vision," in Bordwell, David & Carroll, Noël (eds.), *Post-Theory. Reconstructing Film Studies*, Madison: University of Wisconsin Press, pp. 87–107.

Bordwell, David (1996b). "Contemporary Film Studies and the Vicissitudes of Grand Theory," in Bordwell, D. & Carroll, N. (eds.), *Post-Theory. Reconstructing Film Studies*, Madison: University of Wisconsin Press, pp. 3–36.

Bordwell, David & Carroll, Noël (eds.) (1996). *Post-Theory. Reconstructing Film Studies*, Madison: University of Wisconsin Press.

Bordwell, David, Staiger, Janet & Thompson, Kristin (1985). *The Classical Hollywood Cinema. Film Style & Mode of Production to 1960*, New York: Columbia University Press.

Bordwell, David & Thompson, Kristin (1993). *Film Art – An Introduction*, New York: McGraw-Hill.

Bourg, T. & Stephenson, S. (1997). "Comprehending Characters' Emotions: The Role of Event Categories and Causal Connectivity," in van den Broek, P., Bauer, P. & Bourg, T. (eds.), *Developmental Spans in Event Comprehension and Representation. Bridging Fictional and Actual Events*, Mahwah, NJ: Lawrence Erlbaum Associates, pp. 295–319.

Bower, G., Black, J. & Turner, T. (1979). "Scripts in Memory for Texts," *Cognitive Psychology*, No. 11, 177–220.

Branigan, Edward R. (1984). *Point of View in the Cinema. A Theory of Narration and Subjectivity in Classical Film*, Berlin: Mouton.

Branigan, Edward (1992). *Narrative Comprehension and Film*, London: Routledge.

Braudy, Leo (1976). *The World in a Frame. What We See in Films*, Garden City, NY: Anchor.

Bremmer, Jan (1983). *The Early Greek Concept of the Soul*, Princeton, NJ: Princeton University Press.

Brewer, W. & Lichtenstein, E. (1982). "Stories Are to Entertain: A Structural-Affect Theory of Stories," *Journal of Pragmatics*, Vol. 6, 473–86.

Brewster, Ben (1982). "A Scene at the 'Movies,'" *Screen*, Vol. 23 (August), 4–15.

Brewster, Ben (1990). "Deep Staging in French Films 1900–1914," In Elsaesser, T. (ed.), *Early Cinema: Space – Frame – Narrative*, London: BFI, pp. 45–55.

Brewster, Ben & Jacobs, Lea (1998). "Pictorial Styles of Film Acting in Europe in the 1910s," in Fullerton, John (ed.), *Celebrating 1895. The Centenary of Cinema*, Sydney: Libbey, pp. 253–63.

Briggs, R. & Haviland, V.J. (eds.) (1974). *The Fairy Tale Treasure*, Harmondsworth, England: Puffin.

Britton, B. & Pellegrini, A.D. (eds.) (1990). *Narrative Thought and Narrative Language*, Hillsdale, NJ: Lawrence Erlbaum Associates.

Britton, B. & Graesser, A. (eds.) (1996). *Models of Understanding Text*, Mahwah, NJ: Lawrence Erlbaum Associates.

Brody, Nathan (1994). "Traits," in *Encyclopedia of Human Behavior*, New York: Academic, Vol. 4, pp. 419–25.

Browne, Nick (1982). *The Rhetoric of Filmic Narration*, Ann Arbor, MI: University of Michigan Research Press.

Bruce, V., Green, P. & Georgeson, M. (1996). *Visual Perception. Physiology, Psychology, and Ecology*, Hove, England: Psychological Press.

Bruner, Jerome (1981). "Review and Prospectus," in Lloyd, Barbara & Gay, John (eds.), *Universals of Human Thought – Some African Evidence*, Cambridge: Cambridge University Press, pp. 256–62.

Bruner, Jerome (1983). *Child's Talk. Learning to Use Language*, New York: Norton.

Bruner, Jerome (1986). *Actual Minds, Possible Worlds*, Cambridge, MA: Harvard University Press.

Bruner, Jerome (1990). *Acts of Meaning*, Cambridge, MA: Harvard University Press.

Bull, Peter (1984). *Body Movement and Interpersonal Communication*, Chichester, England: Wiley.

Burch, Noël (1990). *Life to Those Shadows*, London: BFI.

Butterworth, George (1991). "The Ontogeny and Phylogeny of Joint Visual Attention," in Whiten, A. (ed.), *Natural Theories of Mind. Evolution, Development and Simulation of Everyday Mindreading*, Oxford: Blackwell, pp. 223–32.

Byrne, Richard (1995). *The Thinking Ape. Evolutionary Origins of Intelligence*, Oxford: Oxford University Press.

Byrne, Richard & Whiten, Andrew (eds.) (1988). *Machiavellian Intelligence. Social Expertise and the Evolution of Intellect in Monkeys, Apes, and Humans*, Oxford: Clarendon.

Cantor, N. & Mischel, W. (1979). "Prototypes in Person Perception," in L. Berkowitz (ed.), *Advances in Experimental Psychology*, New York: Academic, Vol. 12.

Carroll, John (1980). *Toward a Structural Psychology of Cinema*, The Hague: Mouton.

Carroll, Noël (1988). *Mystifying Movies. Fads and Fallacies in Contemporary Film Theory*, New York: Columbia University Press.

Carroll, Noël (1990). *The Philosophy of Horror. Paradoxes of the Heart*, New York: Rutledge.

Carroll, Noël (1993). "Toward a Theory of Point-of-View Editing: Communication, Emotion, and the Movies," *Poetics Today*, Vol. 14, No. 1, 123–42. Reprinted in Carroll, 1996a, 125–38.

Carroll, Noël (1996a). Theorizing the Moving Image, New York: Cambridge University Press.

Carroll, Noël (1996b). "Film, Attention, and Communication," in van Doren C. & Fuller M. (eds.), *The Great Ideas Today 1996*, London: Encyclopœdia Britannica, pp. 4–49.

Carroll, Noël (1996c). "Prospects for Film Theory: A Personal Assessment," in Bordwell, D. & Carroll, N. (eds.), *Post-Theory. Reconstructing Film Studies*, Madison: University of Wisconsin Press, pp. 37–68.

Carroll, Noël (1996d). "The Paradox of Suspense," in Vorderer, P., Wulff, H. & Friedrichsen, M. (eds.), *Suspense. Conceptualizations, Theoretical Analysis, and Empirical Explorations*, Mahwah, NJ: Lawrence Erlbaum Associates, pp. 71–92.

Chatman, Seymour (1978). *Story and Discourse. Narrative Structure in Fiction and Film*, Ithaca, NY: Cornell University Press.

Chatman, Seymour (1990). *Coming to Terms. The Rhetoric of Narrative in Fiction and Film*, Ithaca, NY: Cornell University Press.

Child, Theodore (1887). "A Note on Impressionist Painting," *Harper's New Monthly Magazine*, Vol. 74, No. 440, January, 314–15. Excerpts of this article are reprinted in Pratt, G.C., (ed.) (1973), *Spellbound in Darkness. A History of the Silent Film*, Greenwich, CT: New York Graphic Society, p. 98.

Churchland, Paul M. (1988). *Matter and Consciousness*, Cambridge, MA: MIT Press.

Cole, Michael (1996). *Cultural Psychology. A Once and Future Discipline*, Cambridge, MA: Belknap.

Cosmides, L., Tooby, J. & Barkow, J. (1992). "Introduction: Evolutionary Psychology and Conceptual Integration," in Barkow, J., Cosmides, L. & Tooby, J. (eds.),

The Adapted Mind. Evolutionary Psychology and the Generation of Culture, New York: Oxford University Press, pp. 3–15.

Cupchik, G. & Laszlo, J. (1994). "The Landscape of Time in Literary Reception: Character Experience and Narrative Action," *Cognition and Emotion*, Vol. 8, No. 4, 297–312.

Currie, Gregory (1995). *Image and Mind. Film, Philosophy and Cognitive Science*, Cambridge: Cambridge University Press.

Cutting, J. & Vishton, P. (1995). "Perceiving Layout and Knowing Distances: The Integration, Relative Potency, and Contextual Use of Different Information about Depth," in Epstein & Rogers (eds.), *Perception of Space and Motion*, New York: Academic, pp. 71–117.

Damasio, Antonio R. (1994). *Descartes' Error. Emotion, Reason and the Human Brain*, New York: Avon.

D'Andrade, Roy (1987). "A Folk Model of the Mind," in Holland, Dorothy & Quinn, Naomi (eds.), *Cultural Models in Language and Thought*, Cambridge: Cambridge University Press, pp. 112–48.

DeConti, Kirsten A. & Dickerson, Donald J. (1994). "Preschool Children's Understanding of the Situational Determinants of Other's Emotions," *Cognition and Emotion*, Vol. 8, No. 5, 453–72.

deCordova, Richard (1990). *Picture Personalities. The Emergence of the Star System in America*, Chicago: University of Chicago Press.

Deleuze, Gilles (1983). *Cinéma 1. L'image-mouvement*, Paris: Éditions de Minuit.

DeMille, Cecil B. (1923). "What Psychology Has Done for the Pictures," in Wing, Ruth (ed.), *The Blue Book of the Screen*, Hollywood: The Blue Book of the Screen, Inc.

Dennett, Daniel (1987). *The Intentional Stance*, Cambridge, MA: MIT Press / A Bradford Book.

Dennett, Daniel (1991a). *Consciousness Explained*, Boston: Little, Brown.

Dennett, Daniel (1991b). "True Believers: The Intentional Strategy and Why It Works," in Rosenthal, David (ed.), *The Nature of Mind*, Oxford: Oxford University Press, pp. 339–50. Originally published 1975.

den Uyl, M. & van Oostendorp, H. (1980). "The Use of Scripts in Text Comprehension," *Poetics*, Vol. 9, 275–94.

Deregowski, J.B. (1980). *Illusions, Patterns and Pictures: A Cross-Cultural Perspective*, London: Academic.

Deregowski, J.B. (1984). *Distortion in Art*, London: Routledge & Kegan Paul.

de Vega, M., Díaz, J. & León, I. (1997). "To Know or Not to Know: Comprehending Protagonists' Beliefs and Their Emotional Consequences," *Discourse Processes*, Vol. 23, 169–92.

de Vega, M., León, I. & Díaz, J. (1996). "The Representation of Changing Emotions in Reading Comprehension," *Cognition and Emotion*, Vol. 10, No. 3, 303–21.

Dubois, Philippe (1984). "Le gros plan primitif," *Revue Belge du Cinéma*, No. 10, 11–34.

Egri, Lajos (1946). *The Art of Dramatic Writing*, New York: Simon and Schuster.

Eisenstein, S. (1957). *Film Form*, Leyda, J. (trans.), New York: Meridian.

Eisenstein, S. (1974). "En gros plan," in Aumont, Jacques (ed.), *Au-dela des etoiles*, Paris: Union Générale d'Editions, Vol. 1. Aumont, Jacques, Eisenschitz, Bernard,

Mossé, Sylviane, Robel, Andrée, Luda, M. and Schnitzer, Jean (trans.). This text fragment was originally written in 1940.

Eisenstein, S. (1988). *Writings 1922–1934*, Selected works by Eisenstein, edited and translated by Richard Taylor, London: BFI.

Ekman, Paul (1982). *Emotion in the Human Face* (2nd ed.), Cambridge: Cambridge University Press.

Ekman, Paul (1993). "Facial Expression and Emotion," *American Psychologist*, Vol. 48, No. 4, 384–92.

Ekman, Paul & Friesen, W.V. (1975). *Unmasking the Face: A Guide to Recognising Emotions from Facial Clues*, Englewood Cliffs, NJ: Prentice-Hall.

Elsaesser, Thomas (ed.) (1990). *Early Cinema: Space – Frame – Narrative*, London: BFI.

Epstein, Jean (1921). "Grossissement," in *Bonjour Cinema*, Paris: Editions de la sirène, pp. 93–108. Reprinted as "Magnification" in Abel, Richard (ed.), (1988), *French Film Theory and Criticism – a History/Anthology 1907–1939*, Princeton, NJ: Princeton University Press, Vol. I, pp. 235–41.

Evans, J., Newstead, S.E. & Byrne, R.M.J. (1993). *Human Reasoning: The Psychology of Deduction*, Hove, England: Lawrence Erlbaum Associates.

Eysenck, M. & Keane, M. (1995). *Cognitive Psychology. A Student's Handbook*, London: Lawrence Erlbaum Associates.

Feldman, C.F. (1987). "Thought from Language: The Linguistic Construction of Cognitive Representations," in Bruner, J. & Haste H. (eds.), *Making Sense: The Child's Construction of the World*, New York: Methuen.

Freelance (1911). "Seen on the Screen," *The Moving Picture World*, Vol. 8, No. 20, May 20, 1120. Reprinted in Pratt, G.C. (ed.), (1973), *Spellbound in Darkness. A History of the Silent Film*, Greenwich, CT: New York Graphic Society, pp. 90–1.

Friedman, A. (1979). "Framing Pictures: The Role of Knowledge in Automatized Encoding and Memory for Gist," *Journal of Experimental Psychology: General*, Vol. 108, No. 3, 316–55.

Fry, A.M. & Willis, F.N. (1971). "Invasion of personal space as a function of the age of the invader," *Psychological Record*, Vol. 21, 385–9.

Frye, Douglas & Moore, Chris (eds.) (1991). *Children's Theories of Mind: Mental States and Social Understanding*, Hillsdale, NJ: Lawrence Erlbaum Associates.

Fullerton, John (ed.) (1998). *Celebrating 1895. The Centenary of Cinema*, Sydney: Libbey.

Gagg, M.E. (1958). *The Farm*, Loughborough, England: Wills & Hepworth.

Gaudreault, André (1985). "The Infringement of Copyright Laws and Its Effect (1900–1906)," *Framework*, Vol. 29. Reprinted in Elsaesser, T. (ed.) (1990). *Early Cinema: Space – Frame – Narrative*, London: BFI, pp. 114–22.

Gaut, Berys (1995). "Making Sense of Films: Neoformalism and Its Limits," *Forum for Modern Language Studies*, Vol. XXXI, No. 1, 8–23.

Gaut, Berys (1997). "Film Authorship and Collaboration," in Allen, R. & Smith, M. (eds.), *Film Theory and Philosophy*, New York: Oxford University Press, 149–72.

Genette, Gérard (1980). *Narrative Discourse. An Essay in Method*, Lewin, Jane E. (trans.), Ithaca, NY: Cornell University Press.

Gentner, D. & Stevens, A.L. (1983). *Mental Models*, Hillsdale, NJ: Lawrence Erlbaum Associates.

Gerrig, Richard J. & Allbritton, David, W. (1990). "The Construction of Literary Character: A View from Cognitive Psychology," *Style*, Vol. 24, No. 3, Fall, 380–91.

Gomery, Douglas (1992). *Shared Pleasures. A History of Movie Presentation in the United States*, London: BFI.

Gómez, J. (1991). "Visual Behavior as a Window for Reading the Mind of Others in Primates," in Whiten, A. (ed.), *Natural Theories of Mind. Evolution, Development and Simulation of Everyday Mindreading*, Oxford: Blackwell, pp. 195–207.

Gorky, Maxim (1896). Review of the Lumière programme at the Nizhni-Novgorod Fair, in *Nizhegorodski* newspaper, July 4th. Reprinted in Leyda, Jay (1960), *Kino. A History of the Russian and Soviet Film*, Swan, Leda (trans.), London: Ruskin House, pp. 407–9.

Graesser, Arthur, Gordon, Sallie & Sawyer, John (1979). "Recognition Memory for Typical and Atypical Actions in Scripted Activities: Tests of a Script Pointer + Tag Hypothesis," *Journal of Verbal Learning and Verbal Behavior*, Vol. 18, 319–32.

Graesser, Arthur, Singer, Murray & Trabasso, Tom (1994). "Constructing Inferences During Narrative Text Comprehension," *Psychological Review*, Vol. 101, No. 3, 371–95.

Greimas, Algirdas Julien (1966). *Sémantique Structurale*, Paris: Larousse.

Griffiths, Alison (1998). "'Animated Geography': Early Cinema at the American Museum of Natural History," in Fullerton, J. (ed.), *Celebrating 1895. The Centenary of Cinema*, Sydney: Libbey, pp. 190–202.

Grodal, Torben (1997). *Moving Pictures. A New Theory of Film, Genres, Feelings, and Cognition*, Oxford: Clarendon.

Grover, L. (1988). "Comprehension of the Manual Pointing Gesture in Human Infants," Ph.D. thesis, University of Southampton, England.

Gunning, Tom (1986). "The Cinema of Attractions. Early Film, Its Spectator and the Avant-Garde," *Wide Angle*, Vol. 8, No. 3/4. Reprinted in Elsaesser, T. (ed.) (1990), *Early Cinema: Space – Frame – Narrative*, London: BFI, pp. 56–62.

Gunning, Tom (1989). "An Aesthetic of Astonishment: Early Film and the (In)credulous Spectator," *Art & Text*, Vol. 34, 34–5.

Gunning, Tom (1990a). "'Primitive' Cinema. A Frame-up? Or The Trick's on Us," in Elsaesser, Thomas (ed.) *Early Cinema: Space – Frame – Narrative*, London: BFI, pp. 95–103.

Gunning, Tom (1990b). "Weaving a Narrative. Style and Economic Background in Griffith's Biograph Films," in Elsaesser, Thomas (ed.), *Early Cinema: Space – Frame – Narrative*, London: BFI, pp. 336–47. First published in *Quarterly Review of Film Studies*, Winter, 1981.

Gunning, Tom (1994). *D.W. Griffith and the Origins of American Narrative Film*, Chicago: University of Illinois Press.

Hall, E.T. (1966). *The Hidden Dimension*, New York: Doubleday.

Hall, S., Hobson, D., Lowe, A. & Willis, P. (1980). *Culture, Media, Language: Working Papers in Cultural Studies*, London: Hutchinson.

Hansen, Miriam (1991). *Babel & Babylon. Spectatorship in American Silent Film*, Cambridge, MA: Harvard University Press.

Harré, Rom & Parrott, W. Gerrod (eds.) (1996). *The Emotions. Social, Cultural, and Biological Dimensions*, London: Sage.

Harris, Paul (1983). "Infant Cognition," in Haith, M. & Campos, J. (eds.), *Handbook of Child Psychology*, New York: Wiley, Vol. II, pp. 689–782.

Harris, Paul (1993). "Understanding Emotion," in Lewis, M. & Haviland, J. (eds.), *Handbook of Emotions*, New York: Guilford, pp. 237–46.

Heider, Fritz & Simmel, Marianne (1944). "An Experimental Study of Apparent Behavior," *American Journal of Psychology*, Vol. 57, No. 2, April, 243–59. Reprinted in Aronson, Elliot & Pratkanis, Anthony (eds.) (1993), *Social Psychology*, Vol. 1, pp. 279–95, Aldershot: Elgar.

Herrnstein Smith, Barbara (1981). "Narrative Versions, Narrative Theories," in Mitchell, W.J.T. (ed.), *On Narrative*, Chicago: University of Chicago Press, pp. 209–32.

Hochberg, Julian (1986). "Representation of Motion and Space in Video and Cinematic Displays," in Boff, K., Kaufman L. & Thomas J. (eds.), *Handbook of Perception and Human Performance*, New York: Wiley, Vol. 1.

Hoffman, H.F. (1912). "Cutting off the feet," *The Moving Picture World*, Vol. 12, No. 1, 53. Reprinted in Pratt, G.C. (ed.) (1973), *Spellbound in Darkness. A History of the Silent Film*, Greenwich, CT: New York Graphic Society, p. 97.

Hoffman, Donald (1998). *Visual Intelligence: How We Create What We See*, New York: Norton.

Holland, D. & Quinn, N. (eds.) (1987). *Cultural Models in Language and Thought*, Cambridge: Cambridge University Press.

Holland, D. & Skinner, D. (1987). "Prestige and Intimacy: The Cultural Models behind American's Talk about Gender Types," in Holland, D. & Quinn, N. (eds.), *Cultural Models in Language and Thought*, Cambridge: Cambridge University Press, pp. 78–111.

Hughes, J. & Goldman, M. (1978). "Eye Contact, Facial Expression, Sex, and the Violation of Personal Space," *Perceptual and Motor Skills*, Vol. 46, 579–84.

Hume, David (1739). *A Treatise of Human Nature*.

Hutchins, Edwin (1980). *Culture and Inference: A Trobriand Case Study*, Cambridge, MA: Harvard University Press.

Intraub, H., Gottesman, C. & Bills, A. (1998). "Effects of Perceiving and Imagining Scenes on Memory for Pictures," *Journal of Experimental Psychology: Learning, Memory, and Cognition*, Vol. 24, No. 1, 186–201.

Iser, Wolfgang (1978). *The Act of Reading. A Theory of Aesthetic Response*, Baltimore: Johns Hopkins University Press.

Jacobs, Lea (1993). "The Woman's Picture and the Poetics of Melodrama," *Camera Obscura*, No. 31 (January–May), 121–47.

Jauss, Hans Robert (1970). "Literary History as a Challenge to Literary Theory," *New Literary History*, Vol. II, No. 1, 1970, 7–38.

Johnson, Mark (1987). *The Body in the Mind. The Bodily Basis of Meaning, Imagination, and Reason*, Chicago: University of Chicago Press.

Jolicoeur, P., Gluck, M. & Kosslyn, S. (1984). "Pictures and Names: Making the Connection," *Cognitive Psychology*, Vol. 16, 243–275.

Kempton, W. (1986). "Two Theories of Home Heat Control," *Cognitive Science*, Vol. 10, No. 1, 75–90.

Kepley, Vance Jr. (1995). "Pudovkin and the Continuity Style: Problems of Space and Narration," *Discourse: Journal for Theoretical Studies in Media and Culture*, Vol. 17, No. 3, 85–100.

Kintsch, Walter (1977). "On Comprehending Stories," in Just M. & Carpenter P. (eds.), *Cognitive Processes in Comprehension*, Hillsdale, NJ: Lawrence Erlbaum Associates, pp. 33–63.

Kirkpatrick, John & White, Geoffrey M. (1985). "Exploring Ethnopsychologies," in White, Geoffrey & Kirkpatrick, John (eds.), *Person, Self, and Experience*, Berkeley: University of California Press, pp. 3–32.

Kleinke, Chris (1986). "Gaze and Eye Contact: A Research Review," *Psychological Bulletin*, Vol. 100, No. 1, 78–100.

Klinnert, Mary, Campos, Joseph, Sorce, James, Emde, Robert & Svejda, Marilyn (1983). "Emotions as Behavior Regulators: Social Referencing in Infancy," in Plutchik R. & Kellerman H. (eds.), *Emotion. Theory, Research, and Experience*, New York: Academic, Vol. 2, pp. 57–86.

Krutnik, Frank (1991). *In a Lonely Street. Film Noir, Genre, Masculinity*, London: Routledge.

Lakoff, George (1987). *Women, Fire, and Dangerous Things. What Categories Reveal about the Mind*, Chicago: University of Chicago Press.

Lakoff, George & Johnson, Mark (1980). *Metaphors We Live By*, Chicago: University of Chicago Press.

Lakoff, George & Johnson, Mark (1999). *Philosophy in the Flesh. The Embodied Mind and its Challenge to Western Thought*, New York: Basic Books.

Lakoff, George & Kövecses, Zoltan (1987). "The Cognitive Model of Anger Inherent in American English," in Holland, D. & Quinn, N. (eds.), *Cultural Models in Language and Thought*, Cambridge: Cambridge University Press, pp. 195–221.

Lakoff, George & Turner, Mark (1989). *More than Cool Reason. A Field Guide to Poetic Metaphor*, Chicago: University of Chicago Press.

Leslie, Alan M. (1991). "The Theory of Mind Impairment in Autism: Evidence for a Modular Mechanism of Development?" in Whiten, Andrew (ed.), *Natural Theories of Mind. Evolution, Development and Simulation of Everyday Mindreading*, Oxford: Blackwell, pp. 63–78.

Linguistic Glossary, The (1997). Produced by The International Linguistics Department of the Summer Institute of Linguistics, Dallas, TX [http://www.sil.org/linguistics/glossary/].

Livingstone, Paisley (1996). "Characterization and Fictional Truth in the Cinema," in Bordwell, D. & Carroll, N. (eds.), *Post-Theory. Reconstructing Film Studies*, Madison: University of Wisconsin Press, pp. 149–74.

Lombard, Matthew (1995). "Direct Responses to People on the Screen: Television and Personal Space," *Communication Research*, Vol. 22, No. 3, 288–324.

Long, Debra & Golding, Jonathan (1993). "Superordinate Goal Inferences: Are They Automatically Generated During Comprehension?" *Discourse Processes*, Vol. 16, 55–73.

Lutz, Catherine (1985). "Ethnopsychology – Compared to What? Explaining Behavior and Consciousness Among the Ifaluk," in White, Geoffrey M. & Kirkpatrick, John (eds.), *Person, Self, and Experience*, Berkeley: University of California Press, pp. 35–79.

Lutz, Catherine (1987). "Goals, events, and understanding in Ifaluk emotion theory," in Holland, Dorothy & Quinn, Naomi (eds.), *Cultural Models in Language and Thought*, Cambridge: Cambridge University Press, pp. 290–312.

Lutz, Catherine A. (1996). "Engendered Emotion: Gender, Power, and the Rhetoric of Emotional Control in American Discourse," in Harré, Rom & Parrott, Gerrod W. (eds.), *The Emotions*, London: Sage, pp. 151–170.

Magliano, J., Dijkastra, K. & Zwaan, R. (1996). "Generating Predictive Inferences While Viewing a Movie," *Discourse Processes*, Vol. 22, 199–224.

Mandler, Jean Matter (1984). *Stories, Scripts, and Scenes: Aspects of Schema Theory*, Hillsdale, NJ: Lawrence Erlbaum Associates.

Martin, Richard (1984). "Effets et paradoxes d'un plan-limite," *Revue Belge du Cinéma*, No. 10, Winter 1984–5, 37–45.

Mayne, Judith (1993). *Cinema and Spectatorship*, London: Routledge.

McCloskey, M. (1983). "Intuitive Physics," *Scientific American*, Vol. 24, 122–30.

Merleau-Ponty, Maurice (1966). "Le cinéma et la nouvelle psychologie" in *Sens et nonsens*, Paris: Nagel.

Messaris, Paul (1994). *Visual Literacy-Image, Mind & Reality*, Boulder, CO: Westview.

Metz, Christian (1982). *The Imaginary Signifier. Psychoanalysis and the Cinema*, Bloomington: Indiana University Press.

Meyrowitz, Joshua (1986). "Television and Interpersonal Behavior: Codes of Perception and Response," in Gumpert, Gary & Cathcart, Robert (eds.), *Inter/Media: Interpersonal Communication in a Media World*, Oxford: Oxford University Press, pp. 253–72.

Mitry, Jean (1997). *The Aesthetics and Psychology of the Cinema*, King, Christopher (trans.), Bloomington: Indiana University Press. This is an abridged version of *Esthétique et psychologie du cinéma*, Paris: Groupe Mame, originally published 1963.

Mulvey, Laura (1975). "Visual Pleasure and Narrative Cinema," *Screen*, Vol. 16, No. 3, Autumn, 6–18.

Münsterberg, Hugo (1916). *The Photoplay: A Psychological Study*, New York: Appelton. Republished 1970 under the title *The Film. A Psychological Study*, New York: Dover. Page references in the text relate to the later edition.

Murray, J.H. (1997). *Hamlet on the Holodeck. The future of narrative in Cyberspace*, New York, NY: Free Press.

Musser, Charles (1990a). *The Emergence of Cinema: The American Screen to 1907*, New York: Scribner's.

Musser, Charles (1990b). "The Nickelodeon Era Begins. Establishing the Framework for Hollywood's Mode of Representation," in Elsaesser, T. (ed.), *Early Cinema: Space – Frame – Narrative*, London: BFI, pp. 256–73. Originally published in *Framework*, Autumn, 1984.

Olson, D. & Astington, J. (1990). "Talking About Text: How Literacy Contributes to Thought," *Journal of Pragmatics*, Vol. 14, 705–721.

Olsson, Jan (1996). "Förstorade attraktioner, klassiska närbilder – anteckningar kring ett gränssnitt," *Aura*, Vol. II, No. 1–2, 34–92.

Olsson, Jan (1998). "Magnified Discourse: Screenplays and Censorship in Swedish Cinema of the 1910s," in Fullerton, John (ed.), *Celebrating 1895. The Centenary of Cinema*, Sydney: Libbey, pp. 239–52.

Oman, Charles M. (1993). "Sensory Conflict in Motion Sickness: An Observer Theory Approach," in Ellis, Stephen R. (ed.), *Pictorial Communication in Virtual and Real Environments*, London: Taylor & Francis, pp. 362–76.

Omdahl, Becky (1995). *Cognitive Appraisal, Emotion, and Empathy*, Hillsdale, NJ: Lawrence Erlbaum Associates.

Orthony, A., Clore, G. & Collins, A. (1988). *The Cognitive Structure of Emotions*, Cambridge: Cambridge University Press.

Palmer, S. Rosch E. & Chase P. (1981). "Canonical Perspective and the Perception of Objects," in Long & Baddeley (eds.), *Attention and Performance IX*, Hillsdale, NJ: Lawrence Erlbaum Associates.

Patterson, Joseph Medill (1907). "Nickelodeons: The Poor Man's Elementary Course in Drama," *The Saturday Evening Post*, Vol. 180, No. 21, November 23, 10–11, 38. Excerpts of this article are reprinted in Pratt, G.C. (ed.) (1973), *Spellbound in Darkness. A History of the Silent Film*, Greenwich, CT: New York Graphic Society, pp. 46–52.

Perkins, V.F. (1972). *Film as Film. Understanding and Judging Movies*, New York: Da Capo.

Perner, J., Leekham, S.R., & Wimmer H. (1987). "Three-Year-Olds' Difficulty with False Belief: The Case for a Conceptual Deficit," *British Journal of Developmental Psychology*, Vol. 5, 125–37.

Persson, P. (1999a). "Understanding Representations of Space: a Comparison of Visualisation Techniques in Mainstream Cinema and Computer Interfaces," in Munro, A., Höök, K. & Benyon, D. (eds.), *Social Navigation in Information Space*, London: Springer, pp. 195–216.

Persson, P. (1999b). "Interactive Narratives: Pros and Cons," paper presentation at closing plenary on Visual Culture and Digital Technology-Cinema, *Screen Studies Conference*, Glasgow, Scotland.

Persson, P. (2000). *Understanding Cinema: Constructivism and Spectator Psychology*, unpublished Ph.D. thesis, Stockholm University.

Persson, P. (2001). "Cinema and Computers: Spatial Practices Within Emergent Visual Technologies," in Munt, Sally (ed.), *Technospaces*, London: Cassell.

Persson, P., Laaksolahti, J. & Lönnqvist, P. (2001). "Understanding Socially Intelligent Agents – A Multi-Layered Phenomenon," *IEEE Transactions on Systems, Man, and Cybernetics*, special issue on "Socially Intelligent Agents – The Human in the Loop," Vol. 31, No. 5, 349–60.

Piaget, J. (1954). *The Construction of Reality in the Child*, New York: Basic Books.

Pittam, J. & Scherer, Klaus R. (1993). "Vocal expression and communication of emotion," in Lewis, Michael & Haviland, Jeanette M. (eds.), *Handbook of Emotions*, New York: Guilford.

Planalp, S., DeFrancisco, V. & Rutherford, D. (1996). "Varieties of Cues to Emotion Naturally Occurring Situations," *Cognition and Emotion*, Vol. 10, No. 2, 137–53.

Plantinga, C. (1994). "Movie Pleasures and the Spectator's Experience: Toward a Cognitive Approach," *Film and Philosophy*, Vol. II. Available at http://www.hanover.edu/philos/film/vol_02/toc_02.htm.

Plantinga, C. (1997). *Rhetoric and Representation in Nonfiction Film*, New York: Cambridge University Press.

Plantinga, C. (1999). "The Scene of Empathy and the Human Face on Film," in Plantinga, C. & Smith, G.M. (eds.), *Passionate Views. Film, Cognition, and Emotion*, Baltimore: Johns Hopkins University Press, pp. 239–55.

Plantinga, C. & Smith, G.M. (eds.) (1999). *Passionate Views. Film, Cognition, and Emotion*, Baltimore: Johns Hopkins University Press.

Pratt, George C. (ed.) (1973). *Spellbound in Darkness. A History of the Silent Film*, Greenwich, CT: New York Graphic Society. First published 1966.

Propp, V. (1928). *Morfológija Skázki*. Published in 1968 as *Morphology of the Folk Tale*, Scott, Lawrence (trans.), Austin: University of Texas Press.

Pudovkin, V. I. (1970). *Film Technique* and *Film Acting*, Montagu, Ivor (ed. and trans.), New York: Grove. *Film Technique* first published in English 1929. *Film Acting* first published in English 1937.

Quinn, Naomi & Holland, Dorothy (1987). "Culture and Cognition," in Holland, D. & Quinn, N. (eds.), *Cultural Models in Language and Thought*, Cambridge: Cambridge University Press, pp. 3–40.

Reeves, B., Lombard, M., & Melwani, G. (1992) "Faces on the screen: Pictures or natural experience?" paper presentation to The Mass Communication Division of the International Communication Association, Miami.

Reeves, Byron & Nass, Clifford (1996). *The Media Equation: How People Treat Computers, Television, and New Media Like Real People and Places*, New York: Cambridge University Press.

Ristau, Carolyn A. (1991). "Before Mindreading: Attention, Purposes and Deception in Birds?" in Whiten, A. (ed.), *Natural Theories of Mind. Evolution, Development and Simulation of Everyday Mindreading*, Oxford: Blackwell, pp. 209–22.

Roseman, Ira, Antoniou, Ann Aliki & Jose, Paul (1996). "Appraisal Determinants of Emotions: Constructing a More Accurate and Comprehensive Theory," *Cognition and Emotion*, Vol. 10, No. 3, 241–77.

Rossell, D. (1998). "Double Think: The Cinema and Magic Lantern Culture," in Fullerton, J. (ed.), *Celebrating 1895. The Centenary of Cinema*, Sydney: Libbey.

Ruble, D.N. & Stangor, C. (1986). "Stalking the Elusive Schema: Insights from Developmental and Social–Psychological Analyses of Gender Schemas," *Social Cognition*, Vol. 4, 227–61.

Russell, James A., Fernández-Dols, José-Miguel, Manstead, Anthony S.R. & Wellenkamp, J.C. (eds.) (1995). *Everyday Conceptions of Emotion. An Introduction to the Psychology, Anthropology and Linguistics of Emotion*, Dordrecht: Kluwer.

Rutter, D.R. (1984). *Looking and Seeing: The Role of Visual Communication in Social Interaction*, Chichester, England: Wiley.

Salt, Barry (1992). *Film Style and Technology: History and Analysis* (2nd ed.), London: Starword. First edition published 1983.

Schank, Roger & Abelson, Robert (1977). *Scripts, Plans, Goals, and Understanding*, Hillsdale, NJ: Lawrence Erlbaum Associates.

Scholes, Robert (1981). "Language, Narrative, and Anti-Narrative," in Mitchell, W.J.T. (ed.), *On Narrative*, Chicago: University of Chicago Press, pp. 200–8.

Shore, Bradd (1996). *Culture in Mind. Cognition, Culture, and the Problem of Meaning*, Oxford: Oxford University Press.

Smith, Murray (1995). *Engaging Characters. Fiction, Emotion, and the Cinema*, Oxford: Clarendon.

Snell, Bruno (1953). *The Discovery of the Mind. The Greek Origins of European Thought*, Cambridge, MA: Harvard University Press.

Sorce, J., Emde, R., Klinnert, M. & Campos, J. (1981). "Maternal Emotional Signaling: Its Effect on the Visual Cliff Behavior of One-Year-Olds," paper presentation at The Meeting of the Society for Research in Child Development, Boston. Reprinted in Klinnert et al. (1983).

Staiger, Janet (1985). "The Hollywood Mode of Production to 1930," in Bordwell, D., Staiger, J. & Thompson, K. (eds.), *The Classical Hollywood Cinema. Film Style & Mode of Production to 1960*, New York: Columbia University Press, pp. 85–154.

Staiger, Janet (1992). *Interpreting Films. Studies in the Historical Reception of American Cinema*, Princeton, NJ: Princeton University Press.

Stam, R., Burgoyne, R. & Flitterman-Lewis, S. (1992). *New Vocabularies in Film Semiotics. Structuralism, Post-Structuralism and Beyond*, London: Routledge.

Stein, N. & Liwag, M. (1997). "Children's Understanding, Evaluation, and Memory for Emotional Events," in van den Broek, P. Bauer, P. & Bourg, T. (eds.), *Developmental Spans in Event Comprehension and Representation. Bridging Fictional and Actual Events*, Mahwah, NJ: Lawrence Erlbaum Associates, pp. 199–235.

Tan, Ed (1996). *Emotion and the Structure of Narrative Film. Film as an Emotion Machine*, Mahwah, NJ: Lawrence Erlbaum Associates.

Tan, Ed & Diteweg, Gijsbert (1996). "Suspense, Predictive Inference, and Emotion in Film Viewing," in Vorderer, P., Wulff, H. & Friedrichsen, M. (eds.), *Suspense. Conceptualizations, Theoretical Analysis, and Empirical Explorations*, Mahwah, NJ: Lawrence Erlbaum Associates, pp. 149–88.

Taylor, Shelly & Crocker, Jennifer (1981). "Schematic Bases of Social Information Processes," in Higgins, E.T., Herman, C.P. & Zanna, M.P. (eds.), *Social Cognition*, (*The Ontario Symposium, Vol. 1*), Hillsdale, NJ: Lawrence Erlbaum Associates, pp. 89–134.

Thompson, Kristin (1985). "The Formulation of the Classical Style, 1909–1928" in Bordwell, D., Staiger, J. & Thompson, K. *The Classical Hollywood Cinema. Film Style & Mode of Production to 1960*, New York: Columbia University Press, pp. 157–241.

Thompson, Kristin (1988). *Breaking the Glass Armor. Neoformalist Film Analysis*, Princeton: Princeton University Press.

Trabasso, Tom (1991). "The Development of Coherence in Narratives by Understanding Intentional Action" in Denhière G. & Rossi S. (eds.), *Text and Text Processing*, Amsterdam: North-Holland, pp. 297–317.

Trabasso, T. & Stein, N. (1997). "Narrating, Representing, and Remembering Event Sequences," in van den Broek, P., Bauer, P. & Bourg, T. (eds.) (1997). *Developmental Spans in Event Comprehension and Representation. Bridging Fictional and Actual Events*, Mahwah, NJ: Lawrence Erlbaum Associates, pp. 237–70.

Trabasso, T. & Suh, S. (1993). "Understanding Text: Achieving Explanatory Coherence Through On-Line Inferences and Mental Operations in Working Memory," *Discourse Processes*, Vol. 16, 3–34.

Trabasso, T., Suh, S. & Payton, P. (1995). "Explanatory coherence in understanding and talking about events" in Gernsbacher M.A. & Givón T. (eds.), *Coherence in Spontaneous Text*, Amsterdam: Benjamins, pp. 189–214.

Trabasso, T., Suh, S., Payton, P., & Jain, R. (1994). "Explanatory Inferences and Other Strategies during Comprehension: Encoding Effects on Recall," in Lorch & O'Brien (eds.), *Sources of Coherence in Text Comprehension*, Hillsdale, NJ: Lawrence Erlbaum Associates, pp. 219–39.

Truffaut, François (1966). *Le Cinéma selon Hitchcock*, Paris: Laffont.

Tsivian, Yuri (1994). *Early Cinema in Russia and its Cultural Reception*, Bodger, A. (trans.), London: Routledge.

Uricchio, William & Pearson, Roberta (1993). *Reframing Culture. The Case of the Vitagraph Quality Films*, Princeton, NJ: Princeton University Press.

van den Broek, P. (1997). "Discovering the Cement of the Universe: The Development of Event Comprehension From Childhood to Adulthood," in van den Broek, P., Bauer, P. & Bourg, T. (eds.) (1997). *Developmental Spans in Event Comprehension and Representation. Bridging Fictional and Actual Events*, Mahwah, NJ: Lawrence Erlbaum Associates, pp. 321–42.

van den Broek, P., Bauer, P. & Bourg, T. (eds.) (1997). *Developmental Spans in Event Comprehension and Representation. Bridging Fictional and Actual Events*, Mahwah, NJ: Lawrence Erlbaum Associates.

van Dijk, T.A. (1994). "Discourse and Cognition in Society" in Crowley D. & Mitchell D. (eds.), *Communication Theory Today*, Stanford: Stanford University Press, 107–26.

van Dijk, T.A. & Kintsch, W. (1983). *Strategies of Discourse Comprehension*, New York: Academic.

Vorderer, P., Wulff, H. & Friedrichsen, M. (eds.) (1996). *Suspense. Conceptualizations, Theoretical Analysis, and Empirical Explorations*, Mahwah, NJ: Lawrence Erlbaum Associates.

Walton, Kendall (1990). *Memesis as Make-Believe. On the Foundations of the Representational Arts*, Cambridge, MA: Harvard University Press.

Watson, Michael (1970). *Proxemic Behavior. A Cross-Cultural Study*, Mouton, The Haque.

Wellman, Henry (1990). *The Child's Theory of Mind*, Cambridge, MA: MIT Press.

Wellman, Henry (1995). "Young Children's Conception of Mind and Emotion," in Russell, J., Fernández-Dols, J., Manstead, A. & Wellenkamp, J.C. (eds.), *Everyday Conceptions of Emotion. An Introduction to the Psychology, Anthropology and Linguistics of Emotion*, Dordrecht; The Netherlands: Kluwer Academic, pp. 289–313.

Weatherford, D. (1985). "Representing and Manipulating Spatial Information from Different Environments: Models to Neighborhoods," in Cohen R. (ed.), *The Development of Spatial Cognition*, Hillsdale, NJ: Lawrence Erlbaum Associates, 41–70.

White, Hayden (1990). *The Content of the Form: Narrative Discourse and Historical Representation*, Baltimore: Johns Hopkins University Press.

White, Peter (1995). *The Understanding of Causation and the Production of Action. From Infancy to Childhood*, Hove, England: Lawrence Erlbaum Associates.

Whiten, Andrew (ed.) (1991). *Natural Theories of Mind. Evolution, Development and Simulation of Everyday Mindreading*, Oxford: Blackwell.

Whiten, Andrew & Byrne, Richard (1988). "The manipulation of attention in primate tactical deception," in Byrne, R. & Whiten, A. (eds.), *Machiavellian Intelligence. Social Expertise and the Evolution of Intellect in Monkeys, Apes, and Humans*, Oxford: Clarendon, pp. 211–23.

Whiten, Andrew & Byrne, Richard (1997). *Machiavellian Intelligence II: Extensions and Evaluations*, Cambridge: Cambridge University Press.

Williams, Linda (1996). "När kvinnor ser – en fortsättning," *Aura*, Vol. II 4/1996, 25–35.

Wilson, George (1997). "On Film Narrative and Narrative Meaning," in Allen, R. & Smith, M. (eds.), *Film Theory and Philosophy*, New York: Oxford University Press, pp. 221–38.

Zacks, J. & Tversky, B. (2001). "Event Structure in Perception and Conception," *Psychological Bulletin*, Vol. 127, No. 1, 3–21.

Zwaan, Rolf (1993). *Aspects of Literary Comprehension. A Cognitive Approach*, Amsterdam: Benjamins.

Zwaan, Rolf (1996). "Toward a Model of Literary Comprehension," in Britton, B. & Graesser, A. (eds.), *Models of Understanding Text*, Mahwah, NJ: Lawrence Erlbaum Associates, pp. 241–55.

Index

100-to-One Shot (Vitagraph, 1906), 54
Abelson, Robert, 31, 165, 166
acting, 198, 221, 231
adjacency, 53, 55, 56
Aiello, John, 103–106, 109
alignment, 148, 149, 150, 153, 158, 159, 202, 257
Allbritton, David, 155, 157
allegiance, 32, 148, 150, 156, 202, 257
Allen, Robert, 21, 116, 236
Andersen, H.C., 219
Anderson, Barbara, 27
Anderson, Joseph, 27, 42
anthropology, 44, 163
anthropomorphism, 178
Arnheim, Rudolf, 28, 29
L'Arrivée d'un train à la Ciotat, (Lumière, 1895), 113, 131
As Seen Through a Telescope (George Albert Smith, 1901), 50
Astington, Janet, 163, 175, 176, 218, 219
Augoustinos, Martha, 155
automatization, 96

Bal, Mieke, 143–146, 148, 154, 156, 186, 256
Ballet mécanique (Fernand Léger, 1925), 35
Baron-Cohen, Simon, 74, 177
Barthes, Roland, 144, 251
Battleship Potemkin, The (*Bronenosets Potyomkin*, Sergei Eisenstein, 1925), 32
Bazin, André, 257
Beetlejuice (Tim Burton, 1988), 38
Bellour, Raymond, 144
Biederman, I., 28, 29
Big Parade, The (King Vidor, 1925), 207, 208, 210, 211, 221, 222, 225

Big Swallow, The (James Williamson, 1900), 114
Birds, The (Alfred Hitchcock, 1963), 79, 80, 93
Blowup (Michelangelo Antonioni, 1966), 189, 190
body-cue competence, 174, 196
Bordwell, David, 20, 21, 24–27, 29, 30, 32–34, 39, 42, 47, 52, 64, 73, 74, 94, 137, 144, 145, 148, 149, 158, 178, 186, 191–193, 214, 217, 218, 238, 247, 249, 253, 257
Bower, Gordon, 10, 11
Branigan, Edward, 47, 125, 148, 217
Brewster, Ben, 47, 50, 53, 224, 225, 240
Bruner, Jerome, 70, 108, 179, 220, 246
Buono, il brutto, il cattivo, Il (Sergio Leone, 1966), 82
Burch, Noël, 21, 78, 82, 83, 111, 118–120, 138, 239
Byrne, Richard, 4, 72, 181

Cabinet des Dr. Caligari, Das (Robert Wiene, 1920), 123, 190
Carroll, Noël, 21, 23, 40, 42, 56, 67, 73, 74, 79, 81, 97, 98, 122, 130, 147, 184, 201, 257
causality, 31, 153, 174, 179, 181, 192, 217, 218, 220, 235, 257, 258
  psychological, 217
character
  active/passive, 145, 244
  alignment with, 148, 149
  allegiance with, 148
  in narratology, 144

character (*cont.*)
   recognition of, 147
   round vs. flat, 155, 192, 203, 216
chase film, 53, 121
Chatman, Seymore, 20, 144–146, 148, 153,
   154, 182, 216–218
Chien andalou, Un (Luis Buñuel, 1929), 96
Chien de Montargis, Le (English
   distribution title, *A Nobleman's Dog*,
   Société Cinématographique des
   Auteurs et Gens de Lettre, 1909), 54,
   55, 119, 120, 122, 185,
Churchland, Paul M., 165
Citizen Kane (Orson Welles, 1941), 128
City of Sadness (*Beiqing chengshi*, Hou
   Hsiao-hsien, 1989), 221
Clover, Carol, 147
cognitive anthropology, 249
cognitive unconscious, 66
coherence, 23
comprehension, 23, 25, 32, 37, 39, 42, 54,
   150, 154, 157, 183, 188, 201, 202,
   218, 242
contingent universals, 73
Cowie, Elizabeth, 147
Crime de Monsieur Lange, Le (Jean Renoir,
   1935), 186, 190, 192, 204, 211, 216,
   220, 222
Crocker, Jennifer, 10
Cutting, J., 252

D'Andrade, Roy, 163, 164, 166, 168
Danton (Andrzej Wajda, 1982), 42
David Copperfield (Hepworth, 1913), 258,
   259
deCordova, Richard, 39, 156
deictic gaze, 44, 48, 66–70, 72–75, 77, 79,
   82, 83, 85, 86, 87 88–92, 96–99, 143,
   177, 181
Dennett, Daniel, 180, 181
depth in space, 28
developmental psychology, 176, 219,
   246
Die Hard (John McTiernan, 1988), 33, 35,
   36, 118, 131, 133, 186–188, 190, 191,
   193, 202–204, 210–212, 214, 216
discourse psychology, 26, 187, 249
dispositions, 67, 75, 77, 97, 99, 101, 102,
   109, 110, 121, 130, 134, 141, 143, 145,
   150, 153, 162, 191, 227, 232, 236, 247,
   248
   to behave, 145

Dr. Jekyll and Mr. Hyde (Thanhouser, 1912),
   51
Drunkard's Reformation, A (D.W. Griffith,
   1909), 61, 82
Dubois, Philippe, 131, 136

Edison Company, 48, 78
Egri, Lajos, 145
Egyptian Mummy, The (Lee Beggs, 1914),
   60, 123, 124, 199
Eisenstein, Sergei, 20, 27, 86, 137,
   155
Ekman, Paul, 256
Elsaesser, Thomas, 21, 52, 233, 235
emotion
   in characters. *See* mental attribution
   in spectator, 4, 33, 47, 86, 117, 125, 131,
      138, 140, 142, 148, 149, 209, 237, 244,
      245
empathy, 4, 66, 138, 147, 149, 173, 245,
   254, 256
End of St. Petersburg, The (Vsevolod
   Pudovkin, 1927), 64
Epstein, Jean, 125, 265
eyeline match, 47, 57, 66, 87. *See also* sight
   link

false-belief test, the, 176, 177
Fatal Opal, The (1914), 228
filtration, 145, 148
final girl, 146
Fischinger, Oskar, 35
focalization, 148
folk-psychology, 161, 173
   and autism, 177
   and children, 176
   and "normality," 181
   as a cultural understanding, 174
   deep psychology, 173
   emotion, 169
   mind, 163
   relativism vs. universality, 177
framing, 121, 225, 258
Friday the 13th: The Final Chapter (Joseph
   Zito, 1984), 135
Fullerton, John, 21, 233, 235

Gaudreault, André, 49
Genette, Gerard, 148, 158, 218
Gerrig, Richard, 155, 157, 218
Girl and Her Trust, The (D.W. Griffith,
   1912), 191

glance shot, 47, 50, 63, 67, 75, 76, 78–80, 82, 83, 84, 86, 88, 91, 93, 100
Graesser, Art, 10, 21, 22, 25, 32, 37, 39, 181, 187
Grandma's Reading Glass (George Albert Smith, 1900), 50, 64
Greaser's Gauntlet, The (D.W. Griffith, 1908), 226
Great Train Robbery, The (Edwin S. Porter, 1903), 54, 111, 114, 115, 118, 234, 235
Greimas, A.J., 144
Griffith, D.W., 54, 59, 61, 62, 65, 76, 82, 89, 94, 119, 120, 201, 226, 234, 236, 238, 239
Grodal, Torben, 5, 21, 25, 27, 28, 35, 38, 39, 41, 206, 249, 252
Gunning, Tom, 21, 33, 47, 49, 50, 52–54, 61, 65, 75, 76, 81, 82, 88, 94, 113, 116, 118–122, 125, 130, 136, 138, 201, 226–228, 233, 234, 236, 259

Hall, E.T., 102, 104, 105, 107, 109, 121, 125
Hall, Stuart, 20, 42
Halloween (John Carpenter, 1978), 79, 84
Hansen, Miriam, 21, 39, 233, 248, 249
Harris, Paul, 69, 163, 176, 177
Heider, Fritz, 179
Herrnstein Smith, Barbara, 252
Hochberg, Julian, 56
Holland, Dorothy, 163, 174, 269
House of Wax (André De Toth, 1953), 137
How It Feels to Be Run Over (Cecil M. Hepworth, 1900), 113, 114
Hutchins, Edwin, 15

identification, 38, 47, 66, 90, 146–150, 223
imagining
    central vs. acentral, 147
implied reader, 146
impression formation, 155
In the Days of '49 (D.W. Griffith, 1911), 241
inference, 174
intentional stance, 180
interpretation, 24, 25, 74, 81, 87, 95, 98, 180, 243, 256
intertitles, 57, 190, 191, 221, 226–228, 240
Intraub, H., 30
Iser, Wolfgang, 19, 23, 37, 39

Jacobs, Lea, 144, 146, 224, 225, 240, 244
Jauss, Hans Robert, 21

Johnson, Mark, 7, 15, 33, 160, 174, 175, 178, 179, 253, 256, 257
joint visual attention. *See* deictic gaze
Joyeux microbes, Les (Emilie Cohl , 1909), 50

Kepley, Vance Jr., 64
Kintsch, Walter, 25, 30
Klovnen (A.W. Sandberg, 1917), 225
Komposition in Blau (Oskar Fischinger, 1935), 35
Krutnik, Frank, 144, 146

L'Année dernière à Marienbad (Alain Resnais, 1961), 37, 227
Ladies' Skirts Nailed to a Fence (Bamford, 1900), 60, 61, 111
Ladri di biciclette (Vittorio De Sica, 1948), 63
Lady and the Mouse, The (D.W. Griffith, 1913), 88–91
Lakoff, George, 15, 33, 160, 174, 175, 178, 179, 256, 257
lantern slides, 48, 54
Letzte Mann, Der (F.W. Murnau, 1924), 199
Lombard, M., 39, 101, 106, 117, 142, 256, 269
Lonedale Operator, The (D.W. Griffith, 1911), 60, 76, 78, 80
Lonely Villa, The (D.W. Griffith, 1909), 54

Maboroshi no hikari (Hirokazu Koreeda, 1995), 221
Magliano, J., 21
Man With a Movie Camera, The (Dziga Vertov, 1929), 86, 92
Mandler, Jean Matter, 10, 28
Marey, Étienne Jules, 48
meaning, 19, 23–25, 30, 32, 36–38, 43, 45, 67, 81, 97, 102, 110, 121, 141, 144, 152, 160, 161, 178, 179, 196, 201, 209, 214, 221, 229, 243, 245, 247, 248, 250, 252, 254, 258
    levels of, 24–34, 150
Meet me In St. Louis (Vincente Minnelli, 1944), 190
Mended Lute, The (D.W. Griffith, 1909), 119
mental attribution, 159, 161, 178, 179, 181–184, 186, 187, 211, 212, 214–217, 220–224, 226–229, 231, 232, 234, 236, 237, 240, 241, 243–246, 257–259
    and time, 213
    intradiegetic, 211
Merleau-Ponty, Maurice, 184

Messaris, Paul, 33, 39, 79, 81, 101, 130, 161
metaphor, 49, 137, 257
Metz, Christian, 138, 144, 146
Meyrowitz, Joshua, 101, 104, 106, 108–110, 121, 130, 142
Mitry, Jean, 19, 47, 67
Monty Python's Flying Circus (Ian MacNaughton, 1972), 206
mood, 148, 180
moral judgment, 38, 141, 148, 173, 204, 258
morale, 32, 118
Mulvey, Laura, 47, 90, 145, 147
Münsterberg, Hugo, 20, 51, 52, 130, 256
Musketeers of Pig Alley, The (D.W. Griffith, 1912), 58, 88, 226, 256
Musser, Charles, 21, 52, 233
mutual gaze, 67, 74, 82, 99, 106
Muybridge, Eadweard, 48
My Life as a Dog (*Mitt liv som hund*, Lasse Hallström, 1985), 188, 203

Napoléon (Abel Gance, 1927), 91
narrative pausing, 224
narratology
   and characters, 145
North by Northwest (Alfred Hitchcock, 1959), 31, 144, 193
Nosferatu (F.W. Murnau, 1922), 127, 128, 135, 136

object shot, 47, 57, 60, 62–64, 67, 75, 76, 78–80, 83, 84, 86–88, 90, 91, 98
offscreen space, 53, 54, 80, 111, 112, 117, 132
Olsson, Jan, xi, 52, 110, 136
Omdahl, Becky, 163, 169, 170, 173, 207, 220, 222, 245, 256

Pearson, Roberta E., 21, 233, 235
Perkins, V.F., 47
personal space, 45, 62, 101, 143, 161, 254
Pickpocket (Robert Bresson, 1959), 91, 192, 198, 258
Plantinga, Carl, 39
Play Time (Jacques Tati, 1968), 188, 220
point-of-view
   and character, 145
POV editing, 30, 46, 198, 199, 201, 227, 231
Pratt, George, 21, 56, 78, 112, 125, 228, 239, 253, 259
predictive inferences, 181, 216, 224
Propp, Vladimir, 144, 186

Psycho (Alfred Hitchcock , 1960), 34, 133, 135, 136
psychoanalysis, 107, 138, 144, 146, 186, 256, 270
Pudovkin, V.I., 46, 253, 268

Quinn, Naomi, 163, 174, 269

Rear Window (Alfred Hitchcock, 1954), 76, 77, 85–88, 199, 253
reception, 1, 19, 146, 182
recognition
   of characters, 29, 147
   of faces, 122, 184, 237
   of objects, 28
   of scenes, 28
Redman and the Child, The (D.W. Griffith, 1908), 65, 76, 119, 201
Reeves, B., 101, 142, 179
Rescued by Rover (Hepworth, 1904), 119
Rosch, Eleanor, 28, 29
Roseman, Ira, 163, 170, 173, 202

Saleslady's Matinee, The (Edison, 1909), 78, 80
Salt, Barry, 49, 50, 54, 55, 57–62, 111, 121, 122, 128, 139, 253
Salvation Army Lass, The (D.W. Griffith, 1908), 94, 95
Schank, Roger, 31, 165, 166
schemas, 11, 150, 154, 163, 171, 172, 174, 176, 181, 182, 209, 249, 253, 254
   cultural models, 176
   event schemas, 249
   folk-psychology, 163
   object schemas, 28
   scene schemas, 28
   social schemas, 153, 163
sets, 60
Seven Samurai (Akira Kurosawa, 1954), 150, 195, 215, 221, 223, 226, 243
Seventh Day, The (D.W. Griffith, 1909), 56
shot–reverse shot (SRS), 30, 62, 225, 226
sight link, 47, 87–89, 91, 254
   monitor vs. nonmonitor, 88
Simmel, Marianne, 179
situation, 25, 30, 31, 34, 61, 65, 70, 71, 76, 80, 83, 84, 89–91, 99, 106–109, 117, 130, 131, 136, 138–140, 147, 148, 152, 153, 161, 162, 165, 169–172, 174, 176, 178, 183, 187, 188, 198, 202, 206, 207, 210, 212, 214, 215, 217, 221–224, 227–229,

231, 235, 240, 241, 244, 245, 250, 253, 254, 256, 257
Smith, Murray, 29, 32, 47, 50, 96, 122, 143, 147–150, 153, 155, 156, 158, 159, 176, 184, 185, 202, 204, 216–218, 223, 245, 251, 272
social psychology, 71, 155, 249, 256
social referencing, 71
social types, 153, 166, 191, 249
Some Like It Hot (Billy Wilder, 1959), 195
Sommaren med Monika (Ingmar Bergman, 1953), 140
spatial immersion, 52
spatial reading strategy, 84, 86, 87, 253
spatiotemporal attachment, 148, 158, 204, 216, 223, 231, 237
Staiger, Janet, 21, 25, 33, 42, 47, 52, 53, 64, 186, 247
stalker films, 33, 64, 146, 209
Stam, Robert, 46, 145, 148
Steamboat Bill, Jr. (Charles Reisner, 1928), 196, 197, 212
Strike (Sergei Eisenstein, 1925), 32, 86, 155, 223, 232
switch-back, 94, 95
Switchman's Tower, The (Edison, 1911), 57
sympathy, 147, 149, 199, 245, 256

Tan, Ed, 1, 10, 38, 145, 148–150, 155–157, 183, 217, 244, 245, 256
Taylor, Shelly, 10
That Obscure Object of Desire (Louis Buñuel, 1977), 185
thematic inferences, 36
Thompson, Kristin, 20, 21, 26, 27, 30, 33, 36, 37, 42, 47–49, 52–54, 56, 57, 62–64, 66, 77, 112, 121–123, 125, 130, 132, 137, 139, 144, 155, 182, 183, 186, 225, 227–229, 234, 235, 237–240, 247, 259
Top Secret (Jim Abrahams & David Zucker, 1984), 38
Trabasso, Tom, 24, 187, 188, 218, 246

trait, 145, 154
traits, 31, 144, 146, 148, 153, 155, 158, 191, 216, 244
Trip to Mars, A (Lubin, 1903), 228
Trois couleurs Bleu (Krzysztof Kieslowski, 1993), 192
true POV, 47, 57, 59, 62, 87, 88, 90, 254
Tsivian, Yuri, 21, 42, 51, 52, 101, 102, 112, 116–118, 120, 125, 126, 233, 235, 239

Uricchio, William, 21, 233, 235

Vacances de Monsieur Hulot, Les (Jacques Tati, 1953), 188, 195, 203
van Dijk, T.A, 25, 30
variable framing, 101
vaudeville, 21, 48–50, 52, 53, 64, 90, 110, 112, 138, 155, 224, 227, 233, 236, 238
Vishton, P., 252
visual cliff studies, 71
Voyage dans la lune, Le (Georges Méliès, 1902), 63, 122, 228, 253

Walker, Ian, 155
Warning, The (Majestic, 1914), 155
Weekend (Jean-Luc Godard, 1967), 185, 188, 189, 191, 203, 206, 207, 216, 220, 222, 229, 232
Wellman, Henry, 163, 165, 168, 170, 176
White Rose of the Wilds, The (D.W. Griffith, 1911), 56
Whiten, Andrew, 4, 72, 163, 176, 181
Williams, Linda, 136
Wilson, George, 94
Wind, The (Victor Sjöström, 1928), 205

Ye Gods! What a Cast! (Luna, 1915), 57

Zwaan, Rolf, 21, 34, 270